THE GATE OF
HEAVEN

THE GATE OF
HEAVEN

Insights on the Doctrines and Symbols of the Temple

MATTHEW B. BROWN

Covenant Communications, Inc.

For my wife

Jamie Lynn Brown

No part of this work may be reproduced by any means without the express written permission of Covenant Communications, Inc. This work is not an official publication of The Church of Jesus Christ of Latter-day Saints. The views that are expressed within this work are the sole responsibility of the author and do not necessarily reflect the position of The Church of Jesus Christ of Latter-day Saints, Covenant Communications, Inc., or any other entity.

Published by Covenant Communications, Inc.
American Fork, Utah

Printed in the United States of America
First Printing: October 1999

04 03 02 01 00 99 98 97   10 9 8 7 6 5 4 3 2 1

ISBN 1-57734-511-8

ABBREVIATIONS

AGQ	*Answers to Gospel Questions*
BYUS	*Brigham Young University Studies*
CR	*Conference Report*
D&C	*Doctrine and Covenants*
DNTC	*Doctrinal New Testament Commentary*
DS	*Doctrines of Salvation*
EM	*Encyclopedia of Mormonism*
HC	*History of the Church*
IE	*Improvement Era*
JD	*Journal of Discourses*
JI	*Juvenile Instructor*
JS–H	*Joseph Smith–History*
JST	*Joseph Smith Translation*
MD	*Mormon Doctrine*
MS	*Millennial Star*
NWAF	*New Witness for the Articles of Faith*
RPJS	*Revelations of the Prophet Joseph Smith*
TPJS	*Teachings of the Prophet Joseph Smith*
TS	*Times and Seasons*
WJS	*Words of Joseph Smith*

CONTENTS

INTRODUCTION

In ancient times the Israelites referred to the temple of God as "the gate of heaven" (Genesis 28:17). To them, the temple was a place where the earthly and heavenly spheres combined and, therefore, a place where mortals could commune with the Lord. There was a great deal of symbolism associated with such a sacred place. These symbols were seen in the architectural decorations, in the furnishings, in the rituals, in the layout of the temple rooms, in the clothing worn by the priests, and even in the building's physical location. Where did all of these symbols come from? What doctrines and concepts did the ancient Israelites associate with these emblems? How are these symbols connected with the temples that are built by The Church of Jesus Christ of Latter-day Saints? The aim of this book is to provide substantive answers to these questions by drawing upon the discoveries of biblical scholarship and upon insights that have been provided by the Lord and His latter-day representatives.

The opening chapter of this book, entitled "In Heavenly Realms," begins with the basics by defining the word "temple." The origin of the temple concept is explained on these pages, and the reader is taken back to the premortal existence where the plan of salvation was laid out and the need for temples was established. As part of this discussion, readers are also introduced to symbolic ideas such as the "center" and shown how this concept relates both to the physical location of God in the universe and our relationship to Him through the gospel of His Son.

"The Patriarchal Pattern" then explores some of the doctrines that are connected with the creation. It is pointed out on these pages that the Garden of Eden served as the earth's first temple, and the plan of salvation was revealed to Adam and Eve after they were expelled from paradise so that they could teach their faithful posterity how to reverse the effects of the Fall and return to God's presence. Evidence is then presented that indicates the ancient patriarchs not only knew the fulness of the gospel of Jesus Christ but also participated in temple activities.

Our focus then turns to the time of Moses and "The Tabernacle of Jehovah." In this chapter it is demonstrated that Mount Sinai served as a natural temple, and the portable tabernacle that was built at its base was not only a horizontal replica of the mountain but also a miniature representation of the Garden of Eden. This chapter takes a look at many of the symbolic aspects of the tabernacle, including the furnishings found in its various compartments, the materials used in its construction, the sacred clothing worn in its precincts, the consecration rituals of the priests, zones of holiness, and the sacrifices that pointed forward to the Atonement of Jesus Christ.

The following chapter, "The Temple on Mount Zion," turns our attention to the permanent temple that was built by King Solomon around 1000 B.C. This discussion emphasizes the close association between many of the symbols found in King Solomon's temple and the ancient emblems of kingship. Topics that are covered include royal coronation rituals, the pillars Jachin and Boaz, the Brazen Sea, the temple as a house of prayer, the royal rite of eternal marriage, covenant-making ceremonies, and the king's role in the ritual drama of creation and salvation.

"Early Christians and the House of the Lord" addresses questions about the Savior's relationship to the House of God that stood during His lifetime. This chapter responds to a variety of questions: Did the Lord or His followers ever abandon the temple? What was the intended symbolism of the tearing of the temple veil when the Lord was crucified? Were temple ordinances still necessary after the Atonement? What type of initiation ceremonies did the earliest Christians engage in? What did the Savior teach His faithful followers during His forty-day ministry after the resurrection? Did the earliest Christians ever have their own temples?

Readers will then be taken forward to the time of the Prophet Joseph Smith in the chapter called "The Restoration of the Temple." These pages contain a substantial mixture of history and doctrine, and also explore some of the architectural symbolism associated with the Kirtland and Nauvoo Temples. Topics examined here include the temple-related keys described in section 110 of the Doctrine and Covenants, the differences between the Kirtland and Nauvoo endowment ceremonies, and the various revelations that were connected with the restoration of temple worship in the latter days.

The next chapter is entitled "The Gate of Heaven," the first half of which examines how temple rites are connected to one's reception of the "fulness of salvation." Some of the doctrinal topics that are touched upon in this part of the book include making one's calling and election sure, the fulness of the priesthood, the more sure word of prophecy, and the Church of the Firstborn. This chapter then shifts its focus from the exaltation of the living to the redemption of the dead, and examines a few widely held views about vicarious temple work that call for clarification. A number of

accounts are also included in this section of personages from the spirit world returning to the earth to request temple work, to assist with this work, or to witness their
own work being done. This chapter ends with a brief discussion on temple work during the Millennium.

The final chapter of this volume, "Stand Ye in Holy Places," addresses the necessity of being properly prepared for the temple experience and the blessings that one
may receive by engaging in the sacred work of the Lord's house. By drawing on the
teachings of latter-day prophets and apostles, this chapter teaches both the great value
of the temple ordinances and their absolute necessity for one's exaltation in the life to
come.

A short appendix then addresses the relationship between "The LDS Temple and
Freemasonry." This section of the book is written in a question-and-answer format
and is designed to briefly address three overall issues: (1) The historical origins of
Freemasonry, (2) the presence of Freemasonry in Nauvoo, Illinois during the lifetime
of Joseph Smith, and (3) the charge by critics of the LDS Church that Joseph Smith
plagiarized Masonic rituals and symbolism in order to create the Nauvoo-era temple
endowment ceremony.

I would like to extend my sincere thanks and appreciation to all of those who have
assisted in the preparation of this book for publication. I am particularly grateful to
those who have provided editing, production, and design skills and who have offered
their valuable comments and critiques on the various drafts of this manuscript. I must
emphasize, however, that even with the help and encouragement of all of these individuals, I am solely responsible for the content and conclusions of this book.

There are three things to which I would like to draw the reader's attention: First,
some of the quotations in this work have been standardized for modern spelling,
punctuation, and grammar but great care has been taken to maintain their original
context and meaning. Second, while the research in this book is extensive, it should
in no way be considered exhaustive. And third, I would strongly encourage the reader
to examine the numerous notes that are found at the end of each chapter as they provide many insights and considerable background information that could not be comfortably included in the main text.

It is my sincere hope that those who carefully examine the pages of this book will
come away from it with a better understanding of the temple, a clearer vision of the
past, and a stronger conviction of the reality of the Restoration.

CHAPTER ONE

In Heavenly Realms

The Lord commanded His ancient covenant people to build temples unto His holy name. He issued this same divine directive when the gospel was restored in the latter days through the Prophet Joseph Smith. This chapter is designed to help readers gain a preliminary understanding of what temples are and why they are necessary. The chapter will address such questions as: Where did the concept of the temple come from? What does the word *temple* mean? Why is the temple considered to be the house of the Lord? What role do temples play in the plan of salvation? What basic symbolic concepts are associated with these sacred structures? To find answers to these questions we must turn our attention to the heavenly realms.

The Nature of the Temple

Let us begin this chapter by defining the word *temple*. A *temple* commonly refers to a consecrated space or sanctuary that has been set apart for religious worship.[1] The word *temple* comes from the Latin *templum,* which signifies an extended open space that has been marked out for the observation of the sky.[2] In what manner is such a space marked out? According to Dr. Hugh W. Nibley, the word *templum* "designates a building specially designed for interpreting signs in the heavens—a sort of observatory where one gets one's bearings on the universe. The root *tem-* in Greek and Latin denotes a 'cutting' or intersection of two lines at right angles, 'the point where the *cardo* and *decumanus* cross,' hence where the four regions come together."[3] A temple is thus a central point from which one can determine the relationship between the motions of the heavens and the four quarters of the earth.

Dr. John M. Lundquist has noted that the "Sumerian word for foundation is *temen,* which can probably be viewed as an historical predecessor of the Greek word *temenos* [meaning 'a sacred enclosure'], which gives us the *tem* root of our word 'temple.'" He goes on to say that in some ancient cultures the *foundation* concept was equated with the *mountain* concept because a mountain was believed to have been the first solid structure to emerge from the waters of chaos that covered the earth at the time of creation (*see* Genesis 1:1-10). Some of the Jews who lived after biblical times taught that the temple mount in Jerusalem was the very first mountain to emerge from these waters, and they therefore looked upon it as the center or navel of the earth. They also taught that this very sacred place was marked by an object called the *Foundation Stone.*

> Just as the navel is found at the center of a human being, so the land of Israel is found at the center of the world. Jerusalem is at the center of the land of Israel, and the temple is at the center of Jerusalem, the Holy of Holies is at the center of the temple, the Ark [of the Covenant] is at the center of the Holy of Holies, and the Foundation Stone is in front of the Ark, which spot is the foundation of the world.[4]

Thus we see that a number of symbolic ideas are associated with the word *temple.* A temple is considered to be the most holy space on the earth; it is equated with a mountain and is thus symbolically seen as being above the plane of the earth and close to heaven; it is the center point where the four cardinal directions join together; it is considered a foundation or place of solidity; and it is an area where individuals take their bearings on their place in the universe.[5]

The Nature of God

The next subject we should address is the origin of the temple concept. One of the most important truths that was restored in the dispensation of the fulness of times was a correct understanding of the nature of God. In the Sacred Grove in the spring of 1820, the Prophet Joseph Smith learned firsthand that God the Father is separate and distinct from all other personages (*see* JS–H 1:17), and he later learned that "in the language of Adam, Man of Holiness is [God's] name" (Moses 6:57; *see also* 7:35).[6] The Prophet therefore taught Latter-day Saints that God the Father is physical in nature and has a perfected and glorified "body of flesh and bones as tangible as man's" (D&C 130:22).[7] In explaining how the Father obtained His body, the Prophet declared,

> God himself was once as we are now, and is an exalted man, and sits enthroned in yonder heavens! That is the great secret. If the veil were rent today, and the great God who holds this world in its orbit, and who upholds all worlds and all things by his

power, was to make himself visible,—I say, if you were to see him today, you would see him like a man in form—like yourselves in all the person, image, and very form as a man; for Adam was created in the very fashion, image and likeness of God, and received instruction from, and walked, talked and conversed with him, as one man talks and communes with another. . . . It is the first principle of the gospel to know for a certainty the character of God, and to know that we may converse with him as one man converses with another, and that he was once a man like us; yea, that God himself, the Father of us all, dwelt on an earth, the same as Jesus Christ himself did. . . .[8]

Since God occupies physical space, it is natural to suppose that He also resides somewhere within the physical universe. From scriptures such as 1 Corinthians 15:40–42[9] and section 76 of the Doctrine and Covenants[10], we learn that the kingdom of God is divided into three general degrees or spheres of glory (called *telestial, terrestrial,* and *celestial)* and that God's throne is located in the highest or celestial sphere (*see* D&C 137:1–4). Some mortals have been privileged to see the various spheres of the spiritual world and even see the place where God the Father resides. One such person was Lorenzo Dow Young. In 1832, before he became a member of the LDS Church, Lorenzo had a visionary dream wherein he was shown his own death. Immediately after his spirit had left his body, he became aware of a heavenly guide in the room who was dressed in pure white and who said unto him: "Now let us go."

Space seemed annihilated. Apparently we went up, and almost instantly were in another world. It was of such magnitude that I formed no conception of its size. It was filled with innumerable hosts of beings, who seemed as naturally human as those among whom I had lived. With some I had been acquainted in the world I had just left. My guide informed me that those I saw had not yet arrived at their final abiding place. All kinds of people seemed mixed up promiscuously, as they are in this world. Their surroundings and manner indicated that they were in a state of expectation, and awaiting some event of considerable moment to them.

As we went on from this place, my guide said, "I will now show you the condition of the damned." Pointing with his hand, he said, "Look!"

I looked down a distance which appeared incomprehensible to me. I gazed on a vast region filled with multitudes of beings. I could see everything with the most minute distinctness. The multitude of people I saw were miserable in the extreme. "These," said my guide, "are they who have rejected the means of salvation, that were placed within their reach, and have brought upon themselves the condemnation you behold."

The expression of the countenances of these sufferers was clear and distinct. They indicated extreme remorse, sorrow and dejection. They appeared conscious that none but themselves were to blame for their forlorn condition.

This scene affected me much, and I could not refrain from weeping.

Again my guide said, "Now let us go."

In a moment we were at the gate of a beautiful city. A porter opened it and we passed in. The city was grand and beautiful beyond anything that I can describe. It was clothed in the purest light, brilliant but not glaring or unpleasant.

The people, men and women, in their employments and surroundings, seemed contented and happy. I knew those I met without being told who they were. Jesus and the ancient apostles were there. I saw and spoke with the apostle Paul.

My guide would not permit me to pause much by the way, but rather hurried me on through this place to another still higher but connected with it. It was still more beautiful and glorious than anything I had before seen. To me its extent and magnificence were incomprehensible.

My guide pointed to a mansion which excelled everything else in perfection and beauty. It was clothed with fire and intense light. It appeared a fountain of light, throwing brilliant scintillations of glory all around it, and I could conceive of no limit to which these emanations extended. Said my guide, "That is where God resides." He permitted me to enter this glorious city but a short distance. Without speaking, he motioned that we would retrace our steps.

We were soon in the adjoining city. There I met my mother, and a sister who died when six or seven years old. These I knew at sight without an introduction.

After mingling with the pure and happy beings of this place a short time, my guide said again, "Let us go."

We were soon through the gate by which we had entered the city. My guide then said, "Now we will return."

I could distinctly see the world from which we had first come. It appeared to be a vast distance below us. To me, it looked cloudy, dreary and dark. I was filled with sad disappointment, I might say horror, at the idea of returning there. I supposed I had come to stay in that heavenly place, which I had so long desired to see; up to this time, the thought had not occurred to me that I would be required to return.

I pled with my guide to let me remain. He replied that I was permitted to only visit these heavenly cities, for I had not filled my mission in yonder world; therefore I must return and take my body. If I was faithful to the grace of God which would be imparted to me, if I would bear a faithful testimony to the inhabitants of the earth of a sacrificed and risen Savior, and his atonement for man; in a little time I should be permitted to return and remain.[11]

In the Midst of All Things

Joseph Smith has provided us with further insights about God's heavenly abode. God and His angels, said the Prophet, reside "on a globe like a sea of glass and fire, where all things for their glory are manifest, past, present, and future, and are continually before the Lord. The place where God resides is a great Urim and Thummim" (D&C 130:7–8).[12] Where in the vast universe is this heavenly habitation located? A passage from the Book of Abraham may provide us with a clue.

> And I, Abraham, had the Urim and Thummim, which the Lord my God had given unto me, in Ur of the Chaldees;
>
> And I saw the stars, that they were very great, and that one of them was nearest unto the throne of God; and there were many great ones which were near unto it;
>
> And the Lord said unto me: These are the governing ones; and the name of the great one is Kolob, because it is near unto me, for I am the Lord thy God: I have set this one to govern all those which belong to the same order as that upon which thou standest.
>
> And the Lord said unto me, by the Urim and Thummim, that Kolob was after the manner of the Lord, according to its times and seasons in the revolutions thereof; that one revolution was a day unto the Lord, after his manner of reckoning, it being one thousand years according to the time appointed unto that whereon thou standest. This is the reckoning of the Lord's time, according to the reckoning of Kolob. . . .
>
> Kolob is after the reckoning of the Lord's time; which Kolob is set nigh unto the throne of God, to govern all those planets which belong to the same order as that upon which thou standest. . . .
>
> Kolob is the greatest of all the Kokaubeam [or stars] that thou hast seen, because it is nearest unto me. (Abraham 3:1–4, 9, 16)

In the explanations attached to facsimile #2 in the Book of Abraham, we also learn from Joseph Smith that figure 1 represents, "Kolob, signifying the first creation, nearest to the celestial, or the residence of God. First in government, the last pertaining to the measurement of time. The measurement according to celestial time, which celestial time signifies one day to a cubit. One day in Kolob is equal to a thousand years according to the measurement of this earth."[13] Since the Prophet stated that the Egyptian papyrus scrolls from which he translated the Book of Abraham discussed "the principles of astronomy as understood by Father Abraham and the ancients,"[14] we would expect *Kolob* to be an authentic ancient word. And, in fact, "Kolob" is used as the name of a deity in an ancient text from Mesopotamia.[15]

Abraham 3:3 seems to indicate that the name Kolob is descriptive: "And the Lord said unto me . . . the name of the great one is Kolob, because it is near unto me." A Semitic word with a root that is similar to Kolob (*qarob*, root *qrb*) means near, next to, or nigh.[16]

One prominent biblical scholar informs us that the Hebrew word *qarob* is sometimes employed as one of the divine titles of Jehovah and means "Near One."[17] Other commentators believe that the word Kolob may derive from the Semitic root *qlb*, the basic meaning of which is heart, center, middle, or midst.[18] These concepts may bear some relation to a passage in the Doctrine and Covenants where it is stated that God "sitteth upon his throne . . . in the bosom of eternity . . . in the midst of all things" (D&C 88:13).

The Heavenly Temple

The Lord's heavenly temple is briefly mentioned in the Bible. For instance, during his apocalyptic vision, the apostle John saw "the temple which is in heaven" and a series of angels coming out of it (Revelation 14:15, 17; 15:5–8). Several scriptures also speak of the Lord's heavenly sanctuary as the place where His throne is located (*see* Psalm 11:4; Revelation 7:15; 16:17). There are a number of ancient Hebrew traditions that specifically state that God resides in a temple that is located in the center of the universe. These traditions symbolically represent the universe as being cubic in shape with the heavenly temple occupying a point exactly in the middle of the cube.[19]

The scriptures tell us that this earth is destined not only to become one of the celestial kingdoms of God but it will also become a replica of the sphere where God resides (*see* D&C 130:9). John the Revelator saw in vision that following the resurrection and judgment of mankind the earth would become "new" (Revelation 21:1–2) and the "curse" of the Fall would be removed (Revelation 22:3; compare Genesis 3:17) so that men and women could once again enter into the presence of the Lord and "see his face" (Revelation 22:4). John was also shown a symbolic image that is intimately connected with entering into the presence of the Lord. He saw the heavenly city of God descending upon the celestialized earth (*see* Revelation 21:1–2, 10). This heavenly structure mirrors the Holy of Holies of the Lord's earthly temples in several different ways. It is called the "tabernacle of God" (Revelation 21:3; Exodus 25:8–9).[20] It has foundations (*see* Revelation 21:19–20; Exodus 26:19). It is cubical in shape (*see* Revelation 21:16; 1 Kings 6:20). It is decorated with glimmering gold (*see* Revelation 21:18; 1 Kings 6:20; Exodus 36:20, 34, 36). Its gates are guarded by angelic sentinels (*see* Revelation 21:12; 1 Chronicles 26:1–19).[21] The throne of God is found within it (*see* Revelation 22:1, 3; Exodus 25:21–22)[22] and therefore the glory of God radiates from it (*see* Revelation 21:11, 23; Exodus 40:34–35; Leviticus 16:2).

Comparison of passages from the books of Exodus and Revelation reveal that the earthly temples of Israel were built after the same pattern as the Lord's temple in heaven.[23] Conversely, the layout of the temple of Jerusalem suggests that the heavenly temple is built in a series of three successive enclosures.[24] The reason for this is that the heavenly temple represents, by its very structure, the three degrees of glory. It embodies "the structure of the universe, so that ascent through the heavenly levels [is] also a journey 'inward' through the temple's concentric areas of increasing holiness to the Holy of Holies at the center."[25] In other words, the temple (whether earthly or heavenly) is a miniature imitation of the structure of the universe.

Some ancient Hebrew and Christian texts speak of various means whereby one is enabled to pass by gates or other barriers and ascend through the various heavens.[26] In one such text, called the Apocalypse of Paul, the angelic guide who escorts the apostle Paul through the heavens prompts him when they arrive at one of the gates by saying, "'Give him [the] sign that you have, and [he will] open for you.' And then I gave [him] the sign," said Paul, and "the heaven opened."[27] The Savior is depicted in one document, known as the Ascension of Isaiah, as passing by guarded gates as he journeys through the heavens. At several gateways we are told that he "gave the password to those who kept the gates."[28] To those who become His sons, says the Lord in the Apocalypse of Elijah, "I will write my name upon their forehead and I will seal their right hand, and they will . . . pass by the thrones" and the angels that are stationed at the gates.[29]

Some scriptural and nonscriptural sources speak of rituals that individuals go through when they reach the highest heaven and enter into the presence of the Lord. In Zechariah 3:1–5, for instance, we read that when Joshua the high priest stood in the Lord's presence, he was clothed by angels in clean garments and a head covering. This is very similar to the white linen robes and golden crowns that are given to the faithful Saints who are in the Lord's presence (*see* Revelation 3:4–5; 4:4; 6:11; 7:9; 19:7–9).[30] Revelation 7:13–15 indicates that white robes are worn by those who are "before the throne of God, and serve him day and night in his temple." Some of the angels who serve before the Lord in His heavenly temple also wear golden sashes (*see* Revelation 1:13; 15:6; Daniel 10:5). The Lord tells His angels in 2 Enoch to "extract Enoch from [his] earthly clothing, and anoint him with my delightful oil, and put him into the clothes of my glory. And so Michael did, just as the Lord had said to him. He anointed me and He clothed me . . . [The oil had a] fragrance [like] myrrh . . . And I looked at myself, and I had become like one of his glorious ones."[31]

In some ancient accounts, a barrier, such as a curtain, conceals the throne of God from the rest of the heavenly world. One scholar has written that this "curtain is the heavenly counterpart of the veil which divided the Holy Place from the Holy of Holies in the earthly Tabernacle and temple (Exodus 26:31; 2 Chronicles 3:14)." He further states that this heavenly veil conceals the ultimate mysteries of Deity and sometimes divine secrets are spoken by a heavenly voice from behind this veil.[32] This veil is said to have "all kinds of lights in the universe" fixed upon it, meaning that it is covered with designs that resemble stars.[33] The Jewish historian Flavius Josephus records that the veil hanging before the Holy Place of the Jerusalem temple was likewise covered with "embroidered" marks that resembled stars.[34]

Some early religious documents describe what individuals do when they enter into the Lord's presence. In 2 Enoch, a text attributed to Rabbi Ishmael the high priest, the rabbi ascends through the heavens until he reaches the final barrier leading to God's throne. There he petitions the Lord in prayer that he might be found worthy to pass by this barrier, and the Lord immediately sends an angel to him. "He grasped me with his hand," said Rabbi Ishmael, "and said to me, 'Come in peace into the presence of the high and exalted King.' . . . Then I entered . . . and he . . . presented me before the throne of glory."[35] Joseph Smith reported that he saw a vision of the gate leading into the celestial kingdom. He described it as being "like unto circling flames of fire" (D&C 137:2). Heber C. Kimball relates that during this vision, the Prophet saw that the Twelve Apostles of the last dispensation "arrived at the gate of the celestial city; there Father Adam stood and opened the gate to them, and as they entered he embraced them one by one and kissed them. He then led them to the throne of God, and then the Savior embraced each one of them and kissed them, and crowned each one of them in the presence of God."[36] This activity is reminiscent of an ascension experience that is attributed to the apostle Paul. In the text that records this ascension we read: "And when I had entered within the gates of Paradise there came to meet me an old man whose face shone as the sun. And he embraced me and said; 'Hail, Paul, dearly beloved of God.' And with a joyful face he kissed me. . . . And I asked the angel and said: 'Who is this, sir?' And he said to me: 'This is Enoch, the scribe of righteousness.'"[37]

The Council in Heaven

Joseph Smith informs us that when he and Sidney Rigdon saw the vision of the three degrees of glory recorded in section 76 of the Doctrine and Covenants, they were shown many "mysteries" that they were not permitted to write down because they concerned things "not lawful for man to utter" (D&C 76:114–115). Verses 12 and 13 of section 76 seem to indicate that among these mysteries were "those things which were from the beginning before the world was, which were ordained of the Father."[38] In a poetic rendition of D&C 76, which was published in 1843 in the *Times and Seasons*, the Prophet hinted that one of the mysteries revealed in the vision was that the premortal Council of Heaven was convened on Kolob.

> For thus saith the Lord, in the spirit of truth,
> I am merciful, gracious, and good unto those
> That fear me, and live for the life that's to come;
> My delight is to honor the saints with repose;
>
> That serve me in righteousness true to the end;
> Eternal's their glory, and great their reward;
> I'll surely reveal all my myst'ries to them,
> The great hidden myst'ries in my kingdom stor'd
>
> From the council in Kolob, to time on the earth,
> And for ages to come unto them I will show
> My pleasure and will, what my kingdom will do:
> Eternity's wonders they truly shall know.[39]

Joseph Smith has provided us with several insights about the premortal council in his public discourses. In offering his own translation of the opening verses of Genesis, the Prophet said that they could be read: "'The head one of the Gods brought forth the Gods.' . . . Thus the head God brought forth the Gods in the grand council. . . . The head God called together the Gods and sat in grand council to bring forth the world. The grand councilors sat at the head in yonder heavens and contemplated the creation of the worlds which were created at the time. . . . In the beginning, the head of the Gods called a council of the Gods; and they came together and concocted a plan to create the world and people it."[40] The idea of a heavenly council is not unique to LDS theology. It is clear that the ancient Israelites also believed that there was a heavenly assembly or council made up of divine beings whose function it was to carry out the plans, designs, and decrees of the Most High God.[41]

Joseph Smith taught that in premortal times the Lord "contemplated the whole of the events connected with the earth, pertaining to the plan of salvation, before it rolled into existence. . . . He comprehended the fall of man, and . . . made ample provision for [mankind's] redemption."[42] When the Lord presented the plan of salvation in the Grand Council, the contention was that "Jesus said there would be certain souls that would not be saved; and the devil said he could save them all, and laid his plans before the grand council, who gave their vote in favor of Jesus Christ."[43] The Prophet further revealed that "we were all present, and saw the Savior chosen and appointed and the plan of salvation made, and we sanctioned it."[44] It is apparent that the members of the Godhead then entered into a covenant with each other to carry out the plan of redemption.[45]

The work and the glory of God, we are told in scripture, is "to bring to pass the immortality and eternal life of man" (Moses 1:39). Joseph Smith was more specific about God's ultimate intentions when he asked: "What was the design of the Almighty in making man? It was to exalt him to be as God."[46] In the *Lectures on Faith* it is indicated that the

> teachings of the Savior most clearly show unto us the nature of salvation, and what he proposed unto the human family when he proposed to save them—that he proposed to make them like unto himself, and he was like the Father, the great proto- type of all saved beings; and for any portion of the human family to be assimilated into their likeness is to be saved.[47]

The plan of redemption centered on "the bringing of men back into the presence of the King of heaven, crowning them in the celestial glory, and making them heirs with the Son."[48] In order to accomplish this, said the Prophet, there were certain ordinances "which God ordained for the salvation of man, to prepare him for, and give him a title to, a celestial glory."[49] Because God is no respecter of persons (*see* D&C 1:35; 38:16; Acts 10:34) He has decreed that all of His children "must be saved on the same principles" and participate in ordinances that were "instituted in the heavens before the foundation of the world, in the priesthood, for the salvation of men."[50] God then "set the ordinances to be the same forever and ever, and set Adam to watch over them, to reveal them from heaven to man, or to send angels to reveal them."[51] "If men would acquire salvation," said the Prophet, "they have got to be subject, before they leave this world, to certain rules and principles, which were fixed by an unalterable decree before the world was"[52] (*see* Alma 41:8). Were these ordinances and principles new? According to Elder Orson Pratt,

> The dealing of God towards his children from the time that they are first born in heaven, through all their successive stages of existence, until they are redeemed, per- fected, and made gods, is a pattern after which all other worlds are dealt with. All gods act upon the same great general principles; and thus, the course of each god is one eter- nal round. There will, of course, be a variety in all [of God's] works, but there will be no great deviations from the general laws which he has ordained. The creation, fall,

and redemption of all future worlds with their inhabitants will be conducted upon the same general plan. . . . The Father of our spirits has only been doing that which his progenitors did before him. Each succeeding generation of gods follow the example of the preceding ones. . . . [When new worlds are organized, their inhabitants] are redeemed after the pattern by which more ancient worlds have been redeemed.[53]

In what manner was it foreordained that the Saints would obtain the necessary ordinances of salvation? Again, the Prophet Joseph Smith informs us that it "was the design of the councils of heaven before the world was, that the principles and laws of the priesthood should be predicated upon the gathering of the people in every age of the world." And what was to be the purpose of this gathering? "The main object was to build unto the Lord a house whereby he could reveal unto His people the ordinances of His house and the glories of His kingdom, and teach the people the way of salvation; for there are certain ordinances and principles that, when they are taught and practiced, must be done in a place or house built for that purpose."[54]

Joseph Smith was the man chosen and foreordained to restore the fulness of the gospel and the ordinances of the temple during the dispensation of the fulness of times. "Every man who has a calling to minister to the inhabitants of the world," said the Prophet, "was ordained to that very purpose in the Grand Council of heaven before this world was. I suppose I was ordained to this very office in that Grand Council."[55] On 3 October 1918, President Joseph F. Smith saw in vision that Joseph Smith and others were indeed prepared in heavenly realms to build temples upon the earth and to stand as saviors upon Mount Zion.

> The Prophet Joseph Smith, and my father, Hyrum Smith, Brigham Young, John Taylor, Wilford Woodruff, and other choice spirits . . . were reserved to come forth in the fulness of times to take part in laying the foundations of the great latter-day work,
>
> Including the building of the temples and the performance of ordinances therein for the redemption of the dead. . . .
>
> I observed that they were also among the noble and great ones who were chosen in the beginning to be rulers in the Church of God.
>
> Even before they were born, they, with many others, received their first lessons in the world of spirits and were prepared to come forth in the due time of the Lord to labor in his vineyard for the salvation of the souls of men. (D&C 138:53–56)

SUMMARY

A *temple* is a symbolic structure that represents the ideas of centrality, solidity, orientation, and ascension. The temple is an imitation on earth of what is found in the heavens or, put conversely, the temple represents heaven on earth. Temple ordinances were foreordained in the premortal world as part of the plan of salvation, and it is only through them that we can become like the Father as a joint heir with His Son. Prophets of God were commissioned in premortal times to restore and implement these vital ordinances during the final dispensation of the gospel.

NOTES

1. C. T. Onions, ed., *The Oxford Dictionary of English Etymology* (Oxford: Clarendon Press, 1966), 908; Walter W. Skeat, *An Etymological Dictionary of the English Language*, rev. ed. (Oxford: Clarendon Press, 1935), 634.

2. Ernest Klein, *A Comprehensive Etymological Dictionary of the English Language* (New York: Elsevier Publishing, 1967), 2:1584–85.

3. Hugh W. Nibley, "What Is a Temple?" in Truman G. Madsen, ed., *The Temple in Antiquity* (Provo, Utah: BYU Religious Studies Center, 1984), 22.

4. John M. Lundquist, "The Common Temple Ideology of the Ancient Near East," in Madsen, ed., *The Temple in Antiquity*, 64–65. In conjunction with the *navel* concept, Dr. Nibley has noted that early in the twentieth century "Sir Aurel Stein discovered some graves in a seventh-century [Chinese] cemetery. In one of the tomb chambers, two veils were found, one still hanging suspended from wooden pegs; they were near life size and showed the king and queen in a formal embrace on the veil, the king holding up the square on the right side and the queen holding the compass on the left. Located at the navel was the sun as the center of the system, from which twelve spokes extended to the white dots in the circle, indicating the twelve-month course of the year, or the life cycle. At the side of the two intertwined figures appears the Big Dipper. It was at once recognized that the scene represents the sacred marriage of the king and queen at the New Year, celebrating the new age and inaugurating the new life cycle with the drama of creation. The compass and square are viewed as the instruments marking out both the pattern of the universe and the foundations of the earth" (Hugh W. Nibley, "On the Sacred and the Symbolic," in Donald W. Parry, ed., *Temples of the Ancient World: Ritual and Symbolism* [Salt Lake City: Deseret Book and FARMS, 1994], 574–75; for further comments on this veil and its markings, see Dr. Nibley's articles "Sacred Vestments" in Hugh W. Nibley, *Temple and Cosmos* (Salt Lake City: Deseret Book and FARMS, 1992), 105–15, "Return to the Temple" [ibid.], 80–81, and "The Early Christian Prayer Circle" in Hugh W. Nibley, *Mormonism and Early Christianity* [Salt Lake City: Deseret Book and FARMS, 1987], 73–75).

5. John M. Lundquist has offered fifteen propositions as a preliminary typology for understanding the ideology of temples in the ancient Near East: (1) The temple is the architectural embodiment of the cosmic mountain. (2) The cosmic mountain represents the primordial hillock, the place that first emerged from the waters covering the earth during the creative process. (3) The temple is often associated with the waters of life that flow from a spring within the building itself. (4) The temple is built on separate, sacral, set-apart space. (5) The temple is oriented toward the four world regions or cardinal directions, and to various celestial bodies, such as the polar star. (6) Temples, in their architectonic orientation, express the idea of a successive ascension toward heaven. (7) The plan and measurements of the temple are revealed by God to the king, and the plan must be carefully carried out. (8) The temple is the central, organizing, unifying institution in ancient Near Eastern society and is associated with abundance and prosperity. (9) Inside the temple, persons are washed, anointed, clothed, fed, enthroned, and symbolically initiated into the presence of deity, and thus into eternal life. Other temple

activities include the enactment of a drama dealing with premortal life and creation, and the carrying out of a sacred marriage. (10) The temple is associated with the realm of the dead and the afterlife. (11) Sacred meals are carried out in connection with temple ritual, often at the conclusion of or during a covenant ceremony. (12) The tablets of destiny are consulted in a special chamber. (13) There is a close interrelationship between the temple and law in the ancient Near East. (14) The temple is a place of sacrifice. (15) The temple and its ritual are enshrouded in secrecy (John M. Lundquist, "What Is a Temple? A Preliminary Typology," in Parry, ed., *Temples of the Ancient World*, 83–117).

6. Orson Pratt reported: "There is one revelation that this people are not generally acquainted with. I think it has never been published, but probably it will be in the Church History. It is given in questions and answers. The first question is, 'What is the name of God in the pure language?' The answer says, 'Ahman.' 'What is the name of the Son of God?' Answer, 'Son Ahman—the greatest of all the parts of God excepting Ahman'" (*Journal of Discourses*, George D. Watt, et. al., eds., 26 vols. [Liverpool: F. D. Richards and Sons, 1854–86], 2:342, hereafter cited as *JD*). Since it is claimed here that *Ahman* is a revealed word, it should be noted that in Hebrew we find the word *aman* (pronounced "aw-man"), meaning to be firm or faithful, to be true, steadfast, and sure (see James Strong, *The New Strong's Exhaustive Concordance of the Bible* [Nashville: Thomas Nelson Publishers, 1996], Hebrew and Aramaic Dictionary, 10, word #539). In Revelation 3:14 Jesus Christ calls himself "Amen, the faithful and true witness" (compare D&C 78:20; 95:17).

7. "That which is without body, parts and passions is nothing. There is no other God in heaven but that God who has flesh and bones. John 5:26 [reads:] 'For as the Father hath life in himself; so hath he given to the Son to have life in himself.' God the Father took life unto himself precisely as Jesus did" (Joseph Fielding Smith, comp., *The Teachings of the Prophet Joseph Smith* [Salt Lake City: Deseret Book, 1989], 181, hereafter cited as *TPJS*). For evidence that this doctrine is a restoration of the original Christian understanding of God, see David L. Paulsen, "Early Christian Belief in a Corporeal Deity: Origen and Augustine as Reluctant Witnesses," *Harvard Theological Review*, vol. 83, no. 2, April 1990, 105–16. On page 105 of this source we read that "ordinary Christians for at least the first three centuries of the current era commonly (and perhaps generally) believed God to be corporeal." The author goes on to say that this belief was gradually abandoned "as Neoplatonism became more and more entrenched as the dominant world view of Christian thinkers." For further reading, see David L. Paulsen, "The Doctrine of Divine Embodiment: Restoration, Judeo-Christian, and Philosophical Perspectives," *Brigham Young University Studies*, vol. 35, no. 4, 1995–96, 7–94. One text from the Dead Sea Scrolls appears to describe God as "a creature of flesh" (see the note by Daniel C. Peterson in *Review of Books on the Book of Mormon*, vol. 7, no. 2, 1995, 101). Those who believe that God is some type of spirit essence point to John 4:24 to support their view. In the King James Bible, this verse reads: "God *is* a Spirit." At first glance this may appear to be convincing evidence but one biblical scholar has declared that to translate this passage as "'God is a Spirit' is the most gross perversion of the meaning" of the Greek text (Charles H. Dodd, *The Interpretation of the Fourth Gospel* [Cambridge: University Press, 1953], 225). Indeed, this particular translation does not hold up well under close scrutiny. To begin with, the word "is" is italicized because it does not exist in the Greek document from which the translation was made but was added to the sentence by the King James translators (see *LDS Bible*

Dictionary, 708). In addition, some biblical scholars believe a few translations of John 4:24 are correct to "omit the indefinite article ['a'] before 'Spirit' . . . Greek has no such article, and we insert it . . . in English as the sense requires" (Leon Morris, *The Gospel According to John* [Grand Rapids, Michigan: Eerdmans, 1989], 271). In other words, the Greek text from which this sentence was created only consists of two words—*theos* (God) and *pneuma* (Spirit). Modern biblical scholars recognize that the book of John has been tampered with over time and that some material has been deleted from it (*see* Urban C. von Wahlde, *The Earliest Version of John's Gospel* [Wilmington, Delaware: Michael Glazier, 1989], 21). The Prophet Joseph Smith, however, recognized in the 1830s that the text of John 4:24 had been damaged over the centuries and was no longer in its original form. By divine directive, and under the inspiration of heaven, the Prophet restored John 4:24 in the Joseph Smith Translation (hereafter JST) to read: "For unto such hath God promised his Spirit" (JST John 4:26), thus incorporating the only two words that have survived the hands of careless transcribers, ignorant translators, and those with religious agendas (*see TPJS*, 327). For informative discussions regarding the LDS and Trinitarian perspectives on the nature of God, see Daniel C. Peterson and Stephen D. Ricks, *Offenders for a Word* (Provo, Utah: Foundation for Ancient Research and Mormon Studies, 1992), 55–95; Stephen E. Robinson, *Are Mormons Christians?* (Salt Lake City: Bookcraft, 1991), 71–89; Edmond LaB. Cherbonnier, "In Defense of Anthropomorphism," in Truman G. Madsen, ed., *Reflections on Mormonism: Judaeo–Christian Parallels* (Provo, Utah: BYU Religious Studies Center, 1978), 155–73.

8. *TPJS*, 345–46. Joseph Smith also taught: "As the Father hath power in himself, so hath the Son power in himself, to lay down his life and take it again, so he has a body of his own. The Son doeth what he hath seen the Father do: then the Father hath some day laid down his life and taken it again; so he has a body of his own" (ibid., 312, see John 5:19–20, 26; 10:17–18). Wilford Woodruff declared that "whoever goes back into the presence of God our eternal Father, will find that he is a noble man, a noble God, tabernacled in a form similar to ours, for we are created after his own image; they will also learn that he has placed us here that we may pass through a state of probation and experience, the same as he himself did in his day of mortality" (*JD*, 18:32).

9. The text of 1 Corinthians 15:40–42 is obviously damaged because even though it states that there are three glories after the resurrection corresponding to the sun, moon, and stars, it only provides names for two of them (the sun=*celestial*, the moon=*terrestrial*). Joseph Smith learned in the vision now known as D&C 76 that the name of the lowest glory, which corresponds to the brightness of the stars, is called *telestial*. After learning this in the vision, the Prophet added *telestial* to the text of 1 Corinthians 15:40 in the Joseph Smith Translation.

10. Paul said in 2 Corinthians 12:4 that while in the third heaven, he "heard unspeakable words, which it is not lawful for a man to utter." In commenting on these verses, Joseph Smith said that he could say with Paul: "we have seen and heard things that are not lawful to utter" (Joseph Smith, Jr., *History of the Church of Jesus Christ of Latter-day Saints*, B. H. Roberts, ed. [Salt Lake City: The Church of Jesus Christ of Latter-day Saints, 1932–51], 5:556, hereafter cited as *HC)*. On another occasion the Prophet remarked: "Paul saw the third heaven, and I more" (*TPJS*, 301), possibly referring to the fact that the Prophet was made aware of three heavens within the celestial kingdom (see D&C 131:1). The Prophet states in D&C 76:114–117 that he and Sidney Rigdon were expressly commanded *not* to write

about certain things that they saw in the vision of the three degrees of glory. On another occasion the Prophet said: "Paul ascended into the third heaven, and he could understand the three principle rounds of Jacob's ladder—the telestial, the terrestrial, and the celestial glories or kingdoms, where Paul saw and heard things which were not lawful for him to utter. I could explain a hundred fold more than I ever have of the glories of the kingdoms manifested to me in the vision [known as D&C 76], were I permitted, and were the people prepared to receive them" (*TPJS*, 304–305).

11. *Fragments of Experience: Sixth Book of the Faith-Promoting Series* (Salt Lake City: Juvenile Instructor Office, 1882), 27–29.

12. This information is also recorded in William Clayton's journal but his entry adds an important insight. According to Clayton, the Prophet Joseph Smith taught that angels "dwell with God and the planet where he dwells is like crystal, and like a sea of glass before the throne. This is the great Urim and Thummim whereon all things are manifest, both things past, present and future and are continually before the Lord. The Urim and Thummim is a small representation of this globe" (cited in Lyndon W. Cook, *The Revelations of the Prophet Joseph Smith* [Salt Lake City: Deseret Book, 1985], 289; compare Revelation 4:1–2, 5–6; Ezekiel 1:22, 26). This concept is paralleled in an interesting way by the text of 3 Enoch 45:1, which states that on the veil before God's throne "are printed all the generations of the world and all their deeds, whether done [past] or to be done [future], till the last generation" (James H. Charlesworth, *The Old Testament Pseudepigrapha* [Garden City, New York: Doubleday, 1983], 1:296). Since this book cites several apocryphal and pseudepigraphical texts, it is appropriate to remind the reader of the Lord's statement to Joseph Smith that the twelve apocryphal books found in his copy of the King James Bible contain "many things" that are true but also "many things" that are not true, but are "interpolations by the hands of men." Many apocryphal and pseudepigraphical books have come to light since the days of the Prophet Joseph Smith. Those who study these types of literature can rely on the Spirit of the Lord, the doctrines of the restored gospel, biblical scholarship, and common sense to help them discern whether the statements they contain are true (see D&C 91:1–6; *LDS Bible Dictionary*, 610–11).

13. Figure 2 of facsimile #2 in the Book of Abraham says: "Stands next to Kolob, called by the Egyptians Oliblish, which is the next grand governing creation near to the celestial or the place where God resides." Figure 4 of facsimile #2 is said to represent, among other things, "a numerical figure, in Egyptian signifying one thousand; answering to the measuring of the time of Oliblish, which is equal with Kolob in its revolution and in its measurement of time." In figure 5 of facsimile #2 we are told that certain stars borrow their light, in some manner, from the revolutions of Kolob. In the Garden of Eden narrative provided by Abraham we read: "And the Gods commanded the man, saying: Of every tree of the garden thou mayest freely eat, but of the tree of knowledge of good and evil, thou shalt not eat of it; for in the time that thou eatest thereof, thou shalt surely die. Now I, Abraham, saw that it was after the Lord's time, which was after the time of Kolob; for as yet the Gods had not appointed unto Adam his reckoning" (Abraham 5:12–13). As pointed out by Milton R. Hunter, "Our first parents would die in the *day* that they partook of the forbidden fruit; and the account in [the book of] Abraham states that the *day* referred to was according to the measurement of time on Kolob which we have already learned was 1,000 years according to the reckoning of time on this earth. The Lord had

reference to a spiritual death . . . [and also to] the mortal death, that took place with Father Adam 930 years after he was cast out of the Garden of Eden, which was 70 years before the close of a day on Kolob" (Milton R. Hunter, *Pearl of Great Price Commentary* [Salt Lake City: Bookcraft, 1965], 113; emphasis added).

14. *HC*, 2:286.

15. See Lundquist's note that *Kolob* is the name of an ancient Near Eastern deity (John M. Lundquist, "Was Abraham at Ebla: A Cultural Background of the Book of Abraham?" in Robert L. Millet and Kent P. Jackson, eds., *Studies in Scripture: Volume Two, The Pearl of Great Price* [Salt Lake City: Randall Books, 1985], 233).

16. Strong, *The New Strong's Exhaustive Concordance of the Bible*, Hebrew and Aramaic Dictionary, 127, word #7138.

17. Mitchell Dahood, *Psalms II: 51–100* (Garden City, New York: Doubleday, 1968), 209, 210 nt. 2; Mitchell Dahood, *Psalms III: 101–150* (Garden City, New York: Doubleday, 1970), 170, 191 nt. 151.

18. Michael D. Rhodes, "The Joseph Smith Hypocephalus . . . Seventeen Years Later," FARMS preliminary report, 1994, 8. For a brief examination of the possible etymology of the word *Kolob,* see Robert F. Smith, "Some 'Neologisms' from the Mormon Canon," in *Conference on the Language of the Mormons* (Provo, Utah: BYU Language Research Center, 1973), 64.

19. See the article by Peter Hayman, "Some Observations on Sefer Yesira: (2) The Temple at the Center of the Universe," *Journal of Jewish Studies*, vol. 37, no. 2, Autumn 1986, 176–82. In the Clementine Homilies we also find the idea of God existing at the center of the universe and the six cubic directions (north, south, east, west, above, below) extending out from His person (see Alexander Roberts and James Donaldson, eds., *Ante-Nicene Fathers: The Clementina* [Peabody, Massachusetts: Hendrickson Publishers, 1994], 8:320–21).

20. It is also called in the book of Revelation "the bride," the "Lamb's wife," the "great city," the "holy city," the "holy Jerusalem," and the "new Jerusalem" (Revelation 21:2, 9, 10).

21. The sentinel angels are posted at the gates to prevent the unworthy from entering into the presence of the Lord (see Revelation 21:27; 22:14–15).

22. Several passages in the Bible speak of the Lord's throne being situated inside of the heavenly temple. For example, in Psalms 11:4 we read: "The Lord is in his holy temple, the Lord's throne is in heaven." Ezekiel, who was a temple priest in Jerusalem, saw an extensive vision of the Lord sitting upon his throne inside of the heavenly temple (see Ezekiel chapters 1 and 10). The apostle Paul speaks of the heavenly sanctuary as "the true tabernacle, which the Lord pitched" and in which is found "the throne of the Majesty" (Hebrews 8:1–2). The Book of Revelation likewise testifies to the reality of the heavenly temple and states that it is the location of God's throne (see Revelation 7:9–15; 14:17; 15:5–6; 16:17).

23. For a convenient chart comparing the earthly and heavenly temples, see Jay A. Parry and Donald W. Parry, "The Temple in Heaven: Its Description and Significance," in Parry, ed., *Temples of the Ancient World*, 521.

24. In one ancient text, which contains the earliest account of a heavenly ascent in Jewish literature, Enoch passes through the three areas of the heavenly temple. "To reach God on his throne Enoch passes through a wall (1 Enoch 14:9), an outer house (14:10–14), and an inner house (14:15–17) in the Ethiopic [version], or three houses in the Greek [version]. More clearly in the Greek but also in the Ethiopic this arrangement echoes the structure of the earthly temple with its vestibule (*ulam*), sanctuary (*hekhal*), and holy of holies (*debir*)" (Martha Himmelfarb, "Apocalyptic Ascent and the Heavenly Temple," in Kent H. Richards, ed., *Society of Biblical Literature 1987 Seminar Papers* [Atlanta: Scholars Press, 1987], 210). There are other Hebrew cosmologies which speak of seven heavens, but the "three-level cosmology is almost certainly older than the more elaborate seven-level version. The two models appear to correspond to the hierarchic structure of the temple" as it existed in the days of Solomon (three levels) and in the days of Herod (seven levels) (C. R. A. Morray-Jones, "Paradise Revisited (2 Corinthians 12:1–12): The Jewish Mystical Background of Paul's Apostolate. Part 1: The Jewish Sources," *Harvard Theological Review*, vol. 86, no. 2, April 1993, 205).

25. C. R. A. Morray-Jones, "Paradise Revisited (2 Corinthians 12:1–12): The Jewish Mystical Background of Paul's Apostolate. Part 2: Paul's Heavenly Ascent and Its Significance," *Harvard Theological Review*, vol. 86, no. 3, July 1993, 268. The author argues that Paul's ascent to paradise, or the third heaven, indicates that he gained "entry into the celestial Holy of Holies" (p. 286). He therefore suggests, on pages 285–86, that Paul's ascent occurred during the vision he had while praying in the Jerusalem temple complex (see Acts 22:17–22). This connection between the earthly and heavenly temples is also seen in the fact that on the earth "Mt. Zion is understood as the place at which heaven and earth intersect; thus Isaiah (ch. 6) sees God enthroned in the Jerusalem temple" (Himmelfarb, "Apocalyptic Ascent," 211).

26. Tabor lists the following elements that are typically found in ancient ascension texts. "1. A mortal is taken up to the highest heaven. 2. The ascent is an extraordinary privilege. 3. The way is fraught with danger and can only be successfully undertaken through divine permission and power. 4. There is great distance between the earthly and heavenly realms with increasing beauty and splendor (or danger for the uninvited) as one moves up, and an increasing sense of alienation from the world below. 5. The ascent itself is a transforming experience in which the candidate is progressively glorified. 6. The climax of the journey is an encounter with the highest god. 7. One is given secret revelations, or shown mysteries. 8. The ascent is followed by a return to the world below to live on as a mortal. 9. What is seen and heard can be selectively passed on to those who are worthy. 10. The one who has ascended faces the opposition of lower spiritual powers upon his return" (James D. Tabor, *Things Unutterable: Paul's Ascent to Paradise in Its Greco-Roman, Judaic, and Early Christian Contexts* [New York: University Press of America, 1986], 87).

27. James M. Robinson, ed., *The Nag Hammadi Library*, rev. ed. (New York: Harper Collins, 1990), 259.

28. Charlesworth, ed., *The Old Testament Pseudepigrapha*, 2:174. The Lord is depicted as giving passwords at heavenly gates at several other places in this text. In a Rabbinical ascension text called the Hekhalot Rabbati, it is stated that there are seven heavenly temples one must pass through in order to reach the throne of God. Angelic gatekeepers guard the entrance of each of these temples, and the one

making the ascent must recite the name of each sentinel and present them with certain "seals" before they are allowed to continue upward (Tabor, *Things Unutterable*, 88).

29. Charlesworth, ed., *The Old Testament Pseudepigrapha*, 1:736–37; compare with Abraham 1:17–18. The guardians of the heavenly gates are sometimes depicted in ancient literature as being seated upon thrones (*see*, for example, Robinson, ed., *The Nag Hammadi Library*, 259; Charlesworth, ed., *The Old Testament Pseudepigrapha*, 2:174). In some ancient literature it is stated that in order to reach the heaven where the Father and the Son dwell, the ascending soul must approach several gates and "persuade the archons [or guardians] to allow him to pass, the soul must address them by name, recite the correct formula, and show to each a 'symbol' (*symbolon*). These 'symbols' may be connected with the 'seal' (*sphragis*) which . . . was bestowed by the Father on the . . . Son" (P. S. Alexander, "Comparing Merkavah Mysticism and Gnosticism: An Essay in Method," *Journal of Jewish Studies*, vol. 35, no. 1, Spring 1984, 2).

30. In a work attributed to Ezra we read: "I Ezra saw on Mount Zion a great multitude, which I could not number, and they all were praising the Lord with songs. In their midst was a young man of great stature, taller than any of the others, and on the head of each of them he placed a crown, but he was more exalted than they. And I was held spellbound. Then I asked an angel, 'Who are these, my lord?' He answered and said to me, 'These are they who have put off mortal clothing and put on the immortal, and they have confessed the name of God; now they are being crowned, and receive palms.' Then I said to the angel, 'Who is that young man who places crowns on them and puts palms in their hands?' He answered and said to me, 'He is the Son of God, whom they confessed in the world" (Charlesworth, ed., *The Old Testament Pseudepigrapha*, 1:528; compare with Revelation 7:9–17).

31. Charlesworth, ed., *The Old Testament Pseudepigrapha*, 1:138. Note that the phrase "clothes of my glory" is paralleled by the temple clothing of Exodus 28 which is referred to as "garments . . . for glory" (vs. 2). The oil scented with myrrh is also paralleled by the myrrh-scented oil used to consecrate the temple priests of ancient Israel (see Exodus 30:22–38; 37:29).

32. Charlesworth, ed., *The Old Testament Pseudepigrapha*, 1:296. Another commentator on this text says: "The Curtain separates the Throne of Glory and its innermost mysteries from the other parts of the highest heaven and from the world of angels in general, just as the curtain veiled off the Holy of Holies in the sanctuary (cf. *TB. Yoma*, 77a). The Curtain hence becomes the symbol of the last secrets of heaven and earth which are kept with the Godhead, hidden even from the angels. Occasional revelations of these secrets—'the reasons of the Creator'—are described either as obtained by 'hearing from behind the Curtain' or expressed by the phrase 'to know from behind the Curtain.' . . . [In some texts] the secrets are represented as 'written down on the (inside of the) Curtain.' . . . Voices from behind the Curtain announce the answers of prayers" (Hugo Odeberg, ed., *3 Enoch or The Hebrew Book of Enoch* [New York: Ktav Publishing House, 1973], part II, 141).

33. Odeberg, ed., *3 Enoch or The Hebrew Book of Enoch*, part II, 27–28.

34. William Whiston, trans., *The Works of Josephus: Complete and Unabridged*, updated ed. (Peabody, Massachusetts: Hendrickson Publishers, 1987), 707, (*Wars*, 5.5.4).

35. Charlesworth, ed., *The Old Testament Pseudepigrapha*, 1:256. In the *Testament of Levi*, the tribal patriarch is represented as having a visionary ascension experience. He finds himself on a high

mountain and the "heavens were opened, and an angel of the Lord spoke to me: 'Levi, Levi, enter!' And I entered the first heaven." Levi is then shown the second heaven, which is brighter than the first, and is told that he will see a third heaven that is brighter still and in which he will "stand near the Lord" (ibid., 1:788). In the Apocalypse of Paul, verse 19, the apostle is represented as saying: "And I followed the angel and he lifted me up to the third heaven and he set me at the door of a gate. And I looked at it and saw that it was a golden gate and that there were two golden pillars before it and two golden tables above the pillars full of letters. And again the angel turned to me and said: 'Blessed are you if you enter in by these gates, because only those are allowed to enter who have goodness and purity of body'" (Edgar Hennecke and Wilhelm Schneemelcher, eds., *New Testament Apocrypha* [Philadelphia: Westminster Press, 1965], 2:771).

36. Orson F. Whitney, *The Life of Heber C. Kimball* (Salt Lake City: Bookcraft, 1992), 93–94. On another occasion Heber C. Kimball again spoke of "the vision that Joseph Smith had, when he saw Adam open the gate of the Celestial City and admit the people one by one. He then saw Father Adam conduct them to the throne one by one, [where] they were crowned Kings and Priests of God" (*JD*, 9:41).

37. Apocalypse of Paul, verse 20, in Hennecke and Schneemelcher, eds., *New Testament Apocrypha*, 2:771–72.

38. Robert J. Woodford suggests that the Prophet's "later writings on the resurrection, . . . pre-earth life, . . . astronomy, . . . and the [three] degrees within the celestial kingdom . . . may all have reflected some of the things he learned in this vision" (Robert J. Woodford, *The Historical Development of the Doctrine and Covenants*, doctoral dissertation, Brigham Young University, 1974, 2:928).

39. Richard N. Holzapfel, "'Eternity Sketch'd in a Vision': The Poetic Version of Doctrine and Covenants 76," in Bryon R. Merrill, ed., *The Heavens Are Open* (Salt Lake City: Deseret Book, 1993), 143; these are stanzas 5–7 of the poem. For further reading, see Larry E. Dahl, "The Vision of the Glories," in Robert L. Millet and Kent P. Jackson, eds., *Studies in Scripture: Volume One, The Doctrine and Covenants* (Salt Lake City: Deseret Book, 1989), 279–308.

40. *TPJS*, 348–49.

41. See E. Theodore Mullen, Jr., *The Divine Council in Canaanite and Early Hebrew Literature* (Chico, California: Scholars Press, 1980), 113–280. See Numbers 11:24–25 and Revelation 4:2–4, 10 where the elements of the temple, throne, and council are closely associated.

42. *TPJS*, 220.

43. Ibid., 357.

44. Ibid., 181.

45. "Everlasting covenant was made between three personages before the organization of this earth, and relates to their dispensation of things to men on the earth; these personages, according to Abraham's record, are called God the first, the Creator; God the second, the Redeemer; and God the third, the witness or Testator" (*TPJS*, 190).

46. Andrew F. Ehat and Lyndon W. Cook, *The Words of Joseph Smith* (Orem, Utah: Grandin Book, 1994), 247; hereafter cited as *WJS*.

47. *Lectures on Faith* (Salt Lake City: Deseret Book, 1985), 79.

48. *TPJS*, 48.

49. Ibid., 198.

50. Ibid., 308. "The order and ordinances of the Kingdom were instituted by the Priesthood in the council in heaven before the world was" (*WJS*, 215). At another time the Prophet spoke of "the ordinances of the gospel which were laid out before the foundations of the world" (*TPJS*, 367).

51. *TPJS*, 168.

52. Ibid., 324.

53. *The Seer*, vol. 1, no. 9, September 1853, 134. This concept of God having "Progenitors" was addressed by Joseph Smith in the following manner: "If Jesus Christ was the Son of God, and John discovered that God the Father of Jesus Christ had a Father [*see* Revelation 1:6], you may suppose that he had a Father also. Where was there ever a son without a father? And where was there ever a father without first being a son? Whenever did a tree or anything spring into existence without a progenitor? And everything comes in this way. Paul says that which is earthly is in the likeness of that which is heavenly. Hence if Jesus had a Father, can we not believe that *he* had a Father also?" (*TPJS*, 373; emphasis in original). Even though 1 Corinthians 8:5–6 declares that there are "gods many, and lords many" the Prophet Joseph Smith emphasized the message of verse 6 which is that "there is but one God—that is *pertaining to us*" (ibid., 370; emphasis in original).

54. *TPJS*, 308. The quote continues: "It was the design of the councils of heaven before the world was, that the principles and laws of the priesthood should be predicated upon the gathering of the people in every age of the world. Jesus did everything to gather the people, and they would not be gathered, and he therefore poured out curses upon them. Ordinances instituted in the heavens before the foundation of the world, in the priesthood, for the salvation of men, are not to be altered or changed. All must be saved on the same principles. It is for the same purpose that God gathers together his people in the last days, to build unto the Lord a house to prepare them for the ordinances and endowments, washings and anointings, etc."

55. Ibid., 365. Samuel W. Richards records that during this lecture the Prophet also said: "At the general and grand Council of heaven, all those to whom a dispensation was to be committed, were set apart and ordained at that time, to that calling. The Twelve also as witnesses were ordained" (*WJS*, 371). My thanks to John Gee for bringing this source to my attention.

CHAPTER TWO
The Patriarchal Pattern

In this chapter we will explore how the plan of salvation was put into operation through the creation of the earth, the peopling of the earth, and the establishment of the Church and kingdom of God upon it. We will also demonstrate that the Garden of Eden served as the first temple upon the earth and that the patriarchs from Adam to Joseph of Egypt were aware of the fulness of the gospel, including its ordinances.

THE CREATION

The creation and temple concepts are tied together in several different ways. In the ancient world, says Dr. Nibley, the "main action at the temple was the *actio*, for which the Greek word is *drama*, with parts played by priestly temple actors and royalty. Creation was celebrated with the Creation Hymn, or *poema*—the word *poem* means, in fact, 'Creation.'"[1] Dr. Nibley further informs us that,

> the rites of the temple are always a repetition of those that marked its founding in the beginning of the world, telling how it all came to be in the first place. The foundation of the sanctuary coincides with the foundation or creation of the earth itself: [Wensinck informs us that the] "first fixed point in the chaotic waters . . . is the place of the sanctuary, which becomes the earthly seat of the world-order, having its palladium in throne and altar. The foundation of the sanctuary, therefore, coincides with the creation." After a lifetime of study Lord Raglan assures us that when we study all the rituals of the world we come up with the discovery that the pristine and original ritual of them all, from which all others take their rise, was the dramatization of the creation of the world. And Mowinckel sums up the common cult pattern of all the earliest civilizations: "It is the creation of the world that is being repeated."

This creation drama was not a simple one for, as the above authorities remind us, an indispenable part of the story is the ritual death and resurrection of the king, who represents the founder and first parent of the race, and his ultimate triumph over death as priest and king, followed by some form of hieros gamos or ritual marriage for the purpose of begetting the race. . . . And if we ask why this drama is performed, we always get the same answer, according to Mowinckel: "Because the Divinity—the First Father of the Race—did so once in the beginning, and commanded us to do the same."[2]

Latter-day Saints are fortunate to have several accounts of the creation available to them beyond the Genesis narrative, as well as the insights provided by latter-day prophets. President Brigham Young, for example, taught that when the earth "was framed and brought into existence and man was placed on it, it was near the throne of our Father in heaven."[3] This may explain why Abraham said that between the time of the Creation and the Fall, eternity was reckoned "after the Lord's time, which was after the time of Kolob; for as yet the Gods had not appointed unto Adam his reckoning" (Abraham 5:13).

In the creation account from the Book of Abraham we are told that the Lord said to those who would assist him: "We will go down, for there is space there, and we will take of these materials, and we will make an earth whereon these [premortal spirits] may dwell" (Abraham 3:24). Joseph Smith placed particular emphasis on the fact that the Hebrew word translated as "create" in the Genesis account (*bara'*) "does not mean to create out of nothing; it means to organize."[4] The Prophet further stated that "God had materials to organize the world out of chaos—chaotic matter, which is element, and in which dwells all the glory. . . . The pure principles of element are principles which can never be destroyed; they may be organized and reorganized, but not destroyed. They had no beginning and can have no end."[5] And where did this material come from? According to Joseph Smith, the earth was "organized or formed out of other planets which were broken up and remodeled and made into the one on which we live."[6]

Once the planning procedures were complete, the creative actions were carried out. "And then the Lord said: Let us go down. And they went down at the beginning, and they, that is the Gods, organized and formed the heavens and the earth" (Abraham 4:1). Who were these deities? Several scriptures specify that the Father created all things through the instrumentality of the Son (*see* D&C 38:1–3; 76:22–24; Hebrews 1:1–2; Colossians 1:16–17; Moses 1:33; 2:1). Heber C. Kimball elaborated when he stated that "the Almighty sent Jehovah and Michael to do the work."[7] Joseph Fielding Smith confirms the idea that Adam, who was Michael the archangel in the premortal world,[8] helped to form this earth and labored alongside Jesus Christ in that creative endeavor.[9]

The question of how long the creation of the earth took is an intriguing one. The scriptures use several different terms to designate the length of the time spans that were involved, and this must be kept in mind when studying this issue. Latter-day prophets have had some interesting insights on this subject that deserve contemplation. George Q. Cannon claimed it was the teaching of Joseph Smith that the six *days* of creation were actually six periods according to the Lord's reckoning of time.[10] John Taylor was of the opinion that the designation *time* in the Abrahamic creation account should be equated with *ages* or *epochs*.[11] Orson Pratt emphasized the fact that the exact amount of time involved in the creation is unknown[12] and he accepted the possibility that the time it took for the dry ground to arise from the primordial sea could have been thousands or even millions of years.[13] Brigham Young viewed the *days* of the bib-

lical creation account as "a mere term." It was sufficient in his mind to understand that the "creation occupied certain periods of time. We are not authorized to say what the duration of these days was, whether Moses penned these words as we have them, or whether the translators of the Bible have given the words their intended meaning."[14] This

FIGURE 1. Early Christian woodcut (ca. 1450 A.D.) of the Creator utilizing an architect's compass in the act of creating the world and its creatures.

is an important point to consider since the "Hebrew word *yom*, often translated 'day,' can also mean 'time' [as in Abraham's account] or 'period.' In other words, the term translated 'day' in Genesis could be appropriately read as 'period.'"[15] Regardless of how long the process actually took, we know that "the Gods watched those things which they had ordered until they obeyed" (Abraham 4:18). It is clear that we do not possess a full understanding of these things at the present time, but the Lord has promised that in the millennial day He will reveal all things pertaining to the creation of the earth (*see* D&C 101:32–34).

Once the world was in a suitable condition, the Lord began placing a variety of life forms upon it. There are four accounts of the Creation available to Latter-day Saints in the books of Genesis, Moses, Abraham, and in the temple. "The temple account, for reasons that are apparent to those familiar with its teachings," explains Elder Bruce R. McConkie, "has a different division of events."[16] He also informs us that "in the temple we receive the clearest understanding of what took place and how it was accomplished."[17]

The placement of man upon the earth was a different type of creative work. And so "when it came to placing man on earth, there was a change in Creators. That is, the Father Himself became personally involved. All things were created by the Son, using the power delegated by the Father, except man. In spirit and again in the flesh, man was created by the Father."[18] How did the creation of man take place? Moses 6:22 declares forthrightly that Adam "was the son of God."[19] Elder McConkie has said that this statement "has a deep and profound significance and also means what it says."[20] According to the teaching of President Joseph F. Smith, the man Adam was "born of woman into this world, the same as Jesus and you and I."[21] Brigham Young was just as straightforward on this matter. God, he said, "created man, as we create our children; for there is no other process of creation in heaven, on the earth, in the earth, or under the earth, or in all the eternities, that is, that were, or ever that will be. . . . There exist fixed laws and regulations by which the elements are fashioned . . . and this process of creation is from everlasting to everlasting."[22] Thus, we may conclude that the accounts of Adam's creation from the dust and Eve's creation from Adam's rib are figurative, or symbolic, and designed to teach us certain truths about the first man and first woman.[23]

THE GARDEN OF EDEN

The scriptures tell us that God planted a garden eastward in the land of Eden[24] and took Adam and placed him within it (*see* Moses 3:8). The scriptures seem to indicate that the garden was a specified location on the terrestrial world and that Adam was created at a location outside of the garden.

Biblical scholars are little more precise in pinpointing the location of the Garden of Eden than to say that it was "far away in an unknown land."[25] Latter-day Saints, however, have added insight on this subject. Early leaders of the LDS Church, such as Brigham Young, said that Joseph Smith declared Jackson County, Missouri to be the location of "the old garden of Eden."[26] "Right where the Prophet Joseph laid the foundation of the [New Jerusalem] temple," said President Young, "was where God commenced the garden of Eden, and there he will end or consummate his work."[27] Joseph Fielding Smith likewise said that "the Garden of Eden was on the American continent located where the City [of] Zion, or the New Jerusalem, will be built."[28]

The Temple Pattern

Why is the temple of the New Jerusalem to be built on the exact spot where the Garden of Eden once stood? One of the reasons may be that the Garden of Eden—in both its form and function—was the first temple on the earth, and the construction of the temple on that site would constitute part of the restoration of all things. Some biblical scholars suggest that the Garden of Eden was "a type of archetypal sanctuary."[29] One apocryphal text asserts that "the Garden of Eden is the holy of holies, and the dwelling of the Lord."[30] This very specific assertion can be largely substantiated by a close examination of several scriptural passages that match the ancient temple pattern. This pattern can be seen in the following eight categories.

1. TERRESTRIAL / CELESTIAL TYPOLOGY: In LDS theology the earth is believed to have been first created in a spirit form in the presence of God and was thus a celestial sphere. It was then clothed upon with physical elements and became a terrestrial sphere where physical beings could dwell.[31] The terrestrial sphere typologically corresponds to the Holy Place of the temple in ancient Israel. But the Garden of Eden, which the Lord Himself planted (*see* Genesis 2:8) and is called the "garden of God" (Ezekiel 28:13), corresponds to the Holy of Holies of the temple in ancient Israel because the Lord's presence was there. This ties in neatly with the fact that the throne of God and the trees of a garden are found in the heavenly City of Zion, which is shaped just like the Holy of Holies of the earthly temple (*see* Revelation 21:10, 15–16; 22:1–2).

2. CENTRALITY: The four rivers of Paradise flowing out to the cardinal directions mark the garden as a point of origin or centrality. In correspondence with this image is the fact that when the ancient Israelites built the tabernacle, they placed it, by divine decree, in the center of their camp (*see* Numbers 2:1–31). The Lord likewise told the prophet Ezekiel during a visionary experience that He intended to establish His holy temple in the midst of His covenant people (*see* Ezekiel 37:26–28).

3. MOUNTAIN: When Ezekiel was shown his vision of the Jerusalem temple, he had to be taken to "a very high mountain" to see it (Ezekiel 40:2). Likewise, when John the Revelator saw the heavenly city of God, he was required to ascend a "high mountain" (Revelation 21:10). It is therefore interesting to note that in Ezekiel 28:11–16 it is implied that the Garden of Eden was located "upon the holy mountain of God" (compare Isaiah 56:7).

4. RIVER: The Bible states that a river flowing from the Garden of Eden divided into four branches, which ran to the four cardinal directions (*see* Genesis 2:10–14). John the Revelator tells us that in the heavenly city of Zion (which matches the cubical shape of the Holy of Holies) there is "a pure river of water of life, clear as crystal, proceeding out of the throne of God" (Revelation 22:1; *see* Psalm 46:4). In conjunction with this idea, Ezekiel reports that during a vision he saw water gushing out from under the threshold of the Lord's sanctuary and flowing eastward until it became a deep river (*see* Ezekiel 47:1–12).

5. MATERIALS: In the Genesis narrative, mention is made of the gold and precious stones that were associated with the lands surrounding the Garden of Eden (*see* Genesis 2:12; Ezekiel 28:13). As readers of the book of Exodus know, large quantities of gold were used in the construction of the tabernacle, and the type of stones that are mentioned in the Genesis text were the very same ones used to decorate the clothing worn by the high priest of the temple.[32]

6. TREE OF LIFE: The tree of life was found "in the midst of the garden" of Eden (Genesis 2:9; 3:3). John the Revelator likewise locates the tree of life "in the midst of" the heavenly

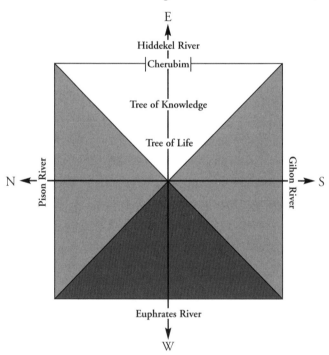

FIGURE 2. Geometric representation of the "Holy Mountain of God," illustrating the various elements that composed the sacred space of the Garden of Eden. These elements were later associated with the temples of ancient Israel.

City of Zion (Revelation 22:2). The walls and doors of Ezekiel's visionary temple were decorated with palm trees which, from the context of his account, are obvious representations of the tree of life (*see* Ezekiel 41:18–20, 23–25).

7. TREE OF KNOWLEDGE: There may be a subtle parallel between the tree of knowledge in Paradise and one of the sacred objects kept inside of the temple. In the Genesis account, the tree of knowledge is described as "pleasant to the eyes" with power to open them and "make one wise" (Genesis 3:6–7). The law of God, which was written on stone tablets and kept inside of the Holy of Holies (*see* Exodus 25:16; Deuteronomy 31:26), is likewise described as "making wise" and "enlightening the eyes" (Psalms 19:7–8).[33] By partaking of the fruit of this tree in the garden, Adam and Eve became "as gods" (Genesis 3:5, 22), and it is in the Lord's heavenly temple upon the heavenly mountain that the gods assemble before the throne of the Most High (*see* Psalms 82:1, 6; Isaiah 14:13–14; Revelation 4:4, 10–11).[34]

8. CHERUBIM: Cherubim and a flaming sword were positioned at the east end of the Garden of Eden as if there were a single entrance located there (*see* Genesis 3:24). Is it merely a coincidence that when the tabernacle was built during the time of Moses, the only entrance that was decorated with cherubim was the veil on the east side of the Holy of Holies (*see* Exodus 26:31–33; 1 Kings 6:31–32)? This does not seem likely. John the Revelator saw that all of the entrances leading into the heavenly city of Zion were also guarded by angels, including the entrances on the eastern side (*see* Revelation 21:12–13).

Falling from the Presence of God

There is some apocryphal material relating to Satan and the Fall that may be of some interest to Latter-day Saints. This material speaks of Satan not as a snake, but as a man who attempts to deceive others about his true nature by appearing as if he were an angel of light (*see* D&C 128:20; 2 Corinthians 11:14). The extracanonical First Book of Adam and Eve says that this most evil of spirits once appeared to Adam and Eve dressed in "a garment of light" and a "bright girdle"[35] in an apparent attempt to imitate the vesture of the holy angels who minister in God's heavenly temple (*see* Daniel 10:5; Revelation 1:13; 15:5–6). On another occasion the adversary and his minions appeared as if they were angels of light while Adam and Eve were engaged in prayer. Adam sensed that something was wrong and so he asked in prayer: "O Lord, is there in the world another God than thou?" God answered Adam's inquiry by sending a legitimate angel to identify Satan and to cast him out.[36] In the apocryphal Book of John the Evangelist, Satan is said to have "sent his ministers" unto Adam and his posterity in order to hide the kingdom of heaven from them by teaching them false ordinances and mysteries. In this document Satan also blasphemously declares unto them: "I am your god and beside me is none other god" (*see* 2 Corinthians 4:3–4).[37]

The LDS perspective on the Fall interprets the expulsion from paradise not only as necessary but also as positive in nature.[38] This view is sometimes encapsulated in the idea that Adam and Eve stepped down but forward. Even though the Fall caused our progenitors to be "shut out from [God's] presence" (Moses 5:4), they were not entirely without hope because they could say with the prophet Jonah: "I am cast out of thy sight; yet I will look again toward thy holy temple" (Jonah 2:4). It was in the setting of the temple that the posterity of our first parents were taught that the blood of the Lamb could overcome the effects of the Fall and redeem them. When Adam and Eve fell, the spiritual substance that sustained them in an immortal condition was replaced by blood.[39] This new substance was symbolic of mortal life and therefore a fallen condition (*see* Leviticus 17:11). Perhaps this is one of the reasons why the Atonement of Jesus Christ was accomplished through the shedding of blood, to signify the shedding of the fallen condition of sin (*see* JST Luke 22:44; Ephesians 1:7; Colossians 1:14).

The Gospel of Redemption

When Adam and Eve were driven from the Garden of Eden, they journeyed to the place that is now known as Davies County, Missouri, but which in primordial times was called Adam-ondi-Ahman (*see* D&C 78:15; 107:53). In the Pearl of Great Price we learn that sometime after the Fall, Adam and Eve offered prayer together and heard the voice of the Lord coming from the direction of paradise. The Lord gave them commandments pertaining to worship and they were instructed that they "should offer the firstlings of their flocks, for an offering unto the Lord" (Moses 5:4–5). Our first parents were obedient in carrying out these instructions even though they had not yet been told the reasons behind what they were doing. In fact, the reason behind the ritual of sacrifice was not revealed unto them for some time.

> And after many days an angel of the Lord appeared unto Adam, saying: Why dost thou offer sacrifices unto the Lord? And Adam said unto him: I know not, save the Lord commanded me.
>
> And then the angel spake, saying: This thing is a similitude of the sacrifice of the Only Begotten of the Father, which is full of grace and truth.

> Wherefore, thou shalt do all that thou doest in the name of the Son, and thou shalt repent and call upon God in the name of the Son forevermore. (Moses 5:6–8)

The scriptural record continues by saying that in that day the Holy Ghost fell upon Adam, and he heard the words of the Savior saying, "I am the Only Begotten of the Father from the beginning, henceforth and forever, that as thou hast fallen thou mayest be redeemed, and all mankind, even as many as will" (Moses 5:9).

But this was not the only method whereby God offered mankind the truths of the gospel. Modern revelation informs us that the gospel "began to be preached, from the beginning, being declared by holy angels sent forth from the presence of God, and by his own voice, and by the gift of the Holy Ghost" (Moses 5:58–59; *see also* Moroni 7:22, 25, 29).[40] Several ancient Christian texts speak of a group of three angels who appeared unto Adam and Eve. These heavenly messengers taught the primal couple about the coming of the Savior and provided them with further instructions.[41]

The Kingship and Priesthood of Adam

Latter-day prophets have taught that Adam held both the positions of a king and a priest.[42] These offices were designed to function as part of the kingdom of God. Joseph Smith declared in the name of the Lord that "the kingdom of God was set up on the earth from the days of Adam." This was necessary, said the Prophet, because "where there is no kingdom of God there is no salvation."[43] The keys of God's kingdom were, therefore, delegated to Adam.[44]

Elder Bruce R. McConkie has indicated that the kingdom established in Adam's day was a patriarchal theocracy. "This theocratic system, patterned after the order and system that prevailed in heaven, was the government of God. He himself, though dwelling in heaven, was the Lawgiver, Judge, and King. He gave direction in all things both civil and ecclesiastical."[45] Adam's kingship was granted unto him when the Lord declared that Adam was to exercise "dominion" over the whole earth (Genesis 1:26–28). Adam reigned on the earth in the Lord's stead but was still subject unto Him.

Some biblical scholars see the clothing given by God to Adam and Eve as royal vestments.[46] In addition, Hebrew legends speak of Adam wearing a crown made from the branches of the tree of life and also possessing a staff or sceptre made from a branch of the same tree.[47] The marriage of Adam and Eve in the Garden of Eden is also seen by some scholars in the context of the ritual marriage of a king and queen.[48]

It is interesting to note that Joseph Smith closely associated Adam's "dominion" (or kingly status) with the "keys" of "the First Presidency."[49]

The Prophet Joseph Smith taught that the "Priesthood was first given to Adam"[50] and he was "the first to hold the spiritual blessings, to whom was made known the plan of ordinances for the salvation of his posterity."[51] Wilford Woodruff elaborated by saying that Adam "received the holy Priesthood in all its power, and its keys and ordinances. He sealed these blessings upon his sons—Seth, Enos, Jared, Cainan, Mahalaleel, Enoch and Methuselah"[52] (see D&C 107:53–54; Moses 6:10–25). In facsimile #2, figure 3 of the Book of Abraham, the Prophet Joseph Smith informs us that Adam was acquainted with "the grand Key-words of the Holy Priesthood," and Joseph Fielding Smith went so far as to say that the fulness of the priesthood was conferred upon Adam.[53]

How did Adam come into possession of these blessings? According to Wilford Woodruff, "he attended to the ordinances of the house of God."[54] This is consistent with the Lord's declaration that His people in all ages are commanded to build a "holy house" unto Him so that He may have a suitable place in which to reveal His ordinances (D&C 124:38–39). Some Jewish legendary material claims that Adam had a "house of worship" where he "offered his prayers."[55] In Isaiah 56:7, it is the temple of Jehovah that is designated as the "house of prayer." A statement by President Ezra Taft Benson implies that Adam and Eve did indeed have access to a house of the Lord.

> When our Heavenly Father placed Adam and Eve on this earth, he did so with the purpose in mind of teaching them how to regain his presence. Our Father promised a Savior to redeem them from their fallen condition. He gave them the plan of salvation and told them to teach their children faith in Jesus Christ and repentance. Further, Adam and his posterity were commanded by God to be baptized, to receive the Holy Ghost, and to enter into the order of the Son of God.
>
> To enter into the order of the Son of God is the equivalent today of entering into the fulness of the Melchizedek Priesthood, which is only received in the house of the Lord.
>
> Because Adam and Eve had complied with these requirements, God said to them, "Thou art after the order of him who was without beginning of days or end of years, from all eternity to all eternity" (Moses 6:67).[56]

There are other evidences that Adam had the priesthood and its blessings. The apostle Peter reportedly told Clement, an early Christian leader, that it is certain Adam was anointed.[57] One of God's commandments to Adam regarding the care of the garden of Eden is significant from a temple and priesthood perspective. Genesis

2:15 says that God took Adam "and put him into the garden of Eden to dress (*ʿabad*) it and to keep (*šamar*) it." In Numbers 3:8 we read that the Levites "shall keep (*šamar*) all the instruments of the Tabernacle of the congregation, and the charge of the children of Israel, to do the service (*ʿabad*) of the Tabernacle." Concerning these parallel passages, one scholar has noted that "if Eden is seen then as an ideal sanctuary, then perhaps Adam should be described as an archetypal Levite."[58]

The Genesis narrative says that before Adam and Eve were driven from the Garden of Eden, God made "coats of skins" for them and "clothed them" (Genesis 3:21). There are several things about this verse that should be noted. First, God is said to have made this clothing, which would mean that it was of a sacred nature. Second, the form of the verb translated as "clothed them" has two main uses in the Bible: (a) to speak of a king "clothing honored subjects (e.g., Genesis 41:42; 1 Samuel 17:38)," or (b) "for the dressing of priests in their sacred vestments, usually put on by Moses. Frequently he clothes them in their tunics (e.g., Exodus 28:41; 29:8; 40:14; Leviticus 8:13). Here again the terminology of the Garden of Eden runs closely parallel to the vocabulary associated with worship in the Tabernacle."[59] Various Jewish legends claim that these clothes were "high-priestly garments" fashioned after the manner of those worn by the angels.[60] The fig leaf aprons worn by Adam and Eve may also be significant in this context since the temple priests of ancient Israel wore ceremonial aprons along with their other priestly vestments.[61] Some Jewish legends claim that the fig leaves from which these aprons were made came from the tree of knowledge, suggesting that the apron could be seen as a symbol of Adam and Eve's mortality.[62]

Finally, in the third chapter of the pseudepigraphical Book of Jubilees we find the claim that once Adam was dressed in the clothing that God gave him, he offered incense as the sun arose.[63] This could be compared with Exodus 30:7, which specifies that the high priest of the temple was to burn "sweet incense every morning" upon the golden altar that stood before the veil.

THE PATRIARCHS

There is sufficient evidence found in scriptural accounts, prophetic teachings, scholarly research, and Jewish legendary material to conclude that the patriarchs were well aware of the temple concept and participated in holy ordinances.

Enoch

Elder Joseph Young Sr. once stated that Enoch was granted a vision of the cities and mansions that are found in the celestial world. He thereby acquired "a superior intelligence and that spirit of refinement and taste which enabled him to instruct his brethren to build [the city of Zion] after the pattern of the heavenly" cities which he had seen.[64] President Brigham Young voiced his opinion that there were temples in the city of Zion and that Enoch officiated within them.[65] Elder Franklin D. Richards of the Quorum of the Twelve Apostles likewise said that he believed that "in the city of Enoch there [were] temples" and when that city returns to the earth those temples will be seen there.[66] This would certainly be consistent with the comment found in Moses 6:21 that Enoch's father Jared taught him "in all the ways of God," and Jewish lore, which claims that Enoch was in possession of the high-priestly garments that were given by God to Adam.[67]

> Enoch's priestly credentials were well-known [among the ancients] and developed in later literature. In Jubilees 4:25 Enoch makes the evening incense offering. In 2 Enoch Enoch's angelomorphic transformation is expressed in terms of priestly investiture (22:8–10) and the concluding chapters (69–73) "are devoted to the succession of the priesthood after Enoch's ascension, clearly implying that Enoch himself served as a priest." So too in the Hekalot text 3 Enoch Enoch's investiture is recognisably priestly (see ch. 12).[68]

In the Joseph Smith Translation we are informed that every individual who is "ordained [as a] high priest after the order of the covenant which God made with Enoch, it being after the order of the Son of God," has power through their faith to "stand in the presence of God."[69] Those in Enoch's city of Zion who did in fact come into the presence of God are identified as "the general assembly of the church of the firstborn" (JST Genesis 9:21–25; see also JST Genesis 14:25–40). In a latter-day revelation we find an additional reference to "the general assembly and church of Enoch, and of the Firstborn" and it is indicated that they are "priests and kings . . . after the order of Enoch, which [is] after the order of the Only Begotten Son" (D&C 76: 56–57, 67).[70] It was the teaching of the Prophet Joseph Smith that a man could only become a king and a priest if he participated in the fulness of temple ordinances.[71]

In Moses 7:69 we read that "Enoch and all his people walked with God, [and God] dwelt in the midst of Zion." It can be seen that this verse has clear temple implications when one realizes that during the time of Moses, the tabernacle of Jehovah was placed "in the midst" of the camp of Israel (Numbers 2:17) so that the Lord could "dwell" among them (Exodus 25:8; 29:45; 1 Kings 6:13) and teach them to "walk" in his ways (Isaiah 2:2–3).

Noah

Scriptures restored in the final dispensation teach that "the Lord ordained Noah after his own order, and commanded him that he should go forth and declare his gospel unto the children of men, even as it was given unto Enoch." Noah then went forward and preached faith in Jesus Christ, repentance, baptism, and reception of the Holy Ghost (Moses 8:19–20, 24). It is evident from another scriptural passage that Noah was aware of such things as Zion, the everlasting covenant that God established with Enoch, and the Church of the Firstborn (*see* JST Genesis 9:21–25).

Joseph Smith taught the Saints that Noah, who is the angel Gabriel, "stands next in authority to Adam in the Priesthood; he was called of God to this office, and was the father of all living in his day, and to him was given the dominion" or kingship.[72] John Taylor echoed this teaching when he stated that Noah was a high priest who held "the keys, rights and powers of the everlasting Priesthood" and he was also a king.[73] These offices were passed on after the flood, said Elder Taylor, as the patriarchal order was introduced among the people and prominent men were made "kings and priests unto God."[74]

In the Joseph Smith Translation we learn that after the flood Noah acted in the capacity of a priest by building an altar and offering sacrifices (JST Genesis 9:4–6). This would be consistent with Jewish legends that claim Noah had the high-priestly robes that God gave to Adam with him in the ark.[75] Joseph Fielding Smith said that Noah "held the fulness of the priesthood"[76] and Joseph Smith explained in facsimile #2, figure 3 of the Book of Abraham that Noah was aware of "the grand Key-words of the Holy Priesthood."

In Genesis 9:20–27 we read of a strange incident after the flood, where Noah pronounced a curse upon his son Ham. This episode makes little sense until one realizes that a mistranslation has obscured the part played by Noah's garment. This additional piece of information is highly significant because the legends of the Jews report that Ham stole the priestly garments of Adam from Noah after they had left the ark.[77]

These insights help to explain several passages in the Book of Abraham. There we read that Ham was married to a woman named Egypt. Their daughter, who was also named Egypt, settled her sons in the land that is now known as Egypt. The name of her firstborn son was Pharaoh, which was the title that was later given to the kings of Egypt (*see* Abraham 1:21–25). Then we learn something very important from the Abrahamic account.

> Now the first government of Egypt was established by Pharaoh, the eldest son of Egyptus, the daughter of Ham, and it was after the manner of the government of Ham, which was patriarchal.
>
> Pharaoh, being a righteous man, established his kingdom and judged his people wisely and justly all his days, seeking earnestly to imitate that order established by the fathers in the first generations, in the days of the first patriarchal reign, even in the reign of Adam, and also of Noah, his father, who blessed him with the blessings of the earth, and with the blessings of wisdom, but cursed him as pertaining to the Priesthood. (Abraham 1:25–26)

Even though Pharaoh, the firstborn son of Egyptus, was "of that lineage by which he could not have the right of Priesthood," the kings of Egypt after him still laid claim to it "from Noah, through Ham" (Abraham 1:27). And what was this "order established . . . in the reign of Adam" that was so earnestly imitated by the Egyptian kings? The answer comes in Joseph Smith's equation of "the order pertaining to the Ancient of Days" and the ordinances of the temple.[78]

The LDS Church obtained several ancient Egyptian papyrus scrolls in the year 1835, and after examining them Joseph Smith stated that Facsimile #2 in the Book of Abraham contained information pertaining to the "Key-words of the Priesthood" (figure 7) and "writings that cannot be revealed unto the world; but [are] to be had in the

FIGURE 3. Facsimile #2 from the Book of Abraham. Joseph Smith indicated that this Egyptian diagram contained information that was "to be had in the Holy Temple of God."

Holy Temple of God" (figures 8 through 21). Dr. Nibley, in his book *The Message of the Joseph Smith Papyri: An Egyptian Endowment*, conducted a study of some of these papyrus scrolls and confirmed that they do indeed contain material from Egyptian temple rites. And even though these rituals are apostate imitations of the true order, and therefore "badly damaged and out of proper context," he feels that they may still serve as confirmatory evidence to the genuineness and antiquity of some Latter-day Saint practices and beliefs.[79] In Dr. Nibley's book we find that the Joseph Smith papyrus scrolls allude to ritual elements such as:

• *Purification Rites:* These rites took place outside the temple proper in a "purification room" (p. 93). Water was used for this cleansing because it is "par excellence the medium of passage: half-way between solid matter and tenuous spirit, it enables bodies to move from one place to another in a state of effortless motion and silent suspension, visibly hovering between the solid earth below and the empty sky above" (94). The washing of Egyptian initiates was followed by an anointing with oil that was meant to sanctify them (98–99). Various parts of the initiate's body were anointed (106–108, 112). This "ordinance insures that each part of the body by virtue of remaining (1) pure and (2) intact will never again lose its proper function. . . . It is specifically an anointing to seal the body up against the day of the resurrection, its total restoration being anticipated by a ritual reversing [of] the effect of the 'blows of death' on each member of the body" (106).[80] The initiate was also clothed "with ritual garments and insignia before entering the inner rooms of the temple" (116). Initiation vestments could include a long white linen robe (144), an apron (119, 199) and white sandals (143). Some ritual texts speak of the initiate receiving a new name (120).

• *Dramatic Presentation:* The Egyptian initiate then went into another room of the temple and viewed a ritual drama that was acted out in the manner of a mystery play (129–30). This drama was centered on a council in heaven and the creation of the earth and man (131). The initiate is described in some ritual texts as being awakened out of sleep when the sun's rays fall upon his face and he finds himself in a new world with a new life (145–48, 151). Some Egyptian temples had garden areas with sacred trees growing within them. These may have been related to ritual texts which speak of a holy garden that is located in between heaven and earth, ritual marriage in the garden, forbidden fruit, and an adversarial serpent who gets cursed (is told his head can be crushed) and is kept at bay by sword and flame (163–81).

• *Long Journey:* Some of the Egyptian initiation ceremonies were concerned with the means whereby the initiate would ascend into heaven. This ascension was seen as a journey that had to be undertaken by all who desired to enter into the presence of deity (183–206). Guides were sent down from heavenly realms to instruct initiates during their journey. In one Egyptian text "three divine beings visit the earth to instruct mankind in the ordinances; they are personified in the temple drama by three actor-priests" (194–95, 148). During the upward journey, the initiate is described as passing through a series of gates at each of which he is tested by creeds, liturgical for-mulas, and passwords (211–12). The royal initiation rituals ended when the king was conducted to a part of the temple that was shut off by a curtain, and here he embraced a deity who transferred power and authority to him (241–53).

Melchizedek

Genesis 14:18 informs us that Melchizedek was both a king and a priest of the Most High God. Melchizedek received the priesthood "through the lineage of his fathers, even till Noah" (D&C 84:14). We learn from JST Genesis 14:25–40 that Melchizedek "was ordained a high priest after the order of the covenant which God made with Enoch, it being after the order of the Son of God" (vss. 27–28). And because he was "ordained after this order" he had the ability, through his faith, "to stand in the presence of God" (vss. 30–31). In the Joseph Smith Translation of the book of Hebrews we also find that "Melchizedek was ordained a priest after the order of the Son of God, which order was without father, without mother, without descent, having neither beginning of days, nor end of life. And all those who are ordained unto this priesthood are made like unto the Son of God, abiding a priest continually" (JST Hebrews 7:3). The Jewish historian Flavius Josephus informs us that Melchizedek was the first priest of God in the city that came to be known as Jerusalem and that he built a temple there.[81] This would be in accordance with Jewish legends stating that Melchizedek was in possession of the priestly garments that were given by God to Adam.[82] Figure 3 of facsimile #2 in the Book of Abraham indicates that Melchizedek was aware of "the grand Key-words of the Holy Priesthood."

Before Melchizedek's day, said the Prophet Joseph Smith, the priesthood "was called *the Holy Priesthood, after the Order of the Son of God.* But out of respect or rev-erence to the name of the Supreme Being, to avoid the too frequent repetition of his name, they, the church, in ancient days, called that priesthood after Melchizedek, or the Melchizedek Priesthood" because this man "was such a great high priest" (D&C 107:2–4). The power and authority of the Melchizedek Priesthood is connected to the spiritual blessings of the gospel, which include "the privilege of receiving the mysteries of the kingdom of heaven," parting the veil between heaven and earth, and coming into the presence of members of the Godhead and the general assembly and Church of the Firstborn (D&C 107:18–19; *see* 84:19–22). According to Joseph Smith, the power of Melchizedek was "not the power of a prophet, nor apostle, nor patriarch only, but of [a] king and priest to God to open the windows of heaven and pour out the peace and law of endless life to man. And no man can attain to the joint heirship with Jesus Christ without being administered to by one having the same power and authority of Melchizedek."[83] All of those who hold "the fulness of the Melchizedek Priesthood," said the Prophet, "are kings and priests of the Most High God, holding the keys of power and blessings. In fact, that Priesthood is a perfect law of theocracy, and stands as God to give laws to the people, administering endless lives to the sons and daughters of Adam."[84]

Abraham

The apostle Paul testified that Abraham knew the "gospel" of Jesus Christ (Galatians 3:8; *see also* Abraham 2:10–11). We find confirmation of this idea in the teachings of the Prophet Joseph Smith[85] and also in JST Genesis 17:3–7 where it states that Abraham was aware of gospel ordinances such as baptism (also called "the burial,")[86] and anointing.

In the Book of Abraham we read that Abraham "sought for the blessings of the fathers," meaning that he desired to become a high priest and an heir to the "right of the firstborn, or the first man, who is Adam" (Abraham 1:1–4). We know from latter-day revelation that "Abraham received the priesthood from Melchizedek" (D&C 84:14) after he had affirmed that he believed all Melchizedek had taught him about the priesthood and the coming of Jesus Christ.[87] Joseph Smith restored the knowledge that Melchizedek, who was a "high priest," blessed the sacramental emblems of bread and wine and administered them unto Abraham and then also blessed Abraham in some manner "according to the covenant which he had made" (JST Genesis 14: 17, 37–40). Joseph Smith clarified the meaning of this statement when he said that Abraham "received a blessing under the hands of Melchizedek, even the last law or a fulness of the law or priesthood which constituted him a king and priest after the order of Melchizedek."[88]

In line with the account of Josephus, which states that Melchizedek built a temple in Jerusalem, a pseudepigraphical work called Pseudo-Eupolemus claims that Abraham entered a temple that was designated as "mountain of the Most High" and he "received gifts from Melchizedek, its ruler [who was also the] priest of God."[89] In one ancient source we read: "The Lord said to Abraham: 'Follow me, and I will make thee a High Priest after the order of Adam, the first man.'"[90] We learn from other ancient texts that Melchizedek taught Abraham all the duties of the priesthood[91] and gave him the priestly garments that were made by God for Adam.[92] Perhaps it was on these occasions that Abraham was made aware of "the grand Key-words of the Holy Priesthood," as mentioned in figure 3 of facsimile #2 in the Book of Abraham.

With the priesthood and its symbolic robes in his possession, Abraham was authorized to build altars and engage in priestly activities. In one biblical passage we read that Abraham built an altar unto the Lord near "a mountain on the east of Bethel" and offered up his prayers before it (Genesis 12:8; *see also* 13:4). An apocryphal work known as the Apocalypse of Abraham depicts the father of the faithful offering prayer upon his knees and requesting that the Lord "teach" him information he had been "promised" he would receive. During this prayer the patriarch employed the curious threefold petition "El, El, El."[93] This same source depicts Abraham on Mount Horeb, the holy mountain of God, where he offers sacrifice and is informed by an angel that he will be shown "the garden of Eden." Satan appears on the scene in disguise and tries to convince Abraham to cease his worshipful activities but an angel of God, who is with Abraham, identifies Satan and commands him to "depart."[94]

FIGURE 4. This illustration, taken from a Christian glass dish (ca. 400 A.D.), depicts Abraham and Isaac standing before a sacred portal with an altar in the foreground.

Even though Abraham was obedient in offering up sacrifices unto the Lord (*see* Abraham 2:17–20), there came a time when this servant of God was required to offer up a supreme sacrifice (*see* Genesis 22:1–18). In the Book of Mormon we are informed that when the Lord commanded Abraham to offer up his son Isaac as a sacrifice, this act was designed to serve as "a similitude of God and his Only Begotten Son" (Jacob 4:5). Some of the typological parallels[95] that can be seen between Isaac and the Savior include:

1. Both Isaac and the Savior were the only begotten sons of their fathers (see Genesis 22:2; Hebrews 11:17–19; 1 John 4:9).
2. Both Isaac and the Savior were in their thirties when they were offered up.
3. Both Isaac and the Savior submitted willingly to being sacrificed.
4. Both Isaac and the Savior were offered up on the mountain where the Jerusalem temple stood.
5. Both Isaac and the Savior carried the wood of their sacrifice upon their backs (see JST Genesis 22:7; John 19:17).
6. Both Isaac and the Savior were bound (see Genesis 22:9; Matthew 27:2).
7. Both Isaac and the Savior were likened unto sacrificial lambs (see Genesis 22:7–8; John 1:29).

The Prophet Joseph Smith taught this very important lesson about Abraham's sacrifice: "The sacrifice required of Abraham in the offering up of Isaac, shows that if a man would attain to the keys of the kingdom of an endless life he must sacrifice all things."[96] The Lord has indicated that the Saints "must needs be chastened and tried, even as Abraham" (D&C 101:4) so that they might eventually receive the same exaltation that has been sealed upon him (*see* D&C 132:37).

Jacob

Jacob had the blessings of the Abrahamic covenant pronounced upon him by his father Isaac on condition that he marry a wife from the covenant lineage. He was commanded, "Take thee a wife from thence" so that God will "bless thee, and make thee fruitful, and multiply thee, that thou mayest be a multitude of people; and give thee the blessing of Abraham, to thee, and to thy seed with thee; that thou mayest inherit the land wherein thou art a stranger, which God gave unto Abraham" (Genesis 28:2–5). On several occasions the Lord Himself appeared to Jacob to confirm upon him the blessings of the Abrahamic covenant (*see* Genesis 28:10–22).[97]

As an inheritor of the blessings of the Abrahamic covenant, Jacob also came into possession of certain ritual objects belonging to the firstborn son who was the heir of the birthright blessings. One Jewish tradition states that,

> To make Jacob's disguise complete, Rebekah felt justified in putting Esau's wonderful garments on him. They were the high-priestly raiment in which God had clothed Adam, 'the firstborn of the world,' for in the days before the creation of the Tabernacle all the firstborn males officiated as priests. From Adam these garments descended to Noah, who transmitted them to Shem, and Shem bequeathed them to Abraham, and Abraham to his son Isaac, from whom they reached Esau as the older

of his two sons. It was the opinion of Rebekah that as Jacob had bought the birthright from his brother, he had thereby come into possession of the garments as well.[98]

An analysis of Jacob's covenant experiences with Jehovah may prove insightful. Jacob had a vision of God at "a certain place" called Bethel (Genesis 28:11–13). *Bethel* is a contraction of two Hebrew words—*Beth*, meaning "house" and *El*, meaning "God." Jacob even uses the phrase "the house of God" to describe the location where his experience with Deity occurred (Genesis 28:17–19). One scholar notes,

> The rendering, "a certain place" does not preserve all the connotations of the Hebrew. The meaning is rather "the well-known place," "the place we are talking about," i.e. the sanctuary at Bethel. The word translated "place" also has the meaning "sanctuary." The implication of the verse is thus that the place was already holy—according to Semitic ideas, a spot at which man could come into effective contact with the divine.[99]

In the apocryphal Book of Jubilees (32:16) it is claimed that Jacob built a temple at Bethel, and it is evident from biblical passages that some type of holy place did, in fact, exist there (*see* 1 Samuel 7:15–17; 10:3). This would help explain why Jacob and his family purified themselves and changed their clothing before they ascended to Bethel (*see* Genesis 35:1–3; compare Exodus 19:10). The "ladder" Jacob saw at Bethel also deserves attention because of its possible temple connection.

> Etymologically, the term (stem sll "to heap up, raise") suggests a ramp or a solid stairway. And archaeologically, the Mesopotamian ziggurats were equipped with flights of stairs leading up to the summit . . . Only such [a] stairway can account for Jacob's later description of it as a "gateway to heaven." . . . The phraseology is much too typical of the temple tower to be merely coincidental, and the underlying imagery cannot be mistaken; the allusion is all the more suggestive when viewed in connection with Jacob's journey to Mesopotamia.[100]

What did Jacob see at this holy place? The text says he saw "the angels of God ascending and descending" the temple stairway (Genesis 28:12). The word used here for "angels" is *mal'ak* and means a messenger of God who is dispatched.[101] Why were these angels being sent down to the earth and then returning to the heavenly realms? Perhaps they were delivering messages pertaining to the Abrahamic covenant that the Lord was establishing with Jacob.[102]

In Genesis 32 we read the astonishing story of Jacob wrestling with a heavenly messenger—and winning! Dr. Nibley helps to clarify the context of this story by comparing some of its elements to ritual actions that were practiced in the ancient Near East.

> One of the most puzzling episodes in the Bible has always been the story of Jacob's wrestling with the Lord. When one considers that the word conventionally translated by 'wrestled' *(yeaveq)* can just as well mean "embrace," and that it was in this ritual embrace that Jacob received a new name and the bestowal of priestly and kingly power at sunrise (Genesis 32:24ff), the parallel to the Egyptian coronation embrace becomes at once apparent.[103]

In addition to receiving the new name of *Israel,* the patriarch Jacob also requested that the divine being reveal his name.[104] We are not told what the exact response of the heavenly messenger was, but we are informed that "he blessed him there" (Genesis 32:26–29). Who was this being from beyond the veil? Jacob called the place where this incident occurred *Peniel* because, he said, he had "seen God face to face" and yet his life was preserved (Genesis 32:30).[105]

Joseph of Egypt

We know from the Bible that Jacob's son Joseph received the birthright among the twelve tribes of Israel (*see* 1 Chronicles 5:1–2). It was Joseph's investiture with the so-called "coat of many colors" that signaled that he was the birthright son (*see* Genesis 37:3, 23, 32).[106] There are several things that the reader should notice in order to properly understand the nature of Joseph's "coat." First of all, the phrase "coat of many colors" actually comes from the Septuagint, which was the Greek translation of the Old Testament made between 284 and 246 B.C. This is not what the Hebrew text says, however. The word "many" is not present in the Hebrew text and that is why it has been italicized by the translators of the King James Bible. Hence the phrase should simply read "coat of colours."

The next thing to notice about this phrase is that "coat" is translated from the Hebrew word *kuttonet,* and it can mean either garment or robe.[107] This is the very same word used to identify one of the vestments worn by the temple priests of Israel from the time of Moses onward (*see* Exodus 28:39). Indeed, it was understood among later Jewish authors that Joseph's vesture was nothing less than "the holy tunic of the priest."[108]

The Hebrew word translated as "colours" also calls for our attention. In the Joseph narrative, this word is *pas* and refers to a long, sleeved tunic that reached to the wrists and the ankles. It was a type of garment that was worn by royalty in Old Testament times.[109] Interestingly, it is the considered opinion of some biblical interpreters that Joseph's "coat" was not only a "royal garment" but it also signified "the claim of the Joseph tribes to a royal authority independent of the tribe of Judah."[110]

The preceding information points to the conclusion that Joseph's distinctive vesture could be seen as both the clothing of a king and a priest. This comes as little surprise when one considers that in Jewish lore the gift that was given by Jacob to Joseph was exactly what he himself had received as part of the birthright blessing, "the garments made by God for Adam."[111]

SUMMARY

It has been demonstrated throughout this chapter that the ancient Hebrews did not believe that the temple concept originated in the time of Moses. Rather, they taught that temple rituals and doctrines originated with Adam and were handed down among the biblical patriarchs. This is precisely what the Prophet Joseph Smith tried to teach the world during the early 1800s, that the gospel of Jesus Christ is eternal and has been on the earth from the beginning.

NOTES

1. Hugh W. Nibley, "Looking Backward," in Truman G. Madsen, ed., *The Temple in Antiquity* (Provo, Utah: BYU Religious Studies Center, 1984), 48; emphasis in original. For further reading on this subject, see Stephen D. Ricks, "Liturgy and Cosmogony: The Ritual Use of Creation Accounts in the Ancient Near East," in Donald W. Parry, ed., *Temples of the Ancient World: Ritual and Symbolism* (Salt Lake City: Deseret Book and FARMS, 1994), 118–25.

2. Hugh W. Nibley, "What Is a Temple?" in Madsen, ed., *The Temple in Antiquity*, 25–26; emphasis in original.

3. *JD*, 17:143. According to John Taylor, the earth "was first organized, near the planet Kolob" (*The Mormon*, vol. 3, no. 28, 29 August 1857, 2). Brigham Young also taught that the earth will eventually "go back into the presence of God, where it was first framed" (*JD*, 9:317; see also ibid., 7:163; 8:8).

4. *HC*, 6:308. "The word *created* should be *formed* or *organized*" (*TPJS*, 181; emphasis added).

5. *HC*, 6:308–309. The Prophet taught that the "elements are eternal" (*TPJS*, 181) and therefore the earth existed in "an elementary state, from eternity" (*HC*, 3:387; see also *JD*, 19:286; 24:61; 26:27). For an informative article that deals with LDS perspectives on the creation, and also with problems in the King James translation of Genesis, see John A. Tvedtnes, "Science and Genesis," in Wilford M. Hess, Raymond T. Matheny, and Donlu D. Thayer, eds., *Science and Religion: Toward a More Useful Dialogue* (Geneva, Illinois: Paladin House, 1979), 2:39–60.

6. *WJS*, 60. On page 61 of the same source we read that the earth "has been organized out of portions of other globes that [have] been disorganized." Orson Pratt once taught: "We are not to suppose that these elements, before they were collected, were formed into solid masses of rocks and other hard substances: and that these came rushing together—rocks being piled on rocks, breaking, crashing, and rending into millions of fragments. But no doubt through the operation of antecedent forces, there had been a complete disorganization or dissolution of the bodies, composed of these elements in that prior state of existence anterior to the foundation of the present globe: this being the case, the elements being separate, and apart, and widely diffused, were in a condition to come together in a state of particles, instead of aggregate masses. These particles, under the law of force ordained, would collect in the form of a sphere, arranging themselves according to their specific gravities in strata at different distances from the center" (*The Seer*, vol. 2, no. 4, April 1854, 249; see also *JD*, 13:248).

7. *JD*, 10:235. Brigham Young taught: "It is true that the earth was organized by three distinct characters, namely, Eloheim, Yahovah, and Michael, these three forming a quorum, as in all heavenly bodies, and in organizing element" (ibid., 1:51). Elder Bruce R. McConkie specifically lists participants in the creation as "Elohim, Jehovah, Michael" (*Ensign*, June 1982, 11).

8. See D&C 27:11; 107:54; 116:1; 128:21; 138:38.

9. *DS*, 1:74–75. One LDS scholar notes that it is "in the temple account of the Creation that we learn that Adam is Michael, who helped Jehovah in the Creation." He also says that by "using the power of drama and group participation, this account teaches, so far as possible within the limits of dramatic structure, the various steps involved in the Creation, the sequence of events, and the roles of those involved" (Keith Meservy, "Four Accounts of the Creation," *Ensign*, January 1986, 50, 53).

10. "Joseph [Smith] taught that a day with God was not the twenty-four hours of our day; but that the six days of the creation were six periods of the Lord's time" (*JD*, 24:61).

11. Ibid., 25:215.

12. Ibid., 14:234–35.

13. Ibid., 18:316.

14. Ibid., 18:231. In studying the various creation accounts that are available, it is important to remember two facts. (1) "The account of creation in Genesis was not a *spirit* creation" (*DS*, 1:76, emphasis in original), and (2) Even though Genesis 2:5 and Moses 3:7–9 make parenthetical statements acknowledging the spirit creation, there "is no revealed account of the spirit creation" (*MD*, 170). From Elder McConkie we also learn that the "Mosaic and the temple accounts set forth the temporal or physical creation, the actual organization of element or matter into tangible form. They are not accounts of the spirit creation" (*Ensign*, June 1982, 11). These statements are sustained by non-LDS biblical commentators. "Genesis contains not one but two distinct accounts of creation, of which the first begins with the opening chapter of Genesis . . . But this account ends with Genesis 2:3; and the following verse, Genesis 2:4, begins a different narrative. . . . Most biblical scholars today agree that the two creation accounts, originally separate, were later joined to make up the first three chapters of Genesis. The story of Adam and Eve (Genesis 2:4f), told in the language of folklore, is considered the older of the two accounts, dating to 1000—900 B.C.E.; the account now placed first (Genesis 1:1–2:3) dates to postexilic theologians (c. 400 B.C.E.). Jewish teachers in antiquity, like many Christians after them, turned to theological ingenuity rather than historical or literary analysis to account for contradictions in the texts" (Elaine Pagels, *Adam, Eve, and the Serpent* [New York: Random House, 1988], xxi–xxii).

15. Thomas R. Valletta, "Some individuals interpret scriptures to say that the Creation was done in six 24-hour days. Does Abraham's usage of 'time' lead us to understand that the Creation was not confined to six 24-hour days as we know them?" *Ensign*, January 1994, 53. Regarding the creation Elder Bruce R. McConkie asks, "What is a day? It is a specified time period; it is an age, an eon, a division of eternity; it is the time between two identifiable events. And each day, of whatever length, has the duration needed for its purposes. . . . There is no revealed recitation specifying that each of the 'six days' involved in the Creation was of the same duration" (*Ensign*, June 1982, 11). "The Hebrew word for *day* used in the creation account can be translated as 'day' in the literal sense, but it can also be used in the sense of an indeterminate length of time (see Genesis 40:4, where *day* is translated as 'a season'; Judges 11:4, where a form of *day* is translated as 'in the process of time'; see also Holladay, *Hebrew and Aramaic Lexicon of the Old Testament*, pp. 130–31). Abraham says that the Gods *called* the creation periods days (*see* Abraham 4:5, 8). If this last meaning was the sense in which Moses used the word *day*, then the apparent conflict between the scriptures and much of the evidence seen by science as supporting a very old age for the earth is easily resolved. Each era or day of creation could have lasted for millions or even hundreds of millions of our years, and uniformitarianism could be accepted without any problem" (*Old Testament: Genesis—2 Samuel, Student Manual*, rev. ed. [Salt Lake City: The Church of Jesus Christ of Latter-day Saints, 1981], 28–29; emphasis in original).

16. Bruce R. McConkie, "Christ and the Creation," *Ensign*, June 1982, 11.

17. *MD*, 169–70.

18. Bruce R. McConkie, *The Promised Messiah* (Salt Lake City: Deseret Book, 1978), 62. Elder McConkie wrote on another occasion that with God "there are two creative events that are his and his alone. First, he is the Father of all spirits, Christ's included; none were fathered or created by anyone else. Second, he is the Creator of the physical body of man. Though Jehovah and Michael and many of the noble and great ones played their assigned roles in the various creative events, yet when it came time to place man on earth, the Lord God himself performed the creative acts" (Bruce R. McConkie, *A New Witness for the Articles of Faith* [Salt Lake City: Deseret Book, 1985], 63; hereafter cited as *NWAF*).

19. Luke 3:38 says exactly the same thing. In the Joseph Smith Translation of this passage (JST Luke 3:45), the Prophet modified this passage to say that Adam "was formed of God."

20. Bruce R. McConkie, *Doctrinal New Testament Commentary* (Salt Lake City: Bookcraft, 1965), 1:95.

21. *Deseret Evening News*, 27 December 1913, section 3, Church News, 7.

22. *JD*, 11:122. Heber C. Kimball taught that we were all "born and begotten by our Father and our God before we ever took these bodies; and these bodies were formed by him, and through him, and of him, just as much as the spirit was; for I tell you, he commenced and brought forth spirits; and then, when he completed that work, he commenced and brought forth tabernacles for those spirits to dwell in. I came through him, both spirit and body" (ibid., 6:31). The First Presidency of the LDS Church once published the declaration that mankind is "the direct and lineal offspring of Deity" (*Improvement Era*, November 1909, 81; hereafter cited as *IE).*

23. On the dust and rib explanations being figurative, see Bruce R. McConkie, "Christ and the Creation," *Ensign*, June 1982, 15; Vivian M. Adams, "Our Glorious Mother Eve," in Joseph Fielding McConkie and Robert L. Millet, eds., *The Man Adam* (Salt Lake City: Bookcraft, 1990), 95–99.

24. The basic meaning of the Hebrew word *'eden* is "delight" or "pleasure" (James Strong, *The New Strong's Exhaustive Concordance of the Bible* [Nashville: Thomas Nelson Publishers, 1996], Hebrew and Aramaic Dictionary of the Old Testament, 103, words #5730 and #5731).

25. G. Johannes Botterweck and Helmer Ringgren, eds., *Theological Dictionary of the Old Testament* (Grand Rapids, Michigan: Eerdmans, 1978), 3:37. Morris believes that it is futile to try to match pre-Flood descriptions of the topography and geography associated with the Garden of Eden with post-Flood locations because the antediluvian world "perished" during the deluge (see 2 Peter 3:6). "Those who have tried to identify the garden of Eden as in the present Tigris-Euphrates region fail to realize that these antediluvian rivers were completely obliterated by the Flood, and have no physical connection with their counterparts in the present world. The garden of Eden was, of course, also destroyed in the Flood, so that it is quite impossible to locate it now in terms of modern geography" (Henry M. Morris, *The Genesis Record* [Grand Rapids, Michigan: Baker Book House, 1976], 89–90).

26. Scott G. Kenney, ed., *Wilford Woodruff's Journal* (Midvale, Utah: Signature Books, 1984), 5:33, under the date of 15 March 1857. George Q. Cannon said that "God in his revelations has informed us that it was on this choice land of Joseph where Adam was placed and the Garden of Eden was laid out. The spot has been designated, and we look forward with peculiar feelings to repossessing that land" *(JD,*

11:337). Heber C. Kimball was more specific when he stated that "the spot chosen for the garden of Eden was Jackson County, in the state of Missouri, where Independence now stands; it was occupied in the morn of creation by Adam and his associates" (ibid., 10:235).

27. *Deseret News*, vol. 10, no. 38, 21 November 1860, 297.

28. *DS*, 3:74. See also *JD*, 10:235; 11:337.

29. Gordon J. Wenham, *Genesis 1–15* (Waco, Texas: Word Books, 1987), 86.

30. This comes from the Book of Jubilees 8:19, cited in C. T. R. Hayward, *The Jewish Temple: A Non-Biblical Sourcebook* (New York: Routledge, 1996), 89. For a look at possible parallels between the Garden of Eden and the temples of ancient Israel, see Donald W. Parry, "Garden of Eden: Prototype Sanctuary," in Parry, ed., *Temples of the Ancient World: Ritual and Symbolism*, 126–51.

31. *MD*, 210–11. The earth's existence seems to follow a chiastic pattern. The earth was first created in spirit form in the presence of God (celestial). It then took on physical form, becoming a place of habitation for physical beings with a spiritual substance flowing through their veins (terrestrial), and then fell when our first parents partook of the forbidden fruit and became mortal (telestial). During the Millennium the earth will regain its paradisiacal glory (terrestrial) and after that period will become a habitation for angels and gods (celestial).

32. See Gordon J. Wenham, "Sanctuary Symbolism in the Garden of Eden Story," in *Proceedings of the Ninth World Congress of Jewish Studies* (Jerusalem: World Union of Jewish Studies, 1986), 22.

33. Ibid., 22–23.

34. See especially E. Theodore Mullen, Jr., *The Divine Council in Canaanite and Early Hebrew Literature* (Chico, California: Scholars Press, 1980), 113–280. See also the translation of Psalm 89:5–7 and the brief comments on the heavenly council that sits before God's throne in Willem A. VanGemeren, ed., *New International Dictionary of Old Testament Theology and Exegesis* (Grand Rapids, Michigan: Zondervan, 1997), 4:1316.

35. See the text of the First Book of Adam and Eve, sometimes called the Conflict of Adam and Eve, in Rutherford H. Platt, Jr., ed., *The Forgotten Books of Eden* (Cleveland, Ohio: Collins World, 1974), 40.

36. Ibid., 19. In the Second Book of Adam and Eve, it is explained to Adam that Satan sometimes takes on the form of an angel or a god in order to deceive others (ibid., 62). In the First Book of Adam and Eve it is said that Satan appeared to Adam and Eve while Adam was praying at a stone altar "with his hands spread unto God" (ibid., 48). My thanks to Matt Roper for bringing these sources to my attention.

37. Montague R. James, trans., *The Apocryphal New Testament* (Oxford: Clarendon Press, 1969), 190. It is claimed in the First Book of Adam and Eve that Satan taught Adam how to swear an oath while giving a handclasp (see Platt, Jr., ed., *The Forgotten Books of Eden*, 50). An early Egyptian-Christian text seems to indicate that this type of ritual activity was sanctioned by God. In the text, angels appear to a man named Shenoute and "seal a covenant with a handclasp of right hands" (C. Wilfred Griggs, *Early Egyptian Christianity: From Its Origin to 451 C.E.* [Leiden: E. J. Brill, 1990], 200). It would therefore appear that Satan used a legitimate ritual in an illegitimate way (without divine authorization) in order to lead the posterity of Adam astray.

38. See Robert J. Matthews, "The Fall of Man," in McConkie and Millet, eds., *The Man Adam*, 37–64. Orson F. Whitney taught that the Fall "had a twofold direction—downward, yet forward" (Forace Green, comp., *Cowley and Whitney on Doctrine* [Salt Lake City: Bookcraft, 1963], 287.

39. See Robert J. Matthews, "The Fall of Man," in McConkie and Millet, eds., *The Man Adam*, 45–46.

40. D&C 29:42 informs us that several angels were sent by the Lord unto Adam and his posterity to teach them of repentance and redemption through faith on the name of the Only Begotten Son.

41. See Stephen E. Robinson, "The Apocalypse of Adam," *BYUS*, vol. 17, no. 2, Winter 1977, 135, 141–42. On page 141 Robinson mentions that in the Apocalypse of Adam, the first man "falls into a sleep during which three men come to him and say 'Arise, Adam.' . . . The 'awakening of Adam' occurs elsewhere. See the Apocryphon of John 70:20–21 and 79:4–25." After the awakening in the Apocalypse of Adam, it is said that Satan appears to both Adam and Eve "and insists that he is their god" (ibid., 135).

42. John Taylor wrote that Adam presided over his posterity as "patriarch, prophet, priest, and king" (*Times and Seasons*, vol. 6, no. 10, 1 June 1845, 921). Rudger Clawson likewise stated that Adam was "a king and a priest" and Eve was "a queen and priestess" (see *CR*, April 1939, 119).

43. *TPJS*, 271–72. On these pages the Prophet also asks: "What constitutes the kingdom of God? Where there is a prophet, a priest, or a righteous man unto whom God gives his oracles, there is the kingdom of God; and where the oracles of God are not, there the kingdom of God is not."

44. Wilford Woodruff stated that Adam was a high priest and held "the keys of the kingdom of God" (*JD*, 13:319). Jewish legend also refers to Adam as a king (see Ginzberg, *The Legends of the Jews*, 1:166).

45. *NWAF*, 35.

46. Engnell sees a "royal robe" behind the clothing given by God to Adam in Genesis 3:21 (I. Engnell, "'Knowledge' and 'Life' in the Creation Story," in M. Noth and D. Winton Thomas, eds., *Wisdom in Israel and in the Ancient Near East* [Leiden: E. J. Brill, 1955], 113).

47. John M. Lundquist, "The Common Temple Ideology of the Ancient Near East," in Madsen, ed., *The Temple in Antiquity*, 69; Geo Widengren, *The King and the Tree of Life in Ancient Near Eastern Religion* (Uppsala: A. B. Lundequistska Bokhandeln, 1951), 21–22, 29–30, 59.

48. Engnell notes that the sacred marriage of Adam and Eve "belongs to the royal pattern" of the ancient Near East (Engnell, "'Knowledge' and 'Life' in the Creation Story," 113).

49. *TPJS*, 157. Joseph Fielding Smith indicates that the keys of "presidency" are synonymous with the power of giving "direction" (*DS*, 2:250–51).

50. *TPJS*, 157. In D&C 107:40–41 we read that the order of the priesthood "was confirmed to be handed down from father to son, and rightly belongs to the literal descendants of the chosen seed, to whom the promises were made. This order was instituted in the days of Adam, and came down by lineage." Hence, we read that Adam bestowed the priesthood upon his sons through ordination (see D&C 84:6–16; 107:41–52). One biblical scholar writes that a "number of passages within the pseudepigraphical corpus and in early rabbinic midrashim speak of the first man as exercising priestly functions. Early sources suggest that the concept of the priesthood of Adam played a greater role in early postbiblical Judaism than extant literatures indicate" (Stephen N. Lambden, "From Fig Leaves

to Fingernails: Some Notes on the Garments of Adam and Eve in the Hebrew Bible and Select Early Postbiblical Jewish Writings," in Paul Morris and Deborah Sawyer, eds., *A Walk in the Garden: Biblical, Iconographical and Literary Images of Eden* [Sheffield, England: JSOT Press, 1992], 79).

51. *TPJS*, 167. The Prophet also said that Adam "received revelations, commandments and ordinances at the beginning" (ibid., 168).

52. *JD*, 16:264. At another time Wilford Woodruff said that Adam "ordained his sons to the Melchizedek Priesthood" (ibid., 13:319).

53. "To Adam, after he was driven from the Garden of Eden, the plan of salvation was revealed, and upon him the *fulness* of the priesthood conferred" (*DS*, 3:81, emphasis in original).

54. *JD*, 13:319. It is significant that when Joseph Smith introduced the Nauvoo-era endowment ceremony on 4 May 1842 he referred to it as "the order pertaining to the Ancient of Days" (*HC*, 5:2), meaning the order pertaining to Adam (compare D&C 27:11; 116:1; 138:38).

55. Louis Ginzberg, *The Legends of the Jews* (Philadelphia: The Jewish Publication Society of America, 1937), 1:93; see also 5:117, nt. 109.

56. *Ensign*, August 1985, 8. Joseph Smith saw in vision the gathering of Adam and his righteous posterity in the valley of Adam-ondi-Ahman. "He called together his children and blessed them with a patriarchal blessing. The Lord appeared in their midst. . . . This is why Adam blessed his posterity; he wanted to bring them into the presence of God" (*TPJS*, 158–59).

57. Alexander Roberts and James Donaldson, eds., *Ante-Nicene Fathers: The Clementina* (Peabody, Massachusetts: Hendrickson Publishers, 1994), 8:90.

58. Wenham, "Sanctuary Symbolism in the Garden of Eden Story," 21.

59. Wenham, *Genesis 1–15*, 84.

60. Ginzberg, *The Legends of the Jews*, 5:104. "They were the high-priestly raiment in which God had clothed Adam" (ibid., 1:332). "Adam and his descendants wore them as priestly garments at the time of the offering of the sacrifices" (ibid., 5:103). "And what were those garments? The vestments of the High Priesthood, with which the Almighty clothed them because Adam was the world's first-born" (Menahem M. Kasher, *Encyclopedia of Biblical Interpretation* [New York: American Biblical Encyclopedia Society, 1953], 1:137). "Adam's garment was a High-priestly robe" (Robert Graves and Ralph Patai, *Hebrew Myths: The Book of Genesis* [New York: Crown Publishers, 1983], 78). "The tradition that Adam's garments were the high priestly robes, handed down through successive generations until they reached Aaron, is well known from Rabbinic writings: *jer. Meg.* 1:11; *Gen. Rab.* 20:12; 97:6; *Num. Rab.* 4:8; *Tanhuma B. Toledot* 67 and *Berešith* 9; *Aggadath Berešith* 42; FTP of Gen. 48:22; PJ of Gen. 27:15; *Tanhuma Toledot* 12; and *Midrash Abkir* on Gen. 3:21 all testify to it, as does Jerome in *Quaestiones Hebraicae in Genesim* on Genesis 27:15. It also occurs in Syriac sources, a fact which very likely indicates its antiquity" (Hayward, *The Jewish Temple: A Non-Biblical Sourcebook*, 45). For further reading, see John A. Tvedtnes, "Priestly Clothing in Bible Times," and Stephen D. Ricks, "The Garment of Adam in Jewish, Muslim, and Christian Tradition," both in Parry, ed., *Temples of the Ancient World*, 649–704 and 705–39, respectively.

61. See Matthew B. Brown, "Girded about with a Lambskin," *Journal of Book of Mormon Studies*, vol. 6, no. 2, 1997, 124–51.

62. Graves and Patai, *Hebrew Myths: The Book of Genesis*, 77.

63. Stephen N. Lambden, "From Fig Leaves to Fingernails: Some Notes on the Garments of Adam and Eve in the Hebrew Bible and Select Early Postbiblical Jewish Writings," in Morris and Sawyer, eds., *A Walk in the Garden: Biblical, Iconographical and Literary Images of Eden*, 82.

64. Joseph Young, Sr., *History of the Organization of the Seventies / Enoch and His City* (Salt Lake City: Deseret News Printing, 1878), 13.

65. *JD*, 18:303. There is some speculation that Enoch may have been the angel Raphael, who appeared to Joseph Smith (see D&C 128:21) and restored certain keys to him that were necessary for the final dispensation (see *MD*, 618). In *JD*, 21:94 we read that Enoch appeared to Joseph Smith at some time.

66. *JD*, 25:236–37.

67. Ginzberg, *The Legends of the Jews*, 1:177.

68. Crispin H. T. Fletcher-Louis, "The High Priest as Divine Mediator in the Hebrew Bible: Daniel 7:13 as a Test Case," in *Society of Biblical Literature 1997 Seminar Papers* (Atlanta: Scholars Press, 1997), 177.

69. In D&C 107:53–57 we learn that Enoch was among a group of Adam's righteous posterity who had gathered together at Adam-ondi-Ahman to receive a blessing from the first man. It is recorded in this scriptural passage that the Lord appeared unto this group of faithful disciples. Enoch stood face to face with the Lord on another occasion when he ascended a mountain (which is considered a natural temple) and was shown many marvelous visions of "the world for the space of many generations" (Moses 7:2–4).

70. In language similar to that found in Exodus 19:6 and 1 Peter 2:9, Joseph Smith called Enoch's people "a kingdom of Priests, a holy people" (*TPJS*, 202).

71. See *TPJS*, 308–309, 322.

72. *WJS*, 8. Notice the Adamic pattern. Noah was king with dominion over a new world and he was also called the "father of all living"—a title given to Adam (compare D&C 27:11; 138:38; *WJS*, 39). Language found in the Genesis account of the creation of Adam is also applied to Noah in JST Genesis 9:13–14.

73. John Taylor, *Mediation and Atonement* (Salt Lake City: Stevens and Wallis, 1950), 185.

74. *JD*, 17:207.

75. Ginzberg, *The Legends of the Jews*, 1:177, 332; Graves and Patai, *Hebrew Myths: The Book of Genesis*, 78, 125.

76. *DS*, 3:83.

77. Ginzberg, *The Legends of the Jews*, 1:177; Graves and Patai, *Hebrew Myths: The Book of Genesis*, 125, 147. See Hugh Nibley's comments and his proposal that the Genesis account of this incident has been mistranslated (Hugh W. Nibley, *Lehi in the Desert / The World of the Jaredites / There Were Jaredites* [Salt Lake City: Deseret Book and FARMS, 1988], 168–70). One biblical scholar points out that even though Genesis 9:23 mentions "a garment" being draped over Noah by his sons, the Hebrew text of this verse literally reads "*the garment*— [i.e.,] Noah's" (Kasher, *Encyclopedia of Biblical Interpretation*, 2:70; emphasis added).

78. *HC*, 5:2.

79. Hugh W. Nibley, *The Message of the Joseph Smith Papyri: An Egyptian Endowment* (Salt Lake City: Deseret Book, 1975), xi–xiii.

80. For more of Dr. Nibley's writings on this subject, see Hugh W. Nibley, *Approaching Zion* (Salt Lake City: Deseret Book and FARMS, 1989), 265–70.

81. William Whiston, trans., *The Works of Josephus: Complete and Unabridged*, updated ed. (Peabody, Massachusetts: Hendrickson Publishers, 1987), 750, (*Wars*, 6.10.1).

82. Graves and Patai, *Hebrew Myths: The Book of Genesis*, 147.

83. *WJS*, 245. The vast majority of non-LDS Christians interpret the Greek word *aparabatos* in Hebrews 7:24 ("unchangeable" in the KJV) to mean that the Melchizedek Priesthood is not transmittable from one person to another. To interpret this word to mean "'that doth not pass from one to another,' . . . is not only untenable, and contrary to the constant usage of the word, but does not adequately fit with either the preceding or the succeeding context" of Hebrews 7:24 (William E. Vine, *Vine's Expository Dictionary of Old and New Testament Words* [Old Tappan, New Jersey: Fleming H. Revell Co., 1985], New Testament Words, part 4, 166). Despite the fact that *aparabatos* in Hebrews 7:24 "is usually interpreted [as] *without a successor . . . this meaning is found nowhere else. [This word] rather has the sense *permanent, unchangeable*" (William F. Arndt and F. Wilbur Gingrich, *A Greek-English Lexicon of the New Testament and Other Early Christian Literature* [Chicago: The University of Chicago Press, 1979], 80, emphasis in original; see also Henry G. Liddell and Robert Scott, *A Greek-English Lexicon* [Oxford: Clarendon Press, 1989], 178). It must also be taken into account that throughout the book of Hebrews mention is made of the "order (*taxis*) of Melchizedek" (Hebrews 5:6, 10; 6:20; 7:11, 17, 21). This is the very same word used to designate the "order (*taxis*) of Aaron" (Hebrews 7:11). *Taxis* refers to a "succession" (Strong, *The New Strong's Exhaustive Concordance of the Bible*, Greek Dictionary, 89, word #5010; see also S. Kent Brown, "The Dead Sea Scrolls: A Mormon Perspective," *BYUS*, vol. 23, no. 1, Winter 1983, 56–57).

84. *TPJS*, 322.

85. Ibid., 60.

86. One ancient source declares that Abraham was most certainly baptized (see Hugh W. Nibley, "Setting the Stage: The World of Abraham," *IE*, January 1970, 62).

87. According to Joseph Smith, the patriarch Abraham said to Melchizedek, "'I believe all that thou hast taught me concerning the priesthood and the coming of the Son of Man'; so Melchizedek ordained Abraham" (*TPJS*, 322–23). In JST Genesis 15:12 we read that Abraham was granted a vision of "the days of the Son of Man."

88. *WJS*, 246.

89. James H. Charlesworth, ed., *The Old Testament Pseudepigrapha* (Garden City, New York: Doubleday, 1985), 2:880.

90. Nibley, "Setting the Stage: The World of Abraham," *IE*, January 1970, 64.

91. "According to the Midrash (Mid. Rab., 44) Melchizedek himself instructed Abraham in all the functions of the high priest" (Nibley, "Setting the Stage: The World of Abraham," *IE*, January 1970, 64). A few Jewish sources indicate that God showed Abraham the entire "temple-worship" (ibid., 61). Other texts say that Abraham built three altars in order to advance "from grade (or step) to grade" and

also so that he could provide his children with instructions (ibid., 61–63). Yet another source claims that Abraham dedicated Mount Moriah as the site of the future temple (ibid., 61).

92. Graves and Patai, *Hebrew Myths: The Book of Genesis*, 147. Page 78 of this same source also relates that Abraham came into possession of Adam's "high-priestly robe" because he "could claim the firstborn's right" (compare Abraham 1:1–4). Ginzberg, *The Legends of the Jews*, 1:332, not only says that Abraham received the garments of Adam but also that he passed them on to his son Isaac.

93. Charlesworth, ed., *The Old Testament Psedepigrapha*, 1:696–97.

94. Ibid., 1:694–95.

95. These parallels are drawn mostly from Gerald N. Lund's article "Types of Things to Come," in Gerald N. Lund, *Jesus Christ: Key to the Plan of Salvation* (Salt Lake City: Deseret Book, 1991), 54–75.

96. *TPJS*, 322.

97. The Lord also appeared unto Isaac and pronounced the blessings of the Abrahamic Covenant upon him (see Genesis 26:1–5, 24–25). Isaac subsequently built himself an altar and prayed there unto the Lord (see Genesis 26:24–25). The stipulations of the covenant were that the recipient would receive the promised blessings if they were obedient to the voice of the Lord and kept his charges, commandments, statutes, and laws (see Genesis 26:3–5). Notice that part of the covenant involved the Lord bestowing a new name upon the one entering into it (see Genesis 17:1–8, 15–16; 32:24–30; 35:9–13). Another aspect of the covenant was the reception of a ritual wound (circumcision) that was called "a token of the covenant" (Genesis 17:11). The promise of divine protection and the payment of tithing were also associated with the Abrahamic Covenant (see Genesis 28:15, 20–22).

98. Ginzberg, *The Legends of the Jews*, 1:332.

99. George A. Buttrick, ed., *The Interpreter's Bible* (New York: Abingdon Press, 1952), 1:689.

100. E. A. Speiser, *Genesis* (Garden City, New York: Doubleday, 1986), 218, 20. The translation "stairway" is found in *Tanakh—The Holy Scriptures: The New JPS Translation According to the Traditional Hebrew Text* (New York: The Jewish Publication Society, 1988), 43. Joseph Smith commented that "Paul ascended into the third heaven [see 2 Corinthians 12:2], and he could understand the three principal rounds of Jacob's ladder—the telestial, the terrestrial, and the celestial glories or kingdoms, where Paul saw and heard things which were not lawful for him to utter" (*TPJS*, 304–305). Marion G. Romney likewise observed: "Temples are to us all what Bethel was to Jacob" ("Temples—The Gates to Heaven," *Ensign*, March 1971, 16).

101. Strong, *The New Strong's Exhaustive Concordance of the Bible*, Hebrew and Aramaic Dictionary, 78, word #4397.

102. In speaking to those in the heavenly assembly the Lord is reported to have said, "Let us go down," before they descended to the earth to perform a task (Genesis 11:7). In sending his son Joseph on an errand, Jacob used the words "Go . . . see . . . and bring me word again" (Genesis 37:14). Moses played the role of a heavenly messenger when God told him to descend Mount Sinai and inform the Israelites that if they would be obedient to the covenant they would become "a kingdom of priests." Moses delivered the message assigned to him and then "returned the words of the people unto the Lord" (Exodus 19:3–8). In Ezekiel 9:1–11 the Lord sends an angel "clothed with linen" out from His

presence to perform a task. When the angel completed his assignment, he "reported the matter, saying, I have done as thou hast commanded me."

103. Nibley, *The Message of the Joseph Smith Papyri: An Egyptian Endowment*, 243. Another scholar notes that the word translated in this story as "wrestled" is a by-form of the word found in Genesis 29:13, 33:4, and 48:10 that means "to embrace" (Gordon J. Wenham, *Genesis 16–50* [Dallas, Texas: Word Books, 1994], 295; see also H. D. M. Spence and Joseph S. Exell, eds., *The Pulpit Commentary* [Grand Rapids, Michigan: Eerdmans, 1961], 1:394). A major Jewish translation of Genesis 28 states that "the Lord was standing beside" Jacob (vs. 13) at "the gateway to heaven" (vs. 17) when he pronounced the blessings of the Abrahamic covenant upon the patriarch (*Tanakh—The Holy Scriptures*, 43). In regard to Jacob's reception and bestowal of the birthright blessings, one scholar believes that "it is fair to say that elements which had their original home in ritual and cult create the structural underpinning of Genesis 27 and 48. The formal summons to the son to be blessed, the subsequent identification of that son, the symbolic kiss exchanged between blesser and blessed, and the formulaic pronouncement of blessing are all motifs redolent with the language of ceremony and cult" (Susan Ackerman, "The Deception of Isaac, Jacob's Dream at Bethel, and Incubation on an Animal Skin," in Gary A. Anderson and Saul M. Olyan, eds., *Priesthood and Cult in Ancient Israel* [Sheffield, England: JSOT Press, 1991], 93–94). Some ancient Hebrews believed that in the resurrection God would "embrace them and kiss them and bring them into the life of the world to come" (Friedrich, ed., *Theological Dictionary of the New Testament*, 9:125, nt. 124). Compare this statement with the elements that are present in Genesis 48:9–12. Embraces wherein blessings are bestowed are also mentioned in 1 Kings 17:21–22 and 2 Kings 4:34–35.

104. Compare this with Judges 13:17–18: "And Manoah said unto the angel of the Lord, What is thy name, that when thy sayings come to pass we may do thee honour? And the angel of the Lord said unto him, Why askest thou thus after my name, seeing it is secret?"

105. The Hebrew word *peni'el* literally means "face of God" (Strong, *The New Strong's Exhaustive Concordance of the Bible*, Hebrew and Aramaic Dictionary, 115, word #6439). Jacob's experience may be seen in a temple context since Jehovah commanded all male Israelites to appear three times a year "before" him (*see* Exodus 34:23–24; Deuteronomy 16:16). The Hebrew word translated as "before" in these passages is *panim* and literally refers to the "face" of the Lord. Thus the "true sense of the phrase is 'see the face of' Jehovah, *i.e.* visit him" in his temple. "The phrase *see the face of* is used elsewhere [in the Old Testament] of courtiers or others enjoying access to the royal presence" (S. R. Driver, *A Critical and Exegetical Commentary on Deuteronomy* [New York: Charles Scribner's Sons, 1895], 198; emphasis in original). One should also consider Jacob's statement about his experience in light of D&C 84:19–22 and 107:18–19 which indicate that no one can "see the face of God," or enter his "presence," without the power, authority, and ordinances of the Melchizedek Priesthood.

106. One respected biblical scholar believes that the "coat" represented "the right of the firstborn" (see Alfred Edersheim, *Bible History: Old Testament* [Grand Rapids, Michigan: Eerdmans, 1987], 1:144).

107. Strong, *The New Strong's Exhaustive Concordance of the Bible*, Hebrew and Aramaic Dictionary, 67, word #3801. One biblical commentator voices his opinion that Joseph's "coat" was a "ceremonial robe" (Speiser, *Genesis*, 289–90). Other scholars likewise feel that Joseph's "coat," which is called *ketonet*

passim in Hebrew, was more like a robe *(me'il)* rather than a sleeved garment *(kuttonet)* because Mesopotamian temple documents refer to a "ceremonial robe" by the very similar designation *kitu pišannu* (Botterweck, Ringgren, and Fabry, eds., *Theological Dictionary of the Old Testament*, 7:385–86).

108. Ginzberg, *The Legends of the Jews*, 5:326, nt. 11.

109. Strong, *The New Strong's Exhaustive Concordance of the Bible*, Hebrew and Aramaic Dictionary, 115, word #6446. According to one writer, the phrase "coat of many colours" should be translated in accordance with Mishnaic material as "an upper garment in which figures are woven" (Ginzberg, *The Legends of the Jews*, 5:329, nt. 43).

110. Buttrick, ed., *The Interpreter's Bible*, 1:749.

111. Ginzberg, *The Legends of the Jews*, 2:139.

CHAPTER THREE

The Tabernacle of Jehovah

During the time of Moses, the Israelites were commanded to build a tabernacle for Jehovah so that he could "dwell among" His covenant people (Exodus 25:8; 29:44–46). The term *tabernacle* is translated from two different words in the Old Testament. The first word is *miškan,* which means residence, dwelling, or habitation.[1] The second word is *ohel,* which means tent or covering.[2] Hence, the tabernacle could be viewed as a type of tent that served as a temporary abode for Deity when He visited the earth.

The purpose of this chapter is to explore the many symbolic elements that were associated with the tabernacle of Jehovah including its layout, architecture, building materials, and rituals. But before we explore these topics it would be beneficial to examine the links between Moses and the patriarchs of prior dispensations.

Moses and the Patriarchal Pattern

In the Joseph Smith Translation we learn that Moses' father-in-law, Jethro, was the "high priest" of Midian (JST Exodus 18:1). One of the revelations given through the Prophet Joseph Smith states that it was Jethro who bestowed the Melchizedek Priesthood upon Moses (*see* D&C 84:6). Psalm 99:6 confirms that Moses was one of Jehovah's priests, and rabbinical tradition insists that Moses wore a white linen priestly garment and served as a high priest while the Israelites were in the wilderness.[3] As a recipient of the higher priesthood, Moses was qualified to learn "the mysteries of the kingdom" through "ordinances" and take upon himself "the power of godliness," which would enable him to enter into the presence of the Lord (D&C 84:19–22). Some Jewish legendary sources claim that Moses, like the great patriarchs before him, came into possession of both the high priestly garments of Adam and also his rod or sceptre that was made from a branch of the tree of life.[4] There are some indications from biblical context and tradition that Moses was considered to be a king as well as a priest.[5] Moses is typologically identified with Adam in a variety of ancient texts, and in one instance he is even called the "second Adam."[6]

There is a corpus of legendary material that likens Moses' ascent of Mount Sinai to an ascension into heaven. The ritual elements that are mentioned in these rabbinic legends are familiar motifs from the consecration of priests and the coronation of kings. As part of his ascension experience, Moses is said to have been washed, anointed, clothed in heavenly garments, called with names of honor, enthroned, and initiated into heavenly secrets.[7] This is all especially interesting in light of the comment by Joseph Smith that Moses received the temple endowment while on a mountain top and was there given "the keys of the Kingdom," which included "certain signs and words."[8]

The Presence of the Lord

For the context of what follows it is important to understand that the Israelites who lived during the time of Moses were aware of the gospel of Jesus Christ (see Hebrews 4:2; 1 Corinthians 10:1–4). After Moses had led the children of Israel out of bondage in Egypt, he took them to the foot of Mount Sinai, which was also known as "the mountain of God" (Exodus 3:1; 4:27; 18:5). There the Lord promised them that if they would obey His voice and keep His covenant He would make them "a kingdom of priests" and a holy nation (Exodus 19:1–6). The Israelites agreed to these stipulations and proceeded to build an altar at which they entered into a covenant to be obedient to divine laws (see Exodus 24:1–8). Following this solemn ceremony, the Lord allowed several Israelite leaders, including "seventy of the elders of Israel," to ascend the mountain and see him from a distance (Exodus 24:1–2, 9–10). After this experience, the Lord revealed the pattern for the tabernacle to Moses (see Exodus 25–31) and directed that it be erected in the camp of the Israelites so that He could "dwell among them" (Exodus 25:8–9; 29:45–46).

But the tabernacle was also built for another purpose. In the Doctrine and Covenants the Lord tells us that He commanded Moses to build the tabernacle so that He could reveal certain ordinances unto His people (see D&C 124:37–41). Moses "plainly taught" the children of Israel about the need for these ordinances and "sought diligently to sanctify his people that they might behold the face of God" as he had. But unfortunately the Lord's covenant people "hardened their hearts and could not endure his presence" (D&C 84:19–25).[9] They became so hardened and rebellious, in fact, that they fashioned and worshipped a golden calf. This act of idolatry was all the more atrocious because it took place right before the holy mountain of God (*see* Exodus 32:1–8).[10]

Because of their extremely wicked behavior, Moses took the stone tablets, whereon God himself had written the laws of the covenant, and destroyed them (*see* Exodus 24:12; 32:15–16, 19). Some biblical interpreters feel that this action signified that the covenant had been broken. These tablets had contained "the words of the everlasting covenant of the holy priesthood" that would have made it possible for the children of Israel to enter into the Lord's presence (JST Deuteronomy 10:2). It is from the Joseph Smith Translation that we learn what happened next.

> And the Lord said unto Moses, Hew thee two other tables of stone, like unto the first, and I will write upon them also, the words of the law, according as they were written at the first on the tables which thou brakest; but it shall not be according to the first, for I will take away the priesthood out of their midst; therefore my holy order, and the ordinances thereof, shall not go before them; for my presence shall not go up in their midst, lest I destroy them.
> But I will give unto them the law as at the first, but it shall be after the law of a carnal commandment; for I have sworn in my wrath, that they shall not enter into my presence, into my rest, in the days of their pilgrimage. Therefore do as I have commanded thee, and be ready in the morning, and come up in the morning unto mount Sinai. (JST Exodus 34:1–2; emphasis added)

This remarkable restoration of scripture, and the Prophet's assertion that the "law revealed to Moses in Horeb never was revealed to the children of Israel,"[11] finds support in ancient Jewish tradition. In the *Zohar*, for instance, we read that the first set of stone tablets given to Moses "emanated from the tree of life" but the second set "came from the side of the tree of good and evil." And according to Jewish kabalah, the first tablets "were the light and doctrine of the Messiah, the outpouring of universal deliverance, the source of eternal life on earth" while the second pair "represented the indirect or 'fragmented' manifestation of this light."[12]

Because the children of Israel chose to be "lawless and disobedient" and to believe in precepts that were "contrary to sound doctrine" (1 Timothy 1:9-10), the Lord "added" the Law of Moses unto the gospel as a strict "schoolmaster"[13] to prepare them for the coming of the Messiah (JST Galatians 3:19–20, 24). At that time the Savior would once again invite all Israelites to participate in the ordinances of the temple and thereby qualify to enter into the presence of the Lord.[14]

TABERNACLE SYMBOLISM

During a forty-day sojourn on the top of Mount Sinai, Moses was shown the "pattern" (*tabnit*) of the tabernacle and was commanded to build an exact copy of what he had seen (Exodus 25:9, 40; 26:30; 27:8; Numbers 8:4). While biblical scholars differ in their opinions about the exact nature of what Moses saw on the mountain, the linguistic evidence points to the conclusion that the *tabnit* was some type of model or replica of the Lord's heavenly temple.[15]

The tabernacle was referred to by the term *ohel mo'ed* which, according to one scholar, should be translated as "tent of assembly." In the biblical world, this descriptive title was connected with the council or assembly of the gods which convened on top of the heavenly mountain (*see* Isaiah 14:13). By way of parallel, it is interesting to note that the council of Israel convened at the tabernacle, and their meetings were seen as taking place before Jehovah.[16]

This brings us to one of the primary symbolic features of the tabernacle. There is a direct connection between the tabernacle of Jehovah and the Lord's holy mountain. The horizontal layout of the tabernacle imitated the vertical layout of Mount Sinai. In other words, the tabernacle represented a mountain that had been laid out horizontally.[17]

> Mount Sinai is the archetype of the Tabernacle, and is similarly divided into three gradations of holiness. Its summit is the Holy of Holies; God's voice issues forth from there (Exodus 19:20) as from the inner shrine (Exodus 25:22; Numbers 7:89); the mountaintop is off limits to priests and layman alike (Exodus 19:24) and its very sight is punishable by death (Exodus 19:21), and so with its Tabernacle counterpart (cf. Leviticus 16:2 and Numbers 4:20); finally, Moses alone is privileged to ascend to the top (Exodus 19:20; see 34:2) just as later, the high priest is permitted to enter the inner shrine under special safeguards (Leviticus 16:2–4).
>
> The second division of Sinai is the equivalent of the outer shrine, marked off from the rest of the mountain by being enveloped in a cloud (Exodus 20:21; 24:15–18) just as the cloud overspreads the entirety of the Tabernacle (Numbers 9:15–22). . . .
>
> Below the cloud is the third division. . . . Here is where the altar and stelae are erected (Exodus 24:4). It is equivalent to the courtyard, the sacred enclosure of the Tabernacle.[18]

Creation

The Lord commanded that the various materials needed for the creation of the tabernacle be offered freely by those who had "a willing heart" (Exodus 35:4–19). "And they came, every one whose heart stirred him up, and every one whom his spirit made willing, and they brought the Lord's offering [for use in] the work of the tabernacle" (Exodus 35:21; compare D&C 124:26–27). The willingness of the Lord's people to offer the necessary materials was so great that they eventually had to be restrained from bringing anything further since there was more than enough to build the tabernacle (*see* Exodus 36:3–7).

The structure of the narrative that recounts the creation of the tabernacle mirrors the Genesis narrative that recounts the creation of the world.[19] "The function of these correspondences is to underscore the depiction of the sanctuary as a world, that is, an ordered, supportive, and obedient environment, and the depiction of the world as a sanctuary, that is, a place in which the reign of God is visible and unchallenged, and his holiness is palpable, unthreatened, and pervasive."[20] The connection between the tabernacle and creation is further strengthened by the fact that the tabernacle was "erected 'on the first day of the first month' [Exodus 40:2], which is New Year's day, a powerful symbol of the beginning of the creation of the world, the transformation of chaos into cosmos."[21]

As a place of beginnings (through rituals of renewal and regeneration), the tabernacle exemplified the principle that "sacred space is rooted in creation" or sacred time. Indeed, "the concept of the holiness of time takes precedence over that of the holiness of space" in the biblical value system. Hence, the tabernacle of the Creator "was conceived to initiate a *new era* in the life of the community of Israel" but was not assigned to any permanent location.[22]

Zones of Holiness

There were several zones of holiness surrounding the tabernacle that were designed to protect it from being defiled by anything that was considered unclean. In fact, any Israelite who was ritually unclean was required to remain completely outside of the camp boundaries because the Holy One of Israel dwelt within the midst of the camp (*see* Numbers 5:1–4). This was a graphic way to teach the Lord's people "the difference between the holy and profane, and cause them to discern between the unclean and the clean" (Ezekiel 44:23; *see also* Leviticus 10:10).

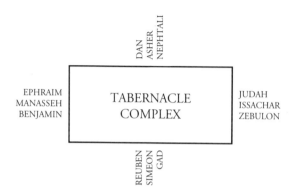

FIGURE 5. Diagram illustrating the position of the twelve tribes of Israel as they encamped around the tabernacle of Jehovah.

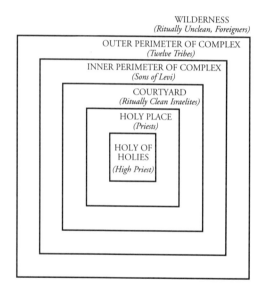

FIGURE 6. Diagram illustrating the zones of holiness that were associated with the temples of ancient Israel. These zones reinforced the distinction to be maintained between the sacred and the profane.

• OUTER BARRIER: In the book of Numbers we read that the Lord dictated exactly how the Israelites were to arrange themselves around the tabernacle. The "camp of the Israelites in the wilderness was arranged in the form of an enormous square with the tabernacle in the center, and with the twelve tribes pitched around it—three on each side"[23] (*see* Numbers 2:1–31). It becomes obvious when one compares the configuration of the camp of Israel around the tabernacle with John the Revelator's description of the heavenly city of Zion that the Lord's intent was to imitate heaven on earth (*see* Revelation 21:9–16).

• INNER BARRIER: In addition to the outer barrier, there was an inner barrier consisting of members of the tribe of Levi. This chosen tribe was commanded by the Lord to encamp along the four sides of the tabernacle courtyard. Those who desired to enter the tabernacle complex had to literally pass by the bearers of the priesthood (sons of Aaron) at the eastern entrance (*see* Numbers 1:53).

• GUARDED ENTRANCES: The entryways of Israelite temples—located at the courtyard, Holy Place, and Holy of Holies—were guarded by Levitical porters (*see* 1 Chronicles 9:17–27). It is believed by some biblical scholars that these guards also served a ritual function at the tabernacle. "The Levitical guard at the entrance [of the courtyard] would prevent an unauthorized entrance by those who were unclean or who were not going to present a sacrifice" (*see* 2 Chronicles 23:19).[24] The guards who were stationed at the entrance of the tabernacle proper were there to ensure that only ritually clean priesthood bearers entered into the house of the Lord.

The Courtyard

The courtyard of the tabernacle complex measured approximately 150 feet by 75 feet and was defined by sixty wooden pillars that marked out its perimeter (*see* Exodus 27:9–17). Each of the pillars was set into a socketed base that was made of solid bronze.[25] These pillars were topped with silver capitals (*see* Exodus 38:17), silver hooks, and silver rods (*chašuq*)[26] that connected each pillar to the one next to it (*see* Exodus 27:17). One end of a rope was attached to each silver hook on the pillar and the other end of the rope was secured to the ground by a bronze stake[27] (*see* Exodus 27:19). Hence, bronze was associated with the bottom level of the courtyard pillars (bases and stakes) and silver was associated with the top (capitals, rods, and hooks). Hangings (*qela*) or screens[28] of fine twined linen, approximately 7.5 feet high, were hung between 56 of the courtyard's 60 pillars (*see* Exodus 27:9, 11–12). These barriers were apparently hung upon the silver rods that connected the pillars together.

There are a few symbolic elements that call for our attention at this point. The white linen barriers that made up the courtyard seem, from scriptural precedent, to signify that those who enter upon holy ground must themselves be in a state of cleanliness and purity (*see* Alma 5:21, 24, 27; Mormon 9:6). The pillars may also be seen in symbolic terms. In the New Testament, the exalted and glorified Redeemer promises to make each of His faithful disciples "a pillar in the temple" of God (Revelation 3:12). Just as the foot or base of the courtyard pillars were made of bronze ("brass" in the KJV, *see* Exodus 27:10) so too are the feet of some heavenly beings described as being "like unto fine brass" (Revelation 1:15; 2:18; *see also* Daniel 10:6). The bronze stakes are also deserving of our attention. These large nails were driven into the ground to secure the tabernacle complex in place. In some ancient Mesopotamian cultures, bronze nails were driven into temple foundations and this "pounding in of nails was regarded as a fixing, fastening action, and was symbolic of the firm establishment of the temple"[29] (compare Isaiah 33:20; 54:2). These foundation nails were also seen as "a symbol of the union between [the] royal builder and the deity to whom the building [was] dedicated."[30] This same connection may perhaps be seen in ancient Israel. There are three biblical verses that speak of symbolic nails. Ezra the temple priest said that the Lord had given the Israelites "a nail in his holy place" and he makes further mention of "the house of our God" (Ezra 9:8–9). The phrase "holy place" refers, of course, to the outer compartment of the Israelite temple (Exodus 26:33).[31] Another reference to a symbolic nail comes from the temple priest Zechariah. In chapter 10 verse 4 of his writings, we discover that the covenant people anticipated that a leader would come forth from the tribe of Judah who would be known as "the nail." Both Jewish and Christian commentators have viewed this verse as being Messianic in character[32] and it has been noted that "the nail" mentioned here "has an association with royal messianism by virtue of the way it is used in Isaiah [22:21–25]."[33] In these verses, Isaiah speaks of both "the nail that is fastened in the sure place" and "the key of the house of David," a phrase that is clearly connected with the Savior in Revelation 3:7.[34]

In order to understand some of the more subtle symbolism associated with the courtyard, it is necessary to know three Hebrew terms that were used to describe different grades of material and workmanship. The least holy workmanship employed in the tabernacle complex was called *oreg*, the next most holy was known as *roqem*, and the most holy was called *hošeb*. *Oreg* refers to something that is made of only one type of material, has only one color, and contains no designs or "figures" of any kind. *Roqem* refers to a material that contains a mixture of colors or types of material (such as linen and wool), displays designs of various types, but again exhibits no "figures" (such as cherubim) upon it. *Hošeb*, on the other hand, refers to a material that includes a mixture of materials and does have some type of "figures" displayed upon it.[35] The fine-twined linen barriers that were stretched between 56 pillars of the tabernacle courtyard (*see* Exodus 27:9; 38:16) were of *oreg* workmanship, but there was a 30-foot-wide curtain (*masak*)[36] of *roqem* workmanship stretched across the 4 pillars that composed the "gate" (*ša'ar*)[37] of the courtyard's eastern side. Hence, the curtain of the courtyard gate was considered to be more holy than the linen barriers that made up the courtyard.

The curtain of the gate was composed of a mixture of three colors of woolen thread (blue, purple, red) and white linen (*see* Exodus 27:16; 38:18). The combination of wool and linen was seen as a mark of holiness by the Israelites and in consequence, the ordinary citizens of Israel were forbidden to create cloth that included this mixture (*see* Leviticus 19:19; Deuteronomy 22:11). Since the Lord Himself revealed which colors should decorate the curtain of the gate (blue, purple, red, and white) we may safely presume that they carried some symbolic meaning. Blue was the color of the sky and thus was associated with heaven and divinity (*see* Exodus 24:10).[38] Purple "in the ancient Near East was a token of sovereignty and rulership."[39] Red is the color of blood and thus an appropriate representation of "life" and "atonement" (*see* Leviticus 17:11, 14). White was seen by the Israelites as a symbol of purity (*see* Daniel 12:10), a ritual condition that had to be achieved before one could serve the Lord in

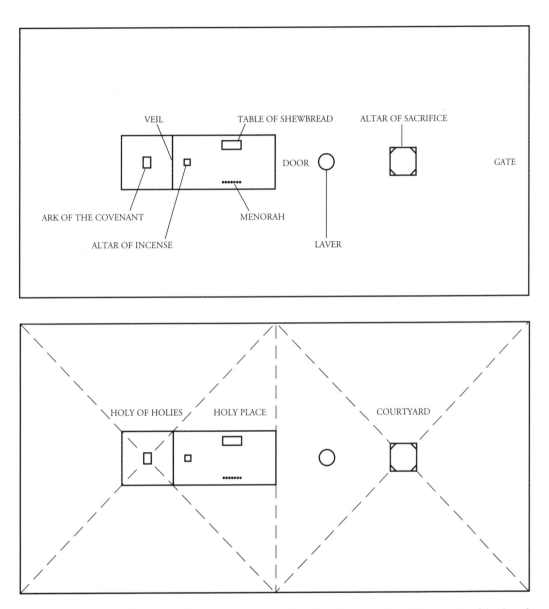

FIGURE 7. Two diagrams of the tabernacle complex, indicating the location of the ritual objects. The centrality of the altar of sacrifice and the ark of the covenant is indicated by the dotted lines in the lower diagram.

His holy house (*see* Numbers 8:21; Ezra 6:20; Nehemiah 12:30). Since the curtain of the gate was of *roqem* workmanship, there were probably some type of "designs" displayed upon it, though their exact nature is unknown.

The Lord directed that an altar and a water basin be constructed and placed inside of the tabernacle courtyard. The altar of sacrifice, or "altar of burnt offering" as it was sometimes called (Exodus 30:28), was built of acacia wood and was completely over-laid with bronze. It measured approximately 7 feet 3 inches square, and 4 feet 4 inches high. A ledge or border molding (*zer*)[40] was located halfway down the vertical side-boards of the altar, and below this ledge the boards were perforated with "a grate of network" that was evidently meant to facilitate the free flow of air throughout the altar. This description makes more sense when one understands that prior to the erection of the tabernacle, the Lord had directed that sacrificial altars be made only of earth or stone (*see* Exodus 20:24–25). When the Lord ordered the building of the tabernacle altar, He provided Moses with the pattern for a more permanent structure than mere earth or stones but that would still make the incorporation of earth or stone possible. To facilitate such an incorporation, the altar of sacrifice was built like a hollow, four-sided box (*see* Exodus 27:8). The empty space between the walls of the altar could then be filled in with either earth or stone, and sacrifices could be burnt upon these natural materials.[41]

There are three symbolic concepts associated with this altar that we will briefly address here. First, the courtyard could be divided geometrically into two perfect squares. The sacrificial altar was placed exactly in the center of the eastern square, which was the area where the common Israelites gathered. The centrality of this object in the court emphasized its great importance and thereby focused attention on its purpose. Second, the fire burning upon this altar was also symbolic in that it was initially kindled by the Lord Himself (*see* Leviticus 9:24; 2 Chronicles 7:1–3). Because of its holy nature, this heavenly fire was kept burning on a perpetual basis (*see* Leviticus 6:12–13). And third, there were four "horns" arising from the corners of the altar (*see* Exodus 27:1–2). Based on comparative Near Eastern studies, some biblical scholars have concluded that these protrusions represented the horns of an animal, such as a bull or a ram, and were thus representative of the strength, force, or power of Deity.[42] The Hebrew word translated as "horn" (*qeren*) does in fact mean "power" in the figurative sense.[43]

The other ritual object that was placed inside of the tabernacle courtyard was the laver or water basin. It was located between the altar of sacrifice and the entrance of the tabernacle (*see* Exodus 30:18; 40:7). This object was evidently round in shape,[44] was made completely of hammered bronze, and sat upon a bronze base. The bronze used in the construction of the laver came from mirrors that had been donated by women who "assembled at the door of the tabernacle" (Exodus 38:8).[45] The Bible does not provide any measurements for the laver's height, width, and diameter, nor are any measurements given for its base.

This ritual basin was filled with water (*see* Exodus 40:7) so that the priests could ritually cleanse their hands and their feet each time they ministered in the tabernacle complex (*see* Exodus 30:17–21; 2 Chronicles 4:6). We are told in the Psalms that only those with "clean hands" could "ascend . . . the hill of the Lord" and "stand in his holy place" (Psalm 24:3–4) because the washing of hands was symbolic of being in a state of innocence (*see* Psalms 26:6; 73:13).

The Tabernacle

The tabernacle of Jehovah was a portable structure that incorporated elements of both a solid sanctuary and a nomadic tent. Together these elements gave the tabernacle a double quality that can best be described as an "ever-moving center." The tabernacle was physically located in the center of the camp of Israel. Its solid portions lent themselves to the symbolism of "endurance and everlasting assurance," even though the structure itself was periodically relocated.[46] Before the Israelites entered the promised land, they were a nomadic people on a pilgrimage (*see* Exodus 6:4; JST Exodus 34:2) and were obliged to live in tents (*see* Exodus 33:8; 2 Samuel 11:11). The Lord stated that the purpose of building the tabernacle was so that He could "dwell" among His chosen people (Exodus 25:8). In Revelation 7:15 the Lord likewise indicated that He would "dwell" among those who served within His temple. The Greek word translated in this verse as "dwell" is *skenoo* and literally means "to tent or encamp"[47] (compare Exodus 29:45–46). Hence, no matter where the Israelites wandered in an unstable form of life, the Lord would always "tent" among them and provide a stable or enduring center.

The solid portion of the tabernacle consisted of 48 acacia wood boards or frames,[48] each measuring approximately 14 feet 7 inches high and 2 feet 2 inches wide. These structures were overlaid with a coating of pure gold. One biblical scholar notes that gold is extremely stable and remains unchanged throughout the generations of time. In his view, it is therefore a fitting material for a structure that "represents the living God who abides forever."[49] When the tabernacle was fully assembled, it measured about 45 feet long and 15 feet wide. In order to provide this large structure with unity and stability, four rows of gold rings were attached to the back side of each board, and gold-covered acacia wood bars were passed through each row of rings. In addition, a fifth bar was passed through the center of all of the boards along their width, running parallel with the other bars (*see* Exodus 36:20–34). On the bottom end of each board, there were two tenons (dowels or projections) designed to be set into two separate, socketed foundation pieces that were made from molten silver.

These silver bases were symbolic in several respects. Because the Lord had taken the life of every firstborn Egyptian in order to free His people from bondage (*see* Exodus 11:4–7; 12:21–29), He consecrated and sanctified every firstborn Israelite male as His own personal possession and required their service in His tabernacle (*see* Numbers 3:12–13; 8:13–19). In order to be freed from this responsibility, the Israelites were required to pay a "ransom" (*kopher*) of a silver half-shekel "to make an atonement" or in other words, cancel the debt that they owed to Jehovah (*see* Exodus 30:11–16). It was this ransom, or redemption, silver that was used to cast the foundation sockets for the sanctuary (*see* Exodus 38:25–27; 34:20). The typological parallels to the Redeemer are fairly obvious. Not only is He likened unto a "foundation" (1 Corinthians 3:11) and called "a ransom for many" (Matthew 20:28), but it was through the Atonement that His disciples were "bought with a price" and redeemed (1 Corinthians 6:19–20).

The solid structure of the tabernacle was overspread by four separate and distinct coverings. The innermost of these enclosures was a "tabernacle" (*miškan*) made of fine-twined linen followed by a "tent" (*ohel*) of black goat's hair,[50] a "covering" (*mikseh*) of ram skins that had been dyed red, and then a "covering" (*mikseh*) of dolphin skins[51] (*see* Exodus 36:8–19).

All of the tabernacle's coverings could be seen in symbolic terms. The innermost "tabernacle" was made from fine-twined linen and was decorated with figures of cherubim woven in the sacred colors blue, purple, and scarlet (*see* Exodus 36:8). Those serving inside of the tabernacle would have seen the cherubim on the ceiling (and through the walls, if frames were employed instead of solid boards) and thus been reminded that they were serving in a holy and heavenly realm.[52] The black goat hair tent may have reminded the Israelites of the "thick cloud" they saw when Jehovah made His appearances (Exodus 19:9, 16–18; 40:34–35; 2 Samuel 22:12; 1 Kings 8:10–11; Job 22:13–14) or the fact that He dwelled in "thick darkness" to shield mortals from the brilliant glory of His presence (Exodus 20:18, 21; 24:15–18; 1 Kings 8:12–13; 2 Chronicles 6:1–2; Psalm 97:1–2; Matthew 17:5).[53] The covering of red ram skins could be interpreted from two symbolic perspectives. First, some ancient Near Eastern nomadic tribes carried a portable tent shrine with them constructed of red leather, which could be seen from a distance, and set it apart as a sacred structure. "When the tribe pitched camp, the tent shrine was unloaded and set up beside the tent of the sheik. People would come to it seeking oracles."[54] Second, rams were used in the sacrificial rites of the tabernacle (*see* Exodus 29:1, 31), and it is not hard to see the red dye as being emblematic of sacrificial blood (compare 1 Peter 1:18–19; *see also* Isaiah 63:1–3; D&C 133:48).

The outermost covering of dolphin skins may have been tied to ancient Near Eastern mythology about the tent of El (Elohim) that was pitched "on the mount out of which spring the sources of the cosmic rivers . . . in the midst of the fountains of the double-deep" or sea.[55] The dolphin skins may also have been chosen as an outermost layer to protect the tabernacle against inclement weather. This idea finds support in the fact that the Hebrew word used to describe it (*mikseh*, translated "covering") refers to a weather-proof barrier.[56] In addition, it should be noted that when the main ritual objects of the tabernacle were moved through the wilderness, almost all of them were covered by an outer layer of dolphin skins (*see* Numbers 4:5–15). One scholar has made the observation that Exodus 40:18-19, which describes the erection of the tabernacle, does not mention the placement of the dolphin skin covering on the top of the sanctuary.[57] This would seem to indicate that under normal weather conditions, the tabernacle was seen from the outside as a red leather tent.

Across the east end of the tabernacle stood five acacia wood pillars that had been overlaid with gold. Each of these pillars was topped by a gold capital, was connected to the one next to it by a gold-covered rod,[58] was equipped with a gold hook near its top, and was set into a socketed base made of bronze (*see* Exodus 26:37; 36:38). Attached to the gold hooks on the back side of these pillars was a curtain (*masak*) that concealed the entire entryway. This curtain, like the one at the courtyard entrance, was of *roqem* workmanship and therefore had some type of unspecified designs displayed upon it of "blue, and purple, and scarlet, and fine twined linen" (Exodus 26:36). But unlike the courtyard "gate," this entryway was designated as a "door" (*petah*) or opening.[59] This brings to mind the words of the Savior who declared "I am the door, by me if any man enter in, he shall be saved" (John 10:9).

The Holy Place

The tabernacle's spacial area could be understood geometrically as a series of three cubes of equal proportion. The area consisting of the first two cubes directly behind the tabernacle entrance was known as the Holy Place. Within this sacred space, there were three ritual objects known as the table of shewbread, the menorah, and the altar of incense. Each of these objects merits discussion here.

• THE TABLE OF SHEWBREAD: The table of shewbread was an acacia wood structure that had been completely overlaid with pure gold. It measured approximately three feet long, eighteen inches wide, and twenty-six inches high. This holy table was decorated with an ornamental gold molding (*zer*) that surrounded its top perimeter, had a three-inch wide molded gold frame joining and reinforcing its legs,[60] had gold rings attached to the legs at the height of the frame, and could be carried by passing two acacia wood poles that had been overlaid with gold through the rings. This table was stationed near the north wall of the Holy Place (*see* Exodus 25:23–30; 40:22–23).

There were several objects placed upon the golden table of shewbread. First, there were twelve loaves of unleavened bread stacked in two rows of six loaves each (*see* Leviticus 24:5–6). In Hebrew, "shewbread" actually consists of two separate words— (*paneh*, face) and (*lehem*, bread)[61]—hence a literal translation would be "bread of the face" (the bread that sits before the face of Jehovah) or, as many translators prefer, "bread of the presence" (the bread that sits in the presence of Jehovah). This bread is the only offering in the tabernacle that is said to pertain to "an everlasting covenant" (Leviticus 24:8). The priests were to gather inside the Holy Place every Sabbath day and consume the bread that lay upon the golden table (*see* Leviticus 24:8–9). Biblical texts indicate that pitchers and cups of pure gold were also set upon the table of shewbread.[62] Some biblical scholars believe that these vessels were used for the purpose of distributing and consuming wine along with the bread every Sabbath day.[63] This may find some corroboration in the account of the seventy elders of Israel who were allowed to ascend partway up Mount Sinai (which has been shown above to correspond to the Holy Place) and who ate and drank in close proximity to the Lord's presence (Exodus 24:1, 9–11). An interesting parallel can be seen in the Savior's visit to the Nephites at the temple in Bountiful after His resurrection when they partook of sacramental bread and wine (*see* 3 Nephi 18:1–9). It will also be recalled that the Kirtland Temple was equipped with sacrament tables.[64] It has been noted by one scholar that Abraham's reception of bread and wine from Melchizedek might be seen as part of an ancient Near Eastern enthronement ritual[65] (*see* Genesis 14:18). By way of typological sym-

FIGURE 8. The golden table of shewbread served as a station where Israel's temple priests would partake of holy bread and wine each Sabbath day.

bolism it will be remembered that Jesus Christ is identified in scripture as the "true bread" (John 6:31–35, 48–58) and also the "true vine" from which comes the sacramental wine (John 15:1–6).

• MENORAH: Near the south wall, opposite the table of shewbread, was a golden lampstand called the *menorah*.[66] Even though exact measurements for the *menorah* are not provided in the Bible it has been estimated from iconographical evidence, Jewish traditions, and the amount of material used in its manufacture that it was between forty-two and sixty inches high and about forty-two inches wide.[67] This lampstand was not created from a poured mold but was hammered out of sheets of pure gold. In design, the *menorah* consisted of a hollow central shaft with three hollow "branches" (*qaneh*)[68] protruding from either side of it. The shaft and branches alike were deco-

rated with three repeating motifs: almond-shaped buds,[69] crown-shaped disks,[70] and blossoming flowers.[71] One oil lamp was placed on the top of each of the seven branches of the *menorah* so that light would be provided for the tabernacle's interior (*see* Exodus 25:31–40). Because of its arboreal shape and floral decorations, many biblical interpreters have concluded that the tabernacle *menorah* was a stylized representation of the tree of life.[72] The image is enhanced when one considers that the *menorah* sat upon a three-pronged or tripedal base that imitated the pattern of tree roots.[73]

FIGURE 9. The *menorah*, or golden lampstand, is identified by some biblical scholars as a representation of the Tree of Life.

The lamps that sat atop the seven branches of the *menorah* contained pure olive oil. By divine decree these lamps were to burn continually (*see* Leviticus 24:2), thus presenting the image of a burning or luminescent tree that was never consumed. Biblical commentators have not failed to notice a connection between this burning tree and the burning bush that was seen by Moses on the holy mountain of God.[74] The positioning of the *menorah* directly across from the table of shewbread also adds a significant dimension to its symbolism. A direct connection between these two sacred objects is suggested in one Book of Mormon passage where the Savior is recorded as saying: "Come unto me and ye shall partake of the fruit of the tree of life; yea, ye shall eat and drink of the bread and the waters of life freely" (Alma 5:34; *see also* 32:26–43). Hence, the fruit of the tree of life may be seen as a representation of the emblems of the sacrament, which in turn are emblems of the Lord Jesus Christ. In the marvelous visions of the tree of life that are recorded in the Book of Mormon, it is explained by an angel of God that the tree is symbolic of the Son of God.[75] Indeed, the *menorah* is explicitly identified as a symbol of "the Lord of the whole earth" in Zechariah 4:1–14. In the book of Revelation, the Savior is portrayed standing directly before the lampstand in the heavenly temple, as if readers were meant to see a connection between the two (*see* Revelation 1:12–13).

• ALTAR OF INCENSE: Moses was commanded to build an incense altar for the tabernacle and to place it before the veil that divided the Holy Place from the Holy of Holies. This altar measured approximately eighteen inches square and thirty-six inches high. It was constructed out of acacia wood, had four "horns" or projections on each of its top four corners, and was completely overlaid with pure gold. A decorative gold border molding (*zer*) surrounded the perimeter of the altar, and two gold rings were placed underneath this border. Two gold-covered acacia wood poles were also built for the altar, and they could be passed through the golden rings whenever the altar needed to be transported (*see* Exodus 30:1–10).

A special mixture of pure incense made with sweet spices was burnt upon the golden altar every morning and every evening (*see* Exodus 30:7–8; 37:29). The symbolism behind this act can be discerned from a passage in the book of Revelation

where we read that in the heavenly temple an angel "came and stood at the altar, having a golden censer; and there was given unto him much incense, that he should offer it with the prayers of all saints upon the golden altar which was before the throne. And the smoke of the incense, which came with the prayers of the saints, ascended up before God out of the angel's hand" (Revelation 8:3–4). This connection between the incense smoke and rising prayers is also seen in the petition: "Lord . . . give ear unto my voice . . . Let my prayer be set forth before thee as incense" (Psalm 141:1–2). Hence the altar of incense, which stood before the veil, was an altar of prayer.

FIGURE 10. Smoke rising from the altar of incense symbolized prayers ascendng unto God.

The type of incense burnt on the altar seems to have had symbolic connotations as well. The aromatic spices that were mixed together with the incense granules were evidently meant to provide the tabernacle with a fragrant and purified atmosphere similar to that enjoyed by Jehovah in heaven. Therefore Jehovah would feel at home when He visited His holy house on the earth. The same principle applies to the sweet-smelling spices used in the anointing oil. The priests of the tabernacle could be readily identified as the authorized servants of Jehovah because they bore about them the exclusive, and pleasant, aroma of Jehovah's holy realm.[76]

The Holy of Holies

There were four pillars that separated the space between the Holy Place and the Holy of Holies. Each of these pillars was made of acacia wood, was overlaid with gold, had a gold hook located near its top, and was set into a single base made of silver (*see* Exodus 26:32). Upon the golden hooks of these pillars hung a partition called a "veil" (*paroket*).[77] The tabernacle veil was of the most holy workmanship, called *hošeb,* and it was therefore decorated with "figures" of cherubim in the sacred colors blue, purple, scarlet, and white (*see* Exodus 26:31). Throughout the Bible, cherubim are depicted as guardians of holy places (*see* Genesis 3:24; Exodus 25:18, 22; 1 Kings 6:23–28; Ezekiel 10; 11:22; Hebrews 9:5). The cherubim of the tabernacle can be seen from the context of other ancient Near Eastern cultures where temple doorways and gates were seen as symbolic meeting places between men and deities. Because of their sanctity, these portals were guarded by doorkeepers whose task it was to admit the just and exclude the unworthy[78] (compare D&C 132:19).

The Holy of Holies was shaped like a perfect cube. In the temple built by King Solomon, this room was decorated with pure gold (*see* 1 Kings 6:20). When these two themes are considered together, the possibility arises that the Holy of Holies was an earthly representation of the heavenly city of Zion, for it was also perfectly cubical and adorned with pure gold (*see* Revelation 21:10–18). The perfect square, when "amplified into a cube, was the symbol of truth, because from whatever point of view it may be contemplated it is always the same."[79] Throughout the scriptures, "truth" is listed as one of the primary qualities of the character of God.[80]

It is in the heavenly city of Zion that the throne of God is to be found (*see* Revelation 22:1–3). This leads us to consider the character of the only object that was placed in the most holy room of the tabernacle. In the center of the cubical Holy of Holies, and consequently in the very center of the second large square that formed the western side of the courtyard, was the ark of the covenant. This sacred chest measured approximately forty-four inches long, twenty-six inches wide, and twenty-six inches high. It was made of acacia wood and was overlaid both on the inside and on the outside with pure gold. The ark was decorated, like the table of shewbread and the altars of sacrifice and incense, with a border molding (*zer*) of gold around its perimeter and was equipped with four gold rings near its corner edges. The Ark was different from all of the other tabernacle objects in that its gold-covered acacia-wood carrying poles were left permanently in their rings (*see* Exodus 25:15).

On the top of the ark of the covenant was a solid cover of pure gold whose measurements matched that of the chest that it covered, forty-four inches long and twenty-six inches wide. On each end of this cover was the figure of a cherub that had been hammered out of sheets of gold. The cherubim faced toward each other, had their heads bowed downward, and were fashioned with wings that stretched out over the pure gold cover (*see* Exodus 25:10–22).

A considerable amount of symbolism was associated with the ark of the covenant. The ark itself served as a container for several holy objects. First and foremost, it was designed as a container for the two stone tablets or "testimony" (*'edut*)[81] that God gave to Moses on Mount Sinai (*see* Exodus 24:12; 25:16, 21; 31:18). Aaron's rod (which represented legitimate priesthood authority) and a golden pot filled with manna (which represented the bread of life) were also kept inside the ark of the covenant (*see* Hebrews 9:4).

The cherubim on the lid of the ark also had symbolic associations. Cherubim are generally regarded as guardians of sacred things. While their exact nature is not discernable from the scriptural record, some scholars believe that the cherubim represented "redeemed and glorified manhood" or "glorified saints and angels."[82] But "Hebrew angels were men, and were not winged,"[83] a fact that was emphasized by the Prophet Joseph Smith.[84] So why did the cherubim on top of the ark of the covenant have wings? The wings evidently served as a symbol. The Israelites viewed the tabernacle as the Lord's earthly palace,[85] and the ark of the covenant represented His

FIGURE 11. The ark of the covenant served as a symbolic representation of the throne of Jehovah.

throne.[86] Some scholars are of the opinion that the outstretched wings of the cherubim served as the seat of the throne[87] while the container below them served as the throne's footstool.[88] In D&C 77:4, we learn that when wings are associated with heavenly beings, they are "a representation of power, to move, to act, etc." And, indeed, the scriptures speak in poetic language of Jehovah moving through the firmament "upon a cherub . . . upon the wings of the wind" (2 Samuel 22:11).[89] Thus, the wings of the cherubim could be seen as a symbol of the power of Israel's King to move among His countless dominions.

The wings of the cherubim "covered" or shielded the lid of pure gold that rested on top of the ark of the covenant.[90] The Hebrew word that designates the golden lid that they were guarding (*kapporet*) is translated in the King James Bible as "mercy seat," but it more properly means "atonement piece"[91] or "place of atonement."[92] Once a year on the Day of Atonement, the blood of atonement was sprinkled on the place of atonement or lid of the ark. This ritual blood was a symbol of the purging of sin (*see* Leviticus 16:15)[93] and, of course, was also a symbolic shadow of the atoning blood of the Lamb that would, in the meridian of time, be shed to purge the sins of the repentant (*see* John 1:29).

The observation has been made by one biblical scholar that the slab of pure gold was "the locus of God's presence in Israel, conceived of as a 'pure plane.' The critical feature of the *kapporet* is neither its outward form nor its precise structural description nor its position 'above the ark,' which appears to qualify it as a 'cover,' but its symbolic representation of a theological reality: the sign marking the boundary of the transcendent realm and therefore the site of God's condescension."[94] Since the wings of the cherubim formed the seat of the Lord's earthly throne, it is only natural that some scholars would see the pure gold slab as the place where His feet rested.[95] Such an observation correlates well with the fact that when the Lord appeared to Joseph Smith and Oliver Cowdery in the Kirtland Temple, He was "standing upon the breastwork of the pulpit . . . and under his feet was *a paved work of pure gold*" (D&C 110:2, emphasis added; *see* Exodus 24:10). This parallel is all the more arresting when it is realized that the early Saints in Kirtland called the area where these pulpits were located "the Holy of Holies" or "the most holy place."[96]

Dedication

Once the individual components of the tabernacle complex had been constructed and put into their proper place, Moses applied holy anointing oil to all of them and they became "sanctified" (Leviticus 8:10–11).[97] The sanctification of these objects made them "most holy" in the sight of the Lord, and anything coming into physical contact with them was brought into a similar state of holiness (Exodus 30:25–29; compare Leviticus 11:44).

Once the sanctuary had been sanctified, "a cloud covered the tent of the congregation, and the glory of the Lord filled the Tabernacle. And Moses was not able to enter into the tent of the congregation, because the cloud abode thereon, and the glory of the Lord filled the tabernacle" (Exodus 40:34–35; Numbers 9:15-16). An identical manifestation occurred during the dedication services of King Solomon's Temple (*see* 1 Kings 8:10–11; 2 Chronicles 5:13–14; 7:1–2). This cloud, called the *Shekinah* by Jews in later ages, radiated light because it shielded the Lord who stood within it (*see* Exodus 13:21–22; 14:24; 19:16–18; 24:15–17; 33:9–11; Leviticus 16:2; Numbers 12:5; Matthew 17:5). This brilliant cloud was thus a symbol of the Divine Presence.

PRIESTLY CONSECRATION

Before members of the tribe of Levi (specifically the sons of Aaron) were allowed to serve as priests in the tabernacle, they were required to go through a series of initiation rituals that would prepare them for their experience. After it was determined that the candidate was of the proper lineage and age, he was washed with water, anointed with oil, clothed in priestly vestments, and given symbols pertaining to the priestly office. Let us briefly examine each of these ceremonies.

Priesthood

The Lord chose the sons of Aaron to serve as tabernacle priests instead of the first-born males from each of the twelve tribes of Israel (*see* Numbers 8:13–19). This privilege was afforded to them, in part, because they had proven their faithfulness unto the Lord (*see* Exodus 32:26). Deuteronomy 10:8 states that "the Lord separated the tribe of Levi, to bear the ark of the covenant of the Lord, to stand before the Lord to minister unto him, and to bless in his name." An apocryphal work called Jubilees claims that while at Bethel, Jacob's son Levi dreamed that he and his sons would be ordained as priests of the Most High God forever. The text also states that "Jacob counted his sons . . . and Levi fell to the portion of the Lord. And [Jacob] put garments of the priesthood on him and filled his hands. . . . And Levi served as priest in Bethel before his father Jacob" (32:1–9). In commenting on this story, one writer has noted that Jacob was counting his sons so that, along with all of his other possessions, he could offer the Lord appropriate tithing from among them. "Counting backwards from the youngest, Jacob thus designates the tenth, Levi, as a kind of human tithe, 'the portion of the Lord.'"[98] In other legendary material, Levi says of a visionary experience he had,

> And I saw seven men in white raiment saying unto me: Arise, put on the robe of priesthood, and the crown of righteousness, and the breastplate of understanding, and the garment of truth, and the plate of faith, and the turban of the head, and the ephod of prophecy. Then each of them brought forward a thing and put it on me, and said unto me: From henceforth become a priest of the Lord, thou and thy seed forever. And the first man anointed me with holy oil, and gave me a staff of judgment. The second washed me with pure water, fed me with bread and holy wine and clad me with a holy and glorious robe. The third clothed me with a linen vestment like an ephod. The forth put round me a girdle like unto purple. The fifth gave me a branch of rich olive. The sixth placed a crown on my head. The seventh placed on my head a priestly diadem and filled my hands with incense, that I might serve as priest to the Lord, God. And they said unto me: "Levi, thy seed shall be divided into three dominations, as a sign of the coming glory of the Lord. The first one shall be great. Yea, greater than it none shall be. The second one shall be in the priesthood. The third one shall be called by a new name because a king shall arise in Judah and establish a new priesthood to all peoples, after the fashion of the Gentiles. His coming is beloved because he is a prophet of the Most High, and comes from the seed of Abraham our father."[99]

The customary method whereby an Israelite was invested with authority was by ordination through the laying on of hands (*see* Numbers 27:18–23; Deuteronomy 34:9; Acts 6:5–6; 13:3).[100] There is some evidence that temple priests were ordained to their office by the laying on of hands (*see* Numbers 8:9–10; 1 Chronicles 9:22).[101] When the priests or other Israelites needed an animal to serve as their proxy representative for the purpose of sacrifice, they laid their hands upon its head in order to transfer their representational authority to it (*see* Exodus 29:10, 15, 19; Leviticus 1:4; 3:2, 8, 13; 4:4; 8:14, 18, 22; 16:21).[102]

The tabernacle priests had to be of the proper lineage (*see* Ezra 2:62) and had to be thirty years of age before they could serve in the Lord's sanctuary (*see* Numbers 4:3). It is interesting to note that the New Testament not only begins with the genealogy of Jesus Christ (*see* Matthew 1:1–17), but we are informed that the Savior began His ministry at the age of thirty (*see* Luke 3:23) and was identified as a "high priest" (*see* Hebrews 3:1).

It is a commonly held view among Latter-day Saints that the temple priests of ancient Israel were only ordained to the Aaronic Priesthood, and this lesser authority was all that was had among the Israelites after the time of Moses. But this is not the view held by some LDS commentators. Elder Bruce R. McConkie has stated that Aaron and his sons "held the Melchizedek Priesthood and were numbered with the elders of Israel when the Lord first conferred the lesser authority [or Aaronic Priesthood] upon them. This is precisely what we do today when we take a holder of the Melchizedek Priesthood and ordain him a bishop in the Aaronic Priesthood."[103] President John Taylor likewise believed that "Aaron and the seventy elders of Israel . . . had the Melchizedek Priesthood,"[104] and according to Joseph Fielding Smith "Samuel, Isaiah, Jeremiah, Daniel, Ezekiel, Elijah, and others of the prophets held the Melchizedek Priesthood."[105]

Washing

Before the priests could serve the Lord in His tabernacle, they were required to become holy and clean (*see* Leviticus 10:8–11). In order to place the priests in such a ritual condition, the Lord directed Moses to take them "unto the door of the Tabernacle of the congregation, and wash them with water" (Exodus 40:12; Leviticus 8:6).[106] Since this ritual washing took place at the tabernacle door, Moses and the priests would have been standing next to the laver that had been filled with water (*see* Exodus 40:7). It is therefore likely that Moses used the water in the laver to ritually cleanse the priests.

The water used in this initiation rite was apparently of a specific nature. In Leviticus 15:13 we read that the type of water used in ritual cleansing was "running water." The Hebrew word translated as "running" is *chay*, which in the literal sense means "living."[107] According to one prominent biblical scholar, this was "spring water," such as that found in an artesian well.[108] "The insistence upon the use of running water in such instances [as Leviticus 14:5–6, 50–52 and 15:13] probably goes back to an era when divine power was thought to reside in stream or fountain."[109] Indeed, Jehovah symbolically calls Himself "the fountain of living waters" in Jeremiah 2:13 and 17:13 (compare 1 Nephi 11:25; Revelation 7:17). It is plain from John 4:6–14 that these are the waters of life (*see* Revelation 21:6; D&C 10:66). Several biblical texts inform us that the water of life originates as a fountain at the temple of God and flows out of the sacred compound as a life-giving river (*see* Ezekiel 47:1–12; Zechariah 14:8; Joel 3:18; Revelation 22:1–2).[110]

Since the washing of the priests was of a ritual nature, it was "necessary that the entire body be washed."[111] This washing was "in preparation for their consecration."[112] One ancient Jewish source indicates that the washing ceremony took place behind a linen curtain that had been set up inside the tabernacle's courtyard.[113]

The temple that stood during the lifetime of Jesus Christ was equipped with approximately forty ritual bathing pools (*miqva'ot*) alongside the monumental staircases that led up to its southern gates. Before any lay Israelites could enter the courtyards of the temple, they were required to ritually cleanse themselves in one of these pools.[114] This information naturally raises the question of whether lay Israelites also had to be ritually purified before they entered the tabernacle complex (compare Genesis 35:2–3).

Anointing

In addition to the ceremonial washing, the Lord directed that the tabernacle priests be consecrated to their service by an anointing ritual. The substance used for this anointing was olive oil that had been perfumed with liquid myrrh, sweet cinnamon, sweet calamus, and the bark of the cassia tree. When the aromatic extracts of these spices were combined with the olive oil, they produced a compound of "holy anointing oil" that was forbidden to be replicated for secular use (*see* Exodus 30:22–33).

Several scriptures indicate that the anointing oil was stored inside a "horn" that was kept within the tabernacle (1 Kings 1:39; 1 Samuel 16:1, 13).[115] There are several symbolic concepts that are connected with this horn. King David referred to the God of Israel as "the horn of my salvation" (2 Samuel 22:3; Psalm 18:2), and "the horn of David" mentioned in Psalm 132:17 was viewed among the Jews as a title of the Messiah.[116] Jesus Christ is explicitly identified in the New Testament both as the "horn of salvation," raised up out of the house of David (Luke 1:69), and also as the Messiah (*see* John 1:41; 4:25–26). The connection between these two concepts lies in the fact that the title *Messiah* (*mašiah*) means "anointed"[117] (*see* Acts 4:27; 10:38), and the holy anointing oil was kept inside the horn. In other words, the horn represented the *Anointed One*. And since "horn" in Hebrew figuratively means "power,"[118] an anointing with oil from the horn could perhaps be seen as symbolic of sharing in the power of the Messiah.[119]

This power came in the form of the Spirit of the Lord. When the prophet Samuel anointed Saul to be the king of Israel, he promised that the Spirit of the Lord would come upon him in such a powerful manner that it would change his heart and turn him into another man (*see* 1 Samuel 10:1, 6, 9). When Samuel anointed David as the king over Israel, "the Spirit of the Lord came upon David from that day forward" (1 Samuel 16:13). Isaiah provides us with the same imagery: "The Spirit of the Lord God is upon me; because the Lord hath anointed me" (Isaiah 61:1). And finally, we read in the book of Acts that "God anointed Jesus of Nazareth with the Holy Ghost and with power" (Acts 10:38). There may be an even more direct symbolic connection here since some scholars believe that olive oil is a symbol of the Holy Ghost.[120]

The Bible does not provide very much information about the form of the priestly anointing ceremony. What is known for certain is that the priests were anointed in the same manner as the high priest (*see* Exodus 40:15). Anointing oil was poured upon the head of the high priest, and he was then "anointed" (Leviticus 8:12; Exodus 29:7; Psalm 133:2 and footnote 2*a*). There is some indirect evidence, however, that may help us to fill in the gap of our missing knowledge. In an ordinance that closely parallels one of the priestly consecration rites, we read that the priest would pour oil into the palm of his left hand, dip the index finger of his right hand into the oil, and apply the oil to the right ear-lobe, right thumb, right big toe, and head of the person who was receiving the ordinance (*see* Leviticus 14:15–18; compare Exodus 29:20).[121] Some scholars are of the opinion that the anointing oil was applied to the tabernacle's components "with a single stroke."[122] The Hebrew word for "anoint" (*mašah*) means "to rub,"[123] and according to one scholar, the "original meaning of the root *mašah* was 'to wipe or stroke with the hand.'"[124]

Investiture

In studying the priestly vestments of the Bible, it must be borne in mind that their exact form "remains a matter of conjecture." They have "been given widely different forms by a succession of illustrators throughout the ages, probably with varying degrees of historical inaccuracy."[125] This is partly because most illustrators garner their mental images of this clothing from the archaic and sometimes inaccurate language of the King James Bible. The translators of 1611 A.D. did not have a detailed knowledge of Hebrew or ancient Near Eastern history, and so they presented a translation based upon their level of understanding. And while we still cannot claim to fully understand all of the ancient texts of the Bible that speak of priestly clothing, we can at least present a clearer picture than our ancestors did.

The Lord commanded Moses to dress the tabernacle priests in clothing that was designed to endow them with glory and honor (*see* Exodus 28:40–41).[126] The fact that God Himself revealed the pattern for these vestments should alert us to the possibility that they imitate the clothing that is worn by heavenly beings. And indeed, there is some evidence to support this view. A post-biblical Jewish commentary on the book of Exodus explains that the high priest's garments were like those worn by the Lord.[127] And one extrabiblical source also describes an angel wearing eight garments, alluding to those worn by the earthly high priest.[128] With this connection between the heavens and the earth, it is little wonder that they were called "holy garments" (Exodus 28:2, 4; 31:10; Leviticus 16:4).

There were three different types or sets of priestly garments that were worn in the tabernacle precincts. First, there were the five items worn by the ordinary priests—breeches, coat, ephod, girdle, and cap. Second, there were the eight items worn by the high priest—breeches, coat, robe, ephod, turban, girdle, breastplate, and crown.[129] And third, there were the all-white vestments worn by the high priest when he entered into the Holy of Holies on the Day of Atonement—breeches, coat, girdle, and cap.[130] Let us briefly examine each component of the priestly apparel.

• BREECHES: The breeches were an inner "garment, extending from the waist to just below the knee or to the ankle, and covering each leg separately."[131] They were made out of fine-twined linen (*see* Exodus 28:42; 39:28; Leviticus 6:10),[132] and since

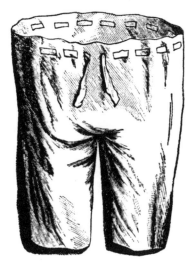

they were considered to be one of the "holy garments" belonging to the House of the Lord (Leviticus 16:4), they could only be worn by the priests, not by any of the other Israelites.

The priestly vestments are referred to in the Bible as "linen garments" (Ezekiel 44:17–18; compare Exodus 39:27–29). In 2 Chronicles 5:12, the Levites are specifically said to have been "arrayed in white linen." Linen fabric possesses several symbolic aspects that are relevant to our discussion. The fine linen worn by heavenly beings is described as "clean and white" or "pure and white" and is therefore an appropriate symbol of worthiness or righteousness (*see* Revelation 3:4–5; 15:6; 19:8).[133] Since linen is not the product of an animal that is

FIGURE 12. Reconstruction of the breeches that were worn by the temple priests of ancient Israel.

subject unto death, or "corruption" as it is called, it is also a fitting symbol of immortality, which is also called "incorruption" (*see* 1 Corinthians 15:52–54).[134]

• COAT: Also among the priestly vestments was a "holy linen coat" (Leviticus 16:4), otherwise known as the "coat of fine linen" (Exodus 28:39) and the "linen garment"

(Leviticus 6:10). This fine linen garment was shaped like a shirt or tunic and, like the breeches, was worn next to the skin.[135] The word translated as "coat" in the priestly narratives is *kuttonet*, the same word that is used to designate the "coats of skins" worn by Adam and Eve (Genesis 3:21) and also the "coat of many colours" owned by the patriarch Joseph (Genesis 37:3).[136] In the case of the high priest, he wore this piece of clothing underneath his robe.[137]

Exodus 39:27 indicates that both the "coats" of the high priest and the ordinary priests were of *oreg* workmanship (translated as "woven work" in the King James Bible). But the scriptures further indicate that the garment of the high priest was embroidered in some manner (*see* Exodus 28:4, 39).[138] The exact

FIGURE 13. Reconstruction of the tunic worn by ancient Israel's temple priests when they served in the Lord's house.

nature of this embroidery is still a matter of debate, however.[139]

• ROBE: Over his white linen garments, the high priest wore a free-flowing, ankle-length blue robe that was woven entirely of wool.[140] This particular type of apparel was worn in the ancient Near East almost exclusively by people of high rank and authority (*see* 1 Samuel 18:4; 24:4, 11; 2 Samuel 13:18; Ezekiel 26:16).[141] In form, the high priest's robe was a woven strip of cloth (thus seamless) with a reinforced hole in the middle of the material for the head to pass through (*see* Exodus 28:31–32; 39:22–23).[142] One extra-biblical source states that Jehovah "strengthened Aaron with emblems of power including the 'long robe.'"[143] We should also note that blue, the color of the heavens or sky, was associated in ancient times with royalty and also with Jehovah.[144]

White linen robes are often associated in scripture with kings, priests, saints, angels, and Gods (*see* 1 Chronicles 15:27; Psalm 104:1–2; Ezekiel 9:2–3, 11; Mark 9:3; Revelation 3:4–5; 6:11; 7:9; 15:6; 19:8). In fact, the Hebrew word used to designate the high priest's robe (*me'il*) is believed to be etymologically related to the Egyptian word *m'r* which refers to the faultless, or defectless, clothing of gods.[145]

Upon the hems of the high priest's robe, there was an alternating pattern of pure gold bells and pomegranate-shaped tassels dyed with the sacred tabernacle colors of blue, purple, red, and white (*see* Exodus 28:33–35; 39:24–26).[146] The melodious tinkling of the small golden bells, concludes one biblical interpreter, was meant solely to summon the attention of Jehovah as the high priest crossed the curtained threshold between the courtyard and the Holy Place.[147] This was necessary, says another writer, because "it is unseemly to enter the royal palace suddenly; propriety demands that the entry should be preceded by an announcement."[148] And why were pomegranates associated with the tabernacle of Jehovah? There are at least two plausible reasons. First of all, pomegranates were one of the fruits identified with the promised land (*see* Deuteronomy 8:7–8; Numbers 13:23) and because of their numerous seeds they were ideal symbols of abundance and prosperity.[149] Secondly, the crown-like shape of the pomegranate's flowered end made this fruit a symbol of royalty. One Jewish tradition claims that "Solomon's coronet was modeled on the pomegranate's crown,"[150] and this royal connection may help to explain why hundreds of pomegranates were used to decorate King Solomon's Temple (*see* 1 Kings 7:18, 42; Jeremiah 52:22–23).[151]

• GIRDLE: The priestly girdle or sash (*abnet*) was of two different types. First, there was the elaborate sash of the high priest that was made primarily of fine-twined linen and then decorated in *roqem* workmanship with threads of blue, purple, and red wool (*see* Exodus 39:29).[152] Second, there were the sashes worn by the ordinary priests. Nowhere in the Old Testament is it stated that these sashes were designed in the same manner as the high priest's sash. Instead, we are simply informed that the ordinary priests wore "girdles" (*see* Exodus 28:40; 29:8–9; Leviticus 8:13). On the Day of Atonement the high priest was required to dress like an ordinary priest. Since the high priest wore a plain white linen sash on this occasion, we can safely conclude that the ordinary priests wore white linen sashes as well.[153]

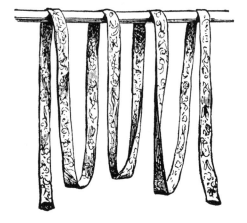

FIGURE 14. The sash worn by the high priest of the temple was elaborately decorated with blue, purple, and red threads and was also interwoven with thinly cut threads of gold.

High Priest on Day of Atonement	Ordinary Priest
(Leviticus 16:4)	*(Exodus 39:27–29; Leviticus 6:10; 8:13)*
Linen Breeches	Linen Breeches
Linen Coat	Linen Coat
Linen Mitre *(misnepet)*	Linen Bonnet *(pa'arey migba'ah)*
Linen Girdle	Girdle (unspecified fabric)

The sash worn by the priests of the Aaronic order was rather long. It was "wound under the breast, twice around the body, was tied in an ample bow or loop, and the ends reached the ankles. It was thrown over the left shoulder while the priest was officiating."[154] The angelic priests in the heavenly temple wear golden sashes over their white linen robes (*see* Revelation 1:13; 15:6; *see also* Daniel 10:5). Beyond the references to the priestly sash, the word *abnet* is only mentioned in Isaiah 22:21 where it belongs to the regalia of a royal official.[155] From this evidence we could conclude that the *abnet* was only worn by those of royal or priestly status. The sash is represented in several Old Testament scriptures as a symbol of strength (*see* Psalm 18:32, 39; Proverbs 31:17; Isaiah 22:21).

• BONNET: There were two types of headcoverings worn by members of the tabernacle priesthood. The headdress of the ordinary priests was made of fine linen and in Hebrew was called a *pa'arey migba'ah,* which may be translated as "decorated cap" (*see* Exodus 39:28).[156] This priestly headpiece was "a nonconical—that is, flattish—cap."[157] It was bound onto the head of the priest in some unspecified manner.[158]

The high priest, on the other hand, wore a different type of headress that was called *misnepet* in the Hebrew language. Like the headgear of the ordinary priests, it too was made of fine linen (*see* Exodus 28:39; 39:28), but it was of the distinctive design worn by royalty.[159] On the Day of Atonement, the high priest also donned a *misnepet* before he entered the Holy of Holies, but this particular headpiece was made of plain linen (*bad*) instead of fine linen (*šeš*).[160]

• CROWN: Over his fine linen cap, the high priest wore a plate of pure gold that was engraved with the words "HOLY TO YAHWEH" but translated in the King James Bible as "HOLINESS TO THE LORD" (Exodus 28:36–38). This golden plate, which was positioned across the forehead, was also called "the holy crown" (Leviticus 8:9). This crown was secured to the forehead of the high priest by a single blue *pathil,* which is translated as "lace" in the King James Bible (Exodus 28:37) but which can be more accurately rendered as "a thread, line, cord."[161] The pure gold crown was an obvious symbol of kingship (*see* Psalms 21:3). The blue string, on the other hand, was symbolically related to the robe of the high priest, being of the same color.

The crown was considered to be holy because it was engraved with the name of the God of Israel.[162] The Lord's name played an important role in the temple theology of ancient Israel for the Lord said, "in all places where I record (*azkir*, "make to be remembered")[163] my name I will come unto thee, and I will bless thee" (Exodus 20:24). The temple is specifically referred to in scripture as the house of the Lord's name (*see* Deuteronomy 12:5; 2 Samuel 7:13; 1 Kings 9:3, 7; 2 Chronicles 7:16) and it was in that holy house that the holy name was transmitted to the covenant people.

> Only the priests in the temple were allowed to pronounce the sacred name and were enjoined to do so when blessing the people, in accordance with Numbers 6:27: "And they shall put my name upon the children of Israel, and I will bless them." . . . The priests, when pronouncing the name in their blessing, did it in a whisper. . . . An ancient Baraita says: Formerly the quadraliteral name . . . was transmitted to everybody, but when the insolent ones increased it was transmitted only to the discreet ones (z'nuim) among the priesthood.[164]

In Exodus 33:19, the Lord promised Moses: "I will proclaim (i.e., 'pronounce')[165] the name of the Lord before thee." This promise was fulfilled in Exodus 34:5 when the Lord "descended in the cloud, and stood with him there, and proclaimed ('pronounced') the name of the Lord." The proper context of these statements is that what Moses heard being pronounced was "the name LORD [i.e.,] the tetragrammaton: YHVH."[166] Why is this significant? In Exodus 3:15 we read that YHVH is the Lord's name "forever" but it has been noted by some biblical commentators that the form of the word that is in the Hebrew text can be translated as "hidden."[167] Several scholars have further noted that this is the "covenant name" that is revealed at the time of covenant renewal.[168]

• EPHOD: The word *ephod* was left untranslated in the King James Bible and its exact identity, form, and function have been debated in scholarly circles for several centuries.[169] A sizeable number of biblical interpreters, however, have come to the conclusion that this item of ritual apparel was an apron that extended from the loins to the thighs[170] and covered only the "lower front part of the body."[171] It also had a belt attached to its top edge so that it could be girded to the priest by tying the two ends of the belt together behind his back.[172] The book of Exodus leaves one with the impression that only the high priest wore an ephod. But there is evidence from other books of the Bible indicating that linen aprons were worn by all of the temple priests (*see* 1 Samuel 2:18; 22:18) and also by at least one of the kings of Israel (*see* 1 Chronicles 15:27; 2 Samuel 6:14). There are also several references in the Dead Sea Scrolls to the angelic priests of the heavenly temple wearing an *ephod*.[173] Based upon the fact that the high priest's apron was of *hošeb* workmanship, we may conclude that it was decorated with some type of "figures."[174]

The apron was viewed as the most important of the priestly vestments.[175] The reason for its preeminence can be seen in both the nature and design of the elaborate apron that was worn by the high priest. This item of apparel must have been stunning to behold because its main body and belt were composed of threads of gold (*see* Exodus 39:3) that were combined with the sacred mixture and colors of the tabernacle—blue, purple, and red wool with fine-twined linen (*see* Exodus 28:5–6, 8; 39:2–3, 5). In the ancient Near East, golden garments were worn primarily by exalted beings (compare Daniel 10:5; Revelation 1:13; 15:6).[176]

• BREASTPLATE: Attached to the horizontal belt of the high priest's apron were two vertical straps of unspecified material that ran up to and over his shoulders. On the top of each of these shoulderpieces was an onyx stone that was encased in a framework of gold and engraved with the names of six of the tribes of Israel (*see* Exodus 28:9–12). Hebrew tradition indicates that the names of the six older sons of Jacob were engraved into the stone on the right shoulder and the names of the six younger sons on the left shoulder.[177] Since they were located on the high priest's shoulders, only the Lord could read them from his vantage point in the heavens (compare 1 Kings 9:3). The shoulder stones thus served the function of continually exhibiting or memorializing the names of the children of Israel "before the Lord" (Exodus 28:12) so that He would always remember the covenant that He had made with Abraham, Isaac, and Jacob (*see* Exodus 2:24–25; 6:2–8).

Between the two shoulder straps of the high priest's *ephod* hung an object called the "breastplate of judgment" (Exodus 28:15). A more accurate title for this pectoral decoration would perhaps be "pouch[178] of decision."[179] This breastpiece consisted of a rectangular piece of cloth that had been woven in the same manner, and of the same sacred materials, as the high priest's apron (gold threads; blue, purple and red wool; white linen). The cloth was folded double and sewn at the sides to create an approximately nine-inch-square pocket that served as a receptacle for the Urim and

Thummim (*see* Exodus 28:30). There is a great amount of debate among scholars about the form and function of these mysterious objects whose names literally mean "lights" (Urim) and "perfections" (Thummim).[180] One scholar who has conducted a substantial amount of research on the Urim and Thummim has gathered several early traditions that claim these objects were stones of some type (compare JS–H 1:34–35).[181] His overall conclusions are of interest to Latter-day Saints because he believes that these stones, through which detailed revelations were received,[182] existed prior to the time of Moses (compare Ether 3:21–28; Abraham 3:1, 4),[183] and when they were activated a "miraculous light verified that the message given by the high priest was indeed from God"[184] (compare Mosiah 8:13–18; Alma 37:21–23).

The front face of the breastpiece was decorated with twelve different stones that had each been encased in a gold framework and engraved upon its surface with one of the names of the twelve tribes of Israel (*see* Exodus 28:17–21).[185] Like the stones on the shoulderpieces, these stones served as a memorial "before the Lord" but only when the high priest entered into the Holy Place of the tabernacle (Exodus 28:29). Why would it be necessary to display this second set of tribal names in the Holy Place? Perhaps so that when Jehovah was seated upon His throne in the Holy of Holies, He could view the names from eye level and, again, remember the promises of the Abrahamic covenant.[186]

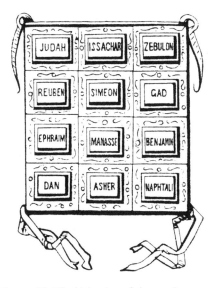

FIGURE 15. The high priest of the temple wore a breastplate that was decorated with twelve stones that represented the twelve tribes of Israel.

The Lord directed that the breastpiece was to be positioned over the high priest's heart (*see* Exodus 28:29–30), and in order to keep it in place He revealed the pattern for a series of fastening devices. A gold ring was attached to each of the four corners of the breastpiece and two gold rings were likewise attached at the points where the horizontal belt of the apron and the vertical shoulderpieces of the apron met. A blue cord was attached between the bottom set of gold breastpiece rings and those found at the intersection of the apron's belt and shoulderpieces. But the top attachments were considerably more elaborate. Twisted chains of pure gold were permanently attached on one end to the gold rings on the upper corners of the breastpiece, and on the other end to open frameworks of gold that were slightly larger than the gold-encased stones on the shoulders of the high priest. The gold frameworks were simply slipped over the shoulderstones in order to secure the breastpiece into its proper place (*see* Exodus 28:13–14, 22–28; 39:15–21).

The high priest's breastpiece had several symbolic aspects that are well worth mentioning. It has been observed by one writer that the stones decorating the high priest's chest "are identical with the precious or semi-precious stones that, according to the tradition reflected in Ezekiel 28:13, were to be found in Eden, the garden of God. . . . [The high priest], when making atonement for the iniquities of the children of Israel, was to wear on his garments the gold and the precious stones that implicitly symbolized the situation [prevalent] in the Garden of Eden [*see* Genesis 2:11–12], when man was free from all sin. This, apparently, is the primary significance of the stones of the pouch."[187] There are also a significant number of direct parallels between the high priest's pectoral and the heavenly city of Zion. For instance, the celestial city has a foursquare foundation, it is adorned with twelve precious stones and pure gold, and its twelve gates are in four sets of three and are named after the twelve tribes of Israel (*see* Revelation 21:9–21). The fact that the breastpiece was located over the high priest's heart (*see* Exodus 28:30) may also represent a connection with the celestial city of Zion since we are told in D&C 97:21 that Zion consists of "THE PURE IN HEART." And finally, there may be a connection between the light of God that fills Zion as if reflected from "a stone . . . clear as crystal" (*see* Revelation 21:11, 23–25) and the stone inside the breastpiece called "Urim," which some biblical scholars translate as "lights" (compare D&C 130:6–9).[188]

Because of its physical attachments, the breastpiece was seen as an integral part of the high priest's apron. The main purpose of the breastpiece, of course, was to serve as a place to store the Urim and Thummim over the high priest's heart (*see* Exodus 28:30). In this context, one can readily see why one ancient document that describes the priestly vestments says that the "apron" represented "prophetic power."[189]

Filling the Hands

Moses was commanded to take Aaron and his sons after their investiture "and consecrate them . . . that they may minister unto [the Lord] in the priest's office" (Exodus 28:41). The term "consecrate" is actually the translation of two Hebrew words; *male'*, meaning "to fill"[190] and *yad*, meaning "a hand, the *open* one."[191] Hence, the translation would more accurately read, "you shall fill their hand."[192] One scholar has noted that "an expression corresponding to this idiom, word for word, is found in Akkadian in the sense of 'installing,' the original meaning being to fill the hands of the appointed person with the material for the work entrusted to him and with the tools required for executing it."[193] What were the temple priests' hands filled with?

• SACRIFICIAL EMBLEMS: "The priest in the temple slaughtered with his right hand, and received the blood in his left."[194] Then specific parts of the sacrificial animal and other emblems of consecration were put into "the hands of Aaron, and in the hands of his sons" in order to "sanctify them" (Exodus 29:24, 33; *see also* Leviticus 8:27–28). A portion of the meat offering was also put into one hand of the priest who then burnt it upon the altar of sacrifice (*see* Leviticus 9:17).

• OLIVE OIL: "And the priest shall take some of the log of oil and pour it into the palm of his own left hand. And the priest shall dip his right finger in the oil that is in his left hand, and shall sprinkle of the oil with his finger seven times before the Lord. And of the rest of the oil that is in his hand shall the priest put upon the tip of the right ear of him that is to be cleansed, and upon the thumb of his right hand, and upon the great toe of his right foot. . . . And the remnant of the oil that is in the priest's hand he shall pour upon the head of him that is to be cleansed" (Leviticus 14:15–18).

• INCENSE: The Israelites were commanded to make "spoons" of pure gold to be used inside of the Holy Place of the tabernacle (Exodus 25:29). During the period of King Solomon's Temple these "spoons" were referred to as "censers of pure gold" (1 Kings 7:50; 2 Chronicles 4:22), and hence were used by the temple priests for burning incense (*see* Numbers 7:84, 86).

The word translated here as "spoon" is *kaph* and literally means "the hollow hand or palm" and refers to the shape seen in "the bowl of a dish."[195] Several incense ladles have been recovered in Israelite archeological sites which have a repesentation of a hand carved on the convex side of the ladle's cup. This connection between the incense ladle and the hand is seen in Revelation 8:3–5, where an angel in the heavenly temple took a golden censer to the golden altar of incense which is before the throne of God. There the angel offered up the incense, and its smoke "ascended up before God out of the angel's hand."[196]

FIGURE 16. Incense ladles with hands carved on the underside have been found in Israelite archeological sites dating from as early as the 8th century B.C.

SUMMARY

The tabernacle was rich in symbolic associations. The pattern for this divine dwelling was revealed unto Moses when he ascended Mount Sinai to meet with the Lord. The tabernacle was an earthly replica of the heavenly temple where the throne of the Lord is located. The ark of the covenant was a symbolic representation of the Lord's heavenly throne. Even the clothing worn by the tabernacle priests was fashioned in imitation of the clothing worn by the angels who ministered in the temple of heaven. The tabernacle was thus a place where heaven and earth combined. It was a sacred space where the children of Israel could have close communion with God.

NOTES

1. James Strong, *The New Strong's Exhaustive Concordance of the Bible* (Nashville: Thomas Nelson Publishers, 1996), Hebrew and Aramaic Dictionary, 87, word #4908.

2. Ibid., Hebrew and Aramaic Dictionary, 3, word #168.

3. See Jacob Milgrom, *Leviticus 1–16* (New York: Doubleday, 1991), 555.

4. The "Samaritan *Asatir* . . . teaches that both the rod and garments of Adam were received by Moses (9.22; cf. the Syriac *Book of the Bee* 30)" (Stephen N. Lambden, "From Fig Leaves to Fingernails: Some Notes on the Garments of Adam and Eve in the Hebrew Bible and Select Early Postbiblical Jewish Writings," in Paul Morris and Deborah Sawyer, eds., *A Walk in the Garden: Biblical, Iconographical and Literary Images of Eden* [Sheffield, England: JSOT Press, 1992], 88). References to the rod of Moses can be found in Exodus 4:2–4, 17; 7:15–17, 20; 9:22–23; 10:12–13; 14:16; 17:5, 9–12; JST Genesis 50:34. It is referred to as "the rod of God" in Exodus 4:20 and 17:9. The rod of Aaron is mentioned in Exodus 7:9–12; 8:5–6, 16–17.

5. See Milgrom, *Leviticus 1–16*, 557. "In many respects Moses has the traits of the ideal sacral king, uniting in his person the three functions of king, priest, and prophet, as does Adam according to late Jewish traditions" (Geo Widengren, *The Ascension of the Apostle and the Heavenly Book* [Uppsala: A. B. Lundequistska Bokhandeln, 1950], 28). For other traditions of Moses as "King and Priest," see Wayne A. Meeks, *The Prophet-King: Moses Traditions and the Johannine Christology* (Leiden: E. J. Brill, 1967), 181–83, 232–37.

6. Wayne A. Meeks, "Moses as God and King," in Jacob Neusner, ed., *Religions in Antiquity* (Leiden: E. J. Brill, 1968), 365, see also 363. Jesus Christ is called "the last Adam" in 1 Corinthians 15:45.

7. Joseph P. Schultz, "Angelic Opposition to the Ascension of Moses and the Revelation of the Law," *The Jewish Quarterly Review*, vol. 61, no. 4, April 1971, 295. Other sources speak of Moses receiving a "robe of light," a "crown of light," and a "sceptre of sovereignty" (Meeks, "Moses as God and King," 358). The heavenly garments Moses received are said to have been symbolic of God's favor and protection (see Schultz, "Angelic Opposition," 292). The book of 3 Enoch describes how, as an angel, Enoch revealed to Moses "the mysteries . . . and all the secrets of creation" (ibid., 296) while 4 Ezra 14:4–6 states that secret teachings were delivered to Moses on Mount Sinai, and God commanded him not to reveal them to others (see Meeks, "Moses as God and King," 368). Some ancient texts speak of Moses becoming deified when he received the name *Elohim* while on top of Mount Horeb (ibid., 359–61).

8. *WJS*, 119–20.

9. "Moses sought to bring the children of Israel into the presence of God, through the power of the Priesthood" (*WJS*, 9).

10. This sin was so serious that the chief participants in the act were executed by the sons of Levi, and the Lord brought a plague upon the remainder of the people (see Exodus 32:25–35; see also JST Exodus 32:14). The Lord even refused, in his anger, to allow Moses to see his face when they met

together (see JST Exodus 33:18–23). The Lord threatened to destroy the entire nation except for Moses and commanded the Israelites to remove their "ornaments" (Exodus 33:4–6). The Septuagint (or ancient Greek version of the Old Testament) adds that the Israelites had on "robes of . . . glory" and they were required to remove them also (Curtis Vaughan, ed., *Twenty-Six Translations of the Bible* [Chattanooga, Tennessee: AMG Publishers, 1985], 1:295). These robes may be related to the "garments . . . for glory" (i.e., temple robes) worn by the Israelite priests (see Exodus 28:2). This brings us to the subject of the *tallit*. The Lord commanded that each Israelite place four marks on their garment (white linen tassels, each with a blue wool thread) to remind them to live holy lives by keeping God's commandments (see Numbers 15:37–40; Deuteronomy 22:12). One prominent biblical scholar believes that these marks transformed the Israelite's vesture into "a priestly garment" that also signified the wearer's royal status (see Jacob Milgrom, "Of Hems and Tassels," *Biblical Archaeology Review*, May/June 1983, 65; compare Exodus 19:6 where the Israelite nation is called "a kingdom of priests"). Today some Jews wear a white garment with the four prescribed marks, called a *tallit katan*, underneath their regular clothing (see Cecil Roth, ed., *Encyclopaedia Judaica* [Jerusalem: Keter Publishing House], 15:743–45; Frankel and Teutsch, *The Encyclopedia of Jewish Symbols*, 168–70). The removal or destruction of any of the marks makes this garment "ritually unfit" (Roth, ed., *Encyclopaedia Judaica*, 15:745; 16:1188) and then the garment will no longer provide "protection" to its wearer (Isaac Landman, ed., *The Universal Jewish Encyclopedia* [New York: The Universal Jewish Encyclopedia, 1941], 4:460–61). It is of interest that one *tallit* recovered at an Israelite archeological site does not have four tassels at its corners but rather four marks shaped like the right-angled Greek letter *gamma* (see Yigael Yadin, *The Finds from the Bar Kokhba Period in the Cave of Letters* [Jerusalem: Israel Exploration Society, 1963], 238).

11. *WJS*, 244.

12. Leo Schaya, *The Universal Meaning of the Kabbalah* (London: George Allen and Unwin, 1971), 15–16.

13. "Schoolmaster" is translated from the Greek word *paidagogos* and carries the meaning "instructor" or "tutor" (see Strong, *The New Strong's Exhaustive Concordance of the Bible*, Greek Dictionary, 66, word #3807).

14. In his comments on the Savior's lament found in Matthew 23:37, Joseph Smith directly connected the concept of gathering the Lord's people with the building of temples and the bestowal of the ordinances of salvation (see *TPJS*, 307–308).

15. See Victor Hurowitz, *I Have Built You an Exalted House* (Sheffield, England: JSOT Press, 1992), 168–70. In some rabbinical literature the idea is put forward that "God showed Moses the heavenly temple and said unto him: 'Make a likeness of it on the earth'" (Raphael Patai, *Man and Temple in Ancient Jewish Myth and Ritual* [New York: Thomas Nelson and Sons, 1947], 130).

16. See Frank M. Cross, Jr., "The Priestly Tabernacle in the Light of Recent Research," in Truman G. Madsen, ed., *The Temple in Antiquity* [Provo, Utah: BYU Religious Studies Center, 1984], 96–97. Notice the connection between the "tent of assembly" for the council in ancient Israel and the "Assembly Room" in early LDS temples where Church leaders met in council (see James E. Talmage, *The House of the Lord*, rev. ed. [Salt Lake City: Deseret Book, 1974], illustration 14).

17. It is admittedly difficult to visualize the completely horizontal tabernacle as imitating a vertical mountain that was divided into three successively higher levels. It is possible that the ascension between the various compartments of the tabernacle complex was illustrated by way of the bases or foundation pieces that marked the perimeter of each successive area. For example, the bases that ran along the perimeter of the courtyard and also across the threshold of its entrance were all made of bronze. The threshold of the Holy Place was also marked by bronze bases, but the bases that ran along the perimeter of this area were all made of silver. And finally, the bases that marked the threshold of the Holy of Holies, as well as its perimeter, were all made of silver. There was also another way whereby the ascension might have been indicated. "The symbolism seems to picture a situation in which the bottom tip of the Tabernacle, i.e., the silver bases, fit into the top tip of the courtyard, i.e., the silver bands [or rods] and hooks [of the pillars]. The Tabernacle proper is a kind of upper story to the courtyard" (Vern S. Poythress, *The Shadow of Christ in the Law of Moses* [Brentwood, Tennessee: Wolgemuth and Hyatt, 1991], 26).

18. Jacob Milgrom, *Studies in Levitical Terminology* (Berkeley: University of California Press, 1970), 44–45. See also Nahum M. Sarna, *Exploring Exodus* (New York: Schocken Books, 1986), 203.

19. See Peter J. Kearney, "Creation and Liturgy: The P Redaction of Exodus 25–40," *Zeitschrift Für Die Alttestamentliche Wissenschaft*, vol. 89, no. 3, 1977, 375–87.

20. Terrence E. Fretheim, *Exodus* (Louisville, Kentucky: John Knox Press, 1991), 269. Fretheim lists common themes between the two narratives such as (a) Presence of the Spirit of God; (b) Liturgical celebration of New Year's day or the first day of creation; (c) Seven divine speeches concluding with the Sabbath; (d) Importance given to shape, order, design, and intricacy; (e) Both creations evaluated and deemed "very good" (ibid., 269–72).

21. Sarna, *Exploring Exodus*, 214. "The Tabernacle thus represented, as it were, a microcosm in which the macrocosmic universe was reflected" (ibid.).

22. Ibid., 214–15; emphasis added.

23. Sarna, *Exploring Exodus*, 204. There seems to be a symbolic correlation between the order of the twelve tribes of Israel around the tabernacle and the cherubim seen in vision by the temple priest Ezekiel (see Ezekiel 1:4, 6–10). See the diagram in E. Raymond Capt, *King Solomon's Temple* (Thousand Oaks, California: Artisan, 1979), 62.

24. Philip P. Jenson, *Graded Holiness* (Sheffield, England: JSOT Press, 1992), 92. The entrance guards may have also served in a ritual capacity. Some biblical scholars believe that Psalms 15 and 24 contain elements of an entrance liturgy. This "sacred rite" supposedly took place at the gate leading into the temple courtyard, involved the priests and those desiring entry, and was in a question and answer format. Those who approached the gate evidently requested to pass through it (see Psalm 118:19–20) and were then required to answer the questions posed by the gatekeepers. One of the answers included the pronunciation of the sacred name of God which served as "the password." There was then a confirmation that the supplicants were "qualified to ascend" (A. A. Anderson, *The Book of Psalms: 1–72* [Grand Rapids, Michigan: Eerdmans, 1981], 202–205; Peter C. Craigie, *Psalms 1–50* [Waco, Texas: Word Books, 1983], 211).

25. The footnotes in the LDS edition of the King James Bible indicate that "brass" should actu-

ally read "bronze." Hence "bronze" will be used throughout this chapter in describing the various parts of the tabernacle.

26. See Strong, *The New Strong's Exhaustive Concordance of the Bible*, Hebrew and Aramaic Dictionary, 50, word #2838.

27. This is where the LDS term "stake" comes from (*see* Isaiah 54:2; D&C 82:14; 133:9). See the comments on stakes in Matthew B. Brown and Paul Thomas Smith, *Symbols in Stone: Symbolism on the Early Temples of the Restoration* (American Fork, Utah: Covenant Communications, Inc., 1997), 18–19, 36 nt. 49.

28. See Strong, *The New Strong's Exhaustive Concordance of the Bible*, Hebrew and Aramaic Dictionary, 126, word #7050.

29. Richard S. Ellis, *Foundation Deposits in Ancient Mesopotamia* (New Haven, Connecticut: Yale University Press, 1968), 79.

30. Joseph Blenkinsopp, *Ezra—Nehemiah: A Commentary* (Philadelphia: Westminster Press, 1988), 183.

31. For confirmation that "his holy place" in verse 8 refers to the temple, see H. G. M. Williamson, *Ezra, Nehemiah* (Waco, Texas: Word Books, 1985), 135. Two biblical commentators are of the opinion that the nail mentioned in verse 8 "must surely be a reference to the tent pegs of sacred architecture" (Carol L. Meyers and Eric M. Meyers, *Zechariah 9–14* [New York: Doubleday, 1993], 202).

32. "Verse 4 is variously interpreted. Those commentators are probably correct who, with the Targum, take it as messianic" (Frank E. Gaebelein, ed., *Daniel—Minor Prophets* [Grand Rapids, Michigan: Zondervan, 1985], 669). "Some say it is spoken concerning the Lord, that he is . . . the nail. It refers to him, no doubt" (Arno C. Gaebelein, *Gaebelein's Concise Commentary on the Whole Bible* [Neptune, New Jersey: Loizeaux Brothers, 1985], 750).

33. Meyers and Meyers, *Zechariah 9–14*, 200; see also 201–202.

34. In likening the rite of baptism to Christ's death by crucifixion, the early Church father Ambrose said: "When you are immersed, you receive the likeness of death and burial, you receive the sacrament of his cross; because Christ hung upon the cross and his body was fastened to it by the nails [see John 20:24–29]. So you are crucified with him, you are fastened to Christ, you are fastened by the nails of our Lord Jesus Christ lest the devil pull you away. May Christ's nail continue to hold you, for human weakness seeks to pull you away" (Edward Yarnold, *The Awe-Inspiring Rites of Initiation: Baptismal Homilies of the Fourth Century* [England: St. Paul Publications, 1971], 118).

35. *See* Menahem Haran, *Temples and Temple-Service in Ancient Israel* (Winona Lake, Indiana: Eisenbrauns, 1985), 160–62.

36. *See* Strong, *The New Strong's Exhaustive Concordance of the Bible*, Hebrew and Aramaic Dictionary, 81, word #4539.

37. Ibid., Hebrew and Aramaic Dictionary, 146, word #8179.

38. The "sapphire stone" that God stands upon in Exodus 24:10 is, of course, deep blue in color. God's throne is also described as having "the appearance of a sapphire stone" in Ezekiel 1:26.

39. Geo Widengren, "Royal Ideology and the Testaments of the Twelve Patriarchs," in F. F. Bruce,

ed., *Promise and Fulfillment* (Edinburgh: T. and T. Clark, 1963), 205.

40. The word translated here as "crown" is *zer* and means "a chaplet, a border moulding" (Strong, *The New Strong's Exhaustive Concordance of the Bible*, Hebrew and Aramaic Dictionary, 39, word #2213).

41. See Umberto Cassuto, *A Commentary on the Book of Exodus* (Jerusalem: Magnes Press, 1983), 362–64.

42. See H. Th. Obbink, "The Horns of the Altar in the Semitic World, Especially in Jahwism," *Journal of Biblical Literature*, vol. 56, 1937, 43–49. There are several biblical texts that speak of actions taking place in association with the horns of the altar. For instance, Psalm 118:27 states that sacrificial animals were bound to the horns of the altar with cords, sacrificial blood was smeared upon the horns of the tabernacle altars on the Day of Atonement (see Leviticus 4:7, 18, 25, 34), and those who sought for refuge or protection would grasp the altar horns (see 1 Kings 1:50).

43. Strong, *The New Strong's Exhaustive Concordance of the Bible*, Hebrew and Aramaic Dictionary, 128, word #7161.

44. The word "laver" is translated from the Hebrew *kiyyor* which properly means "something round" (Strong, *The New Strong's Exhaustive Concordance of the Bible*, Hebrew and Aramaic Dictionary, 64, word #3595).

45. "There has been much debate as to the role of the women who gathered at the Tent of Meeting (1 Samuel 2:22; cf. Exodus 38:8). . . . Most scholars suggest that these women served some cultic role—either praying, fasting, offering sacrifices, or serving as an honor guard at the Tabernacle" (Susan Grossman, "Women and the Jerusalem Temple," in Susan Grossman and Rivka Haut, eds., *Daughters of the King: Women and the Synagogue* [New York: The Jewish Publication Society, 1992], 18). "That Exodus 38:8 may actually speak of women functionaries in the cult whose activity was similar to that of the Levites of the Book of Numbers finds support in the use of the same verbal root *sb'* to describe the service of the Levites in Numbers 4:23 and Numbers 8:24" (Mayer I. Gruber, "Women in the Cult According to the Priestly Code," in Jacob Neusner, Baruch A. Levine, and Ernest S. Frerichs, eds., *Judaic Perspectives on Ancient Israel* [Philadelphia: Fortress Press, 1987], 36).

46. Hugh W. Nibley, *Temple and Cosmos* (Salt Lake City: Deseret Book and FARMS, 1992), 145.

47. Strong, *The New Strong's Exhaustive Concordance of the Bible*, Greek Dictionary, 82, word #4637.

48. The word "boards" is translated from the Hebrew *qerašim* (Strong, *The New Strong's Exhaustive Concordance of the Bible*, Hebrew and Aramaic Dictionary, 128, word #7175). Some biblical commentators believe that the *qerašim* were "frames" (see J. D. Douglas, ed., *New Bible Dictionary*, 3d ed. [Downers Grove, Illinois: Intervarsity Press, 1996], 1145–46) while others have noted that the "boards" of the divine dwelling have precedence in the ancient Near East (see Cassuto, *A Commentary on the Book of Exodus*, 323, 351, 354–58).

49. Jenson, *Graded Holiness*, 112.

50. This covering consisted "specifically of black goats' hair" (Cassuto, *A Commentary on the Book of Exodus*, 347).

51. See Frank M. Cross, Jr., "The Priestly Tabernacle in the Light of Recent Research," 95–96. This interpretation is also endorsed in Sarna, *Exploring Exodus*, 194. The term "badgers' skins" in the

King James Bible is simply a mistranslation.

52. Raphael Patai has expressed his view that there were twenty-four cherubim associated with the tabernacle: two on the ark of the covenant, two embroidered on the veil of the Holy of Holies, and twenty on the linen coverings that were draped over the tabernacle structure (see Raphael Patai, *The Hebrew Goddess*, 3d ed. [Detroit: Wayne State University Press, 1990], 70). This is interesting in light of the fact that there were twenty-four courses of priests serving in the Jerusalem Temple after the monarchy was established (*see* 1 Chronicles 24:3–19) and twenty-four Levitical guards posted at points of importance throughout the temple complex, "chiefly places where entrance could be made into the holy courts" (F. J. Hollis, *The Archaeology of Herod's Temple* [London: J. M. Dent and Sons, 1934], 223). The apostle John also reported that there were twenty-four thrones near the throne of God in the heavenly temple (*see* JST Revelation 4:4–6, 10–11). Notice the parallel to the twenty-four pulpits in the Kirtland Temple that were seen in vision by the entire First Presidency (see Brown and Smith, *Symbols in Stone: Symbolism on the Early Temples of the Restoration*, 53).

53. Other heavenly beings have been seen surrounded by a dark cloud. For instance, George A. Thomas reported that on 12 October 1901 he saw a female angel whose "face and white robe shone brightly, and beyond the light the whole was encircled by a dark cloud" (*Juvenile Instructor*, vol. 36, no. 22, 15 November 1901, 686).

54. Sarna, *Exploring Exodus*, 198; Cassuto, *A Commentary on the Book of Exodus*, 353.

55. Cross, Jr., "The Priestly Tabernacle in the Light of Recent Research," 94–95. Compare with Psalm 104:3, which says that God "layeth the beams of his chambers in the waters," and Ezekiel 28:2, which says "I sit in the seat of God, in the midst of the seas."

56. See Strong, *The New Strong's Exhaustive Concordance of the Bible*, Hebrew and Aramaic Dictionary, 78, word #4372. This is the same Hebrew word used to denote the weather-proof "covering" on Noah's ark (Genesis 8:13). My thanks to John A. Tvedtnes for bringing this item to my attention.

57. See Cassuto, *A Commentary on the Book of Exodus*, 354.

58. This, again, is the word *chašuq* which is translated as "fillets" in the King James Bible (see Strong, *The New Strong's Exhaustive Concordance of the Bible*, Hebrew and Aramaic Dictionary, 50, word #2838).

59. Ibid., Hebrew and Aramaic Dictionary, 118, word #6607.

60. See Cassuto, *A Commentary on the Book of Exodus*, 338.

61. See Strong, *The New Strong's Exhaustive Concordance of the Bible*, Hebrew and Aramaic Dictionary, 69, word #3899; 115, word #6440.

62. The King James translation of the verses describing the vessels of the table (Exodus 25:29–30) is not very clear. For a more precise translation, see Cassuto, *A Commentary on the Book of Exodus*, 339.

63. See Roy Gane, "'Bread of the Presence' and Creator-in-Residence," *Vetus Testamentum*, vol. 42, no. 2, April 1992, 184.

64. See Brown and Smith, *Symbols in Stone: Symbolism on the Early Temples of the Restoration*, 54–55.

65. See Widengren, "Royal Ideology and the Testaments of the Twelve Patriarchs," 207–208.

66. See Strong, *The New Strong's Exhaustive Concordance of the Bible*, Hebrew and Aramaic Dictionary, 80, word #4501.

67. See William Brown, *The Tabernacle: Its Priests and Its Services*, updated ed. (Peabody, Massachusetts: Hendrickson Publishers, 1996), 67–69; James Strong, *The Tabernacle of Israel: Its Structure and Symbolism*, rev. ed. (Grand Rapids, Michigan: Kregel Publications, 1987), 67–68.

68. *Qaneh* refers to a hollow reed, rod, or tube (see Strong, *The New Strong's Exhaustive Concordance of the Bible*, Hebrew and Aramaic Dictionary, 126, word #7070).

69. The King James Bible reads "bowls made like unto almonds" (Exodus 25:33–34). *Bowls* is translated from the Hebrew word *gebiya* and literally means *curvature*, referring to the tapered shape of an egg or the calyx of a flower (see Strong, *The Tabernacle of Israel: Its Structure and Symbolism*, 70–71; Strong, *The New Strong's Exhaustive Concordance of the Bible*, Hebrew and Aramaic Dictionary, 24–25, word #1375).

70. The Hebrew word *kaphtor* is translated in the King James Version as "knops" (Exodus 25:31–35) but it is an architectural term that actually means "to encircle; a chaplet; . . . a wreath-like . . . disk" (Strong, *The New Strong's Exhaustive Concordance of the Bible*, Hebrew and Aramaic Dictionary, 66, word #3730). The LDS edition of the Bible, footnote *a* for Exodus 25:33, calls these objects "crown-shaped circlets." It appears that the function of this crown-like ornament was to act as a flange for the attachment of the lamps on top of each branch of the *menorah* (see Strong, *The Tabernacle of Israel: Its Structure and Symbolism*, 70–71).

71. The word used here is *perach* and means a calyx, bud, or bloom. It is derived from *parach* which means to break forth or out, spread, flourish, blossom (see Strong, *The New Strong's Exhaustive Concordance of the Bible*, Hebrew and Aramaic Dictionary, 116–17, word #6524 and #6525). The idea seems to be that this decoration resembled a flower bud that had begun to bloom or that was partially opened. See the illustration in Strong, *The Tabernacle of Israel: Its Structure and Symbolism*, 71.

72. Carol L. Meyers, *The Tabernacle Menorah: A Synthetic Study of a Symbol from the Biblical Cult* (Missoula, Montana: Scholars Press, 1976), 95–179. See also C. Wilfred Griggs, "The Tree of Life in Ancient Cultures," *Ensign*, June 1988, 28.

73. The tabernacle *menorah* "had a three-legged stand" (Frankel and Teutsch, *The Encyclopedia of Jewish Symbols*, 105). For depictions of the *menorah* with a tripedal base, see Georgette Corcos, ed., *The Glory of the Old Testament* (New York: Villard Books, 1984), 49, 230. The "tripedal base has the form of tree roots" (N. Wyatt, "The Significance of the Burning Bush," *Vetus Testamentum*, vol. 36, no. 3, July 1986, 363. When King Solomon built the Jerusalem Temple it appears that he placed the original tabernacle *menorah* inside the new temple and also made ten ornamental *menorahs* to provide sufficient light for the large sanctuary, five on each side of the Holy Place (see 1 Kings 7:49; 2 Chronicles 4:7. 2 Chronicles 4:6–8 seems to indicate that King Solomon also constructed ten lavers and ten tables of shewbread for the new temple). One scholar has noted the apparent correlation between the 70 lamps of the ornamental *menorahs* and the 70 rulers of the heavenly council that meet with God in the heavenly temple (see Margaret Barker, *The Older Testament: The Survival of Themes from the Ancient Royal Cult in Sectarian Judaism and Early Christianity* [London: SPCK, 1987], 226). As this scholar notes on page 227 there may be some type of connection between the 70 angelic rulers and the 70 elders of Israel

who ascended halfway up Mount Sinai (corresponding to the Holy Place of the temple) to see God from a distance (see Exodus 24:9–10). The account of the 70 elders of Israel gathering around the tabernacle in Numbers 11:24–25 may also be symbolic of the 70 angels of the heavenly council gathering in the celestial temple.

74. See Wyatt, "The Significance of the Burning Bush," 361–65; John I. Durham, *Exodus* (Waco, Texas: Word Books, 1987), 364–65.

75. See Kent P. Jackson, "The Tree of Life and the Ministry of Christ," in Kent P. Jackson, ed., *Studies in Scripture: Volume Seven, 1 Nephi to Alma 29* (Salt Lake City: Deseret Book, 1987), 34–43; Jeanette W. Miller, "The Tree of Life, a Personification of Christ," *Journal of Book of Mormon Studies*, vol. 2, no. 1, Spring 1993, 93–106.

76. See C. Houtman, "On the Function of the Holy Incense (Exodus 30:34–38) and the Sacred Anointing Oil (Exodus 30:22–33)," *Vetus Testamentum*, vol 42, no. 4, October 1992, 458–65.

77. See Strong, *The New Strong's Exhaustive Concordance of the Bible*, Hebrew and Aramaic Dictionary, 117, word #6532.

78. See Arvid S. Kapelrud, "The Gates of Hell and the Guardian Angels of Paradise," *Journal of the American Oriental Society*, vol. 70, 1950, 152–53, 155.

79. Maurice H. Farbridge, *Studies in Biblical and Semitic Symbolism* (New York: E. P. Dutton and Co., 1923), 118.

80. See Deuteronomy 32:4; Daniel 4:37; John 14:6; Ether 3:12, 4:12; D&C 93:36; Moses 1:6, 7:31.

81. The word used here for "testimony" (*'edut*) is derived from the word that means "witness" (*'ed*) (Strong, *The New Strong's Exhaustive Concordance of the Bible*, Hebrew and Aramaic Dictionary, 102, word #5707 and #5715). Thus, the stone tablets were a witness or testimony of the covenant between Jehovah and the nation of Israel.

82. William Wilson, *Old Testament Word Studies* (Grand Rapids, Michigan: Kregel Publications, 1978), 75. "The origin and meaning of the word *cherub*, a transliteration of the Hebrew *krub*, is uncertain. A fanciful rabbinic interpretation connected it with Aramaic *k-rabia*, 'like a growing child.' This may well have been the inspiration for the conventional depiction of the cherub by Renaissance artists as a child with wings" (Sarna, *Exploring Exodus*, 212, emphasis in original).

83. George A. Buttrick, ed., *The Interpreter's Bible* (New York: Abingdon Press, 1956), 6:111.

84. "An angel of God never has wings" (*TPJS*, 162).

85. See Tryggve N. D. Mettinger, "YHWH SABAOTH—The Heavenly King on the Cherubim Throne," in Tomoo Ishida, ed., *Studies in the Period of David and Solomon* (Winona Lake, Indiana: Eisenbrauns, 1982), 117. "The combination of the temple and the royal palace within a common encompassing wall on [Mt.] Zion (1 Kings 7:12) suggests an ideological link between the heavenly sovereign on the temple's throne of cherubim and the Davidic king in the palace" (ibid., 136).

86. See Patai, *Man and Temple in Ancient Jewish Myth and Ritual*, 130; C. F. Keil and F. Delitzsch, *Biblical Commentary on the Old Testament: Pentateuch* (Grand Rapids, Michigan: Eerdmans, 1949), 2:169. "From the ark [of the covenant] in the Holy of Holies, God reaches out to Israel; from the altar of sacrifice, the Israelites reach out to God. Each seems to be located exactly at the point of intersec-

tion of the diagonals of the [two] squares" that make up the tabernacle's courtyard (Nahum M. Sarna, *The JPS Torah Commentary: Exodus* [Philadelphia: The Jewish Publication Society, 1991], 156).

87. The "seat itself is formed of the outspread wings of the cherubim. . . . The wings, spread horizontally, form the throne proper" (Haran, *Temples and Temple-Service in Ancient Israel*, 252). In several Old Testament passages, the Lord is referred to as he who "dwellest *between* the cherubim" (Psalm 80:1; 2 Kings 19:15; Isaiah 37:16; 1 Samuel 4:4; 2 Samuel 6:2) or "sitteth *between* the cherubim" (Psalm 99:1). In each case the word "between" is italicized because it is not in the Hebrew text but was added by the King James translators. The word translated in the above passages as "dwellest" is *yašab* and carries the primary meaning of "to *sit* down" (Strong, *The New Strong's Exhaustive Concordance of the Bible*, Hebrew and Aramaic Dictionary, 60, word #3427, emphasis in original). Hence, some modern biblical scholars translate these passages to say that Jehovah is "enthroned on the cherubim" (E. Theodore Mullen, Jr., *The Divine Council in Canaanite and Early Hebrew Literature* [Chico, California: Scholars Press, 1980], 187; Elie Borowski, "Cherubim: God's Throne?" *Biblical Archaeology Review*, July/August 1995, 37). This correlates with one scholar's translation of 1 Kings 8:13 which speaks of the Jerusalem Temple and reads: "I have built a royal house for thee, an established place for thy *throne* forever" (Mettinger, "YHWH SABAOTH—The Heavenly King on the Cherubim Throne," 117; emphasis added).

88. The Lord told the prophet Ezekiel that the earthly temple is "the place of my throne, and the place of the soles of my feet" (Ezekiel 43:7). In Psalm 132:7 the Lord's "footstool" is said to be located inside the tabernacle (*miškan*) and this object is paralleled in verse 8 by the "ark." In 1 Chronicles 28:2, King David also speaks in parallel language of the "ark" and the "footstool" of the Lord. In several ancient Near Eastern cultures, the "testimony" or legal record of a covenant would be deposited inside a temple beneath the feet of a deity so that there would be both a divine witness to the transaction and a constant observer of the execution of the covenant stipulations. Biblical scholars believe that this is the most probable reason why the "two tables of testimony" (Exodus 31:18) were deposited inside the "ark of the testimony" (Exodus 31:7), which in turn was placed inside the most holy room of the "tent of the testimony" (Numbers 9:15) (see Cassuto, *A Commentary on the Book of Exodus*, 330–31; Sarna, *Exploring Exodus*, 209–10; Haran, *Temples and Temple Service in Ancient Israel*, 254–55).

89. Compare this scripture with Ezekiel 1:4–28 and 10:1–20 where the Lord's throne is moved about by winged cherubim. 1 Chronicles 28:18 speaks of "the chariot of the cherubim, that spread out their wings, and covered the ark of the covenant." Psalm 104:3 says that God "maketh the clouds his chariot . . . [and] walketh upon the wings of the wind." In Isaiah 66:15 we read: "For, behold, the Lord will come with fire, and with his chariots like a whirlwind." In the passages from 1 Chronicles and Isaiah, the word used for "chariot" is *merkabah*. This is the term that is traditionally applied to the vehicle seen by Ezekiel in his vision.

90. The Hebrew word that is used almost exclusively in describing the wings of the cherubim covering the ark is *sakak,* and it means "cover over, protect . . . defend" (Strong, *The New Strong's Exhaustive Concordance of the Bible*, Hebrew and Aramaic Dictionary, 99, word #5526). Examples of the use of this word include: "And the cherubim shall stretch forth their wings on high, covering the mercy seat with their wings" (Exodus 25:20); "And the cherubim spread out their wings on high, and

covered with their wings over the mercy seat" (Exodus 37:9); "For the cherubim spread forth their two wings over the place of the ark, and the cherubim covered the ark" (1 Kings 8:7); "the cherubim, that spread out their wings, and covered the ark of the covenant" (1 Chronicles 28:18); "O covering cherub" (Ezekiel 28:16).

91. G. Johannes Botterweck, Helmer Ringgren, and Heinz-Josef Fabry, eds., *Theological Dictionary of the Old Testament* (Grand Rapids, Michigan: Eerdmans, 1995), 7:297.

92. R. Laird Harris, ed., *Theological Wordbook of the Old Testament* (Chicago: Moody Press, 1980), 1:453. The Hebrew word *kapporet* comes from the same root (*kpr*) as the word *koper*, which means "ransom" and is parallel to the word "redeem" in Psalms 49:7. The Hebrew word *kopar* means "to atone by offering a substitute." The word *kapporet* is thus "derived from the root [that means] 'to atone.'" Throughout the Old Testament *kapporet* is translated as "mercy seat" even though the word "is not related to mercy." In the Septuagint, the Greek equivalent of *kapporet* is usually *hilasterion,* which means "place or object of propitiation" (ibid.). Notice that the same exact word (*hilasterion*) is found in both Romans 3:25 and Hebrews 9:5. In Romans it is appropriately translated as "propitiation" and is associated with "redemption" (vs. 24) and the "blood" of Jesus Christ (vs. 25). But in Hebrews this word is mistranslated as "mercy seat." "The translation 'mercy seat' does not sufficiently express the fact that the lid of the ark was the place where the blood was sprinkled on the day of atonement" (ibid.).

93. See Jacob Milgrom, "The Temple in Biblical Israel: Kinships of Meaning," in Truman G. Madsen, ed., *Reflections on Mormonism: Judaeo-Christian Parallels* (Provo, Utah: BYU Religious Studies Center, 1978), 57–65.

94. Botterweck, Ringgren, and Fabry, eds., *Theological Dictionary of the Old Testament*, 7:298.

95. Ibid., 7:298.

96. See *HC*, 2:429; A. Karl Larson and Katharine Miles Larson, eds., *Diary of Charles Lowell Walker* (Logan, Utah: Utah State University Press, 1980), 2:563.

97. See Strong, *The New Strong's Exhaustive Concordance of the Bible*, Hebrew and Aramaic Dictionary, 124, word #6942.

98. James Kugel, "Levi's Elevation to the Priesthood in Second Temple Writings," *Harvard Theological Review*, vol. 86, no. 1, January 1993, 5. In Jubilees 30:18 it is stated that the seed of Levi were chosen to minister before the Lord always, just as the angels in heaven do. In Jubilees 31:14–16, Isaac blesses Levi with the words: "May the Lord give you and your seed very great honor. May he draw you and your seed near to him from all flesh to serve in his sanctuary as angels of the presence and the holy ones"—thus indicating that the temple priests on earth symbolized the angelic priests in the heavenly temple (ibid., 6). Other traditions mention that Levi was made aware of secret heavenly knowledge or the unspeakable mysteries of the Most High. This esoteric knowledge may be reflected in Malachi 2:4–7, where it is said that "'the priest's lips will keep knowledge'—that is, keep this knowledge *secret*, because it is 'unspeakable'" (ibid., 34; emphasis in original).

99. H. Ludin Jansen, "The Consecration in the Eighth Chapter of Testamentum Levi," in *The Sacral Kingship* (Leiden: E. J. Brill, 1959), 356–57.

100. "A special type of blessing through laying on of hands occurs in rites of ordination. So Moses ordained Joshua as his successor (Numbers 27:18, 23; Deuteronomy 34:9)—a ceremony adopted in

later times for ordination to the rabbinate" (George A. Buttrick, ed., *The Interpreter's Dictionary of the Bible* [New York: Abingdon, 1962], 2:521).

101. "Laying On of Hands. An act symbolizing dedication to a special purpose. The Israelites placed their hands on the heads of the Levites, dedicating them to the service of the Lord at the Tabernacle in the place of the firstborn of all the tribes. They pressed down their hands upon the heads of the Levites, doubtless with the intention of signifying thereby that, with God's permission and by his authority, they transferred their own obligation to service to the Levites (Numbers 8:5–20)" (Henry S. Gehman, ed., *The New Westminster Dictionary of the Bible* [Philadelphia: Westminster Press, 1970], 553). The "assembly" of the children of Israel in Numbers 8:9–10 who laid their hands upon the priests to ordain them may have consisted of the twelve tribal leaders who served as the executive body of the nation (see Milgrom, *Leviticus 1–16*, 498).

102. When an individual is given divine authority through the laying on of the hands by someone who already possesses it, is the same as if the Lord himself were performing the act (see D&C 36:2).

103. Bruce R. McConkie, *The Promised Messiah* (Salt Lake City: Deseret Book, 1978), 411. On another occasion, Elder McConkie stated that Aaron "held the Melchizedek Priesthood" and was "called of God to preside over the lesser priesthood, which ever thereafter would bear his name. He was the presiding bishop of the Church, as it were, and the office was ordained of God to be hereditary, to go from father to son" (Bruce R. McConkie, *The Mortal Messiah* [Salt Lake City: Deseret Book, 1979], 1:245–46; see also Bruce R. McConkie, *Doctrinal New Testament Commentary* [Salt Lake City: Bookcraft, 1973], 3:156).

104. John Taylor, *Items on Priesthood* (Salt Lake City: George Q. Cannon and Sons, 1899), 4.

105. *DS*, 3:85. The Prophet Joseph Smith said: "All Priesthood is Melchizedek, but there are different portions or degrees of it. That portion which brought Moses to speak with God face to face was taken away [from the Israelites when the Lord took Moses out of their midst]; but that which brought the ministry of angels remained. All the prophets had the Melchizedek Priesthood and were ordained by God himself" (*TPJS*, 180–81).

106. This initiatory washing, which was conducted by Moses, is not to be confused with the washing of the hands and feet that occurred each time a priest ministered inside the tabernacle or at the courtyard altar after he had been initiated (see Exodus 30:17–21; 40:30–32).

107. Strong, *The New Strong's Exhaustive Concordance of the Bible*, Hebrew and Aramaic Dictionary, 42, word #2416.

108. Milgrom, *Leviticus 1–16*, 923. This author specifically notes that water which is stored in a cistern or drawn from a normal well is not included in the category of *living water* (ibid.). See also pages 836–37.

109. Buttrick, ed., *The Interpreter's Bible*, 1:975.

110. In ancient Near Eastern ideology the "temple is often associated with the waters of life which flow from a spring within the building itself—or rather the temple is viewed as incorporating within itself such a spring or having been built upon the spring. The reason that such springs exist in temples is that they were perceived as the primeval waters of creation, *nun* in Egypt, *abzu* in Mesopotamia, *tehom* in Israel. The temple is thus founded upon and stands in contact with the waters of creation.

These waters carry the dual symbolism of the chaotic waters that were organized during the creation and of the life-giving, saving nature of the waters of life" (John M. Lundquist, "The Common Temple Ideology of the Ancient Near East," in Madsen, ed., *The Temple in Antiquity*, 57; emphasis in original. For further discussion on this topic, see ibid., 66–67).

111. A. Noordtzij, *Bible Student's Commentary: Leviticus* (Grand Rapids, Michigan: Zondervan, 1982), 94. Another scholar has concluded from textual evidence in the book of Exodus that the entire body of each priest was washed during this initiation rite (see Milgrom, *Leviticus 1–16*, 501).

112. Geoffrey W. Bromiley, ed., *The International Standard Bible Encyclopedia* (Grand Rapids, Michigan: Eerdmans, 1988), 4:1022.

113. The rabbinical reference for this information is Yoma 3.4. From a biblical commentary we read that after the high priest performed certain duties at the altar of sacrifice, he "proceeded to a screened area, adjacent to the Tent, where he disrobed, bathed, and donned his golden vestments. Mishnah Middot 5.3 and Mishnah Yoma 3.3 refer to a bureau in the temple complex on whose roof was a place for ablutions, called *beit ha-tevilah*, 'the place of immersion.' One assumes that in the tabernacle described by the priestly tradition there was also an area for disrobing and bathing, acts quite frequently called for in the performance of the sacrificial cult" (Baruch A. Levine, *The JPS Torah Commentary: Leviticus* [Jerusalem: The Jewish Publication Society, 1989], 108).

114. See Stephen D. Ricks, "*Miqvaot*: Ritual Immersion Baths in Second Temple (Intertestamental) Jewish History," *Brigham Young University Studies*, vol. 36, no. 3, 1996–97, 279. Josephus (*Wars*, 2.1.1) tells us that at least one non-priestly visitor to the temple complex wore a white garment (see William Whiston, trans., *The Works of Josephus: Complete and Unabridged*, updated ed. [Peabody, Massachusetts: Hendrikson Publishers, 1987], 597). "In the rabbinic period, white garments were worn on Shabbat and the High Holy Days, and it was customary to clothe the dead in a white shroud" (Frankel and Teutsch, *The Encyclopedia of Jewish Symbols*, 191). Lay Israelites, like the priests, removed their shoes before entering the temple complex (see Herbert Danby, trans., *The Mishnah* [New York: Oxford University Press, 1933], 10).

115. Based upon Psalm 92:10, it would appear that the horn containing the oil of anointing might have been the horn of an ox—"But my horn shalt thou exalt like the horn of an unicorn: I shall be anointed with fresh oil." The word "unicorn" is, of course, a mistranslation of *re'em* which properly means a wild bull or a wild ox (see *LDS Bible Dictionary*, 786; JST Isaiah 34:7).

116. "The phrase 'horn of David' (*keren David*), refers to the Messiah, who like David will be anointed with a horn of oil" (Frankel and Teutsch, *The Encyclopedia of Jewish Symbols*, 76).

117. Strong, *The New Strong's Exhaustive Concordance of the Bible*, Hebrew and Aramaic Dictionary, 87, word #4899.

118. Ibid., Hebrew and Aramaic Dictionary, 128, word #7161.

119. Notice the connection between the image of the horn and kingship in 1 Samuel 2:10; Daniel 7:7–8, 20–24; Revelation 13:1; 17:12.

120. See John A. Tvedtnes, "Olive Oil: Symbol of the Holy Ghost," in Stephen D. Ricks and John W. Welch, eds., *The Allegory of the Olive Tree: The Olive, the Bible, and Jacob 5* (Salt Lake City: Deseret Book and FARMS, 1994), 427–59; Donald W. Parry, "Ritual Anointing with Olive Oil in Ancient

Israelite Religion," (ibid., 279–81).

121. Leviticus 14:18 has been mistranslated in the King James Bible. Instead of "he shall *pour* upon the head," the Hebrew text reads "he shall *put* on the head" (J. P. Green, Sr., ed., *The Interlinear Bible: Hebrew-Greek-English*, 2d ed. [Grand Rapids, Michigan: Baker Book House, 1986], 99; emphasis added). Hence, the implication is that the oil was smeared upon the head just as it was upon the other parts of the body. One scholar insists that "the forehead is clearly intended [in this passage]. This is the part of the body that is the focus of oil rituals elsewhere in the ancient Near East" (Milgrom, *Leviticus 1–16*, 855). "Talmudic tradition also tells of the exact way in which kings and priests were anointed. In the case of kings the oil was applied to their heads in the form of a wreath (i.e., around the head), while in the case of priests it was applied in the form of the Greek letter *X* [*see* B. Horayot 12a; B. Keretot 5b]" (Ralph Patai, *On Jewish Folklore* [Detroit: Wayne State University Press, 1983], 124).

122. Milgrom, *Leviticus 1–16*, 518.

123. Strong, *The New Strong's Exhaustive Concordance of the Bible*, Hebrew and Aramaic Dictionary, 87, word #4886.

124. C. R. North, "The Religious Aspects of Hebrew Kingship," *Zeitschrift Für Die Alttestamentliche Wissenschaft*, vol. 50, 1932, 15.

125. Gaalyahu Cornfeld, ed., *Pictorial Biblical Encyclopedia* (New York: Macmillan, 1964), 605.

126. "Beauty," in this passage, has been changed to "honour" because the phrase "glory and honour" matches the same temple-related phrase found in D&C 124:33–34, 95 and because "honour" is a viable alternative according to Strong, *The New Strong's Exhaustive Concordance of the Bible*, Hebrew and Aramaic Dictionary, 154, word #8597.

127. "For this reason did God give unto [the high priest garments] after the pattern of the holy garments" that were worn by him (S. M. Lehrman, trans., *Midrash Rabbah: Exodus* [New York: Soncino Press, 1983], 456–57). In Jewish lore we read: "God said to Abraham: 'Thou occupiest thyself with showing loving-kindness to mankind, and art thus doing the same work as I. I shall therefore clothe thee with the same garments with which I am clad when appearing to the prophets'" (Ginzberg, *The Legends of the Jews*, 5:259, nt. 274). "Clad in the garment of glory . . . Abraham becomes like 'one of the glorified beings'" in heaven (ibid., 5:229, nt. 114).

128. See Charlesworth, ed., *The Old Testament Pseudepigrapha*, 1:265, nt. 12a.

129. The high priest's wardrobe is called the "clothes of service" in Exodus 31:10; 35:19; 39:1, 41. The title "high priest," as applied to Aaron and his successors, should not be confused with the office of "high priest" in the Melchizedek Priesthood. The high priest of the tabernacle was the head of those priests who held the Aaronic Priesthood and would more properly be considered the "chief priest" of the Aaronic order. This position is similar to that of the Presiding Bishop in the LDS Church (see McConkie, *The Mortal Messiah*, 1:245–46; see also *DS*, 3:92–93).

130. In Leviticus 16:4 these white linen vestments are called "holy garments." This simple attire symbolized the angelic identity of the high priest who, by passing into the Holy of Holies, was figuratively passing into the heavenly assembly or council (see Milgrom, *Leviticus 1–16*, 1016).

131. James Orr, ed., *The International Standard Bible Encyclopaedia* (Grand Rapids, Michigan:

Eerdmans, 1960), 1:518, see illustration. Another commentary says that the breeches "reached to the knees" (Bromiley, ed., *The International Standard Bible Encyclopedia*, 1:545).

132. There is a slight discrepancy in biblical texts regarding the exact type of material used in making the breeches. "In the first list, Exodus 28, only the fabric of the breeches is given: they are breeches of *bad*, which is plain linen [BDB, white linen]. In Exodus 39, however, they are called 'breeches of *bad*, of *šeš mišzar*'; that is, 'of plain linen, of twined fine linen.' Perhaps we should translate *bad* as a simple generic, 'linen', and read, 'breeches of linen, [specifically] of fine, twined linen.' Josephus is quite clear: the breeches were of 'fine twined [or twisted] linen' (*ek bussou klostes*). That is, before being put on the loom the linen thread was twined so as to be thick" (E. P. Sanders, *Judaism: Practice and Belief 63 BCE—66 CE* [London: SCM Press, 1992], 94).

133. In Mishnah *Yoma* 3.6, the Talmudic sages maintain that the priestly attire was white in color. The linen worn by angels who have access to the heavenly temple is "pure and white" (Revelation 15:6).

134. See Stephen D. Ricks, "The Garment of Adam in Jewish, Muslim, and Christian Tradition," in Donald W. Parry, ed., *Temples of the Ancient World: Ritual and Symbolism* (Salt Lake City: Deseret Book and FARMS, 1994), 709, 727 nt. 23.

135. See Buttrick, ed., *The Interpreter's Dictionary of the Bible*, 1:655.

136. See Strong, *The New Strong's Exhaustive Concordance of the Bible*, Hebrew and Aramaic Dictionary, 67, word #3801.

137. See Bromiley, ed., *The International Standard Bible Encyclopedia*, 1:727.

138. There are actually two separate words used in these verses. In Exodus 28:4, the Hebrew word *tašbets* (Strong, *The New Strong's Exhaustive Concordance of the Bible*, Hebrew and Aramaic Dictionary, 155, word #8665) is translated as "broidered." And only a few verses later, in Exodus 28:39, the Hebrew word *šabats* (ibid., Hebrew and Aramaic Dictionary, 137, word #7660) is translated as "embroider." The word *tašbets* is derived from *šabats*.

139. The majority of biblical commentators have assumed that the type of embroidery employed on this garment was something like checkerwork, but this interpretation is not at all certain (see Willem A. VanGemeren, ed., *The New International Dictionary of Old Testament Theology and Exegesis* [Grand Rapids, Michigan: Zondervan, 1997], 4:340–41; Sarna, *The JPS Torah Commentary: Exodus*, 184; Milgrom, *Leviticus 1–16*, 502). In the paintings of the Dura Europos synagogue (ca. 245 A.D.), Moses is depicted standing before the tabernacle dressed in a white robe that is decorated at chest and knee level with two different checkered marks (for an illustration see Nibley, *Temple and Cosmos*, 110). Examples of Jewish clothing with marks shaped like the Greek letter *gamma* (Γ) have been recovered in archeological sites at Masada, Bar-Kokhba, and Dura-Europos (see John W. Welch and Claire Foley, "Gammadia on Early Jewish and Christian Garments," *BYUS*, vol. 36, no. 3, 1996–97, 253–58).

140. See Sarna, *The JPS Torah Commentary: Exodus*, 182; Haran, *Temples and Temple-Service in Ancient Israel*, 168; Cassuto, *A Commentary on the Book of Exodus*, 382.

141. See Bromiley, ed., *The International Standard Bible Encyclopedia*, 4:204.

142. It should be noted that Jesus Christ, who is identified as both a King and a Priest (*see* John 1:49; Hebrews 3:1), also wore a seamless robe (see John 19:23).

143. Bromiley, ed., *The International Standard Bible Encyclopedia*, 4:204.

144. Ibid., 1:731. The throne of Jehovah is described as being blue in color in Ezekiel 1:26.

145. Milgrom, *Leviticus 1–16*, 504.

146. See Sarna, *The JPS Torah Commentary: Exodus*, 182. For evidence that the pomegranates were in the form of tassels, see Strong, *The Tabernacle of Israel: Its Structure and Symbolism*, 103; Brown, *The Tabernacle: Its Priests and Its Services*, 95. The King James Bible is inconsistent in its description of the materials used to form the pomegranates (wool, wool and linen). But the Septuagint and Samaritan versions of Exodus correctly supply the words missing in the King James Bible so that the pomegranates are said to be made both of dyed woolen threads and fine-twined linen (see Haran, *Temples and Temple-Service in Ancient Israel*, 169, nt. 44).

147. See C. Houtman, "On the Pomegranates and the Golden Bells of the High Priest's Mantle," *Vetus Testamentum*, vol. 40, no. 2, April 1990, 226.

148. Cassuto, *A Commentary on the Book of Exodus*, 383. This may be analogous to what the Egyptian king did at the temple. "When the king enters the sanctuary for the first time, at the completion of the temple, he performs an act exactly resembling what is done at the door of the church at Easter in the Eastern Orthodox rites, namely, he knocks three times on the door with his white mace, enters, illuminates the shrine with sacred fire, and performs a series of lustrations and circumambulations" (Hugh W. Nibley, *The Message of the Joseph Smith Papyri: An Egyptian Endowment* [Salt Lake City: Deseret Book, 1975], 250). On Jubilee years, the Pope carries out a similar rite when he knocks three times with a golden hammer on the Holy Door, or Holy Gate, of St. Peter's Basilica in Rome (several other basilicas in Rome also have Holy Doors). A medieval medal struck to commemorate this occasion shows the people on one side of the door and the Lord on the other side (see Herbert Thurston, *The Holy Year of Jubilee* [London: Sands and Co., 1900], 50, 244). The words spoken along with this rite make it clear that the ceremony represents entry into God's temple (ibid., 221, see the illustrations on page 85 and on the inside of the front cover). For a color picture of this rite being performed, see Francesco Papafava, ed., *The Vatican* (New York: Harper and Row, 1984), 19. The tradition of the Holy Door is also found in the Russian Orthodox Church. These Christians view this door as "the entrance into the Holy of Holies—the Sanctuary; only the clergy may enter through it, and only at definite moments" (Leonid Ouspensky and Vladimir Lossky, *The Meaning of Icons* [Boston: Boston Book and Art Shop, 1956], 67).

149. John M. Lundquist notes: "The temple is associated with abundance and prosperity, indeed is perceived as the giver of these. . . . One reads that abundance shall come from heaven when the foundation of the temple is laid" (John M. Lundquist, "What Is a Temple? A Preliminary Typology," in Parry, ed., *Temples of the Ancient World: Ritual and Symbolism*, 97).

150. Frankel and Teutsch, *The Encyclopedia of Jewish Symbols*, 128. For an excellent representation of the crown-shaped flower of the pomegranate see Corcos, ed., *The Glory of the Old Testament*, 153.

151. An inscribed ivory pomegranate believed to have come from King Solomon's Temple was acquired by the Israel Museum. Unlike its bronze counterparts that decorated objects in the courtyard of Solomon's Temple, this specimen appears to have been the headpiece of a priestly scepter (*see* André Lemaire, "Probable Head of Priestly Scepter from Solomon's Temple Surfaces in Jerusalem," *Biblical Archaeology Review*, January/February 1984, 24–29; Michal Artzy, "Pomegranate Scepters and Incense

Stand with Pomegranates Found in Priest's Grave," *Biblical Archaeology Review*, January/February 1990, 48–51; Nahman Avigad, "The Inscribed Pomegranate from the 'House of the Lord,'" *Biblical Archaeologist*, September 1990, 157–66). Zechariah 6:11–14 presents the imagery of a temple official who is both a king and a priest.

152. Aaron's sash is also designated as being of *roqem* workmanship in Exodus 28:39 (*roqem* is translated as "needlework" both here and in Exodus 39:29). Notice that fine-twined linen is mentioned first in regard to the high priest's sash (followed by the different colored threads of wool—see Exodus 28:39; 39:29) whereas with all of his other vestments, linen threads are always mentioned last. The only other instance where linen is mentioned first in the tabernacle narratives is in regard to the "tent" or "tabernacle" that was placed closest to, and directly over, the tabernacle's solid structure (*see* Exodus 26:1; 36:8).

153. Josephus reports that during the New Testament period, the temple *priests* (or sons of Aaron) were wearing sashes that were decorated with the same colors found on the high priest's sash (see *Antiquities*, 3.7.2; compare Exodus 39:29). During this same time period Josephus reports that the *Levites* (temple servants from the tribe of Levi) were granted, by a political decree from Herod Agrippa II, the right to wear the priestly robes of the sons of Aaron (see *Antiquities*, 20.9.6). The Lord did not grant the Levites this privilege originally (*see* Numbers 8:5–7); neither did he grant the priests the right to wear the high priest's special colors upon their vesture.

154. Thomas K. Cheyne, *Encyclopaedia Biblica* (New York: Macmillan, 1899), 2:1735. This information is drawn from Josephus (*Antiquities*, 3.7.2).

155. To understand this more clearly, see the entries for the Hebrew word *abnet* under the headings "girdle" and "girdles" in Strong, *The New Strong's Exhaustive Concordance of the Bible*, 504, word #73.

156. The Hebrew phrase *pa'arey migba'ot* is translated in one source as "decorated turbans" (Roth, ed., *Encyclopaedia Judaica*, 13:1067). The singular *migba'ah* can also be translated as "cap" (Strong, *The New Strong's Exhaustive Concordance of the Bible*, Hebrew and Aramaic Dictionary, 71, word #4021), while *pe'er* is translated as "ornaments" in Isaiah 61:10. Thus it would seem that the priestly caps were "ornamented" or "decorated" in some fashion.

157. Sarna, *The JPS Torah Commentary: Exodus*, 185.

158. Exodus 29:9 says of Aaron's sons: "And thou shalt . . . put the bonnets (*migba'ah*) on them." In footnote 9*b* for this verse in the LDS edition of the King James Bible, it is noted that the Hebrew word translated as "put" really means "bind." This translation is confirmed in Green, Sr., ed., *The Interlinear Bible: Hebrew-Greek-English*, 74—"you shall bind on bonnets for them." The imagery of binding, or literally tying (*'anad*), on a headpiece is found in Job 31:36.

159. See Strong, *The New Strong's Exhaustive Concordance of the Bible*, Hebrew and Aramaic Dictionary, 84, word #4701. In Ezekiel 21:25–26 the *misnepet* (translated as "diadem" in the KJV) seems to be a pad for the crown worn by the king of Israel.

160. That which the Bible calls "fine linen," or *šeš*, is the bleached white linen of Egypt mentioned in Genesis 41:42 (Strong, *The New Strong's Exhaustive Concordance of the Bible*, Hebrew and Aramaic Dictionary, 149, word #8336). Leviticus 16:4 informs us that on the Day of Atonement the high priest

wore breeches, a tunic, a sash, and a cap all made from *bad,* or plain, linen (ibid., Hebrew and Aramaic Dictionary, 16, word #906).

161. William Wilson, *Old Testament Word Studies* (Grand Rapids, Michigan: Kregel Publications, 1978), 241. This object is called a "string" in Charles B. Chavel, trans., *Commentary on the Torah: Exodus* (New York: Shiloh Publishing House, 1973), 491–95.

162. Whenever the word "LORD" appears in an Old Testament text of the King James Bible (in all capital letters), it is an indication that the Hebrew word being translated is "YHWH," meaning Yahweh, or Jehovah.

163. Strong, *The New Strong's Exhaustive Concordance of the Bible*, Hebrew and Aramaic Dictionary, 37, word #2142.

164. Kaufmann Kohler, *The Origins of the Synagogue and the Church* (New York: Macmillan, 1929), 50–51. The idea of having the name of the Lord put upon one in the temple seems to be connected with becoming the Lord's possession and thus receiving his protection (see Deuteronomy 28:10; Isaiah 43:1–7; 63:19; Jeremiah 14:9; 15:16; compare D&C 109:22).

165. Strong, *The New Strong's Exhaustive Concordance of the Bible*, Hebrew and Aramaic Dictionary, 127, word #7121.

166. Sarna, *The JPS Torah Commentary: Exodus*, 214. The name JEHOVAH is found in the King James translation of Exodus 6:3; Psalm 8:18; Isaiah 12:2 and 26:4. This name is a combination of the letters of the so-called Tetragrammaton (YHWH or YHVH or JHVH) and the vowels from the title ADONAI (which means "my lords"). Despite the text of Exodus 6:3, the name "YHWH was known to the patriarchs . . . [There are] passages in Genesis where the patriarchs apparently knew and worshipped God under this name (Genesis 15:7; 28:13; etc. [see especially JST Exodus 6:3]) . . . Therefore one need not doubt the biblical tradition that the use of this name was already very ancient by the time of Moses (cf. Genesis 4:26; 9:26)" (Bromiley, ed., *The International Standard Bible Encyclopedia*, 2:507).

167. W. Gunther Plaut, ed., *The Torah: A Modern Commentary* (New York: Union of American Hebrew Congregations, 1981), 408. Compare this idea with Judges 13:17–18, where it is stated by an angel that his name is secret. "According to Midrash Shemu'el xv the scholars explained the words in Exodus 4:28 as meaning that Moses revealed the Four-Lettered Name to Aaron" (Singer, ed., *The Jewish Encyclopedia*, 11:264). This same idea is put forward in Menaham M. Kasher, *Encyclopedia of Biblical Interpretation: Exodus* (New York: American Biblical Encyclopedia Society, 1967), 7:153.

168. See Sarna, *The JPS Torah Commentary: Exodus*, 214; Bromiley, ed., *The International Standard Bible Encyclopedia*, 2:506; Spence and Exell, eds., *The Pulpit Commentary: Numbers*, 2:52.

169. The word *ephod* was left untranslated in the King James Bible due to uncertainty about its origin and meaning. It is the belief of some scholars that the word *ephod* is essentially Egyptian (see Milgrom, *Leviticus 1–16*, 505; John A. Tvedtnes, "Egyptian Etymologies for Biblical Cultic Paraphernalia," in Sarah Israelit-Groll, ed., *Scripta Hierosolymitana* [Jerusalem: Magnes Press, 1982], 28:218–19.

170. Milgrom, *Leviticus 1–16*, 505; John P. Whalen, ed., *New Catholic Encyclopedia* (New York: McGraw-Hill, 1967), 5:461–62. Footnote *a* for Exodus 39:2 in the LDS edition of the King James

Bible identifies the *ephod* as an apron. For further confirmation of this identification, and a survey of ritual aprons in several ancient cultures, see Matthew B. Brown, "Girded about with a Lambskin," *Journal of Book of Mormon Studies*, vol. 6, no. 2, 1997, 124–51.

171. Merrill C. Tenney, ed., *The Zondervan Pictorial Encyclopedia of the Bible* (Grand Rapids, Michigan: Zondervan, 1975), 1:230. See also the comments in Haran, *Temples and Temple-Service in Ancient Israel*, 166–67.

172. The belt of the high priest's apron is called "the curious [or cunningly worked] girdle of the ephod" (Exodus 28:8). "It may be that this apron could be fastened and unfastened at the back, since the text refers to its *mahberet* [coupling, junction] (Exodus 28:27; 39:20). This *mahberet . . .* seems to be at the back of the wearer. . . . We may assume that when the priest wishes to remove the apron from his waist, he need not lift it over his head or let it down to his feet, but can untie the 'joining' at his back and take off the ephod frontwards" (Haran, *Temples and Temple Service in Ancient Israel*, 166–67).

173. "In 4QShirShabb (4Q405 23 ii 5; 11 QShirShabb 8–7 6) the *ephodim* are worn by the angelic priests of the heavenly realm. See also Josephus *Ant.* 3:180 in context, Aristeas 99, Rev. 1:13–16" (Crispin H. T. Fletcher-Louis, "The High Priest as Divine Mediator in the Hebrew Bible: Daniel 7:13 as a Test Case," in *Society of Biblical Literature 1997 Seminar Papers* [Atlanta: Scholars Press, 1997], 188, nt. 103; emphasis added).

174. Haran is sure that the *ephod* was of *hošeb* workmanship, but he is not sure about the type of designs that were upon it (*see* Haran, *Temples and Temple-Service in Ancient Israel*, 167). Other scholars also believe that the *ephod* was "an embroidered apron" (Frankel and Teutsch, *The Encyclopedia of Jewish Symbols*, 131).

175. The centrality of the *ephod* is evidenced by how the other priestly clothing is described in relation to it—"the robe of the *ephod*" (Exodus 28:31; 29:5; 39:22); "the curious girdle [or belt] of the *ephod*" (Exodus 28:8; 29:5; 39:5, 20–21; Leviticus 8:7); "the shoulderpieces of the *ephod*" (Exodus 28:25; 39:18). According to one commentator the "*ephod* was, *par excellence*, the priestly garment" (Spence and Exell, eds., *The Pulpit Commentary: Exodus*, 1:281; emphasis in original. Compare with 1 Samuel 2:18, 28; 14:3; 22:18; Judges 17:5).

176. See A. Leo Oppenheim, "The Golden Garments of the Gods," *Journal of Near Eastern Studies*, vol. 8, 1949, 172–93.

177. Sarna, *The JPS Torah Commentary: Exodus*, 179.

178. The word translated throughout the book of Exodus as "breastplate" is *hošen*. The etymology of this word remains obscure but one scholar has suggested that it is an Egyptian loanword that carries the basic meaning of "a cover for the breast" (Milgrom, *Leviticus 1–16*, 505). It is perhaps preferable to render *hošen* as "pouch" based upon the use to which the breastpiece was put and also upon the fact that the root of this word probably means "to contain" (Cassuto, *A Commentary on the Book of Exodus*, 375; Strong, *The New Strong's Exhaustive Concordance of the Bible*, Hebrew and Aramaic Dictionary, 50, word #2833). *Hošen* is rendered as "pocket" in Green, Sr., ed., *The Interlinear Bible: Hebrew-Greek-English*, 72.

179. The primary meaning of the Hebrew word *mišpat* is "verdict" or decision (Strong, *The New Strong's Exhaustive Concordance of the Bible*, Hebrew and Aramaic Dictionary, 88, word #4941).

180. Strong, *The New Strong's Exhaustive Concordance of the Bible*, Hebrew and Aramaic Dictionary, 4, word #224 and 153, word #8550.

181. *See* Cornelis Van Dam, *The Urim and Thummim: A Means of Revelation in Ancient Israel* (Winona Lake, Indiana: Eisenbrauns, 1997), 27–28, 203–204. Even though Van Dam personally believes the Urim and Thummim "probably consisted of a single gem" (ibid., 230), Exodus 28:30 ("the Urim and the Thummim . . . they"), Leviticus 8:8 ("the Urim and the Thummim"), and Deuteronomy 33:8 ("thy Urim and thy Thummim") all seem to speak of two separate objects. For further reading, see John A. Tvedtnes, "Glowing Stones in Ancient and Medieval Lore," *Journal of Book of Mormon Studies*, vol. 6, no. 2, 1997, 99–123.

182. Based upon all of the biblical evidence, Van Dam concludes that since detailed revelations were received through the Urim and Thummim, they "were not a lot oracle" as so many scholars have speculated (Van Dam, *The Urim and Thummim: A Means of Revelation in Ancient Israel*, 210). Because of a distinct lack of convincing evidence, he also rejects any comparison between the Urim and Thummim and the Egyptian "Pendant of Truth" (ibid., 71) or the Mesopotamian "Tablets of Destiny" (ibid., 46–53). He furthermore fails to find any evidence that the Israelite kings wore anything like the high priest's breastpiece during their coronation rites (ibid.).

183. The "silence in Exodus 28 and 39 concerning the manufacture or description of the [Urim and Thummim] appears to imply the prior existence of the [Urim and Thummim] and the knowledge of this oracular equipment by Israel as a whole. This in turn suggests that the [Urim and Thummim] predated Moses. The inclusion of the [Urim and Thummim] in the breastpiece of Aaron when he was ordained as high priest (Leviticus 8:8) could therefore signal the official incorporation of an ancient means of revelation into the official cult" (Van Dam, *The Urim and Thummim: A Means of Revelation in Ancient Israel*, 236).

184. Ibid., 230. David Whitmer wrote that when Joseph Smith's personal seerstone was activated, a "spiritual light would shine" from it (David Whitmer, *An Address to All Believers in Christ: By a Witness to the Divine Authenticity of The Book of Mormon* [Richmond, Missouri: David Whitmer, 1887], 12). But instead of just seeing a light in his seerstone Joseph Smith viewed scenes of the past, present, or future. Note that the Hebrew word for "priest" (*kohen*) "is the philological equivalent of the Arabic *kahin*, the meaning of which is 'seer'" (North, "The Religious Aspects of Hebrew Kingship," 19).

185. Biblical texts indicate that there were "four rows of stones" on the breastpiece. *First row:* sardius (ruby), topaz, carbuncle; *second row:* emerald, sapphire, diamond; *third row:* ligure (opal), agate, amethyst; *fourth row:* beryl, onyx, jasper (see Exodus 28:17–20; 39:10–13). Though there is no indication in the Bible as to which stone matched which tribal name, one scholar presumes that "the names were in the conventional order of encampment (in which the same division of 4 x 3 occurs)" [top, from right to left: 1. Judah 2. Issachar 3. Zebulon / 4. Reuben 5. Simeon 6. Gad / 7. Ephraim 8. Manasseh 9. Benjamin / 10. Dan 11. Asher 12. Naphtali] (Strong, *The Tabernacle of Israel: Its Structure and Symbolism*, 107, see also 108).

186. It is evident from scriptures such as Exodus 25:21–22; 30:6, 36; Numbers 17:4 and Leviticus 16:2 that the Lord would "appear in the cloud" over, or upon, his throne (the ark of the covenant) and there "meet with" and "commune with" the assigned representatives of the covenant people. There is

no indication, however, that the veil that divided the Holy Place from the Holy of Holies was ever drawn aside during these manifestations. It would therefore appear that those who were granted an audience with Jehovah heard his voice coming through the veil. The exception was Moses, for whom the veil was parted so that he could see the Lord "face to face" (Exodus 33:7–11).

187. Cassuto, *A Commentary on the Book of Exodus*, 375–76.

188. Strong, *The New Strong's Exhaustive Concordance of the Bible*, Hebrew and Aramaic Dictionary, 4, word #224.

189. "And I [Levi] saw seven men in white clothing, who were saying to me, 'Arise, put on the vestments of the priesthood, the crown of righteousness, the oracle of understanding, the robe of truth, the breastplate of faith, the miter for the head, and *the apron for prophetic power*'" (James H. Charlesworth, ed., *The Old Testament Pseudepigrapha* [Garden City, New York: Doubleday, 1983], 1:791, emphasis added).

190. Strong, *The New Strong's Exhaustive Concordance of the Bible*, Hebrew and Aramaic Dictionary, 78, word #4390.

191. Ibid., Hebrew and Aramaic Dictionary, 53, word #3027; emphasis in original.

192. For a listing of biblical passages where "consecrate" should be translated as "fill the hand," see Lynn M. Hilton, "The Hand as a Cup in Ancient Temple Worship," *Newsletter and Proceedings of the Society for Early Historic Archaeology*, no. 152, March 1983, 4.

193. Cassuto, *A Commentary on the Book of Exodus*, 386.

194. Jacob Neusner, *Lectures on Judaism in the History of Religions* (Atlanta: Scholars Press, 1990), 49. The actions of slaughter and collecting blood in the hand are called "cultic gestures" in this source (ibid.).

195. Strong, *The New Strong's Exhaustive Concordance of the Bible*, Hebrew and Aramaic Dictionary, 66, word #3709.

196. For pictures of Israelite incense ladles with hands carved on the back of their bowls, see J. D. Douglas and Merrill C. Tenney, eds., *The New International Dictionary of the Bible: Pictorial Edition* (Grand Rapids, Michigan: Zondervan, 1987), 466; Yigael Yadin, *Hazor* (New York: Random House, 1975), 179; G. Ernest Wright, ed., *Great People of the Bible and How They Lived* (Pleasantville, New York: The Reader's Digest Association, 1974), 179; Moshe Pearlman and Yaacov Yannai, *Historical Sites in Israel*, rev. ed. (Secaucus, New Jersey: Chartwell Books, 1978), 46. Zacharias was offering incense (probably with a ladle) at the altar before the veil of the Holy of Holies when an angel appeared and informed him that his prayer had been heard (see Luke 1:5–13).

CHAPTER FOUR
The Temple on Mount Zion

Nearly 1,000 years before the birth of Jesus Christ, King Solomon built a magnificent temple of God on the top of Mount Zion. The main purpose of this temple, like the tabernacle, was to provide a holy place upon the earth where the Lord could come and dwell among His covenant people (*see* 1 Kings 6:12–13; 8:12–13). The Lord had revealed the pattern for the temple to King David just as He had revealed the pattern for the tabernacle to Moses (*see* 1 Chronicles 28:11–19). But the Lord did not allow King David to actually build the temple because He had chosen Solomon to perform that task before he was born (*see* 2 Chronicles 6:7–10).[1] Even though King David was denied the opportunity to build the Lord's house, he nevertheless "prepared abundantly" for its eventual construction by procuring the temple site, arranging for a sizable workforce, and gathering building materials such as stone, timber, gold, silver, iron, and bronze (*see* 1 Chronicles 21:18—22:19).

Once Solomon became the king of Israel and began to build the temple, it took him seven long years to complete the project (*see* 1 Kings 6:38). The overall measurements of the temple were approximately 105 feet long, 30 feet wide, and 45 feet high. The dimensions of the Holy Place and Holy of Holies inside Solomon's Temple were exactly twice those of the corresponding rooms inside the tabernacle. It is recorded that the tabernacle and its sacred vessels were brought to the Solomonic Temple and stored within its chambers on the day that the temple was dedicated (*see* 1 Kings 8:4; 2 Chronicles 5:5).[2]

The Temple Site
The site where the temple was built had several symbolic associations. The temple was located on the top of a mountain. Because the sanctuary was located halfway

between heaven and earth, it served as an ideal meeting place for God and man. The mountain itself, Mount Moriah, was the place where Father Abraham offered up Isaac in similitude of the sacrifice of the Son of God, and where unblemished male lambs later served the same function at the temple altar (*see* Genesis 22:2; 2 Chronicles 3:1).

During the time period when the Jerusalem Temple was being built, the mountain upon which it stood was known as Mount Zion. While there is some uncertainty about the exact meaning of the Hebrew word *Zion,* most scholars agree that it is related to concepts such as protection, refuge, fortress, shield, and defense (*see* Psalm 48:1–3, 11–13).[3] The ideology attached to this term is quite clear, however. Zion is closely connected with the concepts of enthronement and kingship.[4] In D&C 105:32 we read that "the kingdom of Zion is in very deed the kingdom of our God" and the prophet Isaiah states that the Lord, as King, "shall reign in mount Zion" (Isaiah 24:23). Those who achieve the status of kings, taught the Prophet Joseph Smith, "come unto Mount Zion" (D&C 76:54–58, 66–67; *see also* Hebrews 12:22–24; Revelation 14:1).

In the ancient Hebrew conception of the universe, God was thought to reside near the North Star, "the point around which the constellations turned, where was located the summit of the heavenly mountain and the throne of the Most High."[5] This was the "mount of the congregation" located "in the sides of the north" (Isaiah 14:13).[6] The name of this heavenly mountain, among the Hebrews, was *Mount Zion* (*see* Hebrews 12:22). When the temple was built in the ancient city of Jerusalem, it was placed on the top of a mountain that was located in the northern part of the city and was called *Mount Zion*, possibly to replicate on earth what was in heaven (*see* Psalm 48:1–2).[7] The temple on Jerusalem's Mount Zion was thus conceived of as the dwelling place of Jehovah (*see* Psalm 76:2; Isaiah 8:18).

Zion is imbued with symbolic imagery in several scriptures. In Isaiah 51:3, for example, Zion is associated with the Garden of Eden. Psalm 46:4 speaks of "a river, the streams whereof shall make glad the city of God," perhaps alluding to the river that "went out of Eden to water the garden; and from thence it was parted, and became . . . four heads" (Genesis 2:10). In the writings of Ezekiel, the prophet "seems to refer to Zion as the 'navel' of the earth, the place where God sustains this planet (38:12)."[8] We also find the Lord Himself saying in one scripture: "Behold, I lay in Zion for a foundation a stone, a tried stone, a precious cornerstone, a sure foundation" (Isaiah 28:16; *see also* 1 Peter 2:6).

The temple was built on what had previously been the site of a threshingfloor. An angel who spoke in the name of the Lord commanded King David to erect an altar unto the Lord on this elevated spot. The king obeyed this divine directive and, after fire from heaven consumed the sacrifices that were placed upon the altar, he called that location "the house of the Lord" (*see* 1 Chronicles 21:18–22:1; 2 Samuel 24:18–25). One authority on symbolism states that the threshingfloor is an *omphalos,* or navel symbol, because the hemispherical hub of grain, which the oxen tread a circular path around, resembles the point at which the navel cord is bound.[9] And indeed, the temple on Mount Zion was looked upon by the Hebrew people as the sacred center or navel of the earth.[10]

THE SYMBOLISM OF SOLOMON'S TEMPLE

The ancient Israelites understood that God reigns as "the King of all the earth" (Psalm 47:7), and so when they built His temple on Mount Zion they referred to its main chamber as the *hekhal,* which in Hebrew means *temple, middle area,* and *palace.*[11] One biblical scholar has noted the following points of similarity between the Jerusalem Temple and the sanctuaries and royal palaces that were built throughout the ancient Near East.

> As we proceed into the temple, and finally into the Holy of Holies, we find increasingly valuable, sophisticated and elaborate decoration. This gradation corresponded to a progression from profane space to sacred space and finally to most sacred space. The material gradation focused attention on the divine presence resident in the divine palace.
>
> The furnishings of the *hekhal* [or Holy Place] were those of a house—a table, lampstands and an incense altar. The cult [or system of religious worship] sustained by such implements would be similar to the daily routine of a resident.
>
> Since God was king [see Psalms 47:7; 89:18; 95:3], and kings lived in palaces, the temple was not just a simple house. It was God's palace; the Holy of Holies was his throne room. The immense cherubim, similar to cherubim found on royal thrones from neighboring peoples, represented the divine throne on which the deity sat. The ark [of the covenant] was the divine footstool. It contained the tablets of the covenant. In a similar fashion in foreign temples, treaty documents were deposited at the feet of divine statues. The cherubim engraved on the doors kept watch over the palace, just as the cherubim who guarded the way to the Garden of Eden acted as its gatekeepers (Genesis 3:24). . . . The cherubim engraved on the walls may have represented the angelic ministers of the royal council, like the seraphim witnessed by Isaiah in his great throne vision (Isaiah 6:1–2). . . .
>
> The houses of gods and kings were often surrounded with gardens, and the floral motifs that covered the walls and doors of Solomon's Temple, as well as the lamp-

stands decorated with flowers, represented the vegetation of such a garden. The pillars Jachin and Boaz, crowned with lilies and pomegranates, may have represented the trees in the Garden of Eden (1 Kings 7:20). The *mekhonot or* bases for the water basins *(kiyyorot)* were decorated with both lions and cattle, perhaps symbolizing the co-existence of wild and tame animals, typical of divine gardens in the past, as well as in the eschatological future as portrayed by the prophets [see Isaiah 11:6]. The wood with which the temple was panelled was reminiscent of the Lebanon mountains that were the traditional dwellings of deities in the ancient Near East. . . . A cedar-panelled temple not only looked like the natural divine habitat but smelled like it too.

Divine palaces were also situated on the sea, at the confluence of rivers. This too was represented in the temple courtyard by the great bronze sea *(yam)* and the water basins *(kiyyorot).*[12]

Paradise Motifs

There were at least ten points of parallelism between the temple on Mount Zion and the Garden of Eden.

(1) MOUNTAIN: The temple was built on the top of a mountain and one had to ascend a stairway to enter into it because it was built on a raised platform as well (*see* Ezekiel 40:49).[13] By way of parallel, "Eden the garden of God" is referred to in one scriptural passage as "the holy mountain of God" (Ezekiel 28:11–16), as if the garden had been planted on a mountain top. This image of the garden being located at a higher elevation than the surrounding terrain is bolstered when one recalls the four rivers that flowed outward from the garden toward the cardinal points. Waters flowed down into the garden from the heights of Eden, where they then separated to go out and water the four corners of the world (*see* Genesis 2:10–14).

(2) ENCLOSURE: The temple was enclosed by a courtyard made of three courses of hewn stone and one course of cedar beams, like a fence (*see* 1 Kings 7:12). The Hebrew word, *gan*, used to designate the "garden" of Eden refers specifically to a "fenced" garden. *Gan* is derived from the word *ganan*, which means to "hedge about, protect, or defend."[14]

(3) DIRECTION: The entrance to the Solomonic temple was found on its eastern side (*see* Ezekiel 47:1). Likewise, the Garden of Eden appears to have had only one entrance on its eastern boundary (*see* Genesis 3:24).

(4) BUILDING MATERIALS: The inner surfaces of the temple were lavishly covered with gold and also garnished with a number of "precious stones" (2 Chronicles 3:6) that had been imported (*see* 1 Kings 10:11).[15] A comparison between Genesis 2:10–12

and Ezekiel 28:13 seems to indicate that these materials may have been included in the temple's decorations in order to imitate the primordial landscape of Eden. Notice also that King David gathered "iron in abundance . . . and brass in abundance" for the temple's construction (1 Chronicles 22:3), these being the two metals mentioned by Moses as symbols of the promised land (*see* Deuteronomy 8:9).

(5) ABUNDANT WATER: There was an abundance of water found within the temple courtyard, both in the massive bronze "sea" and in ten separate water basins that stood on either side of it (2 Chronicles 4:2–6; *see also* Joel 3:18). The biblical narrative notes that a river provided water for Eden (*see* Genesis 2:10) and that "the garden of the Lord" was "well watered" (Genesis 13:10). Abundant water is one of the symbols of the promised land (*see* Deuteronomy 8:7). "When Ezekiel tells us [in Ezekiel 47:1] that the head of all waters issued from the temple precincts he is alluding to this idea that the temple contained the garden of God."[16]

(6) LUSH VEGETATION: The Garden of Eden was filled with a variety of trees (*see* Genesis 2:8–9; 3:2). The fir and cedar trees that were used to cover the floors and walls of Solomon's Temple (*see* 1 Kings 6:9, 15) happen to be listed among "the trees of Eden, that were in the garden of God" (Ezekiel 31:8–9). The wood of the olive tree was also used to beautify the Lord's house (*see* 1 Kings 6:23, 31–33).[17] Hebrew tradition names the olive tree as one of the trees that were planted in paradise,[18] and in Deuteronomy 8:8 it is named as one of the representative symbols of the promised land.[19] Psalm 52:8–9 compares a righteous Saint to "a green olive tree in the house of God." Aside from the woods of these trees, there were actual representations of date palms decorating the walls, doors, and courtyard furnishings of the Solomonic Temple (*see* 1 Kings 6:29, 32, 35; 7:36; Ezekiel 40:16, 22, 26, 31, 34, 37; 41:18-20). The palm tree and its fruit were a symbol of the promised land (*see* Deuteronomy 8:8).[20] In Psalm 92:12–13 we read: "The righteous shall flourish like the palm tree. . . . Those that be planted in the house of the Lord shall flourish in the courts of our God."[21]

In addition to the trees there were also numerous floral motifs to be seen throughout the temple complex. For instance, the Bronze Sea located in the courtyard was surrounded below its brimline by two rows of floral buds (*peqaʿ*)[22] (*see* 1 Kings 7:24) while the brim itself was decorated with blooming lotus flowers (*perach šošan*)[23] (*see* 1 Kings 7:26). The lotus (*šošan*) design also graced the top of the two bronze pillars that were stationed at the front of the temple's forecourt (*see* 1 Kings 7:19). Additionally, all seventy of the branches of the ten golden candlesticks found in the Holy Place of the temple were topped by blooming floral bulbs (*perach*)[24] (*see* 1 Kings 7:49). And finally, partially opened floral buds (*peqaʻ*) decorated the four walls of the Holy Place (*see* 1 Kings 6:17–18) while fully opened flowers (*patuwr tsiyts*)[25] of an unspecified type adorned the doors and walls of the Holy Place as well as the doors and walls of the Holy of Holies (*see* 1 Kings 6:18, 29, 32, 35).

(7) FRUIT: A total of 400 bronze pomegranates decorated the pillars that stood before the temple (*see* 1 Kings 7:42) while an unspecified number of pomegranates adorned the hems of the high priest's robe (*see* Exodus 28:33–34). Pomegranates are mentioned by Moses as one of the symbols of the promised land in Deuteronomy 8:8. The palm trees decorating the temple precincts (*see* 1 Kings 6:29) were likely depicted with their fruit, the date, which was also one of the symbols of the promised land.[26] While there is no scriptural record specifying that pomegranates or dates grew in the Lord's garden, we are assured that some of the trees in paradise bore various types of fruit (*see* Genesis 3:2).[27]

(8) ANIMALS: Lions, oxen, and winged creatures were displayed throughout the areas of the temple complex (*see* 1 Kings 6:23, 29, 32; 7:25, 29, 36, 44). These correspond closely to three categories of animals that God created and placed inside the Garden of Eden: beasts, cattle, and fowls (*see* Genesis 2:19–20).

(9) TREE OF LIFE: The tree of life was "in the midst of the garden" of God (Genesis 2:9) while the *menorah*, which was a representation of the tree of life,[28] was placed in the middle section of King Solomon's Temple (*see* 1 Kings 7:49).[29]

(10) CHERUBIM: Figures of cherubim were profusely displayed in the courtyard, forecourt, Holy Place, Holy of Holies, and on the veil of King Solomon's Temple (*see* 1 Kings 6:23–29, 32, 35; 7:29, 36; 2 Chronicles 3:14; Ezekiel 41:18–20, 23–25). And, of course, cherubim are mentioned in the Garden of Eden narratives as guardians of sacred space (*see* Genesis 3:24).

The only thing that seems to have been missing in this replica of the Garden of Eden were symbolic representations of Adam and Eve. In the apocryphal book of Jubilees, it is noted that the Garden of Eden was holier than any other place on the earth (3:12). In chapter 8 verse 19 of this same book, it is stated that Noah understood that the Garden of Eden was "the holy of holies, and the dwelling of the Lord." Taking this into account, one scholar has proposed that "Adam and Eve were brought into the Holy of Holies prior to their disobedience; their expulsion from Eden thus signifies their removal from the place where God's presence on the earth is most immediate for Israel. The high priest's entry into the Holy of Holies on Yom Kippur [or the Day of

Atonement] might, then, in some manner typologically correspond to the first man's return to Eden, for a season, to be reconciled with his Maker face to face."[30]

Oracle

The Holy of Holies, or "most holy place," in King Solomon's Temple was exactly twice the size of the corresponding room in the tabernacle (*see* 1 Kings 6:20). This chamber is consistently referred to in the scriptures as the "oracle" (*see* 1 Kings 6:5, 16, 19–23, 31; 7:49; 8:6, 8; 2 Chronicles 3:16; 4:20; 5:7, 9; Psalm 28:2). In Hebrew, the word for "oracle" is *debir* and it is derived from the word *dabar,* which means "to speak."[31] Hence, one could approach the Holy of Holies to hear the Lord's words and revelations. At times the Lord would personally appear in the Holy of Holies and speak from behind the veil that separated the two rooms of the temple (*see* Exodus 25:21–22; 29:42–43; 30:6, 36; Leviticus 16:2; Numbers 17:4). When prophets declared the revelations that they had received from the Lord, they often included "the set phrase of the oracles, *ne'um YHWH,* '(the word) whispered by Yahweh.'"[32]

Inside the Holy of Holies, King Solomon placed two free-standing representations of cherubim that were approximately 15 feet tall. These angelic guardians had been sculpted from olive wood and were adorned with gold. Their outer wings touched the walls and their inner wings touched each other in the exact center of the cubical room (*see* 1 Kings 6:23–28). These enormous sentinels "stood on their feet, and their faces were inward" (2 Chronicles 3:13), perhaps because they bowed their heads toward the ark of the covenant, which they were overshadowing with their wings (*see* 1 Kings 6:19). In addition, they may have looked down because, as a larger version of the cherubim on the lid of the ark whose wings formed God's throne, they too offered a sign of worship and submission in the presence of their King (*see* Exodus 4:31).[33]

Jachin and Boaz

Standing at the entrance to the forecourt, or *ulam,* of King Solomon's Temple were two hollow, cast bronze pillars.[34] Each pillar was approximately twenty-six feet high, over seventeen feet in circumference, three inches thick (*see* Jeremiah 52:21), and topped by a seven-foot-tall capital of cast bronze. The bottom eighteen inches of each capital were shaped like a partially flattened globe whose surface was decorated with seven cords that overlapped each other to create a net-like design. Both above and below this protrusion there was a row of 100 bronze pomegranates that were attached to a chain.[35] The top five and a half feet of these capitals were decorated with "lily work," meaning a design that resembled a lotus flower[36] (*see* 1 Kings 7:15–22; 2 Chronicles 3:15–17).

Both of these massive bronze pillars were given symbolic names. The pillar on the south side of the forecourt was called *Jachin,* which means "he will establish," and the pillar on the north side was called *Boaz,* meaning "in him is strength."[37] Both of these phrases are connected to the concept of kingship. In wording that seems to correspond to the meaning of *Jachin,* the Lord said of King Solomon: "I will establish his kingdom. . . . I will stablish the throne of his kingdom forever"; and of King David He also promised: "thy kingdom shall be established forever before thee: thy throne shall be established forever" (2 Samuel 7:12–13, 16); "I have made a covenant with my chosen, I have sworn unto David my servant, Thy seed will I establish forever, and build up thy throne to all generations" (Psalm 89:3–4). Likewise, in wording that seems to correspond to the meaning of *Boaz* we read: "The Lord reigneth [as King] . . . the Lord is clothed with strength" (Psalm 93:1); "the Lord made the heavens . . . strength and beauty are in his sanctuary . . . the Lord reigneth [as King]" (Psalm 96:5–6, 10).[38]

Based upon these passages it seems apparent that the king of Israel was associated with the pillar called *Jachin,* and the Lord, who was the King of the whole earth (*see* Zechariah 14:9, 16), was associated with the pillar called *Boaz.* This insight may help explain 2 Kings 11:13–14, which states that at his coronation ceremony the "king stood by a pillar, as the manner [custom] was." This passage is clarified by 2 Chronicles 23:13, which explains that "the king stood at *his pillar*" at the entrance to the temple.[39] Similarly, we read in 2 Kings 23:3 that "the king stood by a pillar, and made a covenant before the Lord," whereas 2 Chronicles 34:31 (which is a parallel description) states that "the king stood in *his place,* and made a covenant before the Lord."[40] It is perhaps significant that the pillar on the north end of the forecourt (Boaz) was associated with the Lord because, as mentioned above, the Israelites believed that He resided "in the sides of the north" (Isaiah 14:13), meaning the northern part of the heavens.

The idea that a pillar can represent a king is found in the New Testament as well as in the Old Testament. The Lord told the apostle John that those of His Saints who hold fast to their "crown" will be made "a pillar in the temple" of God (Revelation 3:11–12). John, in fact, informs us that he himself had been made a king (*see* Revelation1:6), and he is referred to in one scriptural passage as one of the "pillars" of the Church (Galatians 2:9). The physical decorations of Jachin and Boaz also seem related to the concept of kingship. As mentioned in the previous chapter, the pomegranate was a symbol of kingship because the shape of its flowered end resembled a crown. The 400 bronze pomegranates hanging upon the Solomonic temple pillars must surely have been placed there for symbolic reasons. Perhaps there was a connection between this fruit, with its abundant seeds, and the promise of Jehovah that the "seed" of King David would rule upon his throne "forever" if they remained righteous (*see* Psalm 89:3–4, 29; 2 Samuel 7:12–13; 1 Kings 9:2–5).

FIGURE 17. Two massive bronze pillars, called Jachin and Boaz, stood before the temple built by King Solomon. The names of these pillars appear to be connected with the ideology of ancient Near Eastern kingship. The various decorations on the capitals also seem to be symbolic of royal concepts.

The net-like design on the capitals may have been symbolic of the Lord's triumph over the forces of chaos during the creation. "The reign of the Lord as the Great King is based on the poetic imagery that he has battled with and defeated chaos . . . This martial victory establishes the Lord's kingship, which in turn necessitates the building of a temple."[41] One scholar has noted that in several Old Testament passages, Jehovah is depicted in symbolic fashion as using a net to catch the creature that represented chaos. By subduing *chaos* the Lord brought *order* to creation.[42] And finally, the lotus flower (*šošan*) atop the pillars may be seen as a symbol of the house of Israel (*see* Hosea 14:5). In language that evokes the image of a flower, the Lord promised: "Israel shall blossom and bud" (Isaiah 27:6). As representatives of the entire nation, the kings of Israel could appropriately be identified with the lotus flower.

By way of summary, the bronze pillars that stood before the temple of Solomon may confidently be looked upon as symbols of kingship. The Lord revealed their pattern when kingship was established in Israel (during the period of David and Solomon)[43] but they did not decorate the house of the Lord when Israelite kings no longer reigned over the covenant nation (during the era of Jesus Christ). It would appear that the pillar named *Jachin* signified the divinely appointed kings of the Davidic lineage and the pillar named *Boaz* stood for the Kingship of the God of Israel.[44]

The Bronze Sea

In the tabernacle, a small laver made of hammered bronze was placed in the courtyard to serve as a water receptacle for ritual washings. For King Solomon's Temple, however, the laver was transformed into an enormous circular basin made of cast bronze. It was so large, in fact, that it was called a "sea" (yam)[45] but it still served the very same function as the tabernacle laver; it was a place "for the priests to wash" before they carried out their sacred duties (2 Chronicles 4:6).[46] From biblical texts we know that the bronze sea was approximately fourteen feet six inches in diameter, seven feet high, forty-four feet in circumference, and three inches thick. Scholars have estimated that this basin had the capacity to hold about 11,500 gallons of water.[47] The top portion of the basin flared outward like the brim of a cup and was decorated with blooming (perach)[48] lotus flowers (šošan).[49] Underneath the brimline there were two rows of floral buds (peqaʿ)[50] that were cast in bronze at the same time that the basin was created.[51] Each individual bud was approximately two inches in size, and there were ten of them per each eighteen-inch span (see 1 Kings 7:23–24).[52]

The "sea" rested on the backs of twelve bronze oxen. These symbolic animals were grouped in four sets of three with each set facing out to one of the four cardinal directions—north, south, east, and west (see 1 Kings 7:25). In one scholar's view the twelve oxen upon which the water basin rested "pointed to the twelve tribes of Israel as a priestly nation, which cleansed itself here in the persons of its priests, to appear clean and holy before the Lord. Just as the number twelve unquestionably suggests the allusion to the twelve tribes of the covenant nation, so, in the choice of oxen or bullocks as supporters of the basin, it is impossible to overlook the significance of this selection of the first and highest of the sacrificial animals to represent the priestly service."[53] While there is no scriptural text that directly equates the twelve oxen under the bronze basin with the twelve tribes of Israel[54] there are a few passages that are suggestive of this connection. For instance, when the twelve tribes were encamped around the tabernacle, they were arranged by divine decree just like the oxen—in four sets of three, on the north, south, east, and west sides of the Lord's sanctuary (see Numbers 2:1–31).[55] The next point that draws our attention is the fact that after Moses "had fully set up the

FIGURE 18. The brazen sea in the courtyard of King Solomon's Temple served as a station where the priests would ritually cleanse their hands and feet before participating in temple functions.

tabernacle, and had anointed it, and sanctified it," the twelve princes over the tribes of Israel each brought an ox and offered them "to do the service of the tabernacle." The Lord commanded Moses to accept the twelve oxen and to give them to the Levitical priests who would use them to transport portions of the tabernacle whenever the tribes journeyed in the wilderness (Numbers 7:1–9). In addition, the head of each of the twelve tribes offered one ox as a burnt offering when the tabernacle altar was dedicated (*see* Numbers 7:87). Thus, there is a definite connection between the oxen and the Lord's house, and there is also a strong sense that the twelve oxen did indeed represent the twelve tribes of Israel.[56]

Some scholars are of the opinion that the bronze water basin was referred to as a "sea" because it may have symbolically "stood for the subterranean fresh-water ocean from which the ancients believed all life and fertility were derived."[57] If so, this object would rightly stand as a symbol of paradise—the four sets of oxen facing the four cardinal directions representing the four rivers of Eden that watered the four quarters of the earth (*see* Genesis 2:10–14). This correlation is strengthened when one recalls that the temple seen in vision by Ezekiel did not have a water reservoir or laver in its courtyard. Instead, water gushed out from underneath the eastern threshold of the temple, "from the right [or south] side of the house" (Ezekiel 47:1; compare Joel 3:18; Zechariah 14:8; Revelation 21:6)—precisely the same location where the "sea" stood in the courtyard of Solomon's Temple "on the right [or south] side of the house"[58] (1 Kings 7:39; 2 Chronicles 4:10). It is obvious from Ezekiel's vision that these were the waters of life (*see* Ezekiel 47:9) and thus corresponded to the fountain and river of paradise (*see* Revelation 22:1–2).[59]

A HOUSE OF SACRIFICE

The temple of Jehovah was a house of sacrifice (*see* Ezra 6:3,10) and, like the tabernacle, it was equipped with a bronze altar. This altar, however, was considerably larger than the one built for the tabernacle. It measured approximately twenty-nine feet square and almost fifteen feet high (*see* 2 Chronicles 4:1). It is believed by some commentators that this altar was placed near the northeast corner of the temple to symmetrically offset the Bronze Sea that was placed at its southeast corner. "In the description of Solomon's dedicatory sacrifices (1 Kings 8:64), the sanctification of space for sacrifice in the *middle* of the courtyard area is reported, an act that took place because the altar itself was too small for all the offerings of the occasion. Perhaps the middle space was available because the enormous appurtenances, sea and altar, were already in place on the [North] and [South] sides of the front of the temple."[60]

The Lord had introduced the law of sacrifice to Adam and Eve after their expulsion from the Garden of Eden and then later sent an angel to explain that their offerings were symbolic of "the sacrifice of the Only Begotten of the Father" (Moses 5:4–7; *see also* D&C 138:12–13). "Whenever the Lord [Jesus Christ] revealed himself to men in ancient days," said the Prophet Joseph Smith, "and commanded them to offer sacrifice to him, . . . it was done that they might look forward in faith to the time of his coming, and rely upon the power of that atonement for a remission of their sins."[61] The sacrifices associated with the law of Moses were designed to serve the very same purpose; they were types, shadows, and reminders of the future sacrifice of Israel's Redeemer (*see* Hebrews 10:1; 2 Nephi 25:24–25; Alma 25:15–16; 34:13–14). Elder M. Russell Ballard of the Quorum of the Twelve Apostles points to some of the connections between the ancient temple sacrifices and the sacrifice of the Son of God.

> First, like Christ, the animal was chosen [see Exodus 29:19; compare Luke 23:35]. . . . Second, the animal was to have its life's blood spilt [see Exodus 29:20; compare Matthew 26:28]. Third, it had to be without blemish—totally free from physical flaws, complete, whole, and perfect [see Leviticus 22:18–25; compare 1 Peter 1:19]. Fourth, the sacrifice had to be clean and worthy [see Leviticus 8:18–21; compare John 1:29-34]. Fifth, the sacrifice had to be domesticated; that is, not wild but tame and of help to man (see Leviticus 1:2–3, 10; [compare Isaiah 53:7]). Sixth and seventh, for the original sacrifice practiced by Adam and the most common sacrifice in the law of Moses, the animal had to be a firstborn and a male (see Exodus 12:5; [13:2; compare Romans 8:29]). Eighth, the sacrifice of grain had to be ground into flour and made into breadstuffs, which reminds us of our Lord's title the Bread of Life (see John 6:48). Ninth, the firstfruits that were offered remind us that Christ was the firstfruits of the resurrection (see 1 Corinthians 15:20).[62]

Three other aspects of Old Testament sacrifice should draw our attention. First, the sacrificial animal served as a proxy (*see* Leviticus 1:4) just as the Savior did (*see* Hebrews 2:9). Second, the blood of the animal was a purging agent. On the Day of Atonement, sacrificial blood was used to purge the Lord's house of offenses that were committed unintentionally by individual Israelites (blood smeared on the horns of the altar of sacrifice in the courtyard), those committed unintentionally by the covenant people (blood smeared on the horns of the altar of incense in the Holy Place), and those committed intentionally by the covenant people (blood sprinkled on the lid of the ark of the covenant in the Holy of Holies).[63] In like manner, the sacrificial blood shed by Jesus Christ is utilized for atonement, with power to purge and purify (*see* Revelation 1:5; 7:14; Alma 13:11; Ether 13:10). And third, sacrificial animals were slain on the north side of the altar of sacrifice (*see* Leviticus 1:11). When Jesus Christ offered Himself as a sacrificial lamb on Golgotha, which is the northernmost point of the temple mount, He too was slain north of the temple altar.[64] Once the Lamb of God was slain, the "performances and ordinances of the law of Moses" were all fulfilled (4 Nephi 1:12). After His resurrection, the Lord stated without exception: "And ye shall offer up unto me *no more* the shedding of blood; yea, your sacrifices and your burnt offerings shall be *done away*, for *I will accept none of your sacrifices* and your burnt offerings" (3 Nephi 9:19; emphasis added).

A HOUSE OF COVENANT

Closely associated with sacrifice was the act of covenant making. In Psalm 50:5 we learn that the Lord's "saints" made covenants with Him by sacrifice. The Hebrew word for "covenant" is *berit*.[65] The idiom for making a covenant, however, is *karat berit*, meaning "to cut a covenant."[66] Animals were sacrificed, or cut, during ancient Near Eastern covenant-making ceremonies in order to graphically demonstrate the penalty for not living up to the stipulations that were sworn to by the participating parties. To covenant breakers, the Lord said,

> And I will give the men that have transgressed my covenant, which have not performed the words of the covenant which they had made before me, when they cut the calf in twain, and passed between the parts thereof . . . I will even give them into the hand of their enemies, and into the hand of them that seek their life. (Jeremiah 34:18, 20)[67]

Such a dire penalty was justified because when those who entered into the covenant killed the animal and pronounced the curse formula of the oath, they presumably made a "symbolic gesture, something like our index finger across the throat. Deep behind this lay, in all probability, a ritual act involving the slaughter of animals, to whom the one swearing the oath equated himself. . . . The slaughtered and split animals represent what the oath-taker invites God to do to him if he fails to keep the oath."[68]

A common gesture for swearing an oath in a covenant situation was to raise the right hand toward heaven. The literal meaning of "to swear" in an oath context is "to raise the hand." The symbolism behind this appears to be that the one entering into the covenant pointed his hand toward God's throne and thereby called upon God and those in the heavens to witness the veracity of his oath.[69] Similarly, in the early Christian Church attestations were made "before God, and the Lord Jesus Christ, and the elect angels" (1 Timothy 5:21; *see also* Genesis 31:50). In addition to these heavenly witnesses, there are indications of earthly witnesses being present when covenants were made (*see* Joshua 24:22).

Saying the word *amen* was "the customary response made to an oath" in biblical times[70] (*see* Numbers 5:19–22; Deuteronomy 27:14–26; Nehemiah 5:13). This Hebrew word means "true" or "so be it."[71] In Isaiah 65:16, the Hebrew phrase *elohey amen* is translated as "the God of truth," and in Revelation 3:14 we find that one of the titles of Jesus Christ is "Amen, the faithful and true witness." In Nehemiah 8:5–6, we read that while a group of Israelites stood before him, "Ezra blessed the Lord, the great God. And all the people answered, Amen, Amen, with lifting up their hands: and they bowed their heads, and worshipped the Lord with their faces to the ground."

What type of covenants were entered into in the temple precincts? In 2 Kings 11:17 we read of a covenant entered into by the Israelites "that they should be the Lord's people." The nature of this type of covenant is clarified in Deuteronomy where it is stated that the children of Israel covenanted to walk in the Lord's ways and to obey His commandments, judgments, and statutes (*see* Deuteronomy 29:12–15; 30:1–2, 8–10, 16, 19–20; *see also* 2 Kings 23:3; 2 Chronicles 15:8–12; 23:16).

A HOUSE OF PRAYER

In both the Old and New Testaments, the temple is referred to as "the house of prayer" (*see* Isaiah 56:7; Matthew 21:13; Mark 11:17; Luke 19:46; compare D&C 59:9). Since the Lord continually saw and felt everything that occurred within the walls of His holy house (*see* 1 Kings 8:29; 9:3), it was a logical place to offer one's supplications and praise. There is some indication that even if an Israelite could not be physically present within the temple courts they could still direct their prayers toward the Lord's earthly abode (1 Kings 8:38–39, 44–45, 48–49). Hence, Psalm 28:2 reads:

"Hear the voice of my supplications . . . when I lift up my hands toward thy holy oracle," meaning that the prayer was being directed toward the Holy of Holies or location of God's throne.[72]

Throughout the Bible there are descriptions of individuals raising their hands during prayer. For instance, when King Solomon offered the dedicatory prayer of the Jerusalem Temple, he "stood before the altar of the Lord in the presence of all the congregation of Israel, and spread forth his hands toward heaven" (1 Kings 8:22; *see also* vs. 54). This gesture was also employed when calling down the blessings of heaven, such as when the Israelites sought strength in battle with the Amalekites (*see* Exodus 17:8–15) or when the temple priests called down blessings upon the congregations that assembled before them (*see* Leviticus 9:22–23; Numbers 6:22–27; compare Luke 24:49–51).[73]

It would appear from several biblical passages that prayer was looked upon by the Lord as a type of temple offering (*see* Psalm 119:108; Hebrews 13:15–16; compare D&C 95:16). Thus we read in Psalm 141:2—"Let my prayer be set before thee as incense; and the lifting of my hands as the evening sacrifice." The connection seems to be that the smoke arising either from the altar of incense or the altar of sacrifice was viewed as being symbolic of prayers rising up into heaven. Prayers are directly connected with the rising smoke from the incense offering of the heavenly temple in Revelation 8:3–4. Prayers could be offered both for petitioning the Lord and also praising His holy name. Thus we find the directive to the temple priests who "stand in the house of the Lord. Lift up your hands in the sanctuary, and bless [or praise] the Lord" (Psalm 134:1–2). And again, in Psalm 63:4 we read: "Thus will I bless thee while I live. I will lift up my hands in thy name."

The emphasis of the ancient gesture of uplifted hands seems to have been on the lifting up, or presentation, of one's *hands* to heaven. It is evident from Isaiah 1:15–16 that the Lord's eyes are drawn to those who lift up clean (or innocent) hands to Him while He hides His eyes, or glances away, from those whose hands are unclean. The presentation of one's hands to heaven was thus a way of requesting the Lord's attention and blessings (*see* Psalm 88:9). Notice also that raising the hands essentially exposes the heart to the Lord. Hence we find the directive in Job 11:13 to "prepare thine heart, and stretch out thine hands towards him" and the admonition of Lamentations 3:41: "Let us lift up our heart with our hands unto God in the heavens."[74] These two concepts are combined in the well-known temple scripture: "Who shall ascend into the hill of the Lord? Or who shall stand in his holy place? He that hath clean hands, and a pure heart" (Psalm 24:3–4; compare 1 Timothy 2:8).

It was the assigned duty of the sons of Levi to "stand" every morning and evening "to thank and praise the Lord" (1 Chronicles 23:30) with one voice (*see* 2 Chronicles 5:13). It is possible that this activity is made note of in the book of Psalms. It has been proposed by one LDS author that Psalm 24:6, which is widely acknowledged as part of the Israelite temple liturgy, has been mistranslated and might possibly mention a prayer circle. In his article, this author surveys several divergent translations of Psalm 24:6 and then offers his own rendition: "This is the circle of them that inquire of him, that seek the face of the God of Jacob."[75] This translation is very similar to one Jewish translation that was not included in the author's survey: "Such is the circle of those who turn to [God]."[76] This proposition may perhaps be strengthened by Psalm 26:6–7, wherein King David states that he will ritually cleanse his hands and "compass" or surround (*sabab*)[77] the Lord's altar to offer up prayers of praise and thanksgiving. Even though the biblical evidence for prayer circles in Old Testament times is sparse, Dr. Nibley has gathered a substantial amount of evidence for prayer circles among the early Christians.[78]

THE CORONATION OF KINGS

When someone became a king in ancient Israel, he went through a coronation ceremony that was designed to endow him with symbols of power and authority. Even though the Bible does not provide a complete description of the royal rites, enough fragments have been preserved upon its pages to allow a partial reconstruction of what occurred. To begin with, we know that the coronation ceremony took place in the temple courtyard near the pillars *Jachin* and *Boaz* (*see* 2 Kings 11:11–14). We also know that it was the authorized representatives of Jehovah (prophets and priests) who initiated the king into the royal office (*see* 1 Kings 1:34). Some scholars have noted that the coronation of Israelite kings and the consecration of Israelite priests followed the same basic pattern.[79]

Washing and Anointing

It is believed by some biblical interpreters that "the ceremonial at the installation of the kings of Jerusalem included a rite of purification at the spring" that was called Gihon (*see* 1 Kings 1:33).[80] This spring bore the same name as one of the rivers that flowed out of paradise (*see* Genesis 2:13). If a ritual washing did indeed take place at the Gihon spring, the king would have been symbolically connected with the Garden of Eden. The significance of this connection will become more apparent as this chapter unfolds.

In contrast to the possible washing rite, it is a concretely established fact that the kings of Israel were initiated into their office by an anointing with oil. In fact, the kings were anointed with the very same perfumed olive oil that was used in the initation ceremony of the temple priests. The oil was kept in a horn somewhere inside the temple complex (*see* 1 Kings 1:39), and it appears from the context of Psalm 92:10 that the horn that held the oil was the horn of an ox.[81] King David states explicitly that he was anointed with "holy oil" (Psalm 89:20), and he also specifies that it was applied to his head (*see* Psalm 23:5).[82]

Royal Vestments

Several passages in the Bible indicate that when an individual became the king of Israel, he was clothed with robes (*see* 1 Kings 22:10; 2 Chronicles 18:9) and invested with several other items of royal apparel.

• Robe, Apron, and Sash: Some scholars are convinced that there is a reference in the Hebrew text of Psalm 110 (the correct translation of which is still uncertain) to "the holy robe in which the king has been arrayed."[83] What kind of a robe was this? In 1 Chronicles 15:27, we read that the king of Israel was "clothed with a robe of fine linen" and that he "also had upon him an *ephod* of linen." The word used here for robe is *me'il,* the very same word used to designate the robe worn by the high priest of the temple (*see* Exodus 28:31). It was pointed out in the previous chapter that the word

ephod refers to an apron and that this item of apparel was also worn by the temple priests (*see* 1 Samuel 2:28; 14:3; 22:18).[84] It might seem curious that the king is described as wearing priest-like clothing but it must be remembered that the king was also "a priest"—not from the lineage of Aaron but "after the order of Melchizedek" (Psalm 110:4). It is interesting to note that the word used to designate the type of sash worn by the temple priests (*abnet*) is only used in one other place in the entire Old Testament, and that is to designate the sash worn by Eliakim, the master of the royal household under King Hezekiah (*see* Isaiah 22:21).[85]

Figure 19. Image from a coin of Charles the Great (ca. 742-814 A.D.) wearing a crown, a pleated robe, and an apron that is decorated with a tree. The king also holds the sword, which in ancient times was regarded as a royal weapon.

One symbolic object that was connected with royal apparel was the "key of the house of David." This symbol was placed upon the shoulder of the robe of a royal official (*see* Isaiah 22:21–22).[86] "The heavy key of the palace, carried on a loop slung over the shoulder, gave both symbolic and actual sole power to lock and unlock the principal door."[87] Some biblical commentators suggest that instead of a physical key hanging from the shoulder, the "key of the house of David" may have been something like "the figure of a key . . . worn on the shoulder as an *epaulette* is now, as a sign of office and authority."[88] In one rabbinical commentary this object is connected with the temple in that it is identified as the "key to the sanctuary and dominion of the house of

FIGURE 20. Large keys were commonly carried upon the shoulder in ancient times. The scriptures refer to one such key as "the key of the house of David," and indicate that it is connected with the power to bind or seal.

David."[89] The stated purpose of this key was to enable one to "open, and none shall shut; and . . . shut, and none shall open" (Isaiah 22:22). Because this key is mentioned in a passage that is widely held to be Messianic, some scholars feel that it too was somehow connected with the Messiah.[90] And indeed, the Lord Jesus Christ declared Himself to be "he that hath the key of David, he that openeth, and no man shutteth; and shutteth, and no man openeth" (Revelation 3:7). What purpose did this key serve? In the meridian of time, the Savior promised to bestow the sealing power upon His apostles with the words: "And I will give unto thee the keys of the kingdom of heaven: and whatsoever thou shalt bind on earth shall be bound in heaven: and whatsoever thou shalt loose on earth shall be loosed in heaven" (Matthew 16:19). According to one scriptural commentator "the keys of the kingdom of God are not different from the key of David" and could appropriately be referred to as "the keys of the royal dominion of God."[91] This perspective gives added meaning to Isaiah's prophesy of the Prince of Peace—"the government shall be upon his shoulder" (Isaiah 9:6).

• HEADGEAR: The best-known of the symbols of kingship was, of course, the crown. It appears that the king of Israel had a crown of pure gold placed upon his head during his coronation rites (*see* 2 Kings 11:12; 2 Chronicles 23:11; 2 Samuel 1:10; Psalms 21:3; 132:18). In the book of Revelation, it is stated that golden crowns are symbolic of "glory and honour and power" (Revelation 4:4, 10–11). Indeed, the King of Heaven Himself wears this royal symbol (*see* Revelation 14:14; 19:11–12) and He promises that His faithful followers will someday receive a crown of their own (*see* Revelation 2:10). It is recorded that at least one Israelite king wore a *misnepet* or white linen headdress underneath his crown (*see* Ezekiel 21:26) just as the high priest of the temple wore a *misnepet* underneath his own crown (*see* Exodus 28:36–37).[92]

It is not known exactly what type of crown was worn by the Israelite kings, but we do know that the high priest of the temple wore a crown of pure gold. A single cord, string, or line *(pathil)*[93] was used to secure the golden crown of the high priest onto the front of his white linen headdress (*see* Exodus 28:36–38; Leviticus 8:9). This particular cord was dyed blue (*see* Exodus 28:36–37), suggesting by its color that it was symbolic of royal or heavenly status.[94] It is presumed that this cord was tied off at the back of the head and its excess end or ends hung down freely. Perhaps a parallel can be seen in the long, decorated ribbons or lappets that are so often depicted hanging from the back or sides of the crowns that were worn by the ancient kings of Assyria, Egypt, and other Near Eastern nations.[95]

The king of Israel was given a type of royal insignia during his coronation that is little understood by biblical scholars. Those in charge of carrying out the coronation not only put the crown upon

FIGURE 21. Image from an ancient sculpture in Persepolis showing a royal headdress with a distinctive ribbon hanging from the back. The high priest of the Israelite temple attached a golden crown to the front of his white linen headdress with a blue cord.

the king's head but also put upon him, or upon the crown itself, something called the "testimony" or *ʿedut* (*see* 2 Kings 11:12; 2 Chronicles 23:11).[96] It is the view of some scholars that this object "may have been some material symbol of a covenant."[97] More specifically, others believe that this was some type of "a document embodying the basic terms of Yahweh's covenant with the House of David."[98] It may have even been some kind of royal ornament "which served as a reminder of the covenant, comparable to the priestly diadem inscribed 'Holy to YHWH' (Exodus 28:36)."[99] The term "testimony" appears to be equivalent to the "law" that God gave unto the covenant people at Mount Sinai (*see* Exodus 24:12; 25:16; 31:18; 32:15). We know that the responsibility was laid upon the king to know and to teach the Lord's laws and statutes unto all of the children of Israel (*see* Deuteronomy 17:14–20). The Lord made this

FIGURE 22. The tefillin, or phylactery, worn on the head by devout Jews may be related to a much older object called the "testimony" that was given to the Israelite king during his coronation ceremony.

conditional promise to the king: "The Lord hath sworn in truth unto David; he will not turn from it; Of the fruit of thy body will I set upon thy throne. If thy children will keep my *covenant* and my *testimony* that I shall teach them, their children shall also sit upon thy throne forevermore" (Psalm 132:11–12; emphasis added). From the foregoing we might plausibly conclude that some type of ornament or symbol was attached to the king's crown, or possibly his white linen headdress, that represented his responsibility to know, teach, and rule by the laws of the covenant.

• FOOTWEAR: The feet of the king had several symbolic connotations. In Psalm 27:4–5 and 40:1–2, King David indicates that the Lord hears his prayers in times of trouble, lifts him out of the pit of miry clay that he is figuratively standing in, and sets his feet upon a "rock." These images of stability and salvation are all the more striking when one considers that "Rock" is one of the names of Jehovah and this title is often mentioned alongside "salvation" (*see* Deuteronomy 32:4, 15, 18, 30–31; 1 Samuel 2:2; 2 Samuel 22:2–3, 32, 47; 23:3; Psalms 18:2, 31, 46; 28:1; 31:2–3; 42:9; 61:2; 62:2, 6–7; 71:3; 78:35; 89:26; 92:15; 94:22; 95:1; 1 Corinthians 10:4). Perhaps the prayer of the king was: "Hold up my goings in thy paths, that my footsteps slip not" (Psalm 17:5; *see also* 18:36; 73:2, 17–18; 94:18).

One of the prominent symbolic images of kingship throughout the ancient world was the king placing all of his enemies underneath his feet (*see* Psalms 18:36–38; 47:2–3). It is clear from Psalm 8:6 that to have all things under one's feet is to have dominion over them. This imagery is found in Psalm 110, which is widely acknowledged as a royal coronation text. Verse 1 speaks of the king being enthroned at the right hand of God and the Lord making the king's enemies the footstool of his throne.[100]

There is no reference in the Bible to the king of Israel being shod with royal footwear during his coronation ceremony.[101] There is, however, ample evidence for kings throughout the ancient world receiving royal footwear when they were enthroned.[102] Kings from both Assyria and Persia are depicted on ancient stone monuments wearing what appear to be slippers that cover their entire foot.[103] Some ritual shoes in the ancient world were made of linen and could only be worn when one was standing on holy ground (compare Ezekiel 42:14; 44:19). The reason for this, evidently, was so that one would not mix common or cursed ground (*see* Genesis 3:17) together with holy or consecrated ground.[104] Slippers are worn at the present time by the Christian priests of the Syrian Orthodox Church and also the Coptic Church. When the Syrian

FIGURE 23. This photograph of a stone monument (ca. 680-669 B.C.) depicts the slippers that were worn by King Esarhaddon of Assyria .

priests put on their slippers, they recite the prayer: "May my feet, O Lord God, be shod with the preparation of the gospel of peace so that I may tread underfoot serpents and scorpions and all the power of the enemy, forever"[105] (compare Genesis 3:14–15; Psalm 110:1; Isaiah 52:7; Ephesians 6:15). In the Coptic liturgy "shoes are not allowed inside the sanctuary as a sign of respect for its sanctity and as an implied expression of an inner feeling of security and absence of danger in the house of God; thus, the footwear used by . . . [the] priests . . . is a pair of slippers made of cotton, wool, or knitted material."[106]

Royal Regalia

There were a wide variety of symbolic objects associated with the kings of the ancient Near East. In ancient Israel such objects included the throne, scepter, sword, and cup.

• THRONE: King Solomon built himself a unique ivory throne with a round backpiece. It was decorated with pure gold, equipped with a golden footstool, and could only be reached by ascending a flight of six steps. Representations of lions—the symbol of the tribe of Judah—adorned both the steps and the armrests of this elaborately decorated throne (*see* 1 Kings 10:18–20; 2 Chronicles 9:17–19). As king over all things, God Himself sits upon a heavenly throne (*see* 1 Kings 22:19; 2 Chronicles 18:18; Psalm 11:4; Isaiah 6:1; Ezekiel 1:26–28; Revelation 4:2). The throne of the house of Israel was called "the throne of the kings" (2 Kings 11:19). But in all actuality it was "the throne of the Lord" (1 Chronicles 29:23) because God was the sovereign over the covenant people (*see* 1 Samuel 12:12) and the kings of Israel merely ruled on His behalf (*see* 2 Chronicles 9:8). Holiness, justice, judgment, mercy, truth, and righteousness are characteristics that are frequently associated with the throne of God and His kings (*see* Psalms 47:8; 89:14; 97:2; Proverbs 16:12; 25:5).

There is some evidence that, upon their enthronement, the kings of Israel took upon themselves a new name or throne name.[107] One commentator states that "the accession ceremony in Judah included the conferment of a coronation name by the deity," and he suggests that traces of this conferral can be seen in 2 Samuel 7:9 and 1 Kings 1:47.[108] Generally, the act of "renaming is associated with a change in the status or condition of the person receiving the new name. The giving of the new name can be a sign that the receiver of the name is coming under the authority of the giver of the name."[109] In the Old Testament, new names are often indicative of adoption into someone's household and are thus equivalent to the conferral of a high honour upon the recipient.[110] In the words of another scholar, the king "receives a new disposition expressed, according to oriental custom, in the giving to him of a new name, which indicates his new, intimate relationship with the god who has chosen him, and whom he represents."[111]

• SCEPTER: The King of heaven is reported to possess a rod (*šebet*) and a staff (*miš^eenah*) (*see* Psalm 23:4; Job 21:9). In Psalms 2 and 110, which are generally looked upon as being royal in nature, we find that the rod (*šebet*)[112] and staff (*mattah*)[113] are mentioned as if they were part of the regalia of the Hebrew king (*see* Psalms 2:9; 110:2). Each of these objects could serve as a scepter and perform a distinctive function. Since the king of Israel was referred to as a shepherd (*see* Ezekiel 34:2, 23; Jeremiah 2:8), his staff could be seen as a symbol of the watchful care and protection he was to provide for his flock, the children of Israel. The rod, on the other hand, was an instrument that was used for correction, reproof, and punishment (*see* Proverbs 22:15; 29:15). This duality is clearly illustrated by the crook and flail scepters that symbolized the dominion held by the kings of Egypt. The royal crook of the pharaohs was a shortened shepherd's staff, while the flail was a type of whip.

According to some ancient Near Eastern traditions, the scepter held by both kings and priests symbolized a branch that had been taken from the tree of life.[114] The possession of this branch directly connected the ruler who held it with paradise. It was a sign of his possession of *life* and his ability to distribute that divine force.[115] Perhaps this concept may be connected with the Messiah, who in one instance is referred to as the "Sceptre" (Numbers 24:17). In Jewish traditions it is said that the rod that Adam took with him from paradise was passed down through the patriarchs from Enoch to Noah, Shem, Abraham, Isaac, Jacob, Joseph, Jethro, and Moses.[116]

• SWORD: The sword of the Lord is spoken of in several passages of the Bible (*see* Judges 7:18, 20; Isaiah 27:1; 34:5–6; 66:16; Jeremiah 12:12; 47:6; Ezekiel 21:4–5;

30:24–25; 32:10; Revelation 2:12) Angels, too, wield heavenly swords (*see* Joshua 5:13–15; 1 Chronicles 21:16, 27). In Jewish legend it is related that a special sword was passed down as part of the birthright blessing from Abraham to Isaac to Jacob.[117] At least some of the kings and other members of Israel's royal household possessed their own swords (*see* 1 Samuel 13:22; 1 Kings 19:15–17; Psalm 45:1–3) and the swords of two foreign kings are mentioned in the scriptures (*see* Exodus 18:4; 1 Kings 19:15–17). As noted by one biblical commentator, the "sword is a royal weapon."[118]

In one intriguing passage from the book of Ezekiel, a king is compared to one of the cherubim in the Garden of Eden (*see* Ezekiel 28:11–17). The cherubim wielded flaming swords to protect or defend the garden of God from unauthorized intruders (*see* Genesis 3:24).[119] In some instances the sword is figuratively compared to the word of God or to the Spirit who is the spokesman of that word. Divine words are "sharper than a two-edged sword" because they possess the power to strike or pierce one to the very core (*see* Hebrews 4:12; Ephesians 6:17; Revelation 1:16; D&C 6:2). In one of the Proverbs we read: "A divine sentence is in the lips of the king: his mouth transgresseth not in judgement" (Proverbs 16:10). And in Ecclesiastes 8:4 it is stated: "Where the word of a king is, there is power." Indeed, the king's words were looked upon as those of "an angel of God" (2 Samuel 14:17).

• CUP: The king's cup is a well-attested ritual object in the various cultures of the ancient Near East.[120] Various scriptures indicate that the King of heaven has a symbolic cup with which He pours out either blessings or curses (*see* Psalm 75:8; Isaiah 51:17, 22–23; Jeremiah 25:15–17; Habakkuk 2:16). This may perhaps be the "cup of salvation" that is mentioned in Psalm 116:13. The cup of the king of Israel is spoken of in Psalms 16:5 and 23:5. It has been suggested by some scholars that a ceremonial cup, representing the water of life, was given to the Israelite king while one of the Psalms of the royal liturgy was being read during his coronation ceremony.[121]

Bestowal of Blessings

We are fortunate to have a record of an Israelite coronation ceremony that was practiced in the tenth century A.D. This ceremony followed the general coronation pattern found in the Old Testament but this account adds an interesting detail. A raised platform was constructed inside a synagogue for the coronation rites (compare 2 Chronicles 6:13), and its superstructure was completely concealed by "magnificent coverings of silk, blue, purple, and scarlet," thus imitating the veil of the temple (compare Exodus 26:31). The king (or exilarch) sat in the middle of the platform while the heads of two religious academies sat on either side of him with empty spaces between each of them. This space was necessary so that a canopy could be lowered down over the king. Once this canopy was lowered, a man called the precentor put his head under the front of it and pronounced certain blessings upon him "with a low voice."[122] This canopy or small hut seems to have a parallel in the kingly initiation ceremonies of the ancient Near East. Normally the enthronement ceremonies of Near Eastern kings took place inside of a temple. "It would appear, however, that at times the enthronement might have taken place in a ritual hut, a hut which was constructed both as a symbol of the order of the new creation and as a replica of the god's heavenly temple." Among other activities that took place within this ritual hut were the anointing of the king and the bestowal upon him of a "holy garment."[123]

Some ancient Near Eastern kings were "initiated into heavenly secrets and given wisdom" during their enthronement rites.[124] This theme, while not found in the Bible, is found in several apocryphal works. In the Ethiopic Book of Enoch, for example, it is stated by the Lord that whomever He chooses to sit upon His throne will be initiated into "all the secrets of wisdom and counsel." In the Slavonic Book of Enoch we likewise read that the prophet Enoch was enthroned and initiated into divine secrets by being shown the contents of heavenly books and by conversing with the Lord Himself. And finally, the Testament of Levi tells us that when the patriarch Levi ascended to the third heaven, he participated in coronation ceremonies, was "initiated into the heavenly secrets," and shared in the wisdom of God.[125] Aside from these apocryphal works, the very subtle connection should be noted between the Israelite king, who was given wisdom to discern between good and evil (*see* 2 Samuel 14:17; 1 Kings 3:9, 12),[126] and Adam (the first king), who gained the same ability by partaking of the tree of the knowledge of good and evil (*see* Genesis 3:5, 22).

Another blessing that was bestowed upon the Israelite king was his formal adoption as Jehovah's son. Psalm 2:6–7, which is believed to be part of a royal coronation text, appears to have been mistranslated in the King James Bible. There seems to be sufficient reason to amend these verses to say that the king of Israel was "anointed"[127] upon the "holy hill of Zion" (meaning the temple mount) and the Lord said unto him: "I have taken thee to my bosom;[128] Thou art my Son; This day have I begotten thee." Psalm 80:14–17, which has also been mistranslated, likewise speaks of the king of Israel as the Lord's son.[129] In speaking of King Solomon, the Lord said: "I will be his father, and he shall be my son" (2 Samuel 7:14; *see also* 1 Chronicles 22:10; 28:6). In Psalm 89:27, the king is even referred to as the Lord's "firstborn."

Some scholars have noticed that alongside the royal adoption imagery of the Old Testament is the motif of the Lord grasping the hand of the king.[130] Psalms such as 18:35, 63:8, 73:23–24, and 139:10 contain references to Jehovah grasping the right hand of the Israelite sovereign. In providing commentary on one of these verses, an expert on the Psalms has stated that this "points to a royal (might we even say, messianic?) procedure. The formula, 'God grasps one by the hand,' when the king ascends the throne and is inducted into the royal office, denotes the conferring of privilege and charisma on the king (Isaiah 45:1; 42:1)."[131] One ancient Near Eastern text brings the motifs of adoption and handclasp together by describing a treaty ceremony between a Hittite king and his vassal. The king "grasped me with his hand," relays the vassal. And then the king spoke the adoption formula: "I shall make you my son . . . and will make you sit on the throne of your father."[132]

Sacred Marriage

The final ceremony in the royal coronation rites of many ancient Near East cultures was the sacred marriage of the king and queen.[133] Some biblical scholars not only believe that royal weddings took place in ancient Israel but they also feel that Psalm 45 was a hymn that was sung during the regal marriage rites.[134]

The Bible provides only sketchy information about the form of marriage rituals among the Israelites. We may perhaps discern some of the details of those ceremonies by examining scriptural passages that allude to actual marriages and also speak of the metaphorical marriage between the Lord (bridegroom) and the nation of Israel (bride).[135]

• RITUAL PREPARATION: In terms that are unmistakably connected with temple ritual the Lord informs us in Ezekiel 16:9 that his bride was washed with water and then anointed with oil (compare Exodus 40:12–15).[136] The sequence of first being washed and then anointed in connection with marriage is also seen in Ruth 3:3.[137]

• SACRED CLOTHING: Ezekiel 16:10–13 indicates that after the bride was washed and anointed, she was clothed with embroidered vestments (compare Revelation 19:7–8), girded with a fine linen sash, covered with silk (possibly a veil),[138] shod with soft leather footwear,[139] and had a beautiful crown placed upon her head. This type of clothing is very similar to the outfit that was worn by the temple priests. And, in fact, there are two Old Testament passages that, when read together, equate the clothing of the temple priests with that worn by Israelite brides and grooms.

"Let thy priests be clothed with righteousness. . . .I will also clothe her priests with salvation"[140]

Psalms 132:9, 16

". . . for [God] hath clothed me with the garments of salvation, he hath covered me with the robe of righteousness, *as a bridegroom* decketh himself with ornaments, and *as a bride* adorneth herself with her jewels."

Isaiah 61:10

There is a mistranslation in Isaiah 61:10 which, when corrected, strengthens the connection between the clothing worn by the bridegroom and the priests of the temple. The King James Bible states that the bridegroom wore "ornaments," but the Hebrew word behind this text (*pe'er*) is not translated as "ornaments" in any other biblical passage. Instead *pe'er* is one of the words used to designate the caps that were worn by the temple priests (*see* Exodus 39:28).

• ROYAL STATUS: In addition to being connected with the temple priests, the brides and grooms of Israel were also associated with royalty. On their wedding day, the bride and groom enjoyed a "temporary symbolic status as queen and king."[141] Ezekiel 16:12 implies that the bride wore "a beautiful crown" on the day of her wedding, and in like manner "the groom was dressed as much like a king as possible. If he were rich enough to afford it, he wore a gold crown [*see* Song of Solomon 3:11]. Otherwise it would be a garland of fresh flowers. His garments would be scented with frankincense and myrrh, his girdle would be a silken one brilliantly colored, his sandals would be figured and carefully laced."[142]

• WEDDING CANOPY: The Bible makes two brief references to the *chuppah* or wedding chamber of the bride and groom but provides no other information about its form and function (*see* Psalm 19:5; Joel 2:16). The word *chuppah* is derived from the word *chaphah* which means "to *cover*; by implication to *veil*, to *incase*."[143] Hence, the wedding chamber was probably something like an enclosed room or perhaps some type of a tent or booth.[144]

The symbolism behind this chamber appears to be tied to the covenant ceremony at Mount Sinai when God was metaphorically wedded to the nation of Israel and became her husband (*see* Isaiah 54:5; 62:5; Jeremiah 3:14, 20; 31:32). "The rabbis regarded the Jewish marriage service as reflecting the main features of God's covenant with Israel at Mount Sinai. The covenant ceremony of marriage was seen as a replica or reenactment of what happened at Sinai. It was designed to be a reminder of that basic covenant obligation which binds God to his people."[145] It is interesting, and perhaps significant, that the Lord commanded the Israelites to build "booths" or *Sukkot* during the springtime Feast of Tabernacles in order to commemorate the Sinai experience (*see* Leviticus 23:33–44).[146] The word used to designate these booths is *sukkah,* which can be translated as hut, booth, tabernacle, or tent.[147] These huts were to be made from "olive branches, and pine branches, and myrtle branches, and palm branches, and branches of thick trees" (Nehemiah 8:14–15). This list of trees evokes the different varieties of trees that were planted in the Garden of Eden (*see* Genesis 2:8–9).[148] In fact, there is a Jewish tradition that God constructed a canopy in the Garden of Eden for the wedding of Adam and Eve.[149] Notice also that the Israelites held a wedding feast outside the bridal chamber for the same amount of time that they feasted in their booths to commemorate the Sinai experience—seven days (compare Leviticus 23:41–42 and Judges 14:12). Furthermore, it should be noted that "certain biblical scholars hold that the 'booths' which the Bible prescribes as a dwelling place for the period of the seven days of the tabernacles 'originally represented the sacred grove in which the divine marriage was consummated.'"[150] Thus, the Israelite wedding booths seem to have been symbolically tied to the booths of the Sinai wedding commemoration.

There is one final correspondence to make note of before we move on. Some of the ancient Israelites were familiar with a "Lesser Mystery" associated with Aaron and "material" things, and a "Greater Mystery" associated with Moses and centered on "spiritual" things (compare D&C 84:18–22, 31–34; 107:8, 13–14, 68–70). These mysteries constituted "two successive initiations" but only the Greater Mystery could enable the initiate to "approach God" whose symbolic throne (the ark of the covenant) was located in the Holy of Holies of the temple. "The objective symbolism of the Higher Mystery was the Holy of Holies with the Ark" and the "mystery of the Holy of Holies," some Israelites believed, was directly connected with "the mystery of the sacred marriage."[151] It is therefore interesting to note that at some point in ancient Israel's history the cherubim on top of the ark of the covenant were refashioned to resemble a husband and a wife in an intimate embrace.[152]

• OATH AND COVENANT: The scriptures appear to indicate that marriage was ratified by swearing an oath and entering into a covenant (*see* Ezekiel 16:8). The Lord Himself seems to have stood as a witness to the marriage covenant (*see* Malachi 2:14), perhaps because this type of covenant was meant to last for eternity (Hosea 2:19).[153] An Aramaic marriage document from a Jewish community in the 5th century B.C. confirms that at least some Israelite marriage unions were considered to be eternal. In this document the groom says of his bride: "She is my wife and I am her husband from this day and forever."[154] In a lengthy study on biblical marriage as a covenant, one scholar has noted that "there is an unmistakeable formulaic quality about [Adam's] expression, 'this is . . . bone of my bones, and flesh of my flesh.'" It is the author's view that this "relationship formula" may be seen in the context of a "covenant-ratifying oath."[155]

• BLESSING: When Adam and Eve were joined together as husband and wife, the scriptures tell us that the Lord Himself "blessed" them in some manner and then directed them to multiply and fill *(male')*[156] the earth with their posterity (Genesis 1:26–28). Based upon Genesis 24:60 and Ruth 4:10–12, several interpreters of the Bible have concluded that Hebrew wedding rites included a blessing that invoked a numerous posterity for the couple that was being united.[157] It will be remembered that an endless posterity was one of the blessings associated with the Abrahamic covenant (*see* Genesis 15:5; 26:4; 28:14).

• MARRIAGE FEAST: Israelite brides and grooms typically enjoyed a marriage feast after they had been joined to one another. Ezekiel 16:13 and 19 seem to speak of the bride enjoying a wedding feast of fine flour, honey, and oil. It is interesting to note that all three of these food items were utilized as offerings in the House of the Lord (*see* Leviticus 2:4–6; 2 Chronicles 31:5). It should further be noted that when Saul became the king of Israel, he participated in a banquet as part of his installation ritual. This was a sacrificial meal whose elements closely paralleled the consecration rites of the temple priests.[158] These earthly feasts seem to have been symbolic of the heavenly "marriage supper of the Lamb" that will be enjoyed by the Lord's faithful disciples in the world to come (*see* Revelation 19:9; Luke 14:15–24; 22:29–30; JST Matthew 22:1–14).

Ritual Drama

Psalm 2 is believed by some biblical scholars to be related to the king's coronation ceremony. In it, one writer sees "the ritual 'repetition' or 'actualization' of the primordial institution of king and kingship. What happened then to the Patriarch of Kings and Men [i.e., Adam] happens again to the actual 'King' and 'Man' in the Coronation Rite." This writer also believes that it is evident from Psalm 72 "that in the early days of Israel the king [was] regarded as achieving the fertility of Paradise. Ideas of Paradise and of Primordial Man have, therefore, been connected with Israelite kingship."[159]

According to some scholars, the children of Israel "experienced a repetition of the events at the creation of the world" during the New Year festival. They did this through "a 'ritual drama' with the re-creation of the world as its central theme." Through the religious act of "remembrance," the creation was thought of as being tangibly experienced.[160] This "remembrance" would have occurred when the creation account was read as part of the temple liturgy during the New Year's festival, precisely the time when the king received his coronation rites.[161] "The enthronement of a king is always a repetition of a primeval act. It is a repetition of the enthronement of the first king in the days of the beginning, the primeval age. . . . The king, then, is *Primeval Man*. The first man of Genesis 1:26–28 is described as the first ruler of the world."[162] In summary, then, "the creative acts of God and man's dominion over creation were actualized in the annual festival when the king played the role of Adam as the representative of mankind."[163]

It may be possible to understand something about the nature of this royal ritual drama by examining what is known of another ritual drama that was enacted in ancient Israel. One scholarly study on this other ritual drama comes to the following conclusions: The Israelites participated in a ritual Exodus drama that was directly influenced by "a kingship drama," possibly the "ancient enthronement and covenant celebration of Sinai." The Exodus drama was "sacred" in character. It was concerned with the salvation of the Hebrew people, and was "in some way 'renewed,' 'actualised,' [or] 'rendered present.'" It is believed that this ritual drama may have been connected with "the initiation of new members into Hebrew society." There were three parties involved in the acting out of the drama: Jehovah (with Moses and Aaron), the Pharaoh as the antagonist (with his court), and the Hebrews who were present. The role of the Hebrews who were seeing this drama was to function as an audience, as participating actors, and as "witnesses." This drama included "ritually determined actions" as well as "formularized conversations." The main focus of the drama was the "creation" of the Lord's people by means of entering into a covenant.[164]

SUMMARY

This chapter has demonstrated that King Solomon's Temple was an architectural replica of the Garden of Eden, and the king of Israel was a typological representation of Adam, the first king. Thus, when the king entered into the temple, it was as if Adam had regained paradise. This reminds us of a passage in the book of Jonah that has Adamic overtones and seems to encapsulate the entire plan of salvation. It reads: "I am cast out of thy sight; yet I will look again toward thy holy temple" (Jonah 2:4).

NOTES

1. In a letter to the king of Tyre, King Solomon further explained: "Thou knowest how that David my father could not build an house unto the name of the Lord his God for the wars which were about him on every side, until the Lord put them under the soles of his feet. But now the Lord my God hath given me rest on every side, so that there is neither adversary nor evil occurrent. And, behold, I propose to build an house unto the name of the Lord my God, as the Lord spake unto David my father, saying, Thy son, whom I will set upon thy throne in thy room, he shall build an house unto my name" (1 Kings 5:3–5). In another passage King David is more forthright about the reasons for his being denied the opportunity to build the Lord's holy house. "And David said to Solomon, My son, as for me, it was in my mind to build an house unto the name of the Lord my God. But the word of the Lord came to me, saying, Thou hast shed blood abundantly, and hast made great wars: thou shalt not build an house unto my name, because thou hast shed much blood upon the earth in my sight. Behold, a son shall be born to thee, who shall be a man of rest; and I will give him rest from all his enemies round about: for his name shall be Solomon, and I will give *peace* and quietness unto Israel in his days. He shall build an house for my name; and he shall be my son, and I will be his father; and I will establish the throne of his kingdom over Israel forever" (1 Chronicles 22:7–10; emphasis added). There is some subtle symbolism to be seen here. The name *Solomon* means "peaceable" (*LDS Bible Dictionary*, 775). In fact, the building site of the temple was relatively peaceful because the stone was shaped in the quarry "so that there was neither hammer nor axe nor any tool of iron heard in the house, while it was in building" (1 Kings 6:7; compare Deuteronomy 27:5). The prohibition against iron seems to have arisen from the fact that in biblical times iron was viewed as a symbol of war and violence (see Ellen Frankel and Betsy P. Teutsch, *The Encyclopedia of Jewish Symbols* [Northvale, New Jersey: Jason Aronson, 1992], 77).

2. The tabernacle and its furnishings were taken up to Jerusalem and stored inside the newly built temple (see *Antiquities*, 8.4.1 in William Whiston, trans., *The Works of Josephus: Complete and Unabridged*, updated ed. [Peabody, Massachusetts: Hendrickson Publishers, 1987], 219).

3. See David N. Freedman, ed., *The Anchor Bible Dictionary* (New York: Doubleday, 1992), 6:1096; R. Laird Harris, ed., *Theological Wordbook of the Old Testament*, (Chicago: Moody Press, 1980), 2:764.

4. See Freedman, ed., *The Anchor Bible Dictionary*, 6:1099–100.

5. George A. Buttrick, ed., *The Interpreter's Bible* (New York: Abingdon Press, 1956), 5:262.

6. This is not to say that the North Star should necessarily be equated with either Kolob or the celestial sphere where God resides. It simply means that the North Star appeared to those on the earth in ancient times as if it were at the center of the cosmos. Visitors to the Salt Lake Temple will notice that the symbolic representation of the Big Dipper on the west center spire is oriented so that its pointer stars direct one to the actual location of the North Star.

7. The temple was built "to the north" of the City of David (Harris , ed., *Theological Wordbook of the Old Testament*, 2:764). For a topographical map showing the temple at the summit of Mount Zion in the northernmost section of the mountain's building complex, see Alfred Edersheim, *The Temple: Its*

Ministry and Services, updated ed. (Peabody, Massachusetts: Hendrickson Publishers, 1994), 15. Brigham Young explained that the Lord visits elevated locations on the earth such as "the tops of high mountains" because they are "places where sinful man has never marked the soil with his polluted feet" (*JD*, 10:252). This would help explain why the Lord directs his servants to build temples unto him on mountain tops. Such locations are literal meeting places between heaven and earth.

8. Harris, ed., *Theological Wordbook of the Old Testament*, 2:764.

9. Ad de Vries, *Dictionary of Symbols and Imagery*, rev. ed. (London: North-Holland Publishing Co., 1976), 464. For an illustration of oxen treading the threshingfloor around a hub of grain, see Donald W. Parry, ed., *Temples of the Ancient World: Ritual and Symbolism* (Salt Lake City: Deseret Book and FARMS, 1994), 90.

10. According to Jewish tradition, "the sacred space of the Jerusalem temple is set apart from all other spaces of the earth, not only because Yahweh has chosen Zion as his . . . 'resting place,' but also because . . . the site of Zion was related to the navel of the earth. Solomon's temple is built on a rock which is the earth-center, the world mountain, the foundation stone of creation, the extremity of the umbilical cord which provides a link between heaven, earth, and the underworld" (Samuel Terrien, "The Omphalos Myth and Hebrew Religion," *Vetus Testamentum*, vol. 20, no. 3, July 1970, 317). In the apocryphal book of Jubilees (8:19), we read that Mount Zion is the center of the navel of the earth.

11. See G. Johannes Botterweck and Helmer Ringgren, eds., *Theological Dictionary of the Old Testament* (Grand Rapids, Michigan: Eerdmans, 1978), 3:383. The word *hekhal* is translated as "palace" or "palaces" in such places as 1 Kings 21:1; Psalm 45:8, 15; 144:12; Proverbs 30:28; Ezra 4:14; and Daniel 1:4.

12. Victor Hurowitz, "Inside Solomon's Temple," *Bible Review*, April 1994, 36–37. The Prophet Joseph Smith stated: "The architectural designs of the temple at Jerusalem, together with its ornaments and beauty, were given of God" (*HC*, 5:63).

13. The tractate from the Jewish Talmud called Middoth (3:6) states that the broad stairway leading up into Solomon's Temple had two intermediate landings. It does not appear, however, that there was a stairway leading up into the Holy of Holies of the Solomonic Temple (see Hurowitz, "Inside Solomon's Temple," 34–35).

14. James Strong, *The New Strong's Exhaustive Concordance of the Bible* (Nashville: Thomas Nelson Publishers, 1996), Hebrew and Aramaic Dictionary, 28, word #1588 and word #1598. In speaking of 1 Kings 7:12, one scholar has noted that the temple court during the time of King Solomon "was marked off by a low 'fence' of 'three rows (courses) of hewed stones and a row (course) of cedar beams'" (Paul L. Garber, "Reconstructing Solomon's Temple," *Biblical Archaeologist*, vol. 14, no. 1, February 1951, 4).

15. "The interior walls were covered with cedar wainscoting; the floor was covered with boards of cypress. Thus no stonework could be seen anywhere on the inside of the building (1 Kings 6:14–18). According to the English translations, much of this woodwork was 'overlaid' with gold (vss.19–22, 30). This seems exaggerated, even in connection with wealthy Solomon; it has been suggested, with good reason, that the proper word is 'inlaid.' It is unlikely that such splendid woodwork would have been completely covered, even with gold. Ivory inlay is now well known from Palestinian excavations at Samaria and Megiddo; it is likely that gold was used in the same way" (George A. Buttrick, ed., *The*

Interpreter's Dictionary of the Bible [New York: Abingdon Press, 1962], 4:537). "It has been recognized that the writer of Kings is quite generous in his use of gold 'overlay;' for example, 1 Kings 6:30 where the floor of the temple was 'overlaid' with gold. Dr. Wright suggests that 'inlaid' is a more accurate translation of this verb. This appears a more suitable rendering in each of the places where the verb occurs, especially 1 Kings 6:21, 'So Solomon overlaid the house within with pure gold:' with its implication that the elegance of cedar and the artistic wood carvings were all blended in a single covering sheath of gold leaf.' 'Highlighting' the carvings by the use of gold inlay, on the other hand, could have increased the effectiveness of the craftsman's art" (Garber, "Reconstructing Solomon's Temple," 16). Wright translates 1 Kings 6:35 to say that the gold leaf was "fitted into the graven work" (G. Ernest Wright, "Solomon's Temple Resurrected," *Biblical Archaeologist*, vol. 4, no. 2, May 1941, 21). Even the King James rendition of 1 Kings 6:35 implies that only the carved emblems were decorated with gold, not the entire walls. "And he carved thereon cherubim and palm trees and open flowers: and covered *them* with gold fitted upon the carved work" (emphasis added).

16. Frederick H. Borsch, *The Son of Man in Myth and History* (Philadelphia: Westminster Press, 1967), 118.

17. Notice that the wood of the olive tree was only used in association with the Holy of Holies in King Solomon's Temple.

18. "Although the tree of life is not identified in rabbinic sources, apocryphal sources claim it was an olive tree" (Frankel and Teutsch, *The Encyclopedia of Jewish Symbols*, 181). In the introduction to section 88 of the Doctrine and Covenants, the Prophet Joseph Smith speaks of the "olive leaf . . . plucked from the tree of Paradise" (*HC*, 1:316). For a variety of ancient Jewish and Christian sources that identify the tree of life as an olive tree, see Stephen D. Ricks, "Olive Culture in the Second Temple Era and Early Rabbinic Period," in Stephen D. Ricks and John W. Welch, eds., *The Allegory of the Olive Tree: The Olive, the Bible, and Jacob 5* (Salt Lake City: Deseret Book and FARMS, 1994), 464–65. For the imagery of an olive tree in the house of God, see Psalm 52:8. The temple *menorah* is associated with olive tree imagery in Zechariah 4:1–14.

19. Footnote 8*a* for Deuteronomy 8:8 in the LDS edition of the King James Bible notes that the awkward phrase "oil olive" actually refers to "olive trees."

20. It is the opinion of some scholars that the "honey" spoken of in Deuteronomy 8:8 is the syrup extracted from the dates of a palm tree (see Frankel and Teutsch, *The Encyclopedia of Jewish Symbols*, 75, 150). This would mean that the 'promised land' (a designation for paradise), or a "land flowing with milk and honey" (Exodus 3:8; 13:5), could be visualized as a land filled with palm trees. Hence, a temple filled with palm trees could be seen as a representation of paradise.

21. In some ancient Near Eastern cultures the date palm was looked upon as the tree of life. "Jewish literature outside the Old Testament also contains tree of life references. The Books of Enoch, the Testaments of the Twelve Patriarchs, and 4 Ezra are the best known of such books. When Enoch journeyed to the Seven Sacred Mountains, he saw a sacred tree similar to a date palm but more beautiful and grand than any he had ever beheld (see 1 Enoch 29). His guide on the visionary journey, Michael, told Enoch that the fruit of the tree could not be eaten by mortals until they were purified after the judgment and that they would have to enter the temple of God to partake of it (see 1 Enoch 25)" (C. Wilfred

Griggs, "The Tree of Life in Ancient Cultures," *Ensign*, June 1988, 28; see the Egyptian illustrations on page 29 depicting the date palm as the tree of life; see also Revelation 2:7; 22:1–2).

22. Strong, *The New Strong's Exhaustive Concordance of the Bible*, Hebrew and Aramaic Dictionary, 116, word #6497; see also word #6498.

23. Ibid., 117, word #6525; 139, word #7799.

24. Ibid., 117, word #6525.

25. Ibid., 114, word #6358; 120, word #6731.

26. See Frankel and Teutsch, *The Encyclopedia of Jewish Symbols*, 150.

27. It is obvious from the explicit reference to "fig leaves" in Genesis 3:7 that figs were growing in the Garden of Eden. Fig trees are identified by Moses as one of the symbols of the promised land in Deuteronomy 8:8.

28. Frankel and Teutsch, *The Encyclopedia of Jewish Symbols*, 106.

29. Instead of a single golden *menorah*, as in the tabernacle, the temple of Solomon contained at least ten *menorahs*. Five were placed against the north wall and five against the south wall (see 1 Kings 7:49).

30. C. T. R. Hayward, *The Jewish Temple: A Non-Biblical Sourcebook* (New York: Routledge, 1996), 89. In the apocryphal book of Jubilees, it is implied that there is a close tie "between Eden and Zion's temple." Moreover, it should be noted that in the very old poem of ben Sira "the high priest appears . . . as a latter-day Adam" (ibid., 89–90). In one ancient Jewish writing (Pirqe Mashiah, BhM 3:74–75), we read that "from the temple will open the gates of the Garden of Eden" (Raphael Patai, *The Messiah Texts* [Detroit: Wayne State University Press, 1988], 217). My thanks to John A. Tvedtnes for bringing this source to my attention.

31. Strong, *The New Strong's Exhaustive Concordance of the Bible*, Hebrew and Aramaic Dictionary, 30, word #1687 and word #1696.

32. Sigmund Mowinckel, *The Psalms in Israel's Worship* (Nashville: Abingdon Press, 1979), 2:55, nt. 16. "In early times the distinction between priest and prophet does not seem to have been sharp. The Arabian *kahin* was both seer and priest. Samuel was both priest and prophet. Jeremiah and Ezekiel both came out of priestly families. The connection, indeed, of priests and prophets was always close (Isaiah 8:2)" (James Hastings, *A Dictionary of the Bible* [New York: Charles Scribner's Sons, 1902], 4:109). "It is true that certain texts show priests and prophets working together inside the temple (Jeremiah 23:11; 26:7ff). Jeremiah 35:4 speaks of a chamber of the temple reserved for the sons of a 'man of God,' in other words, a prophet; but this could be an instance of a priest who prophesied. It is also true that a cultic background seems apparent in certain oracles of Hosea (6:1ff; 14:2–9)" (Raymond J. Tournay, *Seeing and Hearing God with the Psalms: The Prophetic Liturgy of the Second Temple in Jerusalem* [Sheffield, England: JSOT Press, 1991], 59).

33. "In the Bible, the head represents a person's dignity. To lower . . . one's head is an expression of submission. . . . Because it sits atop the body, the head represents mastery or control" (Frankel and Teutsch, *The Encyclopedia of Jewish Symbols*, 74).

34. The "forecourt" of the temple was not an enclosed area but a low barrier composed of three rows of hewn stone and one row of cedar beams. The courtyard was built in the very same manner (see 1 Kings 6:36; 7:12). For illustrations, see Hurowitz, "Inside Solomon's Temple," 26–27.

35. "The relation between the two rows of pomegranates and the plaited [or braided, interwoven] work is indeed not precisely defined; but it is generally and correctly assumed, that one row ran round the pillars below the plaited work and the other above, so that the plaited work, which was formed of seven cords plaited together in the form of festoons, was enclosed above and below by the rows of pomegranates" (C. F. Keil, *The Books of the Kings* [Grand Rapids, Michigan: Eerdmans, 1950], 98).

36. The word employed in the Hebrew text is *šošan.* This object was a white lily and was most probably the *sšn,* or sacred lotus flower, of Egypt (see Buttrick, ed., *The Interpreter's Dictionary of the Bible,* 3:133).

37. *LDS Bible Dictionary,* 708.

38. For further examples and citations, see R. B. Y. Scott, "The Pillars Jachin and Boaz," *Journal of Biblical Literature,* vol. 58, 1939, 147–49. It has been noted by Meyers that the forecourt (*ulam*) where Jachin and Boaz stood was built precisely in the same manner as the courtyard enclosure (three courses of hewn stone and one course of cedar beams) and should therefore be considered as belonging to the courtyard and not to the temple itself (see Carol L. Meyers, "Jachin and Boaz in Religious and Political Perspective," in Truman G. Madsen, ed., *The Temple in Antiquity* [Provo, Utah: BYU Religious Studies Center, 1984], 138–40). This argument is strengthened by the fact that the altar, "sea," and pillars of Solomon's Temple were all made of bronze—the same material used to construct the altar, laver, pillar bases, and stakes in the courtyard of the tabernacle. In other words, bronze objects belonged to the courtyard, not to the temple proper.

39. Emphasis added. One biblical scholar believes that the phrase "by his pillar at the entrance (to the temple)" refers to either Jachin or Boaz because they "symbolized the association of God and the king" (John Gray, *I & II Kings: A Commentary,* rev. ed. [London: SCM Press, 1970], 575, nt. *e*). It would therefore seem plausible that the royal coronation ceremony took place inside the forecourt (*ulam*) of the temple. It would also seem that the forecourt was associated primarily with kingship.

40. Emphasis added. The full text of this covenant-making ceremony bears recital. "Then the king sent and gathered together all the elders of Judah and Jerusalem. And the king went up into the house of the Lord, and all the men of Judah, and the inhabitants of Jerusalem, and the priests, and the Levites, and all the people, great and small: and he read in their ears all the words of the book of the covenant that was found in the house of the Lord. And the king stood in his place, and made a covenant before the Lord, to walk after the Lord, and to keep his commandments, and his testimonies, and his statutes, with all his heart, and with all his soul, to perform the words of the covenant which were written in this book. And he caused all that were present in Jerusalem and Benjamin to stand to it. And the inhabitants of Jerusalem did according to the covenant of God, the God of their fathers" (2 Chronicles 34:29–32).

41. Willem A. VanGemeren, ed., *New International Dictionary of the Old Testament Theology and Exegesis* (Grand Rapids, Michigan: Zondervan, 1997), 4:1315.

42. See de Vries, *Dictionary of Symbols and Imagery,* 340. Biblical references to the Lord's net include Job 19:6; Ezekiel 12:13; 17:20; 32:3; Hosea 7:12. See especially Matthew 13:47–49.

43. Notice that the two pillars of the forecourt were shown to the prophet Ezekiel during his temple vision (see Ezekiel 40:49), suggesting that they may also have been shown to King David and therefore built by divine decree.

44. For further reading on connections between kingship, twin pillars, and the temple, see John M. Lundquist, "The Legitimizing Role of the Temple in the Origin of the State," in Parry, ed., *Temple of the Ancient World: Ritual and Symbolism*, 217–21.

45. Strong, *The New Strong's Exhaustive Concordance of the Bible*, Hebrew and Aramaic Dictionary, 57, word #3220.

46. Some Latter-day Saints may believe that the Solomonic "sea" with its twelve oxen was a baptismal font—drawing a parallel to fonts with twelve oxen in LDS temples that are used for proxy baptisms. It should be remembered, however, that the ordinance of baptism for the dead was not introduced among the Lord's covenant people until after Jesus Christ died and visited the spirit world to authorize and organize salvational work for the dead (see JST 1 Peter 3:18–21; D&C 138:6–34). Therefore, the Brazen Sea in the courtyard of Solomon's Temple could not have served as a proxy baptismal font. Even though a few early Christians iconographically connected Solomon's Brazen Sea with Christian baptism (see the illustrations in Robert G. Calkins, *Monuments of Medieval Art* [New York: E. P. Dutton, 1979], 127; Hanns Swarzenski, *Monuments of Romanesque Art*, 2d ed. [London: Faber and Faber, 1967], plate 113, figure 258; *Church News*, 9 July 1932, 5), it should be made clear that biblical texts do *not* support the idea that the Brazen Sea was a baptismal font for living individuals. The function of the "sea" was the very same as the laver of the tabernacle which it replaced. The "sea" was a station where the priests would "wash" (*rachats*, "to lave the whole or a part of a thing:—bathe (self), wash (self)" [Strong, *The New Strong's Exhaustive Concordance of the Bible*, Hebrew and Aramaic Dictionary, 131, word #7364]) their own hands and feet each time they were about to serve in the temple complex (see 2 Chronicles 4:6; compare Exodus 30:17–21. The word *rachats* is also used in Judges 19:21 and Song of Solomon 5:3 in reference to the washing of one's *own* feet). Notice that the temple priests did not *immerse* themselves, as in 2 Kings 5:10–14 where a man is completely immersed (*tabal*, "dip, plunge," [Strong, *The New Strong's Exhaustive Concordance of the Bible*, Hebrew and Aramaic Dictionary, 51, word #2881]) in water in order to become clean from physical and ritual impurity. The Brazen Sea was especially "ill adapted for the purpose of cleansing" by the method of baptism (being 7 feet deep and holding about 11,500 gallons of water) and more than likely served as "a receptacle from which water was drawn" for ritual purifications (Edward L. Curtis, *A Critical and Exegetical Commentary on the Books of Chronicles* [New York: Charles Scribner's Sons, 1910], 331). Unlike the KJV, where it is stated that the priests washed "in" the Brazen Sea, the NIV translates 2 Chronicles 4:6 to read simply that "the Sea was to be used by the priests for washing" (John R. Kohlenberger III, ed., *The NIV Interlinear Hebrew-English Old Testament* [Grand Rapids, Michigan: Zondervan, 1987], 3:90).

47. See Frank E. Gaebelein, ed., *The Expositor's Bible Commentary* (Grand Rapids, Michigan: Zondervan, 1988), 4:75.

48. Strong, *The New Strong's Exhaustive Concordance of the Bible*, Hebrew and Aramaic Dictionary, 117, word #6525.

49. This is "a *lily* (from its *whiteness*), as a flower or architectural ornament; also a (straight) *trumpet* (from the *tubular* shape)" (Strong, *The New Strong's Exhaustive Concordance of the Bible*, Hebrew and Aramaic Dictionary, 139, word #7799; emphasis in original). The "lily" decorations on the pillars

and "sea" of Solomon's Temple "may have been inspired by the lotus through Egyptian architectural influence" (Buttrick, ed., *The Interpreter's Dictionary of the Bible*, 3:133).

50. Strong, *The New Strong's Exhaustive Concordance of the Bible*, Hebrew and Aramaic Dictionary, 116, word #6497. The Hebrew word *peqa'* is also used to designate the floral buds that were carved on the walls of the Holy Place (see 1 Kings 6:17–18).

51. Notice that the lilywork and two rows of bud-like ornaments on the bronze basin seem to match, in general design, the lilywork and two rows of pomegranates on the bronze pillars.

52. Keil, *The Books of the Kings*, 103–104.

53. Ibid., 104–105.

54. The twelve oxen underneath the bronze basin are equated with the twelve tribes of Israel in a late (13th century A.D.) kabalistic (i.e., Jewish/Mystic) work from Spain called the *Zohar* (see Soncino Zohar, Bereshith, section 1, page 241a; Soncino Zohar, Shemoth, section 2, page 24b). My thanks to John A. Tvedtnes for bringing these sources to my attention.

55. It is interesting, and perhaps significant, that in Ezekiel's bewildering vision of the cherubim with four faces (see Ezekiel 1:6–10), there seems to be a parallel with the order of the twelve tribes encamped around the tabernacle. "The four cherubim are described [in Ezekiel's account] as each having four faces: lion, ox, man and eagle. These are found to be the emblems of the leading tribes (Judah, Ephraim, Reuben and Dan). Ezekiel further states the 'four creatures' came out of the 'north' (Ezekiel 1:4). Since each face of the 'man' is represented as seen in a front position and coming from the 'north,' the face (lion) on the right would be placed in the 'east,' the face (ox) on the left in the west, and the face (eagle) in the rear or the north. These positions correspond perfectly with the positions assigned to the tribes of Judah, Ephraim, Reuben and Dan in the Wilderness Camp" (E. Raymond Capt, *King Solomon's Temple* [Thousand Oaks, California: Artisan, 1979], 62).

56. For articles on the twelve oxen found beneath LDS temple baptismal fonts, see Edward J. Brandt, "Why are oxen used in the design of our temples' baptismal fonts?" *Ensign*, March 1993, 54–55; Emil B. Fetzer, "Could you tell me a little about the history of our temple baptismal fonts? Why are oxen used to support the fonts?" *New Era*, March 1976, 26–28. Perhaps a secondary symbolism can be seen in the twelve oxen that are underneath LDS temple baptismal fonts. The scriptures inform us that the birthright in Israel belonged to Joseph (see 1 Chronicles 5:1–2) and his son Ephraim (see Jeremiah 31:9). The symbol assigned to the birthright tribe was the ox and one of the responsibilities laid upon that tribe was the gathering of the Lord's people by symbolically pushing them together, from the four quarters of the earth, with oxen horns (*see* Deuteronomy 33:13–17; *see especially* nt. 17*b*). This same imagery was employed by the Lord when he spoke to his latter-day servants about their responsibility to gather Israel (see D&C 58:45; 133:17–34). In this light, it is interesting to note that the twelve oxen underneath the Brazen Sea in King Solomon's Temple (and also those underneath many LDS temple baptismal fonts) were arranged in four groups of three with the horns of each group pointing to one of the cardinal directions of the earth (see 1 Kings 7:23–25; compare 1 Nephi 22:25; 2 Nephi 21:12; 3 Nephi 16:5; D&C 33:6; 45:46; JS-Matthew 1:37). This could be seen as a visual representation of Joseph's responsibility to push together, or gather together, the tribes of Israel from the four quarters of the earth. According to Wilford Woodruff, the tribe of Joseph/Ephraim is "the first

fruits of the kingdom of God in this dispensation," and the other tribes of Israel will get their "endowments, and be crowned under the hands of the children of Ephraim" (*JD*, 4:232).

57. Garber, "Reconstructing Solomon's Temple," 5. While I tend to agree with this assessment, I would also present this cautionary note for consideration. "It has often been claimed that the combination of the bulls and the Sea is related to the pagan myths involving the divine creative activity in overcoming the sea. Actually the word . . . (*boqor*, 'bull') is the generic term for cattle generally and may indicate oxen as well as cows. The distinctive word for 'bull' (*šor*) is not used here. It would be incredible for David and Solomon to try to bring about a syncretization of faith in the Lord with pagan mythology. When occasionally religious forms and terms overlapped with those of the world at large, it was not because biblical revelation adopted pagan superstition. The terms and forms were clearly defined so there could be no mistaking the uniqueness of God's revelation of himself and of the God-ordained way of man's approach to God" (Gaebelein, ed., *The Expositor's Bible Commentary*, 4:75).

58. "The location of the bronze 'sea' recalls Ezekiel's vision of the stream rising at the south side of the east door of the temple (Ezekiel 47:1), which, as in Joel 3:18, and probably in Psalm 46:4, probably draws upon pre-Israelite mythology, probably that of the seat of El, the divine king paramount, at the 'out-welling of the rivers' (*mbk nhrm*) in the Ras Shamra texts. This was locally associated with the spring of Gihon" (Gray, *I & II Kings: A Commentary*, 196).

59. One ancient Jewish commentary on Ezekiel 47:1 (P. Seqal. 6, 50a, 3) states that the water at the temple threshold originates in the Holy of Holies. Another Jewish source (Pirqe Mashiah, BhM 3:74) likewise states that the water "issues from the Holy of Holies until it reaches the threshold" of the temple (Patai, *The Messiah Texts*, 233). My thanks to John A. Tvedtnes for providing me with this source. This concept is in keeping with the report of John the Revelator who saw "a pure river of water of life, clear as crystal, proceeding out of the throne of God and the Lamb" (Revelation 22:1). As mentioned in the previous chapter, the ark of the covenant in the Holy of Holies was symbolic of God's throne.

60. David N. Freedman, ed., *The Anchor Bible Dictionary* (New York: Doubleday, 1992), 6:359, emphasis in original.

61. *TPJS*, 60–61.

62. M. Russell Ballard, "The Law of Sacrifice," *Ensign*, October 1998, 10.

63. See Stephen D. Ricks, "The Law of Sacrifice," *Ensign*, June 1998, 24–29; Jacob Milgrom, "The Temple in Biblical Israel: Kinships of Meaning," in Truman G. Madsen, ed., *Reflections on Mormonism: Judaeo-Christian Parallels* (Provo, Utah: BYU Religious Studies Center, 1978), 57–65.

64. For further reading, see Richard D. Draper, "Sacrifices and Offerings: Foreshadowings of Christ," *Ensign*, September 1980, 20–26; Phillip W. McMullin, "Sacrifice in the Law of Moses: Parallels in the Law of the Gospel," *Ensign*, March 1990, 37–41.

65. For an informative article on ancient Hebrew covenants, see Menahem Haran, "The *Berit* 'Covenant': Its Nature and Ceremonial Background," in Mordechai Cogan, ed., *Tehillah le-Moshe* (Winona Lake, Indiana: Eisenbrauns, 1997), 203–19. On pages 214–15 of this same source, it is noted that the three main components of an ancient Near Eastern covenant were (1) "a spoken declaration, made by the sovereign or his representative, of the 'terms' of the pact," (2) "the immediate expression

of consent on the part of the people to the covenant terms," and (3) "presenting a witness that will serve to remind the two parties, vassal as well as sovereign, of their commitment."

66. Buttrick, ed., *The Interpreter's Dictionary of the Bible*, 3:576. "H. Cazelles has pointed out that the verb for dividing the animals is the piel of *šlš*. It must mean 'cut three times' (and so into four parts) or 'cut into three parts'" (Dennis J. McCarthy, *Old Testament Covenant* [Richmond, Virginia: John Knox Press, 1972], 60). In commenting on the temple sacrifice of the lamb, the Talmud says that after the priest had slain the animal he proceeded to "cut off the head. . . . He tore out the heart . . . [and] cleft the body" (Joseph Barclay, *The Talmud* [London: John Murray, 1878], 248). The same basic description of the cutting of the "burnt offering" is found in Mendell Lewittes, trans., *The Code of Maimonides: Book Eight, The Book of Temple Service* (New Haven, Connecticut: Yale University Press, 1957), 184–85.

67. Notice that in the ritual of the Abrahamic Covenant the patriarch was required to sacrifice animals and split the carcasses of some of them so that the pillar of fire, representing the Lord, could pass between the parts and the oath of the covenant be sworn (see Genesis 15:1–18). One LDS scholar notes: "Though for a different purpose (affecting atonement and not covenant making), a somewhat similar procedure may be seen in the rites described in Leviticus, where the priests were instructed to 'cut it [the sacrificial animal] into his pieces . . . [and] lay them in order on the wood that is on the fire which is upon the altar' (Leviticus 1:12). In the sacrifices mentioned in Leviticus as well as in Genesis, the animal is divided and the pieces set in order. Perhaps the pieces were arranged on the altar in the Levitical rite so that the fire on the altar should represent 'the smoking fire and fiery torch' mentioned in Genesis [15:1–18]" (Stephen D. Ricks, "Oaths and Oath Taking in the Old Testament," in *A Symposium on the Old Testament* [Salt Lake City: The Church of Jesus Christ of Latter-day Saints, 1983], 141).

68. Edward F. Campbell, Jr., *Ruth* (Garden City, New York: Doubleday, 1975), 74. "It is . . . possible that [the slaughter and the gesture] were performed simultaneously, the throat of an animal being slit as the [participant] symbolically cut his own throat" (J. M. Munn-Rankin, "Diplomacy in Western Asia in the Early Second Millennium B.C.," *Iraq*, vol. 18, 1956, 91). One scholar has tentatively interpreted some biblical passages as describing "some kind of public ritual act of execution plausibly understood as a punishment for breach of covenant" and believes that "it is the curse of cutting up that seems to have formed the basis for the technical phrase 'to enter a covenant'" (Robert Polzin, "*HWQY*ᶜ and Covenantal Institutions in Early Israel," *Harvard Theological Review*, vol. 62, no. 2, April 1969, 231, 238). Notice that Nehemiah 10:29 is clarified in the Joseph Smith Translation to read that some Israelites "entereth into an oath, that a curse should come upon them if they did not walk in God's law."

69. See David R. Seely, "The Raised Hand of God as an Oath Gesture," in Astrid B. Beck, ed., *Fortunate the Eyes That See* (Grand Rapids, Michigan: Eerdmans, 1995), 411–21. Another scholar has noted that in the ancient world the raised right hand was the sign of the Cosmocrator, the ruler or King of the cosmos, and was symbolic of his power, omnipotence, and salvation. This sign is believed to have originated among the religious rituals of the Semites and can be seen in various biblical passages where Jehovah is spoken of as raising his right hand. This gesture is frequently displayed in early Christian iconography, being used both by Jesus Christ and his disciples (see the chapter entitled "The Gesture

of Power: Cosmocrator's Sign" in Hans P. L'Orange, *Studies on the Iconography of Cosmic Kingship in the Ancient World* [New Rochelle, New York: Caratzas Brothers, 1982], 139–70). "Only the one having received [Jehovah's] initiation is in possession of this powerful hand" (ibid., 161). "The gesture strengthens the spoken word of prayer. . . . Not only the prayer, but every spoken word is . . . strengthened by stretching out the right hand" (ibid., 165). "It is the gods themselves who in this gesture intervene in the sphere of mortals" (ibid., 147).

70. Allison A. Trites, *The New Testament Concept of Witness* (New York: Cambridge University Press, 1977), 32.

71. Strong, *The New Strong's Exhaustive Concordance of the Bible*, Hebrew and Aramaic Dictionary, 10, word, #543. The Hebrew word *amen* is derived from *aman* which means "to be true or certain . . . to go to the right hand" (ibid., word #539).

72. In comparing the phraseology of this petition with the following passages in the Psalms it would appear that there was a specific set of words that accompanied certain Hebrew prayers. "Hear me when I call, O God . . . hear my prayer" (Psalm 4:1); "Give ear to my words, O Lord" (5:1); "Consider and hear me, O Lord my God" (13:3); "Hear . . . O Lord . . . give ear unto my prayer" (17:1); "hear, O Lord my God" (38:15); "Hear my prayer, O Lord, and give ear unto my cry" (39:12); "Hear my prayer, O God; give ear to the words of my mouth" (54:2); "Give ear to my prayer, O God" (55:1); "Hear my cry, O God; attend unto my prayer" (61:1); "Hear my voice, O God, in my prayer" (64:1); "my prayer is unto thee, O Lord . . . hear me" (69:13); "O Lord God of hosts, hear my prayer: give ear, O God of Jacob" (84:8); "Give ear, O Lord, unto my prayer" (86:6); "O Lord God . . . Let my prayer come before thee: incline thine ear unto my cry" (88:1–2); "Hear my prayer, O Lord, and let my cry come unto thee. . . . Incline thine ear unto me" (102:1–2); "Lord, hear my voice" (130:2); "hear the voice of my supplications, O Lord" (140:6); "Lord . . . give ear unto my voice, when I cry unto thee" (141:1); "Hear my prayer, O Lord, give ear to my supplications" (143:1).

73. Even though the text in the King James Bible seems to say that the temple priests only raised one hand during the blessing ceremony, Milgrom translates Leviticus 9:22 as: "*Then Aaron lifted his hands (wayyissa' aharon et-yadaw; K./Q. ydyw). A posture of prayer (Psalms 28:2; 134:2), which must be carefully differentiated from nasa' yad 'lift the hand' (singular) for the purpose of taking an oath (e.g., Exodus 6:8; Numbers 14:30; Ezekiel 20:5)*" (Jacob Milgrom, *Leviticus 1–16* [New York: Doubleday, 1991], 586–87). Other sources also confirm that the priests raised both of their hands. "The [priestly] blessing [in Numbers 6:24–26] was given with uplifted hands. In the temple service the priests raised their hands above their heads, while in other places [i.e., the synagogues] they lifted them only to their shoulders" (Isidore Singer, ed., *The Jewish Encyclopedia* [New York: Funk and Wagnalls, 1902], 3:244). Also, when the priestly blessing was pronounced in the synagogues during the Second Temple period (539 B.C.–18 B.C.), the word *Adonai* was substituted for *YHWH*, the sacred name of God (see Frankel and Teutsch, *The Encyclopedia of Jewish Symbols*, 70, 130). The practice of spreading the fingers of each upraised hand during the priestly blessing so as to form the Hebrew letter *šin* (resembling an English W and representing the first letter of the word *šaddai*—meaning "Almighty") may have originated in the 12th century A.D. when the Kabbalistic, or mystic Jews of the rabbinical period, began to display the three Hebrew letters of the word *šaddai* on their *tefillin* boxes and with the straps that were attached to them (ibid., 171).

74. When King Solomon dedicated the Jerusalem Temple, he asked the Lord to consider the supplications of those who spread forth their hands in or toward the temple and answer their petitions based upon what was in their hearts (*see* 1 Kings 8:38–39; 2 Chronicles 6:29–30).

75. Donald W. Parry, "Temple Worship and a Possible Reference to a Prayer Circle in Psalm 24," *Brigham Young University Studies*, vol. 32, no. 4, Fall 1992, 58. This article's premise centers on the meaning of the Hebrew word *dor*, which is translated as "generation" in the King James Bible. Several Old Testament scholars have taken the stance that the "basic meaning underlying [the Hebrew word] *dor* is 'circle.' . . . *Dor* refers more specifically to a 'circle of people,' viz., an assembly" (Botterweck and Ringgren, eds., *Theological Dictionary of the Old Testament*, 3:169–70).

76. Harry M. Orlinsky, ed., *Tanakh: A New Translation of the Holy Scriptures According to the Traditional Hebrew Text* (New York: The Jewish Publication Society, 1985), 1132.

77. Strong, *The New Strong's Exhaustive Concordance of the Bible*, Hebrew and Aramaic Dictionary, 97, word #5437.

78. See Hugh W. Nibley, "The Early Christian Prayer Circle," in Hugh W. Nibley, *Mormonism and Early Christianity* (Salt Lake City: Deseret Book and FARMS, 1987), 45–99.

79. See Gray, *I & II Kings: A Commentary*, 575; Raphael Patai, *On Jewish Folklore* (Detroit: Wayne State University Press, 1983), 157.

80. Sigmund Mowinckel, *He That Cometh* (New York: Abingdon Press, 1954), 63. "It is probable that certain water-purifications had a place in the Israelite royal consecration" (Geo Widengren, "Royal Ideology and the Testaments of the Twelve Patriarchs," in F. F. Bruce, ed., *Promise and Fulfillment* [Edinburgh: T. and T. Clark, 1963], 207).

81. Mythical "unicorns" are mentioned in the King James translation of Numbers 23:22, 24:8, Deuteronomy 33:17, Job 39:9–10, Psalms 22:21, 29:6, 92:10, and Isaiah 34:7. The same Hebrew word (*re'em*) is present in the text of each of these verses. In JST Isaiah 34:7, the Prophet Joseph Smith replaced "unicorns" with "*re'em*," which is the Hebrew word for "wild ox" (see Strong, *The New Strong's Exhaustive Concordance of the Bible*, Hebrew and Aramaic Dictionary, 129, word #7214).

82. For further reading on the royal anointing, see Ake Viberg, *Symbols of Law: A Contextual Analysis of Legal Symbolic Acts in the Old Testament* (Stockholm: Almqvist and Wiksell, 1992), 89–119.

83. Mowinckel, *The Psalms in Israel's Worship*, 1:64. Cooke also translates "in the beauties of holiness" (Psalm 110:3) as "in holy vestments, or in holy array . . . the *king* as standing 'in holy array' (i.e., adorned with the accoutrements of rule) before the people on the occasion of his enthronement" (Gerald Cooke, "The Israelite King as Son of God," *Zeitschrift Für Die Alttestamentliche Wissenschaft*, vol. 73, 1961, 219; emphasis in original; see also 222). The "holy array" translation is also presented in Borsch, *The Son of Man in Myth and History*, 110.

84. Since the king of Israel was considered to be the personification of Adam (see below), we might ask whether his apron somehow imitated the fig leaf apron that was worn by Adam (see Genesis 3:7).

85. Though he was only a prince of the royal household, Jonathan wore both a robe and a sash (see 1 Samuel 18:4).

86. One scholar points out that the "terms used [in Isaiah 22:21] for *robe* and *sash* appear elsewhere only for garb worn by the [temple] priests" (John N. Oswalt, *The Book of Isaiah: Chapters 1–39*

[Grand Rapids, Michigan: Eerdmans, 1986], 422; emphasis in original). There is evidence that some ancient Near Eastern priestesses were designated as *key-bearers* and did in fact carry a key upon their shoulder (see Adam Clarke, *Clarke's Commentary* [Nashville: Abingdon, 1977], 4:105).

87. Buttrick, ed., *The Interpreter's Bible*, 5:293.

88. Albert Barnes, *Barnes' Notes on Isaiah* (New York: Leavitt and Allen Bros., 1847), 1:395; emphasis in original.

89. J. Massyngberde Ford, *Revelation* (Garden City, New York: Doubleday, 1975), 416. There were certain Levitical porters assigned to the opening of the temple doors every morning (*see* 1 Chronicles 9:26–27). This commentary says that they were "in charge of the key of the temple" (ibid., 414). Hurowitz has raised the possibility that there were golden keys associated with the Lord's house in ancient Israel (*see* Victor A. Hurowitz, "Solomon's Golden Vessels (1 Kings 7:48–50) and the Cult of the First Temple" in David P. Wright, David N. Freedman, and Avi Hurvitz, eds., *Pomegranates and Golden Bells* [Winona Lake, Indiana: Eisenbrauns, 1995], 159).

90. "Just as the master possesses the key to that house, and has complete authority with respect to permitting anyone to enter or to leave, and so entire authority over the house, so God will give to Eliakim a key to the house or dynasty of David. This key will be placed upon his shoulder, an expression which means that the responsibility of the Davidic government is to rest as a burden upon Eliakim's shoulder. . . . In that the prophet says, *house of David*, and not merely *house of the king* or *house of Hezekiah*, he is referring not alone to the actual incumbent of the throne, but to its Messianic aspect. . . . the king in Old Testament times was truly a type of the Christ" (Edward J. Young, *The Book of Isaiah* [Grand Rapids, Michigan: Eerdmans, 1980], 2:114–15; emphasis in original).

91. Kittel, ed., *Theological Dictionary of the New Testament*, 3:749. On page 748 of this same source, it is indicated that the "key of the house of David" refers, in the ultimate sense, to "the key to God's eternal palace" i.e., to the heavenly temple.

92. In Ezekiel 21:26 the word *misnepet* is mistranslated as "diadem." This is the same exact Hebrew word used to designate the white linen headdress of the high priest of the temple.

93. Strong, *The New Strong's Exhaustive Concordance of the Bible*, Hebrew and Aramaic Dictionary, 118, word #6616.

94. Blue dye was very expensive to make and thus blue clothing, which was highly prized, was usually worn by royalty (see Esther 8:15; Ezekiel 23:6).

95. See the illustrations in J. D. Douglas and Merrill C. Tenney, eds., *The New International Dictionary of the Bible: Pictorial Edition* (Grand Rapids, Michigan: Zondervan, 1987), 103, 242; Merrill F. Unger, *The New Unger's Bible Dictionary* (Chicago: Moody Press, 1988), 264, 303, 483; Alan Millard, *Treasures from Bible Times* (Sidney: Lion Publishing, 1985), 121; Buttrick, ed., *The Interpreter's Dictionary of the Bible*, 1:273; Charlotte Anker and Russell B. Adams, Jr., eds., *Mesopotamia: The Mighty Kings* (Alexandria, Virginia: Time-Life Books, 1995), 83. Widengren lists the reception of a crown among the ten points of an ideal ritual ascension. The kings of India participated in a ceremony called the *rajasuya* in order that they might obtain access to heaven. "The *rajasuya* is without doubt an ascension ritually accomplished. The very first element of it is the *prayaniya*, a term which translates into 'ascension' . . . The king is clothed in sacred garments ('The garment is connected with all the

gods,' says an ancient text); the garments are said to be marked in special ways, representative of the ceremony undertaken by the king. The garment consists of several parts, one of which is worn on the head (Widengren's crown), the ends of which are tied into the upper garment. Throughout the ritual the king is called by the name of the various gods whom he is impersonating. He is taken back into primordial time and performs the same functions symbolically which the gods and the first king did at that time, by virtue of which *they* obtained heaven. The king is then enthroned on a throne which is addressed as being the navel of kingship and the cosmos" (Spencer J. Palmer, ed., *Deity and Death* [Provo, Utah: BYU Religious Studies Center, 1978], 96; emphasis in original).

96. Notice that in both 2 Kings 11:12 and 2 Chronicles 23:11, the words "gave him" are italicized, meaning that they are not present in the Hebrew text but were added by the King James translators. Thus, the sentence should read: "put the crown upon him, and the testimony." The parallelism between the ʿedut and the objects known as *tefillin* (or *phylacteries* as they are called in the New Testament) is of particular interest. *Tefillin* were small containers with four compartments that held four tiny scrolls inscribed with the basic terms of the covenant made between God and the Israelites at Mount Sinai. For a picture of an ancient *phylactery* from the Qumran caves, see Michael D. Coogan, ed., *The Oxford History of the Biblical World* (New York: Oxford University Press, 1998), plate 20; for other illustrations *see* Roth, ed., *Encyclopaedia Judaica*, 15:899–903. The idea of the Jewish *phylacteries* comes from a literal reading of Exodus 13:8–9 and Deuteronomy 6:8; 11:18. It must be remembered, however, that the "date when the phylactery was introduced [among the Israelites] is unknown" (John L. McKenzie, *Dictionary of the Bible* [Milwaukee, Wisconsin: Bruce Publishing, 1965], 677). Biblical scholars warn that a material or historical connection between the object that is mentioned in Exodus and Deuteronomy and *phylacteries* "is *not* to be assumed" (Botterweck and Ringgren, eds., *Theological Dictionary of the Old Testament*, 5:320; emphasis added). The first mention of *phylacteries* is found in the *Letter of Aristeas,* which has been dated no earlier than 250 B.C. and can perhaps be dated even later in time (see Hayward, *The Jewish Temple: A Non-Biblical Sourcebook,* 26–27). Since *phylacteries* are unknown among the Samaritans, it is the conclusion of some scholars that the custom of wearing *phylacteries* must have developed sometime after the Jewish-Samaritan schism that occurred around the 3rd century B.C. (see Bromiley, ed., *The International Standard Bible Encyclopedia,* 3:864). In other words, *tefillin* or *phylacteries* were a late invention that may have been based upon the earlier royal head ornament known as the ʿedut or "testimony."

97. Herbert G. May, "A Key to the Interpretation of Zechariah's Visions," *Journal of Biblical Literature,* vol. 57, no. 2, June 1938, 181. Widengren is of the opinion that the Hebrew construction of 2 Kings 11:12 "clearly shows that the 'testimony' is a concrete thing that can be placed upon the king much in the same way as the diadem. Since the word ['witness'], is the synonymous designation of ['law'], we obviously see, from this passage, that a copy of the law was not only given to the ruler, but even attached to him at his coronation" (Geo Widengren, *The Ascension of the Apostle and the Heavenly Book* [Uppsala: A. B. Lundequistska Bokhandeln, 1950], 25).

98. Aubrey R. Johnson, *Sacral Kingship in Ancient Israel* (Cardiff: University of Wales Press, 1967), 24. Johnson states in another place that at the coronation of King Jehoash, "he was invested with 'the crown and the testimony (*or* testimonies).' The Hebrew term employed in the latter connection is

the technical one in use to denote the solemn promises or pledges to which one was committed under the terms of a covenant; and it seems clear, therefore, that at his coronation the king was made to wear as a part of the insignia of office a document embodying, in principle at least, the terms of Yahweh's covenant with the House of David" (Aubrey R. Johnson, "Hebrew Conceptions of Kingship," in S. H. Hooke, ed., *Myth, Ritual, and Kingship* [Oxford: Clarendon Press, 1958], 210; emphasis in original). Another writer agrees with the view that the *ʿedut* "was a symbol of a covenantal relationship between king and God" (Tryggve N. D. Mettinger, *King and Messiah: The Civil and Sacral Legitimation of the Israelite Kings* [Lund: Wallin and Dahlom, 1976], 288). And another scholar affirms that "*ʿedut* ('testimony') was a feature of the coronation ritual and is specifically associated with the covenant of Yahweh with the Davidic king" (Gray, *I & II Kings: A Commentary*, 573).

99. Mordechai Cogan and Hayim Tadmor, *II Kings* (New York: Doubleday, 1988), 128.

100. Notice that Psalm 8:4–8 is paralleled by Genesis 1:26. In the Genesis account we read that God gave "man" (in Hebrew the word is *adam*) "dominion" over "all the earth," including the fish, fowl, cattle, and creeping things. In addition, his chief enemy was put under his feet (see Genesis 3:14–15). In the Psalm account, "man" (again, the word is *adam*) is reported to have been given "dominion" over God's creations, including fish, fowl, beasts, and cattle. God "hast put all things under his feet." From these passages there would appear to be a connection between the concepts of Adam, kingship, and dominion—signified by having one's enemies under one's feet.

101. There is some evidence that the attendants of Israelite kings wore shoes that covered the entire foot (see David N. Freedman, ed., *The Anchor Bible Dictionary* [New York: Doubleday, 1992], 2:234).

102. Hocart lists the putting on of shoes as one of the common elements of ancient coronation rituals (see A. M. Hocart, *Kingship* [London: Oxford University Press, 1969], 71. For examples, see pages 80, 82, 84, 88, 91, 97). Widengren indicates that in some ancient Mesopotamian circles shoes were donned along with other ritual clothing by kings, priests, and bridegrooms before their "heavenly ascent" (see Geo Widengren, "Heavenly Enthronement and Baptism: Studies in Mandaean Baptism," in Jacob Neusner, ed., *Religions in Antiquity* [Leiden: E. J. Brill, 1968], 553–57).

103. For depictions of ancient Near Eastern kings wearing slippers, see Buttrick, ed., *The Interpreter's Dictionary of the Bible*, 1:273; Pat Alexander, ed., *Eerdmans' Family Encyclopedia of the Bible* (Grand Rapids, Michigan: Eerdmans, 1978), 203; David Alexander and Pat Alexander, eds., *Eerdmans' Handbook to the Bible* (Grand Rapids, Michigan: Eerdmans, 1973), 200; Charlotte Anker, Russell B. Adams, Jr., and Charles J. Hagner, eds., *Persians: Masters of Empire* (Alexandria, Virginia: Time-Life Books, 1995), 84. At his coronation in 800 A.D., the Christian Emperor Charlemagne was shod with special shoes that covered his entire foot (see Herbert Norris, *Church Vestments: Their Origin and Development* [London: J. M. Dent and Sons, 1949], 40). Common people in the ancient Near East wore sandals, and shoes or slippers would have been a sign of high status.

104. See James Hastings, ed., *Encyclopaedia of Religion and Ethics* (New York: Charles Scribner's Sons, 1951), 11:474–75. In this same source, mention is made of "slippers" that were worn in a late Syrian initiation rite (ibid., 475). Special shoes were worn in connection with the kingly coronation rites of ancient India (ibid.). Notice the shoes that are given by the father to the son who returns home to his presence in Luke 15:11–32.

105. The Syrian ceremonial slippers are called *msone*. Since animal products are not permitted in the sanctuary, these slippers cannot be made of leather (Samir Anz, Thomas Joseph, and George Kiraz, "Vestments," 1997, 2, internet manuscript, copy in author's possession).

106. Aziz S. Atiya, ed., *The Coptic Encyclopedia*, (New York: Macmillan, 1991), 5:1478.

107. Both in the ancient Near East generally "and in Israel the custom prevailed that the king should take a new name at his accession" (Mowinckel, *The Psalms in Israel's Worship*, 1:63). For further reading, see A. M. Honeyman, "The Evidence for Regnal Names Among the Hebrews," *Journal of Biblical Literature*, vol. 67, 1948, 13–25. It has been pointed out by one scholar that the new name mentioned in Revelation 3:12 has a definite correlation to ancient coronation practices. "In the giving of a new name to the believer [in Revelation 3:12], we might also see a parallel with the common oriental practice of giving new names to monarchs during the coronation and accession ceremonies" (Richard H. Wilkinson, "The *stylos* of Revelation 3:12 and Ancient Coronation Rites," *Journal of Biblical Literature*, vol. 107, no. 3, September 1988, 500).

108. Gerhard von Rad, *The Problem of the Hexateuch and Other Essays* (New York: McGraw-Hill, 1966), 229.

109. T. David Andersen, "Renaming and Wedding Imagery in Isaiah 62," *Biblica*, vol. 67, no. 1, 1986, 75. One scholar detects in the combination of 2 Kings 24:17 and Ezekiel 17:11–21 a ceremony wherein a king gives a handclasp to the king of Jerusalem, bestows a new name upon him, and enters into a covenant with him by swearing an oath (*see* Viberg, *Symbols of Law*, 37–39).

110. See Otto Eissfeldt, "Renaming in the Old Testament," in Peter R. Ackroyd and Barnabas Lindars, eds., *Words and Meanings* (Cambridge: University Press, 1968), 73.

111. Mowinckel, *He That Cometh*, 66.

112. The Hebrew word *šebet* is translated as "sceptre" in Genesis 49:10; Numbers 24:17; Psalm 45:6; Isaiah 14:5; Ezekiel 19:11, 14; Amos 1:5, 8; Zechariah 10:11.

113. The Hebrew word *mattah* refers to a staff that can be used as a scepter (*see* Strong, *The New Strong's Exhaustive Concordance of the Bible*, Hebrew and Aramaic Dictionary, 76, word #4294). *Mattah* is translated as "staff" in Genesis 38:18, 25; Leviticus 26:26; Psalm 105:16; Isaiah 9:4; 10:5, 15, 24; 14:5; 28:27; 30:32; Jeremiah 48:17; Ezekiel 4:16; 5:16; 14:13. Widengren notes that the "Israelite king in the Old Testament carries a staff, and in the royal Psalms 2 and 110 this term is used in the [Septuagint]" (Widengren, "Royal Ideology and the Testaments of the Twelve Patriarchs," 205).

114. In some ancient Near Eastern iconography "it is a twig from the tree of life that the king or priest holds as his sceptre" (Lundquist, "The Common Temple Ideology of the Ancient Near East," 69).

115. Widengren, "Royal Ideology and the Testaments of the Twelve Patriarchs," 206.

116. Ginzberg, *The Legends of the Jews*, 2:291–93.

117. See ibid., 5:165. For further reading, see Brent L. Holbrook, "The Sword of Laban as a Symbol of Divine Authority and Kingship," *Journal of Book of Mormon Studies*, vol. 2, no. 1, Spring 1993, 39–72; Daniel N. Rolph, "Prophets, Kings, and Swords: The Sword of Laban and Its Possible Pre-Laban Origin," ibid., 73–79; John A. Tvedtnes, "*Rod* and *Sword* as the Word of God," ibid., vol. 5, no. 2, 1996, 148–55.

118. Patai, *On Jewish Folklore*, 139.

119. Notice that because of the blasphemous arrogance of the cherub/king of Ezekiel 28:11–17, he was to be destroyed by "swords" (vs. 7) and by "fire" (vs. 18). These are the same destructive elements that are associated with the cherubim of the Garden of Eden (see Genesis 3:24).

120. See, for example, the material presented in Geo Widengren, *The King and the Tree of Life in Ancient Near Eastern Religion* (Uppsala: A. B. Lundequistska Bokhandeln, 1951), 28–31.

121. See Theodor H. Gaster, *Myth, Legend, and Custom in the Old Testament* (New York: Harper and Row, 1969), 779–80. "The goblet or chalice evidently represents that primordial water which . . . the new king had to absorb in order to acquire divine wisdom and power" (ibid., 780). "From the glyptics and texts of the ancient Near East, we know that a cup in the right (usually) hand of a god or a king is a common feature. . . . Many examples of the cup motif and its religious importance are also found in the Old Testament. For instance, Yahweh is sometimes said to have a cup in his hand, which can pour forth blessings or curses and disaster; cf. Pss. 16:5; 75:9; 116:13; Isa. 51:17ff; Jer. 25:15ff; 51:7; Ob. 15; Hab. 2:16" (G. W. Ahlström, "Heaven on Earth—At Hazor and Arad," in Birger A. Pearson, ed., *Religious Syncretism in Antiquity* [Missoula, Montana: Scholars Press, 1975], 73–74). It is believed by some scholars that Psalm 110 is the text spoken during the king's coronation ritual. The Psalm may be divided into "the Enthronement (vs. 1), the Investiture (vs. 2), especially with the sceptre, the Acclamation (vs. 3), the Ordination as priest (vs. 4), the Promise of victory over enemies (vss. 5–6), and the sacramental cup of water from the Holy Well (vs. 7)" (Aage Bentzen, *King and Messiah* [London: Lutterworth Press, 1955], 23).

122. Benzion Halper, *Post-Biblical Hebrew Literature: An Anthology—English Translation* (Philadelphia: The Jewish Publication Society of America, 1943), 2:65–66. It would appear that one of the other blessings bestowed upon the Israelite king related to the sacred name of God. "Psalm 118:26 appears to reflect a liturgical occasion when the king is blessed by the priests, 'Blessed be he who enters in the name of YHWH' (26a). The priests then bless the festival congregation, 'We bless you from the house of YHWH' (26b). J. W. Wevers has suggested another translation for 26a, 'Blessed be the one coming with the name YHWH' for, 'The one coming into the sanctuary is to be entrusted with the divine name which he may there cultically invoke.' The priests would normally be the persons so entrusted, although the king also could bless in the name of YHWH (2 Samuel 6:18)" (G. H. Parke-Taylor, *Yahweh: The Divine Name in the Bible* [Waterloo, Ontario: Wilfrid Laurier University Press, 1975], 14).

123. Borsch, *The Son of Man in Myth and History*, 95; *see* nt. 2.

124. Ibid., 95–96. Widengren also lists participation in heavenly secrets or mysteries as one of the firmly established themes of the ancient Near Eastern pattern of enthronement (see Geo Widengren, "Baptism and Enthronement in Some Jewish-Christian Gnostic Documents," in S. G. F. Brandon, ed., *The Savior God* [New York: Barnes and Noble, 1963], 206, 213).

125. Widengren, "Royal Ideology and the Testaments of the Twelve Patriarchs," 203, 209–11. Levi inherits "not only the priestly but also the royal position" in the Testament of Levi, and he is also referred to as a "son" of God. Furthermore, he is divinely commissioned to distribute the "light of knowledge" among the Israelites and to declare God's "mysteries" unto them (ibid., 203, 209–10).

126. In both of these passages the Hebrew word *raᶜ* is translated as "bad," but it is the very same word that is translated as "evil" in Genesis 2:9, 17; 3:5, 22, where reference is made to "the tree of the knowledge of good and evil."

127. See the amendation in footnote *6a* of the LDS edition of the King James Bible.

128. C. R. North, "The Religious Aspects of Hebrew Kingship," *Zeitschrift Für Die Alttestamentliche Wissenschaft*, vol. 50, 1932, 27. This idea of the king being taken to the bosom of Jehovah is also discussed briefly in Cooke, "The Israelite King as Son of God," 207. The wording of Proverbs 5:20 implies that to be "taken to the bosom" of someone is to be embraced by them.

129. The word translated as "branch" in Psalm 80:15 is *ben* and should be translated as "son." Borsch presents his translation of Psalm 80:14–17 as, "[14] Turn again, O God of hosts. Look down from heaven, and see; have regard for this vine, [15] the stock which thy right hand planted (and upon the Son whom thou hast reared for thyself). [16] They have burned it with fire, they have cut it down; may they perish at the rebuke of thy countenance. [17] But let thy hand be upon the Man (*iš*) of thy right hand, upon the Son of Man (*ben adam*) whom thou hast made strong for thyself." He then goes on to say that the Son referred to in these verses is the king who was viewed as the Son of God (Borsch, *The Son of Man in Myth and History*, 116–17).

130. Gaster, *Myth, Legend, and Custom in the Old Testament*, 775. For a Mesopotamian ritual text that speaks of a deity grasping the hand of a king "from behind the curtains" and the king's subsequent entrance into the deity's throne room, see E. Jan Wilson, "The Biblical Term *lir'ot et penei yhwh* in the Light of Akkadian Cultic Material," *Akkadica*, vol. 93, May/August 1995, 24.

131. Hans-Joachim Kraus, *Theology of the Psalms* (Minneapolis, Minnesota: Augsburg Publishing, 1986), 173. Some scholars have noted that the handclasp was, in the ancient world, closely connected with the concepts of *oath* and *covenant*. "The giving of a hand may function as an oath-sign by solemnly depicting the covenant commitment. . . . [Reference here is made specifically to] giving the right hand. . . . [T]here are a number of references to handshakes in extrabiblical texts and in ancient Near Eastern iconography which support the biblical evidence for the use of this gesture as a pact or covenant-making rite" (Gordon P. Hugenberger, *Marriage as a Covenant* [Leiden: E. J. Brill, 1994], 211–12).

132. Keith Crim, ed., *The Interpreter's Dictionary of the Bible: Supplementary Volume* (Nashville: Abingdon Press, 1976), 190. One biblical commentator says of the phrase "hold my right hand: . . . that to be grasped by one's right hand is symbolic of being honoured, as a king is raised to dignity by his god (cf. Isaiah 45:1). It is possible that the expression was derived from the royal ritual" (A. A. Anderson, *The Book of Psalms: Volume 2, Psalms 73–150* [Grand Rapids, Michigan: Eerdmans, 1981], 535 [quoting Gressmann]). Isaiah 41:10, 13–14 speaks of how the Lord, who is the "redeemer, the Holy One of Israel," will take hold of the right hand of the men of Israel and strengthen them. The wording in these verses in similar to Psalm 63:8 where King David says that he is upheld by the right hand of the Lord (see also Psalms 18:35; 63:8; 73:23; 89:13, 20–21; 139:10). Isaiah 42:6 speaks of the handclasp in connection with "a covenant." Speaking of those who "take hold of my covenant" in Isaiah 56:4–5, the Lord says, "Even unto them will I give in mine house [i.e., the temple] and within my walls a *hand* and a name better than of sons and of daughters: I will give them an everlasting name" (The translation "hand and name" can be found in Jay P. Green, Sr., ed., *The Interlinear Bible: Hebrew-Greek-*

English, 2d ed. [Grand Rapids, Michigan: Baker Book House, 1986], 573 and John D. W. Watts, *Isaiah 34–66* [Waco, Texas: Word Books, 1987], 243).

133. See Widengren, *The King and the Tree of Life in Ancient Near Eastern Religion*, 59. Widengren lists the *hieros gamos*, or sacred marriage, as the last of the ritual motifs of the ideal Mesopotamian enthronement ceremony (see Widengren, *The Ascension of the Apostle and the Heavenly Book*, 19). Borsch likewise calls sacred marriage the "final stage" in the pattern of events that were central to the ancient Near Eastern rites of kingship (Borsch, *The Son of Man in Myth and History*, 96). The "deification of kings in Mesopotamia was closely associated with their sacred marriage" (E. O. James, "The Sacred Kingship and the Priesthood," in *The Sacral Kingship* [Leiden: E. J. Brill, 1959], 66).

134. See Keith R. Crim, *The Royal Psalms* (Richmond, Virginia: John Knox Press, 1962), 92–96. "Quite probably this hymn was used regularly for royal weddings and became a standard item in the cultic poems of kingship" (ibid., 94). Patai likewise subscribes to the view that Psalm 45 was a royal marriage hymn (see Patai, *On Jewish Folklore*, 135; see also Roland de Vaux, *Ancient Israel* [New York: McGraw-Hill, 1961], 1:109). The "great New Year ritual of the ancient Near East—which was also the reenthronement festival—contained a ceremonial sacred marriage which, in one case at least, was celebrated in a special room on the top of the temple building" (Patai, *On Jewish Folklore*, 123). This room is referred to as both the "sacred hut" and the "bridal chamber" in Johnson, "Hebrew Conceptions of Kingship," 226–27.

135. Notice that Jehovah's bride is called "Zion" in Isaiah 49:14–18.

136. "A clue that Israelite brides may once have been anointed lies in the surviving term for betrothal, *qiddušin* ('consecration'), and in the present-day betrothal formula, 'Behold you are consecrated [*mequddešet*] to me' (cf. *t. Qidd.* 2b)" (Milgrom, *Leviticus 1–16*, 555).

137. Notice that before King David could worship in the temple he had to be washed and anointed and then change his apparel (see 2 Samuel 12:20).

138. Since the context of this passage is marriage, it would be natural for the garments that are listed to correspond to the wedding attire of this time period. There are several verses in the Bible where a veil is mentioned in connection with marriage (see Genesis 24:65–67; 38:14, 19; Ruth 3:3, 15) and one passage where a veil is implied (see Genesis 29:21–25). "The cuneiform sources [of ancient Mesopotamia] show that the bride, referred to as *kallatu* (cf. Hebrew *kalla*), was indeed commonly veiled. The word *kallatu* is etymologically related to the verb *kullulu* 'to veil' or 'to crown.'" However, "the veil did not symbolize the actual state of matrimony but its judicial anticipation, in other words, the betrothal" (see Revelation 19:7–9). It was the practice in some ancient Near Eastern societies for priestesses to have their heads covered "like a bride" when they were invested with the robes of their office (Karel van der Toorn, "The Significance of the Veil in the Ancient Near East," in David P. Wright, David N. Freedman, and Avi Hurvitz, eds., *Pomegranates and Golden Bells* [Winona Lake, Indiana: Eisenbrauns, 1995], 330–31, 333). It would appear from the context of Numbers 5:16–18 that at least some of the married women who entered into the tabernacle courtyard were accustomed to wearing veils.

Women's veils are mentioned in the New Testament in a ritual context. The Apostle Paul, in speaking of the "ordinances" that he had delivered unto the Saints, directed that when women prayed and prophesied, they were to have their heads *covered* (see 1 Corinthians 11:2–13). The Joseph Smith Translation of this epistle brings verse 10 into line with the rest of the passage by changing *power* to *covering*—"For this cause ought the woman to have *a covering* on her head because of the angels." It should be noted that the word translated in verses 5 and 13 as "uncovered" is *akatakaluptos* and means "unveiled" (Strong, *The New Strong's Exhaustive Concordance of the Bible*, Greek Dictionary, 4, word #177) and the word translated in verse 6 as "covered" is *katakalupto* and means "to *cover wholly*, i.e. *veil*" (ibid., Greek Dictionary, 46, word #2619, emphasis in original). The word "power" in verse 10 may have also been mistranslated because of the fact that in Aramaic the roots of the words *power* and *veil* are spelled the same. It is therefore of great interest to note that there are several ancient manuscripts of verse 10 that contain the word *veil* instead of *power* (see Adam Clarke, *Clarke's Commentary* [Nashville: Abingdon Press, 1977], 6:252; Buttrick, ed., *The Interpreter's Bible*, 10:128). When all of these possible changes are taken into consideration, Paul's teachings on women's veils are brought into sharper focus. It is clear that Paul's words reflect a firmly established church practice, as there are a great many early Christian artworks that depict women with upraised hands in prayer and wearing white robes with white veils upon their heads (see, for example, André Grabar, *Early Christian Art: From the Rise of Christianity to the Death of Theodosius* [New York: Odyssey Press, 1968], 66, 100, 101, 120, 121, 130, 137, 142, 210, 211, 242). One of these Christian artworks depicts a woman in the prayer posture with the veil covering her entire face (see V. Davin, *Les Antiquités Chrétiennes Rapportées a la Cappella Greca* [Paris: Gaume et Cie, 1892], plate II). It is known from historical records that some of the early Christians wore veils when they participated in ceremonies of initiation (see Susan Ackerman, "The Deception of Isaac, Jacob's Dream at Bethel, and Incubation on an Animal Skin," in Gary A. Anderson and Saul M. Olyan, eds., *Priesthood and Cult in Ancient Israel* [Sheffield, England: JSOT Press, 1991], 99, nt. 3).

But why were early Christian women required to wear veils during prayer (speaking with God) and while exercising the gift of prophesy (speaking for God)? One should notice, first of all, that Paul's comments on the veiling of women have definite marriage overtones (see 1 Corinthians 11: 3, 11) and they center upon Adam and Eve and the maintainance of the order, or hierarchy, of creation (see 1 Corinthians 11:3, 8–9, 12; see also 1 Timothy 2:12–13; Ephesians 5:22–23). Joseph Smith stated that Paul was aware of all of the ordinances and blessings of the church, including the privilege of coming into the physical presence of "an innumerable company of angels, hav[ing] communion with [them] and receiv[ing] instruction from them" (*WJS*, 10). The Prophet Joseph, citing Hebrews 12:22–24, testified that some of the early Christians did, in fact, stand in the presence of heavenly beings (see *WJS*, 253–54). Paul, in his comments, explained that women wore their veil "*because of the angels*" (1 Corinthians 11:10; emphasis added), and this seems to be the key to understanding the veil's general symbolism. Paul implied on one occasion that the activities of the Saints were seen or witnessed by "God, and the Lord Jesus Christ, and the elect *angels*" (1 Timothy 5:21; emphasis added). According to Joseph Smith, all of the ordinances of the gospel constitute *signs* to God and his *angels,* and unless they are carried out in the divinely prescribed manner, mortals cannot receive the blessings that are attached to them (see *WJS*, 108; compare D&C 82:10). The veil, therefore, may have been a *sign* to unseen *angels* that a woman honoured and maintained *the order of creation* that was established by God, and she was therefore entitled to heavenly blessings (such as the gift of prophesy). Paul did not teach that the *order of creation* meant women were inferior to men for, as he explained, "neither is the man without the woman, neither the woman without the man, in the Lord" (1 Corinthians 11:11).

139. The term "badger's skin" is a mistranslation of the Hebrew word *tahas*. The word, according to some scholars, should be rendered "dolphin's skin" (Frank M. Cross, Jr., "The Priestly Tabernacle in the Light of Recent Research," in Truman G. Madsen, ed., *The Temple in Antiquity* [Provo, Utah: BYU Religious Studies Center, 1984], 95–96). The word *tahas* appears only in this passage from Ezekiel and in a few biblical passages that deal directly with the tabernacle. It is known that in the marriage rites of some ancient Near Eastern cultures the "officiating ministers bound sandals on the feet of the newly-wedded pair." This ceremony "may have symbolized the marriage contract between them" (James Hastings, ed., *Encyclopaedia of Religion and Ethics* [New York: Charles Scribner's Sons, 1951], 12:149–50; see Deuteronomy 25:5–10; Ruth 4:5–10).

140. In the dedicatory prayer of the temple, King Solomon petitioned, "let thy priests, O Lord God, be clothed with salvation" (2 Chronicles 6:41).

141. Frankel and Teutsch, *The Encyclopedia of Jewish Symbols*, 38. Patai concurs that during the wedding ceremony the bride and groom were accorded royal status (see Patai, *On Jewish Folklore*, 121; see also Samuel N. Kramer, *The Sacred Marriage Rite* [Bloomington: Indiana University Press, 1969], 88).

142. Fred. H. Wight, *Manners and Customs of Bible Lands* (Chicago: Moody Press, 1953), 130.

143. Strong, *The New Strong's Exhaustive Concordance of the Bible*, Hebrew and Aramaic Dictionary, 46, word #2645 and word #2646.

144. For a color reconstruction, see Ralph Gower, *The New Manners and Customs of Bible Times* (Chicago: Moody Press, 1987), 68–69.

145. Marvin R. Wilson, *Our Father Abraham: Jewish Roots of the Christian Faith* (Grand Rapids, Michigan: Eerdmans, 1989), 203; see the section entitled "Marriage and Sinai: Two Covenants Compared" (ibid., 203–208). For another discussion on this subject called "The Wedding of God and Israel," see Jon D. Levenson, *Sinai and Zion* (Minneapolis, Minnesota: Winston Press, 1985), 75–80.

146. Jewish tradition indicates that the first *Sukkot* was celebrated at the foot of Mount Sinai (see John A. Tvedtnes, "King Benjamin and the Feast of Tabernacles," in John M. Lundquist and Stephen D. Ricks, eds., *By Study and Also By Faith* [Salt Lake City: Deseret Book and FARMS, 1990], 2:199). The Jewish historian Flavius Josephus states that the Israelites had pitched their tents around the foot of Mount Sinai before the Lord came down upon it to reveal his law unto them (see William Whiston, trans., *The Works of Josephus: Complete and Unabridged*, updated ed. [Peabody, Massachusetts: Hendrickson Publishers, 1987], 84, *Antiquities*, 3.5.1–2).

147. Strong, *The New Strong's Exhaustive Concordance of the Bible*, Hebrew and Aramaic Dictionary, 99, word #5521.

148. Widengren notes that the central idea of ancient Sumerian religion was a holy garden of a divinity wherein was found the tree of life and the water of life. "In this garden too is erected the hut, built from branches and twigs taken from the trees of this garden of paradise, the dwelling where the holy marriage is celebrated." The Sumerian king, who represented the divinity in certain rituals, underwent purification ceremonies in a hut before his own sacred marriage took place (see Widengren, *The*

King and the Tree of Life in Ancient Near Eastern Religion, 59). In the view of other scholars, the booth of the Feast of Tabernacles "is simply an adaptation of what was originally the bridal chamber connected with the sacred marriage and its reinterpretation in terms of the historical traditions of the Hebrews" (Johnson, "Hebrew Conceptions of Kingship," 227).

149. See Singer, ed., *The Jewish Encyclopedia*, 6:506.

150. Patai, *On Jewish Folklore*, 124. On page 154 of this same study, the author lists "ceremonial marriage in a special hut" as one of the features of the ancient Hebrew kingship rituals.

151. Erwin R. Goodenough, *By Light, Light: The Mystic Gospel of Hellenistic Judaism* (New Haven, Connecticut: Yale University Press, 1935), 95–96, 256. Other scholarly sources verify that among at least some of the ancient Israelites "the Holy of Holies . . . represented . . . a Nuptial Chamber" (Raphael Patai, *Man and Temple in Ancient Jewish Myth and Ritual* [London: Thomas Nelson and Sons, 1947], 89).

152. See Ginzberg, *The Legends of the Jews*, 3:159; Raphael Patai, *The Hebrew Goddess*, 3d ed. (Detroit: Wayne State University Press, 1990), 84.

153. It is apparent from the account of the first marriage in the Garden of Eden that Adam and Eve's union was meant to last forever since they were joined together by God while they were in an immortal condition. In Ecclesiastes 3:14 we read that "whatsoever God doeth, it shall be forever." Some readers of the New Testament, however, might conclude from the remarks of Jesus Christ in Matthew 22:23–33, Mark 12:18–27, and Luke 20:27–40 that Israelite marriages were not meant to be of an eternal duration. In these passages we are told that the Sadducees, who did not believe in the resurrection, approached the Savior with a question about whether a certain type of union called a levirate marriage would have any binding validity in the resurrected state. The premise of levirate marriage was that if a man was married but died without producing a son his brother would marry his wife and that couple's firstborn son would be considered the child of the deceased brother. Thus, the name of the deceased brother would be perpetuated on the earth through the firstborn son. This practice, which predated the time of Moses (*see* Genesis 38:6–10), was enjoined as a "duty" upon the Israelites under the Law of Moses. This particular duty, however, could be declined by the living brother if he so chose (see Deuteronomy 25:5–10). The Sadducees asked the Savior who the wife would belong to in the resurrected state if, after her initial marriage, she became the wife of six succeeding levirate husbands and they all died without producing any offspring by her.

The Savior's answer to the Sadducees must be understood from several different perspectives. First and foremost, it must be remembered that John the Baptist referred to the Sadducees as the "offspring (*gennema*) of vipers" (Matthew 3:7) and the Savior directed his disciples not to share "holy" teachings with such people (Matthew 7:6). We, therefore, need not suppose that the Lord's answer to the Sadducees' question was meant to teach them any of the deeper precepts of the gospel. Jesus Christ clearly taught his disciples that husbands and wives joined by the power of God were not to be separated (see Matthew 19:4–6; Mark 10:6–9). The Saints were also plainly told that husbands and wives were to become "heirs together" (1 Peter 3:7) for "neither is the man without the woman, neither the woman without the man, *in the Lord*" (1 Corinthians 11:11; emphasis added). It would only make sense that once Christ delegated the power of God ("the keys of the kingdom") to his Twelve Apostles so that they could bind things on earth and have them bound eternally in the heavens, they would use that power to join husbands and wives in an everlasting bond (see Matthew 16:19; 18:18).

Second, it needs to be pointed out that the very question posed to the Savior concerning levirate marriages and eternal relationships was often a matter of debate between the Sadducees and the Pharisees. The Pharisees taught that the woman in question would be the wife of the first husband in the resurrection (see J. R. Dummelow, ed., *The One Volume Bible Commentary* [New York: Macmillan, 1956], 698; H. D. M. Spence and Joseph S. Exell, eds., *The Pulpit Commentary: Luke* [Grand Rapids, Michigan: Eerdmans, 1962], 16:169). And, indeed, the Old Testament scriptures that speak of levirate marriage (see Genesis 38:6–10; Deuteronomy 25:5–10) indicate that even if a man married his deceased brother's wife, she was still considered to be *his brother's wife*. The Sadducees did not believe either in the resurrection nor in the existence of angels (see Acts 23:8), and so in responding to their question the Savior affirmed the reality of both. He also rebuked the Sadducees because they did "greatly err," not knowing the scriptures nor the *"power of God."* The Joseph Smith Translation of Mark 12:24 adds that the Sadducees did not *know* or *understand* what the scriptures said.

Third, the three New Testament texts which relate this incident make it clear that Jesus Christ was answering a question that was centered on an earthly rite that was designed to provide an earthly blessing. In answering the Sadducees the Lord specifically stated that those who participated in that type of earthly marital union would neither marry nor be given in marriage in the resurrected state but would find themselves in the same condition as the "angels" in heaven. This means, according to D&C 132:15–17, that they would remain separate and single throughout eternity. The account found in Mark 12:23–25 helps to clarify this point. The Sadducees asked: "In the resurrection therefore, when *they* shall rise, whose wife shall she be of them? For the seven had her to wife. And Jesus answering said unto them . . . when *they* shall rise from the dead, *they* neither marry, nor are given in marriage; but are as the angels which are in heaven" (emphasis added). And why would they be denied the companionship of a spouse in the heavenly world? Because, said the Savior, they were the "children of *this* world" (Luke 20:34; emphasis added; see also John 17:14–16), not the "children of light" who accepted and followed his teachings (see Luke 16:8; John 8:23; 12:36; Ephesians 5:6–8; 1 Thessalonians 5:5).

Finally, some scholars believe that the story used by the Sadducees to form their question may have been one found in the apocryphal book of Tobit, which was written between 250 and 175 B.C. and has been discovered among the Dead Sea Scrolls (see William L. Lane, *The Gospel According to Mark* [Grand Rapids, Michigan: Eerdmans, 1974], 427). Within this book is the story of a woman who, after her husband died without producing children, married six brothers under the levirate duty. Unfortunately, each of the six brothers died on their wedding day and therefore did not produce any offspring either. When the Savior told the Sadducees that they did not know the scriptures, he may have been referring to the fact that in this story the woman ended up successfully marrying an eighth man with the approval of heaven and they were joined to each other "forever" (Carey A. Moore, *Tobit: A New Translation with Introduction and Commentary* [New York: Doubleday, 1996], 216). In one version of this story we read that during this couple's wedding ceremony they took each other by the right hand while the officiator pronounced the blessing: "The God of Abraham and the God of Isaac and the God of Jacob be with you, and *may he join you together* and fulfill his blessing in you" (ibid., 222;

emphasis added; see Matthew 19:6 and Mark 10:9). For further reading, see David H. Yarn, Jr., "Inasmuch as Latter-day Saints believe in marriage for eternity, how do we explain Jesus' teachings in Matthew 22:29–30?" *Ensign*, February 1986, 34–35.

154. Bruce M. Metzger and Michael D. Coogan, eds., *The Oxford Companion to the Bible* (New York: Oxford University Press, 1993), 795. A Coptic document from the Nag Hammadi library, known as the Gospel of Philip, reveals that some of the early gnostic Christians believed in the concept of eternal marriage. "Gnosis" is defined as "knowledge of the divine mysteries reserved for an elite" group. The "sacrament of the bridal-chamber" was the highest initiation ritual among these gnostics. It was considered to be a "mystery" and was thus kept secret, was associated with "the Holy of Holies" of the temple, and was designed to bring about one's "perfection." This ritual was deemed to be absolutely necessary: "one *must* receive the bridal-chamber here in order to obtain it in the beyond" (Jorunn J. Buckley, "A Cult-Mystery in The Gospel of Philip," *Journal of Biblical Literature*, vol. 99, no. 4, December 1980, 569–72, 576–77; emphasis in original). Some scholars believe that the bridal-chamber was "mirrored" (ibid., 575). While "the nature of the [gnostic marriage] rite is not altogether clear" the Gospel of Philip does state that, "Those who have been united in the bridechamber cannot be separated again" (Robert M. Grant, "The Mystery of Marriage in the Gospel of Philip," *Vigiliae Christianae*, vol. 15, 1961, 133–34).

155. Hugenberger, *Marriage as a Covenant*, 164–65. "The fact that the 'bone of my bones' formula is well-attested elsewhere within the Old Testament helps to identify these words as a covenant-forming *verba solemnia*" (ibid., 230; emphasis in original. Notice also the 'flesh and bones' imagery in Ephesians 5:30–32, where the metaphorical marriage between Jesus Christ [husband] and the Church [wife] is spoken of). If Adam's naming of Eve "is understood in terms of covenant concepts, there is an especially intriguing parallel for consideration. H. Blocher observes that ancient suzerains often (re)named their covenant partners when entering into a covenant. . . . In terms of this background, Adam names Eve 'woman' or better 'wife' at the moment when they enter into a covenant (of marriage)" (ibid., 164, nt. 162).

156. The King James translators rendered the Hebrew word *male'* as "replenish" in Genesis 1:28 and 9:1 (the only places in the KJV where this English word is found) but in both cases the word could be translated as "fill" as it is in Genesis 1:22.

157. See Merrill F. Unger, *The New Unger's Bible Dictionary* (Chicago: Moody Press, 1988), 818; Wight, *Manners and Customs of Bible Lands*, 131.

158. For specific parallels, see the commentary and footnotes in Patai, *On Jewish Folklore*, 120–23.

159. Bentzen, *King and Messiah*, 42.

160. Ibid., 11–12, 16. According to Ringgren, "one thing can be stated with assurance: on the great festivals, something took place in the temple that could be described as seeing the deeds of Yahweh. Comparative evidence suggests a cultic drama, which would, so to speak, renew the event that took place in the past, so that its effects would be actualized once more and made productive for the people participating in the cult" (Helmer Ringgren, *Israelite Religion* [Philadelphia: Fortress Press, 1966], 183).

161. See Stephen D. Ricks, "Liturgy and Cosmogony: The Ritual Use of Creation Accounts in the Ancient Near East," in Parry, ed., *Temples of the Ancient World: Ritual and Symbolism*, 120–22.

162. Bentzen, *King and Messiah*, 17.

163. Herbert G. May, "The King in the Garden of Eden: A Study of Ezekiel 28:12–19" in Bernhard W. Anderson and Walter Harrelson, eds., *Israel's Prophetic Heritage* (New York: Harper and Brothers, 1962), 171.

164. See J. N. M. Wijngaards, *The Dramatization of Salvific History in the Deuteronomic Schools* (Leiden: E. J. Brill, 1969), 31, 46–52, 57, 62–66, 106–108. "Cult dramas represent the mythical events of the prehistorical, timeless world of origins. They express in dramatic form the profound laws of existence: creation, fertility and death, the relationship of the gods to mankind, the basis of human kingship and of priestly rites. Such cult dramas belong to the category of *collective rituals* which have been defined as fixed rituals which move in the sacral sphere and which express the norms, values, aims and expectations of the group according to accepted, traditional forms. The individual benefits much from his participation in these rituals: he is better integrated into the community; his emotions are directed towards the objects of the cult and his intellectual conceptions are clarified. Moreover, through the cult drama the individual takes part in the divine realities which are brought about by it" (ibid., 67; emphasis in original).

CHAPTER FIVE

Early Christians and the House of the Lord

The magnificent temple built by King Solomon stood on Mount Zion for more than 350 years. Then in 586 B.C. King Nebuchadnezzar of Babylon besieged Jerusalem, ransacked the treasures and golden vessels in the house of the Lord, and took many of the Israelites in Jerusalem captive (*see* 2 Kings 24:10–16). Eleven years later the Babylonians returned. This time they stole the remaining ritual and decorative objects from the temple and then destroyed it (*see* 2 Kings 25:1–17).

In the year 539 B.C., King Cyrus of Persia overthrew the Babylonian empire and issued a decree that allowed the Jews to return to their homeland. In addition, he gave back the temple vessels that Nebuchadnezzar had stolen and declared that the Lord had commanded him to rebuild the Jerusalem Temple (*see* Ezra 1:1–11; 6:3–5). The foundation for a new temple was laid shortly thereafter (*see* Ezra 5:16) but the main work of construction did not begin until the second year of the reign of King Darius (522–486 B.C.). This temple was completed and dedicated unto the Lord in the year 516 B.C. (*see* Ezra 6:15–16). According to Jewish tradition there were five things missing from the temple of Zerubbabel that had previously been available in the temple of Solomon: (1) the holy fire kindled upon the altar by Jehovah, (2) the *Shekinah* cloud that displayed God's glory, (3) the Urim and Thummim, (4) the spirit of prophecy, and (5) the ark of the covenant.[1]

Unfortunately, the temple built by Zerubbabel went through a series of extreme desecrations, plunderings, and pollutions by Israelites and non-Israelites alike. At one point it fell into such physical disrepair that shrubs were growing in its courtyards. In the year 165 B.C., Judas Maccabeus restored and cleansed this temple for its ordained use as a holy house of God.[2] Herod the Great became the king of Judea in 37 B.C,. and in an attempt to gain favor among the Jews, he commenced, about 20 B.C., to rebuild the Jerusalem Temple on a much grander scale. The Jewish historian

Flavius Josephus informs us that the temple structure itself was completed during the year 18 B.C. after only 17 months of construction, even though the entire temple complex was not finished until the year 64 A.D.[3] It was this temple that stood upon Mount Zion when the Savior was sent from the heavens to once again offer the descendants of Jacob the fulness of the gospel and all of its attendant blessings.

SYMBOLISM

Several symbolic aspects of the temple built by Herod are deserving of our attention. These include the Foundation Stone, the golden grapevine, the four crowns, the golden lamp, and the decorated veil leading into the Holy Place. Let us briefly examine each of these symbols.

Foundation Stone

Since the ark of the covenant had disappeared by the time the temple was rebuilt by Zerubbabel, there was no longer a representation of the throne of God inside the Holy of Holies. When the temple was rebuilt by King Herod, however, a hewn rock was placed inside the Holy of Holies and called the Foundation Stone. Ancient sources indicate that this stone was three finger-breadths high and was inscribed with the sacred name of God. The mythology attached to this rock indicated that it was a marker of the center or navel of the earth.[4]

Golden Grapevine and Flowers

It is evident from several historical sources that there were four columns standing before the portal that led into the Holy Place of this temple, two on each side of the doorway. Surrounding these columns were vine-like decorations adorned with flowers of gold. In addition, there was apparently a wooden framework laid across the top of these columns, and from this framework large golden vines with clusters of golden grapes that were as tall as a man.[5] The scriptures indicate that the

FIGURE 24. Door hinge from the Salt Lake Temple in the shape of a flowering vine. A flowering grapevine decorated the facade of the Jerusalem Temple during the time of Jesus Christ. The grape clusters, which were fashioned from gold, stood as tall as a man.

grapevine was a symbol of the promised land (*see* Numbers 13:23–25; Deuteronomy 8:8; 1 Kings 4:25) and also of the Israelites themselves (*see* Psalm 80:8–12; Jeremiah 2:21; Ezekiel 17:5–8). The flowers, of course, evoke images of the Garden of Eden.

Golden Lamp

Between the columns and over the portal of the temple there was a golden lamp that had been given as a gift by queen Helena of Adiabene. This lamp is described as being shaped like a conch shell.[6] Perhaps the Israelites looked upon this light as a reminder of the *Shekinah* cloud that lit up the temple courts in previous ages. There are some Old Testament passages that compare the God of Israel to a lamp. "For thou art my lamp, O Lord . . . the Lord will lighten my darkness" (2 Samuel 22:29; *see also* Psalms119:105; 132:17). Perhaps some in Israel would have viewed this as a symbol of the shining light of Zion that is mentioned in Isaiah 62:1.

Four Crowns

Above the golden lamp there were four windows that provided light for the Holy Place, and above each window was a decoration resembling a crown. Some scholars believe that these four decorative crowns may have represented the four gold and silver temple crowns that are connected with kingship and priesthood in Zechariah 6:10–15.[7] There were two golden chains hanging down the front side of the sanctuary, one on either side of the doorway, which enabled the priests to climb up and clean, repair, and maintain all of the golden decorations on the facade of the porch area, including the crowns.

Outer Veil

The entrance to the Holy Place was closed off both by a set of double doors and a veil that hung in front of them. According to the Jewish historian Flavius Josephus, this veil was woven like a Babylonian tapestry and was embroidered in some manner with the four sacred colors blue, purple, red, and white. He tells us that the Jews of his time considered these four colors to be symbolic of the four elements of creation:

FIGURE 25. Mosaic of the veil hanging before the door of the Jerusalem Temple. During the time of Jesus Christ, this particular veil was decorated with a panorama of stars, thus aptly illustrating the idea that this portal was the gate of heaven.

earth (white), air (blue), fire (red), and water (purple). In addition, Josephus notes that this veil displayed a panorama of the heavens upon it but did not show the signs of the Zodiac.[8]

MY FATHER'S HOUSE

Eight days after the Savior was born, he received the ritual wound of the Abrahamic covenant called circumcision (*see* Luke 2:21). In the Joseph Smith Translation, we learn that this "token of the covenant" was given at the age of eight days as a reminder that children are not accountable before the Lord, and therefore have no need of baptism, until they are eight years of age (*see* JST Genesis 17:3–12). A little more than a month after this ritual had taken place, the Savior was taken to the Jerusalem Temple by his parents that they might offer up the sacrifice pertaining to childbirth. The Holy Ghost had revealed to a man named Simeon that the Lord's Anointed or "Christ" could be found in the temple on that day. When Simeon received this revelation he went into the courts of the Lord's house and, upon finding the Savior's family, took the child "up in his arms, and blessed God, and said, Lord, now lettest thou thy servant depart in peace, according to thy word: For mine eyes have seen thy salvation" (Luke 2:25–30). A prophetess named Anna, who served the Lord continually in the temple, came "in that *hora*" (hour) and she likewise thanked the Lord for sending the Redeemer and she "spake of him to all them that looked for redemption" (Luke 2:36–38).

When he was twelve years old, the Lord's parents "found him in the temple [courts]"[9] during the Passover season, teaching the learned men among the Jews and going about his Father's business (JST Luke 2:46–49). Forty days after his baptism we read that "the Spirit brought him to Jerusalem, and set him on a pinnacle of the temple" (JST Luke 4:9). He cleansed the temple both at the beginning (*see* John 2:13–25) and at the end of his mortal ministry (*see* Matthew 21:1–16). We know that whenever he was in Jerusalem "he taught daily in the temple" (Luke 19:47; Mark 14:49), and people gathered there so that they could hear his teachings (*see* Luke 21:37–38). We read that he participated in temple festivals (*see* John 2:13; 5:1; 10:22-23; 12:1, 12-13) and entered the temple courts triumphantly in his role as the rightful King of Israel (*see* Mark 11:1-11; Luke 19:28–45).

But the Savior's connection to his Father's house does not end here. The earliest Christians viewed Jesus Christ in the role of the High Priest of the temple (*see*

Hebrews 3:1; 5:10). He is even described as wearing a seamless robe similar to the one worn by the high priest (John 19:23; compare Exodus 28:31–32). He pronounced a blessing on his disciples after the manner of the high priest with uplifted hands (*see* Luke 24:50; compare Leviticus 9:22–23; Numbers 6:23–27). He was baptized at age 30, which was the age when temple priests began to serve (Luke 3:21–23; compare Numbers 4:1-4). The prayer that Christ utters in the seventeenth chapter of the book of John is regarded by many biblical scholars to be a high priestly prayer.[10] Christ is also depicted in Revelation 1:12–13 standing in the heavenly temple wearing "the royal and high-priestly garb."[11]

Jesus Christ and the Symbols of the Temple

It would appear that there are several correspondences between the symbols of the temple and the person of Jesus Christ. Starting in the courtyard, we see the doctrine of Christ in the altar of sacrifice where lambs were offered every morning and evening (*see* Exodus 29:38–42). John the Baptist said of the Savior, "Behold the Lamb of God, which taketh away the sin of the world" (John 1:29). Also in the courtyard was the water basin filled with "living water" where the priests became ritually purified so that they might serve the Lord. At Jacob's well, where the Lord paused to quench his thirst, he taught, "Whosoever drinketh of this water shall thirst again: But whosoever drinketh of the water that I shall give him shall never thirst; but the water that I shall give him shall be in him a well of water springing up into everlasting life" (John 4:13–14; *see also* 7:37–38; Revelation 21:6). The golden grapevines that hung before the doors of Herod's temple bring to mind the Lord's words, "I am the true vine; . . . ye are the branches: He that abideth in me, and I in him, the same bringeth forth much fruit: for without me ye can do nothing" (John 15:1, 5). The doors that led into the House of the Lord remind us that the Savior taught, "I am the door: by me if any man enter in, he shall be saved" (John 10:9). Inside the Holy Place were three objects that all silently spoke the doctrine of Christ. In the *menorah*, which gave off perpetual light, we see "the true Light, which lighteth every man that cometh

FIGURE 26. Diagram of correspondences between some of the titles of Jesus Christ and the symbols of the Jerusalem Temple.

into the world" (John 1:9). In the temple during the Feast of Tabernacles, when large oil lamps were lit throughout the compound, Christ declared, "I am the light of the world: he that followeth me shall not walk in darkness, but shall have the light of life" (John 8:12). In the table of shewbread we see "the true bread from heaven," even "the bread of life" (John 6:32–35). At the altar of incense, with its rising smoke representing the prayers of the Saints, we remember that there is "one mediator between God and men," even the Lord Jesus Christ (1 Timothy 2:5; *see also* Hebrews 7:25; 1 John 2:1). Finally, we have the Stone of Foundation engraved with the name of God that was inside the Holy of Holies. In 1 Corinthians 10:4, we read that the "Rock was Christ," and in Acts 4:10–12, it is said of Christ, who is called "the stone," that "there is none other *name* under heaven given among men, whereby we must be saved" (emphasis added).

The Temple and the Atonement

Nearly all Christian religions teach that Jesus Christ rejected the temple and its system of worship, and that after he had offered his life as an eternal Atonement, his disciples completely abandoned that building. This stance can be sufficiently rebutted by responding to the following questions.

• *Did Jesus Christ and his disciples reject and abandon the temple?* Not only did Jesus Christ refer to the temple as "my Father's house" (John 2:16; 14:2), but it was there that he performed miracles and was acclaimed as the King of Israel (*see* JST Matthew 21:1–16). It is recorded in the scriptures that "he taught *daily* in the temple" (Luke 19:47, emphasis added; *see also* 20:1; Matthew 26:55; Mark 12:35; 14:49). Not only could the earliest Christians be found "*continually* in the temple, praising and blessing God" (Luke 24:52–53; emphasis added) but they also assembled "*daily* with one accord in the temple" (Acts 2:46; emphasis added). The apostles prayed in the temple courts and taught there just as their Master had done (*see* Acts 3:1, 11–26; 5:12). The Apostle Paul saw a vision of Christ while praying in the temple, indicating that the temple was a house of revelation for the Christians (*see* Acts 22:17–18). An angel of God even commanded the leaders of the Christian faith to go and teach the words of eternal life within the confines of the temple complex (*see* Acts 5:19–21, 25). In short, they were "*daily* in the temple . . . [and] they *ceased not* to teach and preach Jesus Christ" (Acts 5:42; emphasis added). The earliest Christians did not abandon the Lord's house. They only stopped worshipping and teaching there when they were literally thrown out of its hallowed halls by their enemies (*see* Acts 21:23–30).

• *Did Jesus Christ signal the end of temple worship when he drove the sacrificial animals from the temple courts during his ministry?* While some scholars may choose to interpret the Savior's action in this way to support their own theological beliefs, there is no statement in the Bible confirming that this was the Lord's intention. Instead, the scriptures clearly indicate that the Lord's indignation was directed toward "them that sold and bought in the temple" because, by their actions, they had turned the Lord's holy house into "a den of thieves" (*see* Matthew 21:12–13; Mark 11:15–18; Luke 19:45–46).[12] Interestingly, the account in the book of John is the only one that mentions that Christ drove the sacrificial animals from the temple. It should be noted, however, that when the Lord told those who were selling doves to remove them he clearly stated the meaning behind his action: "Take these things hence; make not my Father's house an house of merchandise" (*see* John 2:13–16). It has been noted by several scholars that Christ was insisting that the merchants were destroying the temple and his "act amounts to an attempt to prevent that destruction. Far from being an attempt to prophesy the ruin of the temple, Jesus' aim was purification, along the lines of stopping the illicit trade (cf. Zechariah 14:21b)."[13] It is true that the offering of blood sacrifices was no longer necessary in the temple *after* the death of Jesus Christ (*see* Hebrews 9:11–14; 3 Nephi 9:19). But there is no evidence that Christ's expulsion of the moneychangers and their merchandise was connected with the Atonement and the cessation of animal sacrifice.

• *Since Christ prophesied that the temple would be so totally destroyed that not one of its stones would be left standing upon another, was he not indicating that the temple's usefulness had come to an end?* Christ foretold the destruction of the entire city of Jerusalem and also its magnificent temple. He indicated, in hyperbolic language, that in *neither* case would one stone be left standing upon another (*see* Luke 19:41–44; Mark 13:1–2; compare Matthew 24:1–2; JS-Matthew 1:2–4; D&C 45:18–20). The temple itself, therefore, was not singled out for destruction. It should also be pointed out that the Lord's unenlightened enemies misunderstood his pronouncements on the destruction of the "temple" of his body and thought he was speaking of the temple building (*see* John 2:18–22; compare Matthew 26:61; 27:40; Mark 14:57–59; 15:29; Acts 6:14).

• *What about the words of the Lord in Matthew 23:38—"Behold, your house is left unto you desolate"—was that not a prophecy of the temple's destruction?* This is simply the quotation of a curse formula from the Old Testament that is directed toward the unrighteous (*see* Psalm 69:25; Jeremiah 12:7–13; 22:1–9; *see also* Acts 1:16–20). It is clear from the verse preceding this quote that Christ was stating that "Jerusalem" would become desolate, not the temple.

• *Did Christ's Atonement nullify the need for all temple ordinances?* No. It must be remembered that even though Christ's Atonement fulfilled the law of Moses and its particular sacrificial ordinances (*see* Matthew 5:17–18), there were many rituals pertaining to the priesthood that existed long before the law of Moses ever did. Furthermore, it should be remembered that the ordinances pertaining to kingship did not originate with Moses' law. This is why the earliest Christians could reject the Mosaic laws and ordinances after the Atonement but still participate in rites that made them "kings and priests" (*see* Revelation 1:6; 5:10).

• *What about the tearing of the temple veil at the crucifixion? Did that dramatic sign typologically signal that the way into God's direct presence (signified by the Holy of Holies) was now open to all believers in Christ and that there was no longer a need for a high priest to act as a mediator for God's people?* The validity of part of this argument rests upon the assumption that the veil which tore at the crucifixion was the veil that divided the Holy Place from the Holy of Holies. Biblical scholars are divided when it comes to deciding which veil actually tore on that occasion[14] but a simple reading of the relevant scriptures makes it clear that the veil at the front of the temple tore, not the one before the Holy of Holies. In all three accounts of this incident it is reported that "the veil of the temple was rent" in two (*see* Matthew 27:51; Mark 15:38; Luke 23:45). Each of these accounts uses "veil" in the singular. In the tabernacle, the temple of Solomon, and the temple of Zerubbabel there was only one veil hanging in front of the Holy of Holies. But in the temple of Herod—the one that existed during the time of Christ— there were actually two veils hanging in that position.[15] Based upon this evidence alone, one is inclined to conclude that it was the outer *veil* that tore when Christ was crucified and thus the typology of direct and unrestricted access to God's personal presence after the crucifixion cannot be valid. The New Testament makes it clear that Christ's followers are to look to Him as a High Priest after the order of Melchizedek (*see* Hebrews 3:1; 5:5–6), who fulfills the function of both a mediator and an intercessor between God and His people (*see* Romans 8:34; Hebrews 7:25; 9:24).

• *What about New Testament passages that speak of the Christian community or Church as a spiritual "temple"? Do they not indicate that a physical temple was no longer necessary because a spiritual assembly had somehow taken its place?* First of all, we should point out that 2 Corinthians 6:16, the passage that provides the strongest statement equating the Christian community or Church with a spiritual temple, may not even be an original part of scripture but an unauthorized addition by someone other than Paul. "The reference is part of a fragment of material (6:14–7:1) that many scholars believe to be non-Pauline, because it radically interrupts the epistle's progression of thought, seems to be a self-contained unit, and contains six words that do not occur elsewhere in the New Testament."[16] Second, it is not clear whether 1 Corinthians 3:16–17 is speaking of the entire Christian community as a "temple of God" where the "Spirit of God" dwells, or just the individual body of each Christian. But since 1 Corinthians 6:19–20 contains an almost exact restatement of this passage, and definitely refers to the individual Christian as a "temple of the Holy Ghost," it would seem safe to believe that both passages have the same meaning. Third, the only other biblical passage where the Christian community is referred to explicitly as a "holy temple in the Lord" is Ephesians 2:19–22. What is not usually noticed about this passage is that Paul refers to the Christian community not only as a "temple" but also as the "household" of God or simply a "habitation" for the Spirit. This is all clearly allegorical since Paul states that this "temple" is built upon a "foundation" of apostles and prophets, with "Jesus Christ himself being the chief cornerstone." This is probably the "spiritual house" mentioned by Peter, who likewise spoke of Christ as the "living stone" and referred to individual Christians as "living stones" who compose the structure of this allegorical "house" (1 Peter 2:4–5).[17] There are several other instances where Paul referred to the Church as a "house" that had been "built" by God (1 Timothy 3:15; Hebrews 3:1–6).

In none of these passages is there any statement that this allegorical "house" or "temple" had replaced the need for a physical, holy space where one could learn about and worship God apart from the world. And indeed, there is ample evidence in the New Testament and various other historical sources demonstrating that the earliest Christians sought for sacred space where they could learn of heavenly things and participate in ordinances that pertained to their eternal salvation.

NEW TESTAMENT TEMPLE TEXTS

There are several texts in the New Testament which seem to indicate that, even though the earliest Christians were not able to worship God in the Jerusalem Temple according to the doctrines, laws, and ordinances of Christ's new covenant, they did so on mountain tops and in private dwellings that had been designated for that purpose.

The Mount of Transfiguration

Several interesting correspondences exist between the Jerusalem Temple and the Mount of Transfiguration. First, the Mount of Transfiguration was an isolated and high mountain (*see* Mark 9:2; Luke 9:28) that was referred to as "the holy mount" by the apostle Peter (2 Peter 1:18). The temple mount in Jerusalem was often referred to as the "holy hill" (Psalms 2:6; 3:4; 15:1; 43:3; 99:9) or as the "mountain of [the Lord's] holiness" (Psalm 48:1).

Second, the Savior went to the Mount of Transfiguration to pray (*see* Luke 9:28). The Jerusalem Temple was looked upon by all Israelites as the "house of prayer" (Isaiah 56:7; *see also* Matthew 21:13; Acts 3:1).

Third, as Christ was praying on the mountain, his face began to shine and his clothing changed to a brilliant white color (*see* Matthew 17:2; Mark 9:3; Luke 9:29). White, of course, was the color of the linen clothing worn by the priests of the temple (*see* Leviticus 16:4; Revelation 15:6).

Fourth, when Moses and Elijah appeared in glory and spoke with the Lord "of his decease which he should accomplish at Jerusalem" (Luke 9:30–31), they may have been discussing much more than just his impending death. The Prophet Joseph Smith indicated that the heavenly messengers "spake of his death, and also his resurrection" (JST Luke 9:31). The word translated as "decease" in the King James Bible is *exodus,* which in Greek refers to a departure or journey.[18] It would thus appear that Christ may have spoken with his heavenly visitors about his ascension or journey into heaven that he would take after he had been resurrected.

Fifth, after the heavenly messengers had departed, the Apostle Peter suggested that three "tabernacles" be erected on the mountain (Matthew 17:4; Mark 9:5; Luke 9:33). The Greek word translated in these verses as "tabernacles" (*skene*) is also the very same word used in Acts 7:44 and the Septuagint (or Greek Old Testament) to designate the tabernacle that was erected by the prophet Moses. It will be recalled that the tabernacle complex was divided into three separate and distinct sections.

Sixth, while Peter was making the suggestion to erect the three tabernacles, a bright cloud overshadowed the mountain and those present heard the voice of God from behind the cloud say, "This is my beloved Son: hear him" (Luke 9:35; Matthew 17:5). The bright cloud is another ancient temple motif. It is recorded in the scriptures that when Jehovah came down upon Mount Sinai, His descent was amidst thick clouds and fire (*see* Exodus 19:16–18). When the children of Israel constructed the tabernacle, the Lord came down into it shielded by a glowing cloud (*see* Exodus 33:9-

11; 40:34–35). The same was true for the temple that had been built in Jerusalem (*see* 1 Kings 8:10–11).

Latter-day revelation indicates that we have not yet received a full account of what happened on the Mount of Transfiguration (*see* D&C 63:21). There are several clues scattered throughout the scriptures and prophetic writings, however. In 2 Peter 1:19, for instance, we learn that the apostles received the more sure word of prophecy on this occasion. This means, according to D&C 131:5, that they were sealed up to eternal life. This is the same as saying that they made their calling and election sure.[19] We are further informed in D&C 63:21 that Peter, James, and John were shown a vision of the transfiguration of the earth while on the mountain, which is another way of saying that they saw the earth in its paradisiacal, or Edenic, state.[20] Joseph Smith said that the Savior, Moses, and Elijah "gave the keys to Peter, James, and John on the mount."[21] These "keys" undoubtedly included the sealing keys of the kingdom that the Lord had promised to give unto Peter (*see* Matthew 16:19) but which were clearly bestowed upon all of the apostles (*see* Matthew 18:18; notice that the Transfiguration episode occurs between these two passages in Matthew 17:1–9). Joseph Smith also said that the Lord received "the fulness of [the] Priesthood or the law of God" while on the Mount of Transfiguration.[22]

As a whole, this evidence has prompted some LDS theologians to conclude that the three apostles received their temple endowment on this occasion.[23] There appears to be some support for this conclusion in a scriptural passage where Peter describes his experience. In 2 Peter 1:16, the chief apostle indicates that he and James and John had "made known" information about Christ's "power" to other Christians. One scholar observes that "the verb 'make known' (*gnorizein*) is almost technical in the New Testament for imparting a divine mystery."[24] Peter also says in this passage that he and his fellow apostles were "eyewitnesses of [Christ's] majesty." The word used here for "eyewitness" (*epoptes*) is not found anywhere else in the New Testament and is the Greek designation for one who has received initiation into a high grade of a mystery religion.[25] In the light of this perspective, it is little wonder that the Lord commanded these men to keep their experience on the holy mountain a secret (*see* Matthew 17:9; Mark 9:9).[26]

The Sermon on the Mount

Based on comparative studies, contextual inferences, and circumstantial evidence, one LDS scholar has suggested that the Sermon on the Mount should be seen as a ritual temple text. This conclusion is drawn from two primary perspectives. First, the

Savior repeated almost the same exact sermon to the Nephites at the temple in Bountiful when He appeared to them after the resurrection (*see* 3 Nephi 11:1). And second, many of the elements found in both the sermon at the temple and the Sermon on the Mount are related to the LDS temple endowment.[27]

The fact that Christ delivered this sermon from a mountain in the Holy Land may also hold some significance. Several biblical scholars see evidence that the earliest Christians viewed this particular mountain as the New Mount Sinai, and they also feel that the book of Matthew (which contains the sermon on the Mount) may be constructed in five parts to mirror the five books of Moses. The sermon would thus represent God's new law, "the Messianic Torah."[28] It has been pointed out in a previous chapter of this book that Mount Sinai did indeed serve as a natural temple before the tabernacle was built.

The Mount of Olives

Jesus Christ taught in the Jerusalem Temple's courts during the daytime but at night we are informed that he sometimes lodged on the Mount of Olives (*see* Luke 21:37–38), probably in the city of Bethany, which was on the mountain's eastern slope (*see* Matthew 21:17; Mark 11:11). Shortly before his crucifixion, the Savior took the twelve apostles, and perhaps others, with him to the Garden of Gethsemane, which is located on the western slope of the Mount of Olives. When they had entered into the garden area, the Lord instructed the majority of his disciples to wait for him while he took Peter, James, and John further into the garden. Then, at some unspecified location, Christ told Peter, James, and John to stay where they were while he "went a little further" into Gethsemane by himself (*see* Matthew 26:30–39; Mark 14:26–36). It was in this third area of the garden that the Savior was visited and strengthened by an angel[29] and where he shed his sacrificial blood (*see* JST Luke 22:43–44). This pattern is intriguing because it seems to match the tripartite division of the people during the Mount Sinai episode (Ground Level—Israelites, Half-Way—Seventy Elders, Top—Moses) and the tripartite division in the temple complex (Courtyard—Israelites, Holy Place—Priests, Holy of Holies—High Priest). It was, of course, in the Holy of Holies on the Day of Atonement that the final rite was performed to purge the sins of the Israelites with sacrificial blood (*see* Leviticus 16:15).

There is one other hint from the scriptures that indicates this episode might be seen in a temple context. In Mark 14:51–52 we read that one of Christ's disciples, who was evidently with the group near the entrance to the Garden of Gethsemane, was wearing "a linen cloth" (*see* JST Mark 14:57). This fragmentary piece of information makes little sense as it stands in the King James Bible, but there is an ancient Christian document attributed to the Apostle Mark which states that this particular disciple prepared himself for six days and then received some unspecified instructions directly from Jesus Christ. This document then states that in the evening, the two met again and the Master "taught him the mystery of the kingdom of God"[30] This episode might well be compared to the initiation of Israel's temple priests, who were not only invested with linen clothing but were also consecrated during a seven-day period (*see* Leviticus 8:6–7, 12–13, 33).

The scriptural record indicates that before the time of Jesus Christ the Hebrews considered the Mount of Olives to be a distinguished and holy site. In 2 Samuel 15:30 and 32, for instance, we read that King David worshipped God on the top of this mountain. In Ezekiel's vision of the Jerusalem Temple he saw "the glory of the

Lord" vacate the sanctuary and rest upon the Mount of Olives (*see* Ezekiel 11:22–23). And then there was the expectation that the Messiah would descend upon this very mountain to save His people from destruction (*see* Zechariah 14:3–5; D&C 45:48; 133:20). Clearly, this mountain was associated with the Lord's presence, and hence could be looked upon as a sacred place. Furthermore, it was from this mountain that the resurrected Redeemer ascended into heaven and on which angels made their appearance (*see* Acts 1:9–12). For several hundred years after the ascension there were Christians who could still point to the place on the Mount of Olives where "the sanctuary of the Lord, that is, the temple" would someday be built.[31]

FIGURE 27. Jesus Christ ascending into heaven after his resurrection from the dead. Drawing of an Italian ivory diptych (ca. 400 A.D.).

The Day of Pentecost

The Christians were promised by the Lord that they would be endowed "with power from on high" while they were in Jerusalem (Luke 24:49). This promise was fulfilled on the day of Pentecost when the Saints were meeting in a "house" that was suddenly filled with a rushing wind, cloven tongues of fire, and the Spirit of God (*see* Acts 2:1–4). The word that is translated as "house" in Acts 2:2 (*oikos*) can refer to a temple[32] and is, in fact, used in several New Testament passages to refer to the house of God.[33] Perhaps this was the same house that contained the "upper room" where the Saints offered "prayer and supplication" (Acts 1:13–14; compare 1 Kings 8:54) as was prescribed for the Jerusalem Temple (*see* Isaiah 56:7; Matthew 21:13). Tradition has it that the Saints' upper room was located just to the southwest of the temple mount on a hill that is today identified as Mount Zion.[34] Joseph Smith may have had this very structure in mind when he said that "God obtained a house where Peter was endowed, etc. on the day of Pentecost."[35]

Latter-day Saints can readily draw a parallel between the heavenly manifestations on the ancient day of Pentecost and the great spiritual outpourings that occurred inside the Kirtland Temple in connection with the administration of temple ordinances.[36] It may also be relevant to this discussion that the Saints in Nauvoo taught that it was a law of the priesthood that temple ordinances be performed in an upper room.[37] In fact, it was in the upper room of Joseph Smith's Red Brick Store that temple ordinances were first administered in the city of Nauvoo.[38]

The Gathering

The Prophet Joseph Smith taught that Jesus Christ tried to gather the Jews during his day so that they could participate in the temple rituals of baptism for the dead, washings, anointings, and endowments. In his comments on the words of the Redeemer that are found in Matthew 23:37, the Prophet said,

> What was the object of gathering the Jews, or the people of God in any age of the world? . . . The main object was to build unto the Lord a house whereby he could reveal unto his people the ordinances of his house and the glories of his kingdom, and teach the people the way of salvation; for there are certain ordinances and principles that, when they are taught and practiced, must be done in a place or house built for that purpose. It was the design of the councils of heaven before the world was, that the principles and laws of the priesthood should be predicated upon the gathering of the people in every age of the world. Jesus did everything to gather

the people, and they would not be gathered. . . . It is for the same purpose that God gathers together his people in the last days, to build unto the Lord a house to prepare them for the ordinances and endowments, washings and anointings, etc. One of the ordinances of the house of the Lord is baptism for the dead. God decreed before the foundation of the world that that ordinance should be administered in a font prepared for that purpose in the house of the Lord.[39]

The 40-Day Ministry

We are informed in the New Testament that the resurrected Lord visited with His disciples during a forty-day period and spoke to them of "things pertaining to the kingdom of God" (Acts 1:3). We know that He opened "their understanding, that they might understand the scriptures" (Luke 24:45) but He also did many other things "which are not written" (John 20:30). Clement of Alexandria, one of the early Christian leaders, reports that Peter, James, and John "were entrusted by the Lord after his resurrection with the higher knowledge. They imparted it to the other apostles, and the other apostles to the Seventy."[40] What type of higher knowledge did the Lord impart to His faithful Saints and what things did He do that are not recorded in the Bible? There are many extrabiblical documents that claim to reveal what the Redeemer did during these forty days. While such accounts must be viewed with caution, some of them do speak of things that are of interest to Latter-day Saints. Taken together, these documents reveal that during His forty-day ministry,

> Jesus teaches the apostles the gospel they should preach to the world. He tells of a premortal life and the creation of the world, adding that this life is a probationary state of choosing between good and evil, and that those who choose good might return to the glory of God. He foretells events of the last days, including the return of Elijah. He also tells the disciples that the primitive church will be perverted after one generation, and teaches them to prepare for tribulation. These apocryphal accounts state that Christ's resurrection gives his followers hope for their own resurrection in glory. Besides salvation for the living, salvation for the dead is a major theme, as are the ordinances: baptism, the sacrament or eucharist, ordination of the apostles to authority, their being blessed one by one, and an initiation or endowment (cf. Luke 24:49, usually called "mysteries"), with an emphasis on garments, marriage, and prayer circles. These accounts, usually called secret (Greek, apokryphon; Coptic, hep), are often connected somehow to the temple, or compared to the Mount of Transfiguration.[41]

EARLY CHRISTIAN INITIATION RITES

While there are many apocryphal documents that claim to describe the Lord's teachings and activities during His forty-day, post-resurrection ministry, there are also a sizable number of orthodox Christian sources that confirm some of those claims. These orthodox sources also lead one to the conclusion that some of the early Christians participated in initiation rituals that parallel those performed in the Israelite temple.

Christian Temples

Under the old covenant, only members of the tribe of Levi could serve in the temple as priests and Levites, participate in all the priestly temple ordinances, and have access to the Holy Place and the Holy of Holies. The book of Hebrews points out, however, that the Aaronic Priesthood and the old covenant system of temple worship could not make anyone "perfect" (*teleioo*, Hebrews 7:11, 19). The head priest of the old covenant was only allowed to enter into the Holy of Holies (symbolic of God's presence) once every year and was then required to retreat. It is evident from several New Testament passages that when Jesus Christ established the New Covenant, He established a new system of temple worship. Under this system Christ Himself was the high priest (*see* Hebrews 3:1) but His Priesthood was after the order of Melchizedek (*see* Hebrews 5:5–6; 7:12–17). This is referred to as the "royal priesthood" in 1 Peter 2:9, and it was received in conjunction with the swearing of an oath (*see* Hebrews 7:21, 28; compare D&C 84:33–41). Unlike the Aaronic Priesthood, the Melchizedek Priesthood did have the power to make its possessors "perfect" (*teleioo*, Hebrews 7:19). While the Greek word that is translated as "perfect" in the book of Hebrews is commonly interpreted to mean "complete" or "finished," it can also be translated as "initiated."[42] The book of Hebrews indicates that any man who is made a priest after the order of Melchizedek can do the following:

- Inherit the promises of the Abrahamic covenant (*see* Hebrews 6:11–15).
- Become "perfect" or fully initiated (*see* Hebrews 7:11–12, 19).
- Become both a king and a priest (*see* Hebrews 7:1; Revelation 1:6; 5:10; 20:6).
- Become like the Son of God (*see* Hebrews 7:3, 28).
- Follow Christ within the veil of the Holy of Holies (*see* Hebrews 6:19–20; 10:19–20).

- Draw near unto God (*see* Hebrews 7:19).
- Receive eternal life (*see* Hebrews 7:16).

Although these privileges had been extended to the early Christians, they did not always have access to the courts of the Jerusalem Temple where kings and priests were traditionally initiated. As pointed out in the paragraphs above, it appears that the early Christians resorted to the mountains (which were natural temples) and to private enclosures to carry out their sacred rituals. Eventually, the early Christians built structures that were referred to as temples. For instance, it is reported that in 201 A.D. in the city of Edessa, "the temple of the Church of the Christians was destroyed by a flood."[43] There is also record of a "spacious Christian temple at Nicomedia" that was destroyed by enemies of the Christian faith in the early part of 303 A.D.[44] A Christian pilgrim to the Holy Land in 333 A.D. described the building erected by Constantine on the supposed site of Christ's resurrection as the "House of the Lord."[45] This is the very same building where Cyril of Jerusalem lectured on the Christian mysteries around 348 A.D. Cyril himself said that this building had an "outer chamber" and an "inner chamber" that was called the "Holy of Holies."[46] The historian Eusebius records that the Emperor Constantine built "consecrated temples" on the spot where Christ gained His victory over death.[47] He also noted that Constantine's mother built "a sacred church and temple on the very summit" of the Mount of Olives to mark the spot of the Savior's ascension. He goes on to say that there is a cave located on that mountain, and "authentic history informs us that in this very cave the Savior imparted his secret revelations to his disciples."[48] In a study on the attitude of some early Christians toward the Lord's house, Dr. Nibley has noted that some early basilicas were designed on the same general plan as the Jerusalem Temple, and they were spoken of in terms that clearly connected them with the Israelite sanctuary.[49]

Christian Mysteries

Contrary to the belief of most Christian sects, there is ample evidence from orthodox sources that the Lord taught His followers a body of knowledge called "mysteries." In the Clementine Homilies, for instance, we are informed that the Apostle Peter spoke of "hidden truths" that were revealed by Jesus Christ to His disciples: "We remember that our Lord and teacher, commanding us, said, 'Keep the mysteries for me and the sons of my house.' Wherefore also he explained to his disciples privately the mysteries of the kingdom of heaven."[50]

Evidence of this type of arcane knowledge can be found in New Testament writings. The apostle Paul stated that he and the other leaders of the Church were "stewards of the mysteries of God" (1 Corinthians 4:1; *see also* Matthew 13:11). The word translated in this verse as "stewards" (*oikonomos*) means "distributor" or "overseer."[51] What kind of mysteries was Paul speaking of? In 1 Corinthians 2:6–7, he elaborated when he said, "We speak wisdom among them that are *perfect*: yet not the wisdom of this world. . . . But we speak the wisdom of God in a *mystery*, even the *hidden* wisdom, which God ordained before the world unto our glory" (emphasis added).[52] Several of the words in this passage call for attention. First, as we have mentioned above, the Greek word that is translated as "perfect" is *teleios*, which some scholars argue should be translated as "initiated."[53] The word translated as "mystery" is *musterion*, which can mean either a "secret teaching" or a "secret rite."[54] This word is connected with "the idea of *silence* imposed by *initiation* into religious rites."[55] The word translated as "hidden" is *apokrupto* and means "to *conceal away* (i.e. *fully*) . . . to *keep secret*."[56] One scholar is convinced that the "wisdom" (*sophia*) mentioned in these verses is "esoteric" in nature and is drawn directly from "Jewish and Christian apocalyptic-wisdom theology."[57] Based on this brief analysis, we could interpret this passage to mean that Paul and other church leaders initiated some of the earliest Christians into secret rituals and thereby taught them the hidden wisdom of God that was foreordained to bestow "glory" upon those who received it (compare D&C 124:33–34, 38–41, 95, 97).

What kind of glory were the Christians trying to gain and how was it to be obtained? In the book of Hebrews, Paul admonished his fellow Saints to "go on unto perfection" (JST Hebrews 6:1) by following the example of Jesus Christ. The Savior obtained the Melchizedek Priesthood (*see* Hebrews 6:20), which possessed the power to make him perfect (*see* Hebrews 5:9; 7:11–28) and to enable Him to enter into the presence and glory of God.[58] This is also known as "entering into the Lord's rest." In the Doctrine and Covenants, we read: "For without [the Melchizedek Priesthood] no man can see the face of God, even the Father, and live. Now this Moses plainly taught to the children of Israel in the wilderness, and sought diligently to sanctify his people that they might *behold the face of God*; but they hardened their hearts and could not *endure his presence*; therefore, the Lord . . . swore that they should not *enter into his rest* while in the wilderness, *which rest is the fulness of his glory*. Therefore, he took Moses out of their midst, and the Holy Priesthood also" (D&C 84:22–25; emphasis added). The Prophet Joseph Smith restored the knowledge of what exactly was taken away during this incident. The Lord said: "I will take away *the priesthood* out of their midst; therefore *my holy order, and the ordinances thereof,* shall not go before them; for my presence shall not go up in their midst. . . . they shall not *enter into my presence, into my rest*" (JST Exodus 34:1–2; emphasis added). Even though the majority of the Israelites in Moses' day lost the privilege of entering into the Lord's rest, we read of the early Christians in JST Hebrews 4:3—"For we who have believed *do* enter into rest."[59] In connection with this concept we should note Paul said in Hebrews 10:19 that the Saints of his day had license or authority "to enter into the holiest,"[60] meaning the Holy of Holies of the temple.

How did Jesus Christ enter into the Father's presence? He ascended to the heavenly temple and passed through the veil that separated the Holy Place from the Holy of Holies, as specified in Hebrews 6:19–20 and 4:14. Hebrews 6:20 indicates that Christ passed through the heavenly veil as a "forerunner" for His disciples, and Hebrews 10:20 says that His passage created "a new and living way" for His followers to pass through that barrier. Why was a forerunner necessary? Perhaps the answer lies in Christ's statement to His apostles: "In my Father's house [i.e., the temple] are many mansions [*monai*] . . . I will come again, and receive [*paralambano*] you unto myself; that where I am, there ye may be also. . . . The way ye know. . . . I am the way . . . no man cometh unto the Father, but by me" (John 14:2–4, 6). This is reminiscent of Christ's teaching that his followers who enter the kingdom of heaven will be required to pass through a narrow gate. Many who desire to enter into the Lord's heavenly kingdom will knock on the door of the gate and request entrance but will be denied that privilege by the Lord, who stands there and speaks with them through the barrier, because they were not His true and faithful followers (*see* Luke 13:23–30; Matthew 7:21–23). Returning now to our passage from the book of John, it is noteworthy that Origen, an early Christian theologian, interpreted the word *monai* as meaning "stations or halts in the journey of the soul to God. Only after testing in these can [the soul] proceed."[61] The Greek word used above for "receive" (*paralambano*) is also relevant to our discussion because a closely related word (*paralambanein*) is a "technical term for the reception of the rites and secrets of the mysteries."[62]

There is further evidence that the early Christians engaged in some type of ritual activity in connection with becoming "perfect." An early Christian leader in Alexandria named Clement (150 A.D.) informs us that when the apostle Mark was in Egypt between 65 and 80 A.D. he wrote a document that was to be read only to those Christians who were "attaining perfection" by being "initiated into the great mysteries."[63]

Mark, then, during Peter's stay in Rome, recorded the acts of the Lord, not however reporting them all, for he did not indicate the mystical ones, but selected those which he thought most useful for the increase of the faith of those undergoing instruction.

When Peter had borne his witness (i.e., suffered martyrdom), Mark arrived in Alexandria, taking his own and Peter's memoirs. From these he copied into his first book the things appropriate for those who were making progress in knowledge but compiled a more spiritual gospel for the use of those who were attaining perfection. Yet not even so did he divulge the unutterable things themselves [see 2 Corinthians 12:2–4], nor did he write down the Lord's hierophantic [initiatory] teaching. But adding to the previously written acts of others also, he presented, over and above these, certain oracles whose interpretation he knew would provide the hearers with mystical guidance into the inner shrine of the seven-times-hidden truth. Thus, then, he made advance preparation—not grudgingly or incautiously, as I think—and on his death he left his composition to the church in Alexandria, where even until now it is very well guarded, being read only to those who are being initiated into the great mysteries.[64]

Notice in this quotation that Mark had the writings of Peter with him. Clement seems to imply that some of these writings contained secret teachings of the Lord to His apostles. The mention of things not to be uttered reminds us, of course, of the "unspeakable words, which it is not lawful for a man to utter" that Paul learned when he ascended into "the third heaven" (2 Corinthians 12:2–4).

Having established from orthodox Christian sources that the early Christians had buildings called "temples," and possessed a body of rituals and knowledge known as the "mysteries," we might enquire: What was the nature of the early Christian mysteries? What were some of the ritual elements included in those ancient teachings and ordinances? The most telling clue comes straight from the New Testament itself. The apostle John states quite plainly that the followers of Jesus Christ were "made . . . kings and priests" unto God (*see* Revelation 1:6; 5:10; 20:6), the same as the Lord's followers had been for thousands of years before them.

Anointing

The most prominent ordinance among the initiation rites of Old Testament kings and priests was, of course, the anointing with oil. "Anointing" is mentioned in a Christian context in two New Testament passages where it is connected with the Spirit of God, just as it is in Old Testament passages (*see* 2 Corinthians 1:21–22; 1 John 2:20, 27). While these New Testament scriptures may be considered by some biblical interpreters simply to be figurative, there is an abundance of historical evidence indicating that the early Christians did indeed perform anointing rituals as part of their initiation ceremonies. Some sources even specify that the Christian anointing symbolized the power of a king and a priest.[65] It is also significant that "the anointing of Christians was identified with the anointing of Aaron by Moses"[66] because this may indicate that some early Christians equated their own anointing with that of Israel's temple priests. Confirmation of this viewpoint may be detected in sources that tell us that perfumed olive oil was used for the Christian anointing rite[67] (compare Exodus 30:22–25), and other sources that say the anointing oil was stored inside a horn[68] (compare 1 Kings 1:39).

Around 350 A.D., Cyril of Jerusalem equated the anointing ceremony that was administered under his direction (of the forehead, ears, nose, and chest) with the "unction" or "anointing" that is spoken of in 1 John 2:20, 27.[69] Basil the Great referred to the early Christian anointing ritual as one of the secret teachings "delivered to us 'in a mystery' by the traditions of the apostles."[70] What did this anointing ceremony consist of? Several historical sources say that the early Saints were anointed on the forehead, ears, nose, eyes, mouth, and chest, and a formula of words was pronounced as the body parts were anointed.[71] Most sources, however, simply say that the Christian's entire body was anointed with holy oil.[72] Some ritual texts indicate that the anointing oil was applied to the initiate's head as a type of "seal," and then the seal was confirmed upon the initiate in the name of the three members of the Godhead.[73] Around 200 A.D. Tertullian wrote that the anointing ritual was administered to Christ's disciples so that they themselves could become "christs," or *anointed ones,* like their Master.[74]

Garments

In Revelation 3:4–5 we read that the Lord's Saints who keep their "garments" undefiled will be "clothed in white raiment" in His heavenly kingdom. And in Revelation 3:18, the Lord directly counsels one of His servants to obtain "white raiment" from him (compare Revelation 16:15). These references are much more than just figurative allusions. Like the anointing ritual, there is abundant evidence that the early Christians, in divergent parts of the world and for hundreds of years, received a tangible white garment when they were fully initiated into the Christian faith.[75] Ancient Christian initiation documents that speak of this garment often refer to it as a piece of "royal" clothing[76] and also call it a "wedding garment" (compare Matthew

FIGURE 28. Some of the early Christians received a white garment when they participated in initiation rituals that were designed to endow them with royal and priestly status.

22:11–12).[77] There is also a strand of tradition found in some of these documents that the white garments of the Christian initiate signify "the glory which Adam wore" while he was in paradise.[78] One of the ancient Christian leaders named Theodore told those who received their garments that they symbolized the immortality of the resurrected state and that they would "need them" until they themselves were resurrected.[79]

One ancient non-Christian source notes that the early Saints recognized each other "by secret marks and signs," meaning that they had "distinguishing marks on the body."[80] This may be connected with the apostle Paul's statement that he bore upon his body "the marks of the Lord Jesus" (Galatians 6:17). There are numerous early Christian artworks that depict the Savior, angels, apostles, and Saints with very distinct marks on their white garments. The two most common marks are in the shapes of a straight line and a right angle. Occasionally a mark that is shaped like an artisan's compass can also be seen on these religious garments.[81] The straight line mark is of particular interest because it is not only depicted in artworks as being woven into Christian garments, but it has also been found in the form of an incision on one early garment (believed to be Christian) that has been recovered in an archeological excavation.

> [The] garment next to the skin is sufficiently well preserved for us to observe that small rosettes have been woven into the material in particular locations. There is one rosette over each breast and one on the right leg near the knee, but there is no corresponding rosette on the left leg. Across the lower abdomen, the material also has a hemmed slit about six inches long.[82]

The shape of this mark brings to mind two measuring instruments that are used by divine beings in the Bible. The first instrument is a measuring line. It is recorded that this was one of the instruments used by the Lord in the process of the creation of the earth (*see* Job 38:5). The Lord also uses a plumbline in some scriptures to measure, and thereby judge, His people (*see* 2 Kings 21:13; Isaiah 28:17; Amos 7:7–8). The second instrument is a measuring reed or rule. In the book of Revelation an angel gives the apostle John "a reed like unto a rod" with which to measure the temple of God (*see* Revelation 11:1). In Ezekiel's vision of the Lord's temple, he sees an angel holding both "a line of flax in his hand, and a measuring reed" (Ezekiel 40:3), both straight instruments that resemble the shape of the Christian garment mark.

The right-angle mark, or *gamma* as it is sometimes called, is by far the most common mark displayed in artistic depictions of early Christian garments. This mark was actually "embroidered on the borders or woven into the texture of ecclesiastical vestments, both in the West and East," but it was only embroidered upon clothing of a white color. "The precise meaning of these marks has not been satisfactorily determined."[83] The only thing scholars are really sure of is that the various Christian clothing "marks had some symbolic force."[84] For some unexplained reason the *gamma* mark was also displayed on veils in early Christian artworks.[85] The carpenter's square, which has the exact same shape, eventually came to be employed by the ancient Christians as a symbol of the Apostle Thomas.[86]

The garment mark with the form of an architect's compass is of interest because in early Christian artworks both the Father and the Son were regularly depicted in the act of creating the universe with a pair of compasses. The inspiration for these artworks is believed to have been derived from Proverbs 8:27, which, in the King James Bible, states that God used a compass in the creative process.[87] The compass and square were frequently displayed together in early Christian churches and other holy places as symbols of geometry[88] and also in contexts where the intended meaning is not clear.[89]

FIGURE 29. Jesus Christ and his apostles wearing clothing with right-angle or gamma marks on them. There are a wide variety of markings found on early Christian garments but their meaning is not yet fully understood by biblical scholars.

In addition to white garments there is physical evidence that some early Christians wore linen robes. An archeological excavation of what is believed to be an early Christian burial site in Egypt has yielded ten robes of plain linen. Two of the robes are decorated on the left shoulder with linen ribbons that have been tied into a complex knot. The other eight robes bear knotted linen ribbons on the right shoulder. These shoulder decorations are thought to perhaps be symbolic of priestly authority.[90]

There is an intriguing tradition related by Eusebius, Clement, and other early Christian sources that ties the early Christians to the vesture worn by the temple priests of Israel. This tradition claims that James and John, the Lord's apostles, both wore a "golden plate" or crown similar to the one worn by the high priest. Furthermore, it is said of James that he "exercised the priestly office after the manner of the old priesthood" and even entered "into the Holy of Holies" under unspecified circumstances.[91]

New Name

It has been pointed out in a previous chapter of this book that the kings of Israel received a new name or throne name when they were initiated into kingship within the walls of the temple complex. It is therefore very interesting that the Lord promises in Revelation 2:17 that He will give a white stone with a secret new name to those of His Saints who overcome the world (compare D&C 130:10–11). Several texts in the 17th chapter of the book of John may speak of this very thing or something similar. The clue that John 17 may be connected with initiation rites comes in verse 23, where the Lord indicates that the Twelve Apostles are to be "made perfect." The Greek word is again *teleioo*, "a term of the mystery religions" that means to "consecrate, initiate."[92] The Lord states in these passages that He "manifested" (vs. 6) or "declared" (vs. 26) the *name* of God to the Twelve. Then in verse 12 the Savior reports to His Father: "While I was with them in the world, I kept them in thy name." The word translated here as "kept" is *tereo*, one of the meanings of which is to "test by observation or trial."[93] Perhaps these biblical verses are somehow connected with an orthodox Christian initiation text that mentions "the word that was given to the apostles, and which the apostles handed on to the priests"[94] (compare John 17:6, 14).

Israelite Ritual Elements

The early Christian initiation ceremonies contained several other ritual elements that are recognizable from ancient Israel's temple rites. For instance, Christians experienced some type of "ritual drama" that was based upon the salvation history of the Exodus and included participants such as "the candidates, the angels, Christ, [and] Satan."[95] A number of early Christian initiation texts compare the male initiates to Adam,[96] whose purpose was to return to paradise.[97] Some texts indicate that when the initiates entered "the Holy of Holies (after baptism)," they symbolically reentered paradise and regained access to the tree of life.[98] Some Christian initiates also entered into a covenant when they formally entered into the community of the Saints.[99] Covenant making, of course, was a common theme of Old Testament ritual and was often associated with the house of the Lord (*see* 2 Kings 23:1–3).

FIGURE 30. On the left part of this early Christian catacomb scene, a woman enters paradise by passing through a portal with the assistance of an angel. On the right part of the scene, she is seated at a heavenly banquet.

Another familiar Israelite ritual element found in the Christian initiation ceremonies is prayer with uplifted hands. This practice is mentioned in the New Testament (*see* 1 Timothy 2:8), and there are numerous early artworks showing

FIGURE 31. A damaged scene from an early Christian catacomb painting that depicts a saint being introduced into paradise by the parting of a curtain.

Christians in this posture of prayer.[100] Some initiation texts state that the initiate would stand, or kneel, with their "hands oustretched in the attitude of prayer" as King Solomon did at the temple altar in Jerusalem (*see* 1 Kings 8:54).[101] While praying in this manner, "appointed ministers" approached the Christian initiates and spoke the words of the angel who appeared in the temple to Zacharias, indicating that his prayer had been heard (*see* Luke 1:13). Dr. Nibley has published an insightful study on ritual prayer forms among the early Christians that shows many similarities between the rituals of prayer under the Old and New Covenants.[102]

One final element of Israelite ritual that we will mention is the adoption of the initiate as a son of God. As mentioned previously in this book, the adoption of sonship pertained to the kings of Israel, as evidenced by the text of Psalm 2:7. Adoption as a son of God is mentioned in Galatians 4:5–7 by the Apostle Paul, but it is interesting to note that the theme of adoptional sonship was incorporated into the early initiation rites of Christianity.[103] In fact, Psalm 2:7 was quoted during some Christian initiation ordinances, and some scholars feel that this scripture succinctly sums up the whole purpose of the initiation ceremony.[104]

Unique Ritual Elements

There are several elements found in the Christian initiation rituals that are not mentioned in the Old Testament rites. These include the separation of men and women during reception of the ordinances,[105] the idea that the initiate is entering into a new world,[106] question and answer dialogues,[107] the renunciation of Satan,[108] an embrace, imitation of Christ's sufferings, and baptism for the dead. Let us briefly examine the last three of these ritual elements.

It is evident from surviving ritual texts that some of the early disciples of Christ received an embrace as part of their initiation ceremony.[109] In some documents it is said that the initiate was embraced by the officiating priest.[110] It may be that the Christians saw this initiation embrace as a precursor of the embrace that they expected to receive from the Lord when they entered into His presence in the life to come.[111]

In his lectures on the Christian mysteries, Cyril of Jerusalem said that the initiates who received the ordinances under his direction somehow imitated the sufferings of the Savior in order to share in His salvation.

> O strange and inconceivable thing! We did not really die, we were not really buried, we were not really crucified and raised again; but our imitation was in a figure, and our salvation in reality. Christ was actually crucified, and actually buried, and truly rose again; and all these things he freely bestowed upon us, that we, sharing his sufferings by imitation, might gain salvation in reality. O surpassing loving-kindness! Christ received nails in his undefiled hands and feet, and suffered anguish; while on me without pain or toil by the fellowship of his suffering he freely bestows salvation.[112]

While it is not clear from this passage just how the disciples of Christ shared in His "sufferings" by an act of imitation, there may be a clue found in some of the other initiation texts of the ancient Christian church.[113] In a Syrian rite dating from 477 A.D., the officiating priest takes the thumb of his right hand and "imprints the forehead, left and right thumb, [and] left and right big toe of each candidate, accompanied by a formula."[114] This seems to have been an act of marking the places where the Savior received His crucifixion wounds; nails in His hands and feet, and the crown of thorns upon His head. As noted by one biblical scholar: "Men show themselves to be the possession of their deity by the imprint of their seal."[115]

Finally, we come to baptism for the dead, which is briefly mentioned in 1 Corinthians 15:29. The nature of this vicarious ordinance, which was inaugurated after Christ visited the spirit world to arrange for the preaching of the gospel to those who were dead (*see* 1 Peter 3:18–21; D&C 138:28–37), has been a matter of great debate among biblical interpreters. Although most Christian scholars would not agree with the LDS understanding of this ordinance, there are some that do. Some prominent non-LDS scholars, for instance, believe that the Apostle Paul is alluding in 1 Corinthians 15:29 "to a practice of the Corinthian community as evidence for Christian faith in the resurrection of the dead. It seems that in Corinth some Christians would undergo baptism in the name of their deceased non-Christian relatives and friends, hoping that this vicarious baptism might assure them a share in the redemption of Christ."[116] There are other biblical commentators that say much the same thing about this verse.

> The normal reading of the text is that some Corinthians are being baptized, apparently vicariously, in behalf of some people who have already died. It would be fair to add that this reading is such a plain understanding of the Greek text that no one would ever have imagined the various alternatives were it not for the difficulties involved. . . . Cf. the opinion of A. Oepke, TDNT, 1:542, nt. 63: "All interpretations which seek to evade vicarious baptism for the dead . . . are misleading" (cf. H. Riesenfeld, TDNT, 8:512–13); and Parry, 228: "[This is] the plain and necessary sense of the words."[117]

In other words, since this scripture speaks of an ordinance which none of the traditional Christian denominations understand, they feel that it is necessary to explain it away. The same feeling prevailed shortly after the Apostasy began. Even though there were some Christian splinter groups that were practicing the ordinance of vicarious baptism for the dead, it was officially abandoned in the sixth canon of the Synod of Hippo in the year 393 A.D.[118]

Apostasy

Both the scriptures and the historical documents of the early Christians indicate that there was to be an apostasy from the pure teachings and ordinances of Jesus Christ only a short while after they had been established on the earth.[119] The initiation rituals of the Christian community were quickly refashioned or altogether abandoned once the Lord's apostles were martyred for their beliefs and were no longer present to control the internal affairs of the Church. As demonstrated in the preceding pages, one can see references to the original rites in the scriptures themselves and frag-

ments of them in documents written several hundred years after the time of the apostles. Many of these preserved ritual fragments were eventually incorporated into the
liturgy of the Roman Catholic church.[120]

Some of these fragments can also be seen in the writings of the more heretical
breakaway Christian groups called the *gnostics*. The *gnostics* claimed to possess the
secret teachings and ordinances revealed by the Lord during His post-resurrection
ministry. From the letter attributed to Clement of Alexandria mentioned above, we
learn how at least one of the *gnostic* Christian sects obtained its so-called "mysteries."
Carpocrates, who arose as one of the original *gnostic* teachers between 117 and 138
A.D., is said to have "used deceitful devices so as to enslave a certain elder of the
church in Alexandria and procured from him a copy of the mystical gospel [of the
Apostle Mark], which he proceeded to interpret in accordance with his own blasphemous and carnal opinion. Moreover, he polluted it further by mixing shameless false-
hoods with the holy and undefiled sayings, and from this mixture the dogma of the
Carpocrations has been drawn out."[121]

SUMMARY

It is clear from the material presented in this chapter that the earliest Christians
never did abandon the temple of Israel but were forced to stop worshipping in it by
their enemies. The available evidence also indicates that Jesus Christ taught His faithful followers certain doctrines and rituals, during His post-resurrection forty-day ministry, that closely resembled those that were practiced in the temples of ancient Israel.
These rituals were practiced in locations considered to be holy by the early Saints.
Orthodox Christian sources testify that these ordinances were practiced for several
hundred years but became increasingly corrupted in form and meaning. Thus, the
need arose for the untainted gospel of Jesus Christ to be restored once again.

NOTES

1. See *LDS Bible Dictionary*, 783.

2. Ibid., 784.

3. Joseph Patrich, "Reconstructing the Magnificent Temple Herod Built," *Bible Review*, October 1988, 17.

4. "Tosefta Yoma (ch. ii) expressly notes that the ark [of the covenant] had been placed upon the stone of foundation. . . . [This stone, known in Hebrew as the *eben šetiyyah*] . . . was a portion of rock projecting three finger-breadths upwards from the floor of the Holy of Holies, covering a cavity which was regarded as the mouth of the abyss, reverenced as the center and foundation of the world, and having the ineffable name of God inscribed upon it" (Thomas Chaplin, "The Stone of Foundation and the Site of the Temple," *Palestine Exploration Quarterly* [London: Richard Bentley and Son, 1876], 24–25, see Mishnah, Yoma 5.2).

5. Patrich, "Reconstructing the Magnificent Temple Herod Built," 24. See also Lawrence D. Sporty, "Identifying the Curving Line on the Bar-Kokhba Temple Coin," *Biblical Archaeologist*, Spring 1983, 121–23.

6. M. Avi-Yonah, "The Facade of Herod's Temple: An Attempted Reconstruction," in Jacob Neusner, ed., *Religions in Antiquity* (Leiden: E. J. Brill, 1968), 333; see also figures 1, 3, and plate III.

7. Patrich, "Reconstructing the Magnificent Temple Herod Built," 25.

8. *Wars*, 5.5.4, in William Whiston, trans., *The Works of Josephus: Complete and Unabridged*, updated ed. (Peabody, Massachusetts: Hendrickson Publishers, 1987), 707.

9. The Savior, because he was not from the priestly tribe of Levi, never did enter into the Holy Place or the Holy of Holies of the Jerusalem Temple. Two Greek words are translated as *temple* in the New Testament (*hieron* and *naos*). The word *hieron* refers to all of the buildings in the temple complex while the word *naos* refers specifically to the temple itself (see J. D. Douglas, ed., *New Bible Dictionary*, 3d ed. [Downers Grove, Illinois: Intervarsity Press, 1996], 1159).

10. See, for example, A. J. B. Higgins, "Priest and Messiah," *Vetus Testamentum*, vol. 3, 1953, 334.

11. G. Widengren, "Royal Ideology and the Testaments of the Twelve Patriarchs," in F. F. Bruce, ed., *Promise and Fulfilment* (Edinburgh: T. and T. Clark, 1963), 206, nt. 20.

12. See Craig A. Evans, "Jesus' Action in the Temple: Cleansing or Portent of Destruction?" in Bruce Chilton and Craig A. Evans, *Jesus in Context: Temple, Purity, and Restoration* (Leiden: E. J. Brill, 1997), 395–439; see especially 429–30. It would appear from the evidence presented in this article that the Savior's actions were prompted by the fact that the temple priests had become greedy and corrupt, charging exhorbitant prices for the opportunity to perform religious duties.

13. Bruce Chilton, "The Whip of Ropes in John 2:15," in Chilton and Evans, *Jesus in Context: Temple, Purity, and Restoration*, 451.

14. Ulansey concludes that the outer veil was the one that tore based on the fact that the heavens were torn open (*schizomenous*) when Christ began his ministry with baptism (see Mark 1:10) and the veil of the temple was torn (*schizo*) when his earthly ministry ended with his crucifixion (see Mark 15:38). The more precise connection (besides the observation that these are the only places where Mark

uses *schizo*) can be seen in the fact that the outer veil of the temple was decorated with stars to represent the heavens (see David Ulansey, "The Heavenly Veil Torn: Mark's Cosmic *Inclusio*," *Journal of Biblical Literature*, vol. 110, no. 1, Spring 1991, 123–25; David Ulansey, "Heavens Torn Open: Mark's Powerful Metaphor Explained," *Bible Review*, August 1991, 32–37). For another scholar who favors the view that the outer veil tore, and presents a sizable bibliography of those who share that view, see Howard M. Jackson, "The Death of Jesus in Mark and the Miracle From the Cross," *New Testament Studies*, vol. 33, no. 1, January 1987, 24, 36 nt.23.

15. "According to Mishnah Yoma v.1 (cf. Middoth iv.7) two curtains a cubit apart from each other separated the [Holy Place] from the Holy of Holies" (Geoffrey W. Bromiley, ed., *The International Standard Bible Encyclopedia*, rev. ed. [Grand Rapids, Michigan: Eerdmans, 1988], 4:774; see also Patrich, "Reconstructing the Magnificent Temple Herod Built," 22, 25). Those who advocate the tearing of the Holy of Holies veil frequently quote the allegorizations found in Hebrews 6:19, 9:3, and 10:20 to support their argument "although no mention is made of a torn veil" in any of those verses (Allen C. Myers, ed., *The Eerdmans Bible Dictionary*, rev. ed. [Grand Rapids, Michigan: Eerdmans, 1987], 1036). Rice has demonstrated, based on a survey of texts from the Septuagint, that one cannot automatically assume that the veil mentioned in Hebrews 6:19–20 is the one hanging before the heavenly Holy of Holies (see George E. Rice, "Hebrews 6:19: Analysis of Some Assumptions Concerning *Katapetasma*," *Andrews University Seminary Studies*, vol. 25, no. 1, Spring 1987, 65–71).

16. Craig R. Koester, *The Dwelling of God* (Washington, D.C.: The Catholic Biblical Association of America, 1989), 127–28.

17. See footnote *a* to 1 Peter 2:5 in the LDS edition of the King James Bible which corrects "lively stones" to "living stones." Paul also spoke allegorically of the Christian community or Church as a "body" in 1 Corinthians 12:12–26 and Ephesians 4:15–16. Notice that his allegorical "body" is "fitly joined together" (Ephesians 4:16) just as his allegorical "temple" is "fitly framed together" (Ephesians 2:21). In other words, Paul could have used *any* allegory to describe the Church. What he was trying to teach in each case was that the Christian community had to be properly united together and cooperative. Since Paul did in fact use multiple allegories to describe the Church it should be apparent that the "temple" designation was simply a teaching device, and nothing else. The Savior himself used allegorical devices when he referred to the members of the Church as sheep (see John 10:1–16) and vine branches (see John 15:1–8).

18. James Strong, *The New Strong's Exhaustive Concordance of the Bible* (Nashville: Thomas Nelson Publishers, 1996), Greek Dictionary of the New Testament, 32, word #1841.

19. *MD*, 109–10.

20. *Article of Faith* #10: "We believe . . . that the earth will be renewed and receive its paradisiacal glory."

21. *TPJS*, 158.

22. *WJS*, 246. The Prophet elaborated on this idea by saying, "If a man gets a fulness of the priesthood of God he has to get it in the same way that Jesus Christ obtained it, and that was by keeping all the commandments and obeying all the ordinances of the house of the Lord" (*TPJS*, 308).

23. Joseph Fielding Smith and Bruce R. McConkie have both stated their opinion that the temple endowment was bestowed upon Peter, James, and John on the Mount of Transfiguration (see *DS*, 2:165; *Mortal Messiah*, 3:58; *DNTC*, 1:400). On one occasion Joseph Fielding Smith made it clear that the early Christians performed temple ordinances as they are understood by Latter-day Saints (see *DS*, 2:163–65). Heber C. Kimball stated forthrightly: "Jesus took Peter, James and John into a high mountain, and there gave them their endowment . . . For the same purpose has the Lord called us up into these high mountains, that we may become endowed with power from on high in the Church and kingdom of God, and become kings and priests unto God, which we never can be lawfully until we are ordained and sealed to that power, for the kingdom of God is a kingdom of kings and priests, and will rise in mighty power in the last days" (*JD*, 9:327).

24. John N. Kelly, *A Commentary on the Epistles of Peter and Jude* (New York: Harper and Row, 1969), 316–17.

25. "The word used for [eyewitnesses], *epoptes*, is an unusual and interesting one. It was commonly used to denote one initiated into the mystery religions" (Michael Green, *The Second Epistle General of Peter and the General Epistle of Jude* [Grand Rapids, Michigan: Eerdmans, 1987], 93).

26. On another occasion when the Lord enjoined secrecy upon his apostles, he is also said to have "charged" them (see Mark 8:30; Luke 9:21). The word translated as "charged" in these particular verses is *epitimao* and carries the meaning of forbidding with censure. A closely related word, *epitimia*, means "penalty" (Strong, *The New Strong's Exhaustive Concordance of the Bible*, Greek Dictionary, 35, words #2008 and #2009).

27. See John W. Welch, *Illuminating the Sermon at the Temple and Sermon on the Mount: An Approach to 3 Nephi 11–18 and Matthew 5–7* (Provo, Utah: Foundation for Ancient Research and Mormon Studies,1999), 47–114.

28. W. D. Davies, *The Sermon on the Mount* (Cambridge: University Press, 1966), 6–27.

29. Bruce R. McConkie believed that this angel may have been Adam (see Bruce R. McConkie, *The Mortal Messiah* [Salt Lake City: Deseret Book, 1981], 4:124–25). In this same source he also refers to the Garden of Gethsemane as a "second Eden."

30. Morton Smith, *The Secret Gospel: The Discovery and Interpretation of the Secret Gospel According to Mark* (New York: Harper and Row, 1973), 78. The implication of this text is that it was the Lord who instructed this disciple to come to his initiation "wearing a linen cloth." Another translation of this text says that the disciple was wearing "a linen robe" (F. F. Bruce, *The "Secret" Gospel of Mark* [London: Athlone Press, 1974], 8). Linen, of course, was the fabric used to make the clothing worn by the Israelite temple priests (see Leviticus 16:4).

31. Hugh W. Nibley, *Mormonism and Early Christianity* (Salt Lake City: Deseret Book and FARMS, 1987), 393.

32. Strong, *The New Strong's Exhaustive Concordance of the Bible*, Greek Dictionary, 62, word #3624.

33. The Greek word *oikos* refers to the "house" of God or temple in Matthew 12:4; 21:13; Mark 2:26; 11:17; Luke 6:4; 19:46; John 2:16; Acts 7:47–49; Hebrews 10:21.

34. See Bargil Pixner, "Church of the Apostles Found on Mt. Zion," *Biblical Archaeology Review*, May/June 1990, 16–35, 60. The building that housed the Upper Room was destroyed in 70 A.D.

when the Roman general Titus laid siege to Jerusalem. Scholars believe that some of the Judeo-Christians returned to Jerusalem after 73 A.D. "to rebuild their sanctuary on the site of the ancient Upper Room—where the Last Supper had been held, where the apostles returned after witnessing Jesus' ascension on the Mount of Olives and where Peter delivered his Pentecost sermon as recorded in Acts [chapter] 2" (ibid., 25). The reconstruction of this building was carried out "under the leadership of Simon Bar-Kleophas, who was the second bishop of Jerusalem after James, 'the brother of the Lord' [Galatians 1:19], and, like Jesus, a descendant of the royal Davidic family" (ibid., 26). "Kleophas was known as a brother of Joseph of Nazareth, therefore Simon was a cousin of Jesus" (ibid., 28). A few of the original stones from this structure still exist and their nature has led some scholars to believe that the Judeo-Christians may have taken stones from the destroyed temple and used them to construct their sanctuary. They may have done this in order to "transfer some of the holiness of the destroyed temple to their place of worship on the new Mt. Zion" (ibid., 28, see also 26–27).

35. *Brigham Young University Studies*, vol. 21, no. 4, Fall 1981, 532; hereafter cited as *BYUS*. This is a correction of the faulty text found in *WJS*, 211, which reads: "where Peter was[hed] and ano[inte]d." Joseph Smith taught on another occasion that the Apostle Peter had received "the endowment" (*WJS*, 331). Orson Pratt once reported: "On the day of Pentecost, a great feast which had been observed by the Jewish nation for many generations, there were gathered at Jerusalem, not only the Twelve Apostles, but also all the disciples of Jesus who had not apostatized, to the number of about a hundred and twenty souls—those of the ministry, the Seventies as well as the Twelve. They were gathered together in one place, in an *upper room of the temple;* and they were engaged in fervent prayer and supplication before the Lord. What for? For the *endowments and qualifications* necessary to assist them in the work of the ministry" (*JD*, 14:174, emphasis added).

36. For a discussion on some of the Pentecostal experiences that occurred in the Kirtland Temple, see Karl R. Anderson, *Joseph Smith's Kirtland: Eyewitness Accounts* (Salt Lake City: Deseret Book, 1989), 169–77.

37. When Joseph Smith performed the endowment rites for the first time in Nauvoo he did so in the "upper part" of his Red Brick Store (*HC*, 5:1–2). Heber C. Kimball referred to the place where the endowment ordinances were performed in the Nauvoo Temple as the "upper room" (Stanley B. Kimball, ed., *On the Potter's Wheel: The Diaries of Heber C. Kimball* [Salt Lake City: Signature Books in association with Smith Research Associates, 1987], 163). During the Nauvoo period, Brigham Young stated that "the ordinances of the endowment . . . must always be attended to in an upper room" (George D. Smith, ed., *An Intimate Chronicle: The Journals of William Clayton* [Salt Lake City: Signature Books in association with Smith Research Associates, 1995], 250).

38. See *HC*, 5:1–2.

39. *TPJS*, 307–308.

40. G. A. Williamson, trans., *Eusebius: The History of the Church from Christ to Constantine* (New York: Dorset Press, 1984), 72. In light of this statement it is worth noting Heber C. Kimball's claim that Jesus Christ was the one who initiated his apostles into the ordinances of the temple (see *JD*, 10:241). It is the consensus of several scholars that Clement, who was the head of the catechetical school in Alexandria, Egypt, believed in a "Christian gnosis, i.e., the secret knowledge of the pro-

foundest truths of the Christian faith to which the elite were initiated" (Raymond E. Brown, Joseph A. Fitzmyer, and Roland E. Murphy, eds., *The Jerome Biblical Commentary* (Englewood Cliffs, New Jersey: Prentice-Hall, 1968), 2:611.

41. John Gee, "Forty-Day Ministry and Other Post-Resurrection Appearances of Jesus Christ," in Daniel H. Ludlow, ed., *Encyclopedia of Mormonism* (New York: Macmillan, 1992), 2:735. See also S. Kent Brown and C. Wilfred Griggs, "The 40-Day Ministry," *Ensign*, August 1975, 6–11, which lists themes found in this literature such as ceremonial washings and anointings, reception of special clothing, premortal life, the heavenly council, the creation story, the Fall, dramatic dialogue between God, Adam, Eve, and Satan, secret teachings of the Savior, the plan of redemption, marriage as part of one's salvation, and three heavens.

42. See Welch, *Illuminating the Sermon at the Temple and Sermon on the Mount*, 75–77. It is of interest to note that "Matthew does not use *teleios* in the Greek sense of the perfect ethical personality, but in the Old Testament sense of the wholeness of consecration to God" (G. Bornkamm, G. Barth, and H. Held, *Tradition and Interpretation in Matthew* [London: SCM, 1963], 101).

43. Walter Lowrie, *Art in the Early Church* (New York: Pantheon Books, 1947), 107.

44. John L. Mosheim, *Historical Commentaries on the State of Christianity* (New York: S. Converse, 1854), 2:422. Christian temples are also mentioned on pages 416–18 and 423–24 of this volume. These references clearly distinguish between Christian churches and Christian temples. An apocryphal work called the Acts of John represents the Savior as saying: "I have temples" (J. K. Elliott, *The Apocryphal Jesus: Legends of the Early Church* [New York: Oxford University Press, 1996], 61).

45. Kenneth J. Conant, "The Original Buildings at the Holy Sepulchre in Jerusalem," *Speculum: A Journal of Mediaeval Studies*, vol. 31, no. 1, January 1956, 12.

46. Philip Schaff and Henry Wace, eds., *Nicene and Post-Nicene Fathers: Cyril of Jerusalem* (Peabody, Massachusetts: Hendrickson Publishers, 1994), 7:146–47. Other sources also demonstrate that the early Christians used the term "Holy of Holies," a distinctive temple term, in relation to their own sacred buildings. See, for example, Edward Yarnold, *The Awe-Inspiring Rites of Initiation: Baptismal Homilies of the Fourth Century* (England: St. Paul Publications, 1971), 73; Hugh M. Riley, *Christian Initiation* (Washington, D.C.: The Catholic University of America Press, 1974), 27, 42, 48, 230; Jacob Vellian, ed., *Studies on Syrian Baptismal Rites* (Kottayam: C.M.S. Press, 1973), 4, 6, 15.

47. Conant, "The Original Buildings at the Holy Sepulchre in Jerusalem," 44.

48. Philip Schaff and Henry Wace, eds., *Nicene and Post-Nicene Fathers: Eusebius* (Peabody, Massachusetts: Hendrickson Publishers, 1994), 531.

49. See Hugh W. Nibley, "Christian Envy of the Temple," in Hugh W. Nibley, *Mormonism and Early Christianity* (Salt Lake City: Deseret Book and FARMS, 1987), 391–434.

50. Alexander Roberts and James Donaldson, eds., *Ante-Nicene Fathers: The Clementina* (Peabody Massachusetts: Hendrickson Publishers, 1994), 336. "That the more learned of the Christians, subsequently to the second century, cultivated, in secret, an obstruse discipline of a different nature from that which they taught publicly, is well known to everyone. Concerning the argument, however, or matter of this secret or mysterious discipline, its origin, and the causes which gave rise to it, there are infinite disputes" (Mosheim, *Historical Commentaries on the State of Christianity*, 1:373). There are sev-

eral early sources that refer to the Christian rites of initiation as "mysteries" (see, for example, Riley, *Christian Initiation*, 10–11; Yarnold, *The Awe-Inspiring Rites of Initiation*, 73; Vellian, ed., *Studies on Syrian Baptismal Rites*, 55).

51. Strong, *The New Strong's Exhaustive Concordance of the Bible*, Greek Dictionary, 62, word #3623.

52. Compare with D&C 124:37–41, which speaks of the temple ordinances that have been "kept hid from before the foundation of the world." JST Colossians 2:2–3 indicates that in God and Christ "are hid all the treasures of wisdom and knowledge."

53. See Bo Frid, "The Enigmatic *alla* in 1 Corinthians 2:9," *New Testament Studies*, vol. 31, no. 4, October 1985, 605 and 608, where the word *teleios* is translated as "initiated." Other scholars note that *teleios* is "a technical term of the mystery religions, which refers to one initiated into the mystic rites, the initiate" (Walter Bauer, William F. Arndt, and F. Wilbur Gingrich, *A Greek-English Lexicon of the New Testament and Other Early Christian Literature*, rev. ed. [Chicago: University of Chicago Press, 1979], 809).

54. Bauer, Arndt, and Gingrich, *A Greek-English Lexicon of the New Testament and Other Early Christian Literature*, 530. The ritual background of this Greek word is well known. "Mysteries are cultic rites in which the destinies of a god are portrayed by sacred actions before a circle of devotees in such a way as to give them a part in the fate of the god. . . . Integral to the concept of the mysteries is the fact that those who wish to take part in their celebration must undergo initiation; the uninitiated are denied both access to the sacred actions and knowledge of them. . . . All mysteries promise their devotees salvation by the dispensing of cosmic life. . . . The holy mystery of the rites is [a] sanctifying union between the suffering deity and the devotees, who in the mysteries acquire a share in the destiny of the god and hence in the divine power of life. . . . The union with the gods is effected supremely by the sacramental actions with divine symbols which differ in the individual mysteries. Thus we find sacred meals and weddings, . . . baptisms, investitures with sacred garments, rites of death and resurrection, or cultically symbolised journeys to . . . heaven" (Gerhard Kittel, ed., *Theological Dictionary of the New Testament* [Grand Rapids, Michigan: Eerdmans, 1967], 4:803–805).

55. Strong, *The New Strong's Exhaustive Concordance of the Bible*, Greek Dictionary, 59, word #3466; emphasis in original.

56. Ibid., Greek Dictionary, 11, word #613; emphasis in original.

57. Robin Scroggs, "Paul: Sophos and Pneumatikos," *New Testament Studies*, vol. 14, no. 1, October 1967, 35. On page 38 of this same source the author states: "There is no reason, without evidence to the contrary, not to take Paul's words at face value. He does have an esoteric wisdom teaching in which he instructs only a few and which the congregation at Corinth seems not even to have heard about. . . . The select few to whom Paul transmits this teaching are called [*teleioi*, 'the perfect']. . . . That Paul's use of the term is formally similar to that of the mysteries has been argued strongly by exegetes, and the evidence is convincing." "D. W. B. Robinson argues that *teleioi* is employed in the mystery-initiate sense (cf. 1 Corinthians 2:6; Colossians 1:28); Hebrew believers were 'the first initiates into God's hidden mystery'" (John J. Gunther, *St. Paul's Opponents and Their Background* [Leiden: E. J. Brill, 1973], 277). For an informative look at certain Jewish esoteric teachings that may be con-

nected with Paul's comments, see William J. Hamblin, "Temple Motifs in Jewish Mysticism," in Donald W. Parry, ed., *Temples of the Ancient World: Ritual and Symbolism* (Salt Lake City: Deseret Book and FARMS, 1994), 440–76.

58. In Hebrews 7:19 and 10:1, the form of the Greek word translated as "perfect" is *teleioo*, which means "to put someone in the position in which he can come, or stand, before God" (Kittel, ed., *Theological Dictionary of the New Testament*, 8:82).

59. Emphasis added. Notice that the focus in Hebrews 3:11, 18–19 and most of chapter 4 (and again in 12:18–29) is on entering into the rest of the Lord and the failure of the Israelites at Mount Sinai to do so. For further reading, see M. Catherine Thomas, "Hebrews: To Ascend the Holy Mount," in Parry, ed., *Temples of the Ancient World*, 479–91.

60. "License" and "authority" are substituted here for "boldness" as an alternate translation from the Greek text. This is noted in footnote 19*a* of the LDS edition of the King James Bible.

61. Kittel, ed., *Theological Dictionary of the New Testament*, 4:580, nt. 2.

62. Ibid., 4:12.

63. Clement of Alexandria saw "the truths of the Christian religion as mysteries. Led by Christ the mystagogue [i.e., "one who initiates into mysteries," Stromata IV, 162, 3ff] the Gnostic [or "knower"] receives initiation and perfection [Protrepticon XII, 120,1] by going through the stages from the little mysteries (e.g., the doctrine of creation) to the great mysteries, in which the mystical initiation takes place [Stromata IV, 3, 1; Protrepticon XII]. The supreme mysteries, to be protected against profanation, must be passed on only in veiled form [Stromata V, 57, 2]" (Kittel, ed., *Theological Dictionary of the New Testament*, 4:825).

64. Bruce, *The "Secret" Gospel of Mark*, 7. Dr. Nibley has provided a translation of an Egyptian-Christian ritual text that may provide some insight into the content of Mark's secret gospel (see Hugh W. Nibley, *Mormonism and Early Christianity* [Salt Lake City: Deseret Book and FARMS, 1987], 83–85, 95–99).

65. See Yarnold, *The Awe-Inspiring Rites of Initiation*, 22. The Christian anointing ritual is also connected with the kings and priests of ancient Israel in Vellian, ed., *Studies on Syrian Baptismal Rites*, 21, 27, 45, 82, 91. "Christian rites of anointing commonly referred to the anointing of prophets, priests, and kings" (Leonel L. Mitchell, *Baptismal Anointing* [Notre Dame: University of Notre Dame Press, 1978], 22). By the early sixth century A.D., the anointing ritual was still being explained to Christian initiates "in terms of a royal and priestly mystery" (ibid., 98).

66. Mitchell, *Baptismal Anointing*, 22.

67. See Riley, *Christian Initiation*, 31, 120, 349, 370. In some instances the olive oil was perfumed with myrrh (Yarnold, *The Awe-Inspiring Rites of Initiation*, 22).

68. See Vellian, ed., *Studies on Syrian Baptismal Rites*, 81.

69. See Schaff and Wace, eds., *Nicene and Post-Nicene Fathers: Cyril of Jerusalem*, 150. See also the translation of this material found in McCauley and Stephenson, eds., *The Works of Saint Cyril of Jerusalem*, 171–73. The words "unction" and "anointing" in 1 John 2:20, 27 are both translated from the Greek word *chrisma*, which means "smearing" and is related to the concept of "endowment" (Strong, *The New Strong's Exhaustive Concordance of the Bible*, Greek Dictionary, 99, word #5545). This word

is derived from *chrio,* which means "to *smear* or *rub* with oil, i.e. (by implication) to *consecrate* to an office or religious service" (ibid., word #5548; emphasis in original). Some may argue that the "anointing" in 1 John 2:20, 27 is simply a metaphorical term that represents the reception of the Holy Ghost. But the reception of the Spirit is precisely what occurred when kings and priests were anointed with holy anointing oil in the Old Testament. Christ's disciples were endowed "with power from on high" when the Spirit descended upon them on the day of Pentecost (see Luke 24:49; Acts 2:1–4) and the Apostle John directly connected the Holy Ghost with "anointing" in 1 John 2:20, 27. For further reading, see Donald W. Parry, "Ritual Anointing with Olive Oil in Ancient Israelite Religion" and John A. Tvedtnes, "Olive Oil: Symbol of the Holy Ghost," both in Stephen D. Ricks and John W. Welch, eds., *The Allegory of the Olive Tree: The Olive, the Bible, and Jacob 5* (Salt Lake City: Deseret Book and FARMS, 1994), 262–89 and 427–59 respectively.

70. "Of the beliefs and practices whether generally accepted or publicly enjoined which are preserved in the Church some we possess derived from written teaching; others we have received delivered to us 'in a mystery' by the tradition of the apostles; and both of these in relation to true religion have the same force. . . . For we are not, as is well known, content with what the apostle or the Gospel has recorded, but both in preface and conclusion we add other words as being of great importance to the validity of the ministry, and these we derive from unwritten teaching. . . . Nay, by what written word is the anointing of oil itself taught? . . . Does not this come from that unpublished and secret teaching which our fathers guarded in a silence out of the reach of curious meddling and inquisitive investigation? Well had they learnt the lesson that the awful dignity of the mysteries is best preserved by silence. What the uninitiated are not even allowed to look at was hardly likely to be publicly paraded about in written documents" (Philip Schaff and Henry Wace, eds., *Nicene and Post-Nicene Fathers: Basil, Letters and Select Works* [Peabody, Massachusetts: Hendrickson Publishers, 1994], 40–42).

71. See Vellian, ed., *Studies on Syrian Baptismal Rites,* 67, 94. In one early Christian text we read: "He is sealed with [anointing oil] . . . upon the organs of sense that they may not be entrances of sin. Again on the forehead that he may be terrifying to [evil spirits]. Again on the joints (members) that they may be instruments of righteousness" (ibid., 4). Another text indicates that "all the senses" were anointed (ibid., 67). In some instances the perfumed olive oil is said to have been "applied to the forehead and the organs of sensation" (Yarnold, *The Awe-Inspiring Rites of Initiation,* 32). Sources that mention the anointing of the forehead, ears, nose, and chest can be seen in Riley, *Christian Initiation,* 372–75. In the apocryphal Gospel of Bartholomew, Jesus Christ is represented as saying, "the Father named me Christ, that I might come down on earth and anoint with the oil of life everyone who came to me" (Edgar Hennecke and Wilhelm Schneemelcher, eds., *New Testament Apocrypha* [Philadelphia: Westminster Press, 1963], 1:501).

72. See Riley, *Christian Initiation,* 49, 146–47, 155; Yarnold, *The Awe-Inspiring Rites of Initiation,* 20–21, 194; Mitchell, *Baptismal Anointing,* 40, 44; Vellian, ed., *Studies on Syrian Baptismal Rites,* 27, 30, 34–35, 42–43, 51, 73, 82, 87–88, 116. Page 107 of this same source mentions that initiates were anointed on "all their limbs."

73. Yarnold, *The Awe-Inspiring Rites of Initiation,* 166. In the *Apostolic Constitutions* 7.22, the oil is referred to as "holy oil" and the administrator of the anointing ordinance is directed: "thou shalt seal

him with the chrism . . . the chrism [being] a seal of the covenants" (cited in Mitchell, *Baptismal Anointing*, 45–46).

74. Everett Ferguson, ed., *Encyclopedia of Early Christianity*, 2d ed. (New York: Garland Publishing, 1997), 1:57. Cyril of Jerusalem also noted that through this anointing, all Christians "were made Christs" (cited in Mitchell, *Baptismal Anointing*, 44).

75. See Riley, *Christian Initiation*, 21, 266, 349–50, 353, 388, 413–51; Mitchell, *Baptismal Anointing*, 20, 41, 75, 98, 127, 129; Yarnold, *The Awe-Inspiring Rites of Initiation*, 28–29, 86–87, 129, 165, 168, 189, 207; Vellian, ed., *Studies on Syrian Baptismal Rites*, 2–3, 6, 14.

76. Yarnold, *The Awe-Inspiring Rites of Initiation*, 165, 168; Riley, *Christian Initiation*, 155, 426–27, 430, 448; Vellian, ed., *Studies on Syrian Baptismal Rites*, 38, 40.

77. Riley, *Christian Initiation*, 414–15, 424–25, 433, 439, 447–48. The initiate is "received from the font and adorned as a bridegroom on the day of his marriage-supper" (Vellian, ed., *Studies on Syrian Baptismal Rites*, 56).

78. Vellian, ed., *Studies on Syrian Baptismal Rites*, 3, 14.

79. Yarnold, *The Awe-Inspiring Rites of Initiation*, 207. "Ambrose means to show the [initiates] that the white robe which they are wearing signifies their participation in the resurrection and ascension of Christ, the King of Glory, depicted also in a white robe. The white robe of Christ, resurrected and ascended, and the baptismal robe of the candidate are one" (Riley, *Christian Initiation*, 439).

80. Rudolph Arbesmann, Emily J. Daly, and Edwin A. Quain, trans., *Tertullian: Apologetical Works* (Washington, D. C.: The Catholic University of America Press, 1962), 336.

81. All three of these marks can be seen on white Christian robes in Nicolas Zernov, *Eastern Christendom* (London: Weidenfeld and Nicolson, 1963), figure 19. A close-up of two of these marks can be seen in F. van der Meer, *Early Christian Art* (London: Faber and Faber, 1967), plate 19.

82. See C. Wilfred Griggs, et. al., "Evidences of a Christian Population in the Egyptian Fayum and Genetic and Textile Studies of the Akhmim Noble Mummies," *BYUS*, vol. 33, no. 2, 1993, 226. For a picture of this garment, see page 227.

83. William Smith and Samuel Cheetham, *Dictionary of Christian Antiquities* (New York: Kraus Reprint Co., 1968), 1:709. A drawing of an ancient Christian garment bearing right angle or *gamma* marks can be seen in Klaus Wessel, *Coptic Art* (New York: McGraw-Hill, 1965), 236. For further reading on ritual garments among the ancient Israelites and early Christians, see Hugh Nibley's article "Sacred Vestments" in Hugh W. Nibley, *Temple and Cosmos* (Salt Lake City: Deseret Book and FARMS, 1992), 91–138 and Blake Ostler, "Clothed Upon: A Unique Aspect of Christian Antiquity," *BYUS*, vol. 22, no. 1, Winter 1982, 31–45.

84. Erwin R. Goodenough, *Jewish Symbols in the Greco-Roman Period* (New York: Pantheon Books, 1964), 9:164. See also the illustrations found on pages 88, 128, and 163.

85. For an example, see George Every, *Christian Legends* (New York: Peter Bedrick Books, 1987), 51.

86. For examples, see Elizabeth E. Goldsmith, *Sacred Symbols in Art*, rev. ed. (New York: G. P. Putnam's Sons, 1911), 162; Clara E. Clement, *A Handbook of Legendary and Mythological Art* (Cambridge: Riverside Press, 1876), 290.

87. See John B. Friedman, "The Architect's Compass in Creation Miniatures of the Later Middle Ages," *Traditio: Studies in Ancient and Medieval History, Thought, and Religion*, vol. 30, 1974, 419–29.

This source contains many early Christian artworks showing the Lord holding an architect's compass. For other examples, see Avril Henry, *The Eton Roundels* (Brookfield, Vermont: Gower Publishing, 1990), 90; *Biblical Archeological Review*, April 1995, 45; Harold Bayley, *The Lost Language of Symbolism* (London: Williams and Norgate, 1912), 1:74.

88. For one example, see Richard Morris, *Cathedrals and Abbeys of England and Wales* (London: J. M. Dent and Sons, 1979), 104.

89. For instance, see the illustration of the labyrinth from the Reims Cathedral where monks on the outer boundaries of the maze are holding these instruments (see Maria-Gabriele Wosien, *Sacred Dance: Encounter with the Gods* [New York: Avon Books, 1974], 104).

90. See Griggs, "Evidences," 225–26. See the photographs of two of these robes on page 272. Along with the ritual clothing already mentioned, there are several texts that list ankle-length white linen garments resembling those "worn by the ancients," sashes, aprons, white linen head coverings, and face veils as part of the garb worn by early Christian initiates (see Yarnold, *The Awe-Inspiring Rites of Initiation*, 10, 30, 121–22; Wolfred N. Cote, *The Archaeology of Baptism* [London: Yates and Alexander, 1876], 53, 55, 70).

91. Smith and Cheetham, *Dictionary of Christian Antiquities*, 2:1214.

92. Bauer, Arndt, and Gingrich, *A Greek-English Lexicon of the New Testament and Other Early Christian Literature*, 810.

93. Henry G. Liddell and Robert Scott, *A Greek-English Lexicon*, rev. ed. (Oxford: Clarendon Press, 1989), 1789.

94. Vellian, ed., *Studies on Syrian Baptismal Rites*, 78.

95. Riley, *Christian Initiation*, 36, 51–52.

96. See Riley, *Christian Initiation*, 145, 446; Vellian, ed., *Studies on Syrian Baptismal Rites*, 3, 12, 14, 43, 46, 50–51; Yarnold, *The Awe-Inspiring Rites of Initiation*, 21, 75, 194.

97. See Riley, *Christian Initiation*, 39, 62–63, 75, 145.

98. See Vellian, ed., *Studies on Syrian Baptismal Rites*, 4, 6, 15.

99. See Yarnold, *The Awe-Inspiring Rites of Initiation*, 186.

100. For examples, see Pierre du Bourguet, *Early Christian Art* (New York: Reynal and Co., 1971), 30, 34, 77, 149; Pierre du Bourguet, *Early Christian Painting* (London: Contact Books, 1965), figures 7, 14, 19, 41, 69, 80, 85.

101. Yarnold, *The Awe-Inspiring Rites of Initiation*, 9; see also 17, 165, 177; Riley, *Christian Initiation*, 29–30, 31–32, 34, 57, 64, 68, 74–75; Vellian, ed., *Studies on Syrian Baptismal Rites*, 5, 10.

102. See Hugh W. Nibley, "The Early Christian Prayer Circle," in Hugh W. Nibley, *Mormonism and Early Christianity* (Salt Lake City: Deseret Book and FARMS, 1987), 45–99. In conjunction with the contents of this article, the reader's attention should be drawn to Matthew 26:30 and Mark 14:26, where it is mentioned that Christ and his apostles sang a hymn in the Upper Room before the Lord ascended the Mount of Olives to the Garden of Gethsemane. This hymn, notes one commentator, "was sung antiphonally: Jesus as the leader would sing the lines, and his followers would respond" (Frank E. Gaebelein, *The Expositor's Bible Commentary: Matthew* [Grand Rapids, Michigan: Zondervan, 1984], 539). The apocryphal Acts of John claims to describe what happened when Christ and his apostles sang

this very hymn. "So he [Christ] told us to form a circle, holding one another's hands, and [he] himself stood in the middle and said, 'Answer *Amen* to me.' So he began to sing the hymn" (Edgar Hennecke and Wilhelm Schneemelcher, eds., *New Testament Apocrypha* [Philadelphia: Westminster Press, 1965], 2:227; emphasis added).

103. See Vellian, *Studies on Syrian Baptismal Rites*, 4, 8, 43, 92, 97; Yarnold, *The Awe-Inspiring Rites of Initiation*, 169; Riley, *Christian Initiation*, 328.

104. See Vellian, ed., *Studies on Syrian Baptismal Rites*, 88–89, 91.

105. Until the ordinances had been completed, the initiates were told, "Let the separation be preserved, the men together and the women together" (William Telfer, ed., *Cyril of Jerusalem and Nemesius of Emesa* [Philadelphia: Westminster Press, 1955], 74). "In the 'Apostolic Constitutions,' a writing compiled in the 4th century, A.D., there is a reference to the custom whereby men sat on one side of the room where a meeting was held, and women on the other side of the room" (William E. Vine, *Vine's Expository Dictionary of Old and New Testament Words* [Old Tappan, New Jersey: Fleming H. Revell, Co., 1985], New Testament Words, 2:296). There is some evidence that female officials attended to the anointing of female initiates (see Yarnold, *The Awe-Inspiring Rites of Initiation*, 21, nt. 96). Wilford Woodruff recorded that the bottom floor of the Kirtland Temple was "divided into four parts by veils, the females occupied two parts and the males the others. . . . The veils were all rolled up together which brought the whole congregation in full view of each other" (Dean C. Jessee, "The Kirtland Diary of Wilford Woodruff," *BYUS*, vol. 12, no. 4, Summer 1972, 386).

106. The instructor in one ancient initiation text speaks to the candidate of "the new world you are entering" (Yarnold, *The Awe-Inspiring Rites of Initiation*, 186).

107. See Riley, *Christian Initiation*, 30, 68.

108. The renunciation of Satan and everything associated with him is a common element in the early Christian initiation texts (see Yarnold, *The Awe-Inspiring Rites of Initiation*, 17–18, 178). In some texts it appears that Satan was considered to be present when this renunciation occurred (see Riley, *Christian Initiation*, 42–43, 49). In one set of initiation texts, the candidate raises one hand while renouncing Satan (see Vellian, ed., *Studies on Syrian Baptismal Rites*, 93).

109. See Yarnold, *The Awe-Inspiring Rites of Initiation*, 169; Vellian, ed., *Studies on Syrian Baptismal Rites*, 43; Cote, *The Archaeology of Baptism*, 55.

110. See Vellian, ed., *Studies on Syrian Baptismal Rites*, 55.

111. The early Christians looked forward to receiving the "embrace and kiss of the Lord" after death (Rose B. Donna, trans., *Saint Cyprian* [Washington, D.C.: The Catholic University of America Press, 1964], 19, 96).

112. Philip Schaff and Henry Wace, eds., *Nicene and Post-Nicene Fathers: Cyril of Jerusalem* (Peabody, Massachusetts: Hendrickson Publishers, 1994), 7:148. In offering his own translation of this text, Dr. Nibley believes that it should be rendered, "O strange and paradoxical thing! We did not die in reality, nor were we really buried, nor did we rise up after having been actually crucified. Rather it was imitation (*mimesis*) by a token (*eikon*), while the salvation part is the real thing. Christ was really crucified, really was buried, and really rose again, and all that for our benefit, so that by sharing his sufferings in imitation we might attain to a real salvation. O love of men overflowing! Christ really

received the nails in his blameless hands and feet and suffered pain; while I, without any pain or struggle, by his sharing of suffering the pain enjoy the fruits of salvation!" (Hugh W. Nibley, *The Message of the Joseph Smith Papyri: An Egyptian Endowment* [Salt Lake City: Deseret Book, 1975], 282).

113. Riley questions the assumption, made by many interpreters of this statement, that Cyril is speaking here of baptism which, after all, is not a symbolic imitation of Christ's crucifixion but of his burial and resurrection. Riley fails to see how Christ's "hands being pierced with the nails" is represented by "imitation through the medium of an image" in the baptismal rite (Riley, *Christian Initiation*, 237–38).

114. Vellian, ed., *Studies on Syrian Baptismal Rites*, 74; see also 83. Compare with the consecration ritual of the Israelite temple priests found in Exodus 29:20.

115. Colin Brown, ed., *The New International Dictionary of New Testament Theology* (Exeter, England: Paternoster Press, 1978), 3:497.

116. Brown, Fitzmyer, and Murphy, eds., *The Jerome Biblical Commentary*, 2:273.

117. Gordon D. Fee, *The First Epistle to the Corinthians* (Grand Rapids, Michigan: Eerdmans, 1987), 763–64.

118. Samuel M. Jackson, ed., *The New Schaff-Herzog Encyclopedia of Religious Knowledge* (Grand Rapids, Michigan: Baker Book House, 1977), 1:454. Commentary on this page reads, "Baptism for the Dead: A custom mentioned by Paul in 1 Corinthians 15:29. It probably consisted in the vicarious baptism of a living Christian for a catechumen who had died unbaptized, the latter being thereby accounted as baptized and so received into bliss." John A. Tvedtnes notes that "the Greek original of 1 Corinthians 15:29 does *not* use the pronoun *they*. It says, 'Otherwise, what will do *the ones being baptized* for the dead?' The text uses a passive participle form, 'the being baptized [ones],' as a substantive (where it is usually accompanied by the definitive article). Participles reflect gender, number, and case, but not person. Hence, there is no third-person plural *(they)* in the Greek original. Stressing the pronoun supplied by the English Bible translators for flow in English distorts Paul's meaning" (*FARMS Review of Books*, vol. 10, no. 2, 1998, 196; emphasis in original).

119. For articles on the apostasy of the early Christians, see Kent P. Jackson, "Early Signs of the Apostasy," *Ensign*, December 1984, 8–16; Kent P. Jackson, "'Watch and Remember': The New Testament and the Great Apostasy," in John M. Lundquist and Stephen D. Ricks, eds., *By Study and Also By Faith* (Salt Lake City: Deseret Book and FARMS, 1990), 1:81–117; Hugh W. Nibley, "The Passing of the Primitive Church: Forty Variations on an Unpopular Theme," in Hugh W. Nibley, *Mormonism and Early Christianity* (Salt Lake City: Deseret Book and FARMS, 1987), 168–208; S. Kent Brown, "Whither the Early Church?" *Ensign*, October 1988, 7–10.

120. See Marcus von Wellnitz, "The Catholic Liturgy and the Mormon Temple," *BYUS*, vol. 21, no. 1, Winter 1981, 3–35.

121. Bruce, *The "Secret" Gospel of Mark*, 7–8.

CHAPTER SIX

The Restoration of the Temple

In the spring of 1820 both the Father and the Son appeared to Joseph Smith in a grove of trees in upstate New York and inaugurated the Restoration of the gospel to the earth for the last time. This divine appearance came in response to the Prophet's prayer asking which of all the divergent Christian congregations was the right one to join. Joseph Smith was informed by Jesus Christ during this visitation that he was not to join himself with any Christian denomination because they were all in a state of apostasy. The Savior also told Joseph Smith "many other things" during this interview that have not yet been revealed.[1]

Three years later, on 21 September 1823, the Prophet prayed for a divine manifestation that would indicate his "state and standing" before God. While the prophet was engaged in this prayer, his room began to fill with light and an angel of God named Moroni appeared before him.[2] The angel immediately began to teach the Prophet about the Restoration of the pure gospel of Jesus Christ to the earth, and he quoted many passages from the Bible that pertain to the last days, including prophecies from Isaiah and Malachi that speak of latter-day temples.[3] Since the angel Moroni "offered many explanations" about the scriptures he was quoting on this occasion,[4] and showed the Prophet visions that pertained to what was being taught,[5] it would seem reasonable to conclude that by 1823 Joseph Smith was aware that temples and temple worship would play a part in the Restoration of the gospel.

THE KIRTLAND TEMPLE

In December of 1830, less than a year after the Church had been formally organized, the Lord commanded His Latter-day Saints to gather themselves together in the state of Ohio (*see* D&C 37:3). The Lord explained in January of 1831 that this was necessary so that He could reveal His "law" unto them and also so that they could become "endowed with power from on high" and sent forth to preach the gospel unto all the nations of the earth (D&C 38:32, 38; 39:14–15; *see also* 43:16). By 27 December 1832 the Lord had commanded the Saints that they were to build a temple in the city of Kirtland, Ohio (*see* D&C 88:119–120).[6]

A Revealed Pattern

President Brigham Young informs us that Joseph Smith "not only received revelation and commandment to build a temple, but he received a *pattern* also, as did Moses for the tabernacle, and Solomon for his temple; for without a pattern, he could not know what was wanting, having never seen one, and not having experienced its use."[7] It is apparent from scriptural sources that by 6 May 1833 the Lord had already revealed to the Prophet the "pattern" for laying out the city of Kirtland in the same manner as the city of Zion, with the temple in the center (*see* D&C 94:1–2). On this same day the Lord also promised that sometime in the future He would reveal both the "pattern" for laying the cornerstones of the temple "according to the order of the priesthood" and the "pattern" for the temple's interior (D&C 94:5–6).

On 1 June 1833 the Lord reiterated His desire that the Kirtland Temple be built so that He could endow His Saints with "power from on high" even as His disciples in Jerusalem had been endowed (*see* D&C 95:8–9; compare Luke 24:49). The Lord also commanded on this occasion: "Therefore, let it be built after the manner which I shall show unto three of you, whom ye shall appoint and ordain unto this power" (D&C 95:14). On the 3rd of June 1833 it was decided that the First Presidency would go before the Lord and receive this promised vision of the temple.[8] Even though the exact date of this vision is not known, there was a sudden flurry of temple-building activity on the 5th and 6th of June,[9] thus hinting that the vision had been received by that time. Elder Orson Pratt said of this vision that God "revealed the pattern according to which that house should be built, pointing out the various courts and apartments, telling the size of the house, the order of the pulpits, and in fact everything pertaining to it was clearly pointed out by revelation. God gave a vision of these things, not only to Joseph [Smith], but to several others, and they were strictly commanded to build according to the pattern revealed from the heavens."[10] President Frederick G. Williams was one of the three men who saw this vision. Truman O. Angell records,

Frederick G. Williams, one of President Smith's counselors, came into the temple, when the following dialogue took place in my presence. Carpenter Rolph said: "Doctor, what do you think of the house?" He answered: "It looks to me like the pattern precisely." Then he related the following: "Joseph [Smith] received the word of the Lord for him to take his two counselors, Williams and Rigdon, and come before the Lord, and He would show them the plan or model of the house to be built. We went upon our knees, called on the Lord, and the building appeared within viewing distance: I being the first to discover it. Then all of us viewed it together. After we had taken a good look at the exterior, the building seemed to come right over us; and the make-up of this hall seems to coincide with what I there saw to a minutia." Joseph was accordingly enabled to dictate to the mechanics, and his counselors stood as witnesses.[11]

Architectural Symbolism

As indicated above, the pulpits of the Kirtland Temple, which served as the seating areas for twenty-four priesthood leaders, were seen in the vision that was shown to the First Presidency. Since the Lord revealed the pattern of these pulpits, one would expect them to have symbolic meaning. There may be a connection between the twenty-four seats in the pulpits, the twenty-four elders of Israel seated upon thrones in the heavenly temple (*see* JST Revelation 4:4, 6), and the twenty-four courses of temple priests mentioned in the Old Testament (*see* 1 Chronicles 24:7-19; 28:11–13, 19). Elder Heber C. Kimball recorded an incident that happened at Adam-ondi-Ahman, Missouri, which links the Kirtland Temple pulpits to the ancient past.

The Prophet Joseph [Smith] called upon brother Brigham [Young], myself and others, saying, "Brethren, come, go along with me, and I will show you something." He led us a short distance to a place where were the ruins of three altars built of stone, one above the other, and one standing a little back of the other, like unto the pulpits in the Kirtland Temple, representing the order of three grades of Priesthood; "There," said Joseph, "is the place where Adam offered up sacrifice after he was cast out of the garden." The altar stood at the highest point of the bluff. I went and examined the place several times while I remained there.[12]

Carved into the interior and exterior surfaces of the Kirtland Temple are many symbols that correspond to those that once decorated the ancient temples of Israel. Some of these symbols can be classified as paradise emblems—flowers, vines, the water of life, and the tree of life. As pointed out in a previous chapter, both the tabernacle built by Moses and the temple erected by King Solomon were decorated so as to represent the Garden of Eden. In addition to these garden motifs, there are other

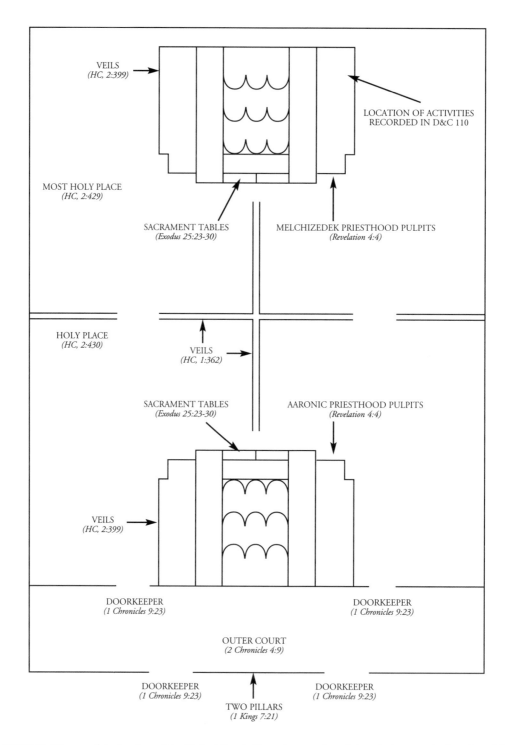

FIGURE 32. Diagram of the first floor of the Kirtland Temple illustrating several parallels to the layout and orientation of the temples of ancient Israel.

symbols such as two pillars, sacrament tables shaped like the yokes of oxen, keystones, veils, and an interesting assortment of geometric emblems.[13] The layout of the Kirtland Temple (as pictured) is also symbolic since the early Latter-day Saints referred to its compartments by the same terms used to designate the rooms of Israel's ancient temples.

THE KIRTLAND ENDOWMENT

There were two sets of endowment ceremonies introduced among Latter-day Saints during the early history of the Church. The first set was administered in the Kirtland Ohio Temple, and a second set was administered in the temple built in Nauvoo, Illinois. While both of these rituals shared various elements between them, it is apparent that the Kirtland rites were geared toward bestowing certain blessings that pertained to this lifetime, while the Nauvoo rites were meant to bestow blessings that pertained to eternity.

An Endowment for Time

It was sometime after the Lord had commanded the building of the Kirtland Temple that He revealed to Joseph Smith the ordinances that were to be administered within its walls.[14] The Kirtland endowment ceremonies were only bestowed upon members of the priesthood quorums because they bore the responsibility of laboring in the Lord's vineyard as messengers of the restored gospel. Joseph Smith said that the Kirtland Temple rites were "necessary ceremonies" that would qualify priesthood bearers to "build up the kingdom of God" on the earth.[15]

From a variety of early sources it can be determined that the Kirtland endowment ceremonies consisted of at least the following eight elements: (1) solemn assemblies for receiving instructions on the doctrines, principles, and laws of the gospel,[16] (2) the ordinances of washing and anointing,[17] (3) a sealing ritual,[18] (4) the making of covenants,[19] (5) partaking of the sacrament in commemoration of the Marriage Supper of the Lamb,[20] (6) the employment of ritual gestures and language,[21] (7) the ordinance of the washing of feet,[22] (8) and the reception of "power from on high" in the form of various spiritual manifestations.[23]

But as President Brigham Young pointed out "those first Elders who helped to build [the Kirtland Temple], received a portion of their first endowments, or we might say more clearly, some of the first, or introductory, or initiatory ordinances, preparatory to an endowment. The preparatory ordinances there administered, though accompanied by the ministration of angels, and the presence of the Lord Jesus, were but a faint similitude of the ordinances of the House of the Lord in their fulness."[24] According to Elder Orson Pratt,

> The Lord told us, when we were living in the state of New York, to go to the Ohio; there to build a temple to the name of the Most High. And there the Lord condescended to bestow upon his servants and people a great endowment, a blessing such as was not known among the children of men. And from thence they should go to the nations of the earth, and publish these tidings. We went to the Ohio; and after we had been sufficiently taught and instructed, the Lord commanded us through Joseph [Smith], to build a temple, giving the pattern thereof, and the size thereof, the size of the inner and outer courts, the size of the several rooms and apartments, and the form of the pulpits and everything pertaining to it, was given by the inspiration of the Almighty that rested upon Joseph, and upon those associated with him.
>
> When the temple was built, the Lord did not see proper to reveal all the ordinances of the endowments such as we now understand. He revealed little by little. No rooms were prepared for washings; no special place prepared for the anointings, such as you understand, and such as you comprehend at this period of the history of the Church! Neither did we know the necessity of the washings, such as we now receive. It is true, our hands were washed, our faces and our feet [see D&C 88:74; compare Exodus 40:30–32]. The Prophet Joseph was commanded to gird himself with a towel, doing this in the temple [see D&C 88:138–141; compare John 13:3–17]. What for? That the first Elder might witness to our Father and God, that we were clean from the blood of that wicked generation, that then lived. We had gone forth according to our best ability, to publish glad tidings of great joy, for thousands of miles, upon this continent. After this we were called in, and this washing of hands and feet was to testify to God that we were clean from the blood of this generation. The holy anointing was placed upon the heads of his servants, but not the full development of the endowments in the anointing. These administrations in the Kirtland Temple were revealed, little by little, corresponding with what I have already been saying, that the Lord does not give the fulness at once, but imparts to us according to his own will and pleasure. Great were the blessings received. We were commanded to seek to behold the face of the Lord; to seek after revelation; to seek after the spirit of prophecy, and the gifts of the Spirit; and many testify to what they saw.[25]

THE RESTORATION OF TEMPLE KEYS

Joseph Smith was evidently under the impression that once he had administered all of the temple ordinances that were thus far revealed to him, the restoration of the ancient Church would be complete. "I then observed to the quorums," said the Prophet, "that I had now completed the organization of the Church, and we had passed through all the necessary ceremonies."[26] But on 3 April 1836, which was both Easter Sunday and the Jewish Passover,[27] the Lord suddenly appeared to Joseph Smith and Oliver Cowdery in the holiest part of the Kirtland Temple[28] and inaugurated the restoration of still more keys of knowledge and power pertaining to His holy house.

The Keys

The visitations that are recorded in section 110 of the Doctrine and Covenants occurred after the emblems of the sacrament had been blessed and passed to those who were congregated in the temple's main room. Once this ordinance had been attended to, Joseph Smith and Oliver Cowdery both retired to the area of the Melchizedek Priesthood pulpits on the west end of the building and lowered the white partitions or "veils" that separated the pulpits from the main room. They then each bowed at the pulpits, offered up a silent prayer, and rose to their feet. It was at this point that the veil between heaven and earth was parted, and they saw a series of angelic beings, standing upon the pulpits, who had come to deliver to them *the keys of power.*[29]

• JESUS CHRIST *(D&C 110:2–10).* Joseph Smith informed W. W. Phelps as early as 11 January 1833 that the Lord had promised the Saints a personal "visit from the heavens" if they would construct the Kirtland Temple.[30] This promise is reflected in D&C 94:8–9, dated 6 May 1833, where the Lord specified that He would personally visit the Kirtland Temple. Even though Joseph Smith acknowledged in the temple's dedicatory prayer that the Lord's house was a place where He might "manifest himself" (D&C 109:5), it is not known if the Prophet was aware that such a visit would occur on 3 April 1836.

Even though one does not get the impression from reading the contents of D&C 110 that the Savior delivered any particular *keys* during this visitation, as did the angelic messengers who appeared after Him, Elder Orson Pratt testified that the Lord did indeed bestow "keys of instruction and counsel and authority" on this occasion.[31] Elder Franklin D. Richards adds that the Lord "conversed with the Prophet Joseph and Oliver, and revealed to them their duties, and informed them that the gospel should go [forth] from there and be preached throughout the nations of the earth."[32] It is apparent from these comments that D&C 110 does not record everything that occurred during this manifestation.[33]

• MOSES (D&C 110:11). After the vision of the Savior had closed, the heavens were once again opened and the prophet Moses appeared upon the Melchizedek Priesthood pulpits. Moses committed unto Joseph Smith and Oliver Cowdery "the keys of the gathering of Israel from the four parts of the earth." These keys pertained to all twelve of the tribes of Israel, including the ten northern tribes that had been taken into captivity around 721 B.C. These ten tribes were scattered throughout the lands north of Israel to such an extent that they no longer had cohesive identities. In this manner they became "lost" among the nations of the earth.[34] Elder Erastus Snow taught that "the keys of Moses" were committed during the final dispensation of the gospel "for the restoration and redemption of the House of Israel."[35]

Why were these keys of gathering necessary? Hadn't the Church already been sending out missionaries prior to Moses' appearance to gather the Lord's people? Yes, but during that time frame the gathering was confined to a limited area of North America and was mostly focused on the birthright tribe of Ephraim, which was responsible for bestowing the blessings of the restored gospel upon the other tribes of Israel (see D&C 133:25–34).[36] The gathering keys brought by Moses were designed to facilitate the restoration of the entire House of Israel and to bestow a very specific type of blessing upon all of its twelve tribes. Joseph Smith asked: "What was the object of gathering the Jews, or the people of God in any age of the world? . . . The main object was to build unto the Lord a house [wherein] He could reveal unto his people the ordinances of his house and the glories of his kingdom, and teach the people the way of salvation; for there are *certain ordinances and principles* that, when they are taught and practiced, must be done in a place or house built for that purpose."[37] The Prophet was more specific on another occasion when he said that "God gathers together the people in the last days to build unto the Lord a house to prepare them for the ordinances and *endowment, washings and anointings, etc.*"[38] To be even more precise, the Prophet further said that the gathering of the Saints was required so that "the *fulness of the Priesthood* might be revealed among them which never can be done but by the gathering of the people."[39]

Joseph Smith knew as early as 23 September 1832 that Moses was aware of certain Melchizedek Priesthood ordinances that would enable the Lord's disciples to enter into His presence (*see* D&C 84:19–25). The Prophet had also learned through his inspired translation of the book of Exodus in the first half of 1833 that Moses understood these ordinances to be part of the "holy order" of God (*see* JST Exodus 34:1–2). Since the Lord told Joseph Smith in November of 1831 that it was his "duty" to "be like unto Moses" (D&C 107:91),[40] one wonders if perhaps the Prophet expected Moses, at some point in time, to deliver keys to him that were related to God's "holy order."

• ELIAS *(D&C 110:12)*. The identity of Elias is somewhat of a mystery until one learns from D&C 27:6–7 that he was the same angel who visited Zacharias the temple priest inside the Lord's house in Jerusalem. In Luke 1:19 this angel identifies himself as Gabriel and, according to Joseph Smith, the angel Gabriel is Noah.[41] Thus, the "Elias" of D&C 110:12 would appear to be the patriarch Noah. This would help to explain why this particular angel was sent to deliver keys associated with the dispensation of Abraham because, according to President John Taylor, Abraham's dispensation "was under the dispensation that was introduced . . . by Noah."[42] The apocryphal Book of Jasher claims that Noah and Abraham were not only contemporaries but that they knew each other.[43]

Curiously, D&C 110:12 does not say that Elias committed any "keys" to Joseph Smith and Oliver Cowdery, but rather it says that he committed unto them "the dispensation of the gospel of Abraham, saying that in [them] and [their] seed all generations after [them] should be blessed" (compare D&C 124:58). This phrase comes directly from the wording of the covenant that God established with Abraham (*see* Genesis 12:3; 18:18; 22:18; Abraham 2:9–11), and so it would seem logical to conclude that Elias restored the blessings of the Abrahamic covenant. Elder Bruce R. McConkie has provided the following thoughts in regard to this subject.

> Now what was the gospel of Abraham? Obviously it was the commission, the mission, the endowment and power, the message of salvation, given to Abraham. And what was this? It was a divine promise that both in the world and out of the world his seed should continue "as innumerable as the stars; or, if ye were to count the sand upon the seashore ye could not number them" (D&C 132:30; Genesis 17; Abraham 2:1–12). Thus the gospel of Abraham was one of celestial marriage. . . . This power and commission is what Elias restored, and as a consequence, the righteous among all future generations were assured of the blessings of a continuation of the seeds forever, even as it was with Abraham of old.[44]

Elder McConkie further teaches that in latter-day temples "faithful couples enter into the ordinance of celestial marriage through which they become parties to the Abrahamic covenant, the covenant of eternal increase, the covenant that in them and in their seed all generations shall be blessed."[45] Those portions of the Abrahamic covenant "which pertain to personal exaltation and eternal increase are renewed with each member of the house of Israel who enters the order of celestial marriage; through that order the participating parties become inheritors of all the blessings of Abraham, Isaac, and Jacob."[46]

• ELIJAH *(D&C 110:13–16)*. On the evening of 21 September 1823, Joseph Smith learned from the angel Moroni that, at some point before the Second Coming, the Lord would send the ancient prophet Elijah to the earth. The Prophet also learned during this visitation that Elijah would somehow "reveal" the priesthood and "plant in the hearts of the children the promises made to the fathers" (D&C 2:1–3).

For untold centuries the Hebrews had expected Elijah to return to the earth at Passover. They even had a tradition that, among other things, Elijah would return to restore temple worship to its pure form.[47] And now here Elijah stood, at Passover, on the Melchizedek Priesthood pulpits in the Kirtland Temple.[48] During his appearance Elijah announced that the biblical prophecy of his return, found in Malachi 4:5–6, was now fulfilled, and he proceeded to commit[49] the "keys of this dispensation" into the hands of Joseph Smith and Oliver Cowdery (*see* D&C 110:14–16).

What exactly were the "keys of this dispensation"? As mentioned above, Elijah's mission was to somehow "reveal" the priesthood (*see* D&C 2:1–3). Joseph Smith identified the dispensation of the fulness of times as "the dispensation of the fulness of the priesthood,"[50] and he had this to say about Elijah's keys:

> Now for Elijah. The spirit, power, and calling of Elijah is, that ye have power to hold the key of the revelations, ordinances, oracles, powers and endowments of the fulness of the Melchizedek Priesthood and of the kingdom of God on the earth; and to receive, obtain, and perform all the ordinances belonging to the kingdom of God, even unto the turning of the hearts of the fathers unto the children, and the hearts of the children unto the fathers, even those who are in heaven. . . . What is this office and work of Elijah? It is one of the greatest and most important subjects that God has revealed. He should send Elijah to seal the children to the fathers, and the fathers to the children. . . . I wish you to understand this subject, for it is important; and if you receive it, this is the spirit of Elijah, that we redeem our dead, and connect ourselves with our fathers which are in heaven, and seal up our dead to come forth in the first resurrection; and here we want the power of Elijah to seal

those who dwell on earth to those who dwell in heaven. This is the power of Elijah and the keys of the kingdom of Jehovah. . . . Then what you seal on earth, by the keys of Elijah, is sealed in heaven; and this is the power of Elijah. . . . The power of Elijah is sufficient to make our calling and election sure.[51]

From this quotation, and several others by the Prophet, we can determine that when Elijah appeared in the Kirtland Temple, he accomplished several distinct but related tasks.

• He revealed all of the powers and blessings that are associated with the holy priesthood of God (*see* D&C 2:1), including the power to seal something on the earth and have it sealed eternally in heaven.[52] The "sealing blessings" are equated with "the Holy Spirit of Promise" in D&C 124:124.[53] Elder Parley P. Pratt informs us that this "last key of the priesthood is the most sacred of all."[54]

• He committed "the keys of the *authority* to administer in all the ordinances of the Priesthood"[55] including the ordinances associated with the fulness of the Melchizedek Priesthood that make one's calling and election sure. It also appears that the "keys of this dispensation" that were brought by Elijah authorized Joseph Smith to have the ordinances of the fulness of the Melchizedek Priesthood revealed unto him at some future time.

• He made it known that the powers of the holy priesthood could be employed for the redemption of the dead as well as the living. The purpose of exercising these keys on behalf of both the living ("children") and the dead ("fathers"), said the Prophet, is to form "a whole and complete and perfect union, and welding together of dispensations" (D&C 128:18). And in order to facilitate this linkage, Elijah revealed "the covenants of the fathers in relation to the children, and the covenants of the children in relation to the fathers."[56]

While section 110 of the Doctrine and Covenants speaks of three angels who committed "the keys of their Priesthood" to Joseph Smith and Oliver Cowdery in the Kirtland Temple, President Joseph F. Smith tells us that "it is very possible also that others of the ancient prophets, who held keys of dispensations appeared in this house at this time, or subsequently, with their keys and authorities."[57] Thus we read that at some unspecified time Joseph Smith received visitations from angels such as Michael, Gabriel, Raphael and "divers angels, from Michael or Adam down to the present time, all declaring their dispensation, their rights, their keys, their honors, their majesty and glory, and the power of their priesthood; giving line upon line, precept upon precept;

here a little, and there a little; giving us consolation by holding forth that which is to come, confirming our hope!" (D&C 128:21).

The Transition

Why did the Lord wait until the Nauvoo period to reveal the ordinances that were connected with the keys committed in the Kirtland Temple on 3 April 1836? First of all, it must be remembered that Kirtland, Ohio, was only a temporary gathering place for the Saints. In May of 1831 the Lord indicated that the Saints would only remain in Ohio "for a little season" until he should "provide for them otherwise, and command them to go hence" (D&C 51:16). On 11 September 1831 the Lord was even more specific when He announced that the Saints would only remain in Kirtland, Ohio, for the space of five years (*see* D&C 64:21), during which time they would lay the foundation for a great work which was yet to come (vs. 33). It was not until near the very end of this time frame that the Kirtland Temple was dedicated and the angels of D&C 110 came to commit their keys. According to Joseph Fielding Smith, the house of the Lord in Kirtland "was only a *preparatory temple*" that "was built *primarily* for the restoration of keys of authority."[58]

Elder George A. Smith indicated that there were other reasons why the Lord only bestowed a portion of his full temple rites upon the Saints during the Kirtland period. He said that during those years the Saints had among them "a great many traditions which they borrowed from their fathers," and some of them were so unstable in the gospel that they apostatized over very trivial matters. Even when the Lord restored the basic temple rituals of the Kirtland period, some of the Saints "apostatized because there was not more of it, and others because there was too much." Elder Smith continues,

> If the Lord had on that occasion revealed one single sentiment more, or went one step further to reveal more fully the law of redemption, I believe he would have upset the whole of us. The fact was, he dare not, on that very account, reveal to us a single principle further than he had done, for he had tried, over and over again, to do it. He tried at Jerusalem; He tried away back before the flood; He tried in the days of Moses; and he had tried, from time to time, to find a people to whom he could reveal the law of salvation, and he never could fully accomplish it; and he was determined this time to be so careful, and advance the idea so slowly, to communicate them to the children of men with such great caution that, at all hazards, a few of them might be able to understand and obey.[59]

All of this raises an interesting question. Since Joseph Smith had the necessary keys, could he have restored and administered the Nauvoo-style temple rites during the Kirtland period? Brigham Young seems to have thought so. After giving a basic outline of the Nauvoo-era temple rites, President Young said that "before these endowments could be given at Kirtland, the Saints had to flee before mobocracy." The Saints then settled in Far West, Missouri, and laid the cornerstones of a temple there but eventually "had to retreat to [Nauvoo,] Illinois to save the lives of those who could get away alive from Missouri." President Young lamented that the Kirtland Temple then fell "into the hands of wicked men, and by them [it was] polluted, like the temple at Jerusalem, and consequently it was disowned by the Father and the Son."[60]

And what about the Far West Temple? Did the Lord plan to restore the full temple ordinances to the Saints in His house at Far West, Missouri? This seems to be a definite possibility. The "pattern" that the Lord revealed for the Kirtland Temple would not have lent itself very well to the administration of the type of ordinances that were practiced during the Nauvoo period. But notice that the Lord was going to "show" the First Presidency the "pattern" for the Far West Temple just as He had for the Kirtland Temple (*see* D&C 115:7–16). Why would this have been necessary unless the "pattern" for the Far West Temple was going to be different than the "pattern" for the Kirtland Temple? As noted above in Brigham Young's statement, persecution and mobocracy prevented the building of the Far West Temple and the Saints did not get another chance to build a House of God until they had settled in Nauvoo, Illinois. Before the Prophet even set foot in Nauvoo, he wrote a member of the Church saying: "I never have had [an] opportunity to give [the Saints] the plan that God has revealed to me."[61]

THE NAUVOO TEMPLE

Joseph Smith moved to Commerce, Illinois, on 10 May 1839. He soon renamed the city Nauvoo and, by divine decree, designated it as the new gathering place for all Latter-day Saints.[62] Shortly thereafter he began to teach temple-related doctrines in earnest. Some of the topics that he spoke on included baptism for the dead, making one's calling and election sure, the Holy Spirit of Promise, the General Assembly and Church of the Firstborn, being sealed up to eternal life, building up Zion, the keys of Elijah, and being brought into God's presence through the power of the priesthood.[63]

It seems apparent from historical sources that the construction of the Nauvoo Temple was considered as early as 19 July 1840.[64] Despite this, the cornerstones for the temple in Nauvoo were not laid out and dedicated until 6 April 1841.[65] As with the Kirtland and Far West temples, the Lord promised to reveal the pattern for the house that would bear His name in the city of Nauvoo.

The Pattern Revealed

On 19 January 1841 the Lord indicated that he would "show" Joseph Smith "all things pertaining to" the Nauvoo Temple (D&C 124:42). Although the exact date when this visionary revelation occurred is not known, it appears to have been sometime before 1 July 1841 since it was announced in the *Times and Seasons* on that date that "the temple will be erected according to the pattern given."[66] When the chief engineer of the temple, William Weeks, disagreed with one of the architectural features that had been planned for the building, the Prophet directed him to carry out the original design. "I have seen in vision the splendid appearance of that building illuminated, and will have it built according to the pattern shown me."[67]

By what means was the pattern of the Nauvoo Temple shown to the Prophet? One source informs us that there "were a great many questions asked Brother Joseph about how he kept the pattern of the [Nauvoo] Temple in his mind so perfect." The Prophet answered: "When a true spirit makes known anything to you, in the daytime, we call it a vision. If it is a true spirit it will never leave you, every particular will be as plain fifty years hence as now."[68] This is consistent with the statement made by Elder Parley P. Pratt to the effect that the Prophet learned "sacred architecture" from "angels and spirits from the eternal worlds."[69]

Architectural Symbolism

The most prominent architectural features of the Nauvoo Temple were the sunstones, moonstones, and starstones that decorated its exterior. It is evident from several sources that at least some of the architectural symbols on the Nauvoo Temple were seen by Joseph Smith in vision. Josiah Quincy reports that the following incident took place on 15 May 1844 while he was being shown around the temple site by the Prophet. "Near the entrance to the temple we passed a workman who was laboring upon a huge sun, which he had chiselled from the solid rock. . . . 'General Smith,' said the man, looking up from his task, 'is this like the face you saw in vision?' 'Very near it,' answered the prophet. . . . [The Nauvoo Temple was] presumably, like something Smith had seen in vision, it certainly cannot be compared to any ecclesiastical building which may be discerned by the natural eyesight."[70]

FIGURE 33. Rare 1847 image of the Nauvoo Temple. The architectural design of this building, including the prominent astronomical decorations that adorned its exterior, was seen in vision by the Prophet Joseph Smith prior to its construction.

What Joseph Smith saw in his vision of the Nauvoo Temple seems to have been very similar to, or the very same as, what the ancient apostle John saw in a vision that is recorded in Revelation 12:1. Wandle Mace, who was one of the construction foremen for the Nauvoo Temple, provides us with confirmation on this point.

> The order of architecture was unlike anything in existence, it was purely original, being a representation of the Church, the Bride, the Lamb's wife. John the Revela[tor] in the 12th chapter, first verse [of the Book of Revelation] says, "And there appeared a great wonder in heaven; a woman clothed with the sun, and the moon under her feet, and upon her head a crown of twelve stars." This is portrayed in the beautifully cut stone of this grand temple.[71]

But why would the Lord show Joseph Smith a symbolic vision of the heavenly Church and then have him incorporate the symbolism associated with that vision into the architecture of the Nauvoo Temple? Perhaps the answer can be found in Joseph Smith's inspired translation of this biblical vision. In JST Revelation chapter 12 verses 1 and 7 we learn that the woman in this vision represented "the church of God" who "brought forth the kingdom of our God and his Christ" and that she was "in the likeness of things on the earth." The Apostle Paul called the heavenly church the "general assembly and church of the firstborn" in Hebrews 12:23. According to Joseph Smith, the ordinances that he restored for use in the Nauvoo Temple consisted of "all those plans and principles by which anyone is enabled to secure the fulness of those blessings which have been prepared for the Church of the Firstborn."[72] Hence, the architectural symbolism on the outside of the Nauvoo Temple indicated the nature of the ordinances that were performed within its walls.[73]

Another symbolic object in the Nauvoo Temple was the baptismal font. The font was first mentioned, by the Lord, in a revelation on the Nauvoo Temple dated 19 January 1841 (see D&C 124:29–33). Joseph Smith taught that "God decreed before the foundation of the world that [the] ordinance [of baptism for the dead] should be administered in a font prepared for that purpose in the house of the Lord."[74] He also stated that this particular type of "baptismal font was instituted as a similitude of the grave, and was commanded to be in a place underneath where the living are wont to assemble" (D&C 128:13), meaning that it was to be placed below the ground level of the building. This font, with twelve oxen underneath its basin, was designed after the pattern of the Brazen Sea in King Solomon's Temple (see 1 Kings 7:23–26). Elder Erastus Snow claimed that Joseph Smith was given "a knowledge of how to build [the] baptismal font" for the Nauvoo Temple.[75]

The doctrine of baptism for the dead was first publicly taught by Joseph Smith on 15 August 1840.[76] Parley P. Pratt listed this doctrine among many that the Prophet learned from heavenly messengers[77] and, indeed, the Prophet indicated that he had "knowledge independent of the Bible" regarding this doctrine.[78] It is of more than passing interest that the Prophet once gave a detailed description of the Apostle Paul[79] since the doctrine of baptism for the dead is only mentioned in Paul's biblical writings (*see* 1 Corinthians 15:29). Perhaps Paul was the heavenly messenger who was sent to restore the knowledge of this doctrine to Joseph Smith.

When the Nauvoo Temple was complete enough to accommodate ordinance work, its attic story was divided into several rooms of various sizes. These included rooms where initiatory rituals took place—the creation room; the garden room; the world, or telestial, room; the terrestrial room; and the celestial room. Patrons who received the rites of the endowment passed through each of these compartments from the initiatory rooms in the west to the Celestial Room in the east.[80] The Telestial, Terrestrial, and Celestial rooms of the Nauvoo Temple symbolically represented the three heavenly degrees of post-resurrectional glory and also corresponded respectively to the Courtyard, Holy Place, and Holy of Holies in the temples of ancient Israel.

THE RITUALS OF THE NAUVOO TEMPLE

Joseph Smith publicly taught many things about the temple ordinances that were restored through him during the Nauvoo period. Among the important insights that he provided on this subject, the Prophet taught that it is necessary for each Latter-day Saint to understand "the designs and purposes of God in our coming into the world, our sufferings here, and our departure hence." He reasoned that,

> Could we read and comprehend all that has been written from the days of Adam, on the relation of man to God and angels in a future state, we should know very little about it. Reading the experience of others, or the revelation given to them, can never give us a comprehensive view of our condition and true relation to God. Knowledge of these things can only be obtained by experience through the ordinances of God set forth for that purpose. Could you gaze into heaven five minutes, you would know more than you would by reading all that ever was written on the subject.[81]

The Prophet further informed the Saints that if they wanted to acquire the fulness of salvation they would need to subject themselves, before leaving this world, "to certain rules and principles, which were fixed by an unalterable decree before the world was." This is necessary, he explained, because the "organization of the spiritual and

heavenly worlds, and of spiritual and heavenly beings, [is] agreeable to the most perfect order and harmony: their limits and bounds [are] fixed irrevocably, and volun-
tarily subscribed to in their heavenly estate." He also stated that Adam and Eve were
obedient to these laws while they were upon the earth and that it was required of all
those who expected eternal life to embrace and subscribe to these very same principles. In rounding out these thoughts he assured the Saints that "truth, in reference to
these matters, can and may be known through the revelations of God in the way of
his ordinances, and in answer to prayer."[82]

On another occasion the Prophet taught that the Lord commanded the Saints to
build temples unto His name so that he "could reveal unto his people the ordinances
of his house and the glories of his kingdom, and teach the people the way of salvation;
for there are certain ordinances and principles that, when they are taught and practiced,
must be done in a place or house built for that purpose."[83] A woman named Mercy R.
Thompson, who lived in Nauvoo, reports: "I received my endowments by the directions of the Prophet Joseph, his wife Emma officiating in my case. In his instructions
to me at that time, he said, 'This will bring you out of darkness into marvelous light.'"[84]

The Endowment

In a revelation given on 19 January 1841, known as Doctrine and Covenants section 124, the Lord outlined the basic elements of the ordinances that were to be practiced in the Nauvoo Temple, and he promised to restore these rites at a future time
through the Prophet Joseph Smith. In this revelation the Lord mentions, in subtle language, that these ordinances are the same as those that were practiced in the ancient
tabernacle built by Moses and in the temple constructed by King Solomon (vs. 38).
According to this revelation, the Nauvoo Temple rites were to include baptism for the
dead (vss. 29–36, 39), washings (vs. 39), anointings (vs. 39), solemn assemblies (vs.
39), an endowment (vs. 39), conversations (vs. 39), oracles (vs. 39), statutes (vs. 39),
judgements (vs. 39), memorials of sacrifices (vs. 39),[85] the keys of the holy priesthood
(vss. 34, 95, 97, 123), sealing blessings (vs. 124), ordinances that have been kept hidden (vss. 38, 40–41), and the fulness of the priesthood (vs. 28).

The exact date when the Nauvoo Temple endowment ceremonies were restored
in their fulness is not presently known. The only thing that can be said with certainty
is that they were restored sometime between 19 January 1841 (when the Lord
promised to reveal them) and 4 May 1842 (when Joseph Smith administered them
for the first time). As demonstrated in the appendix of this book, there is ample evi-

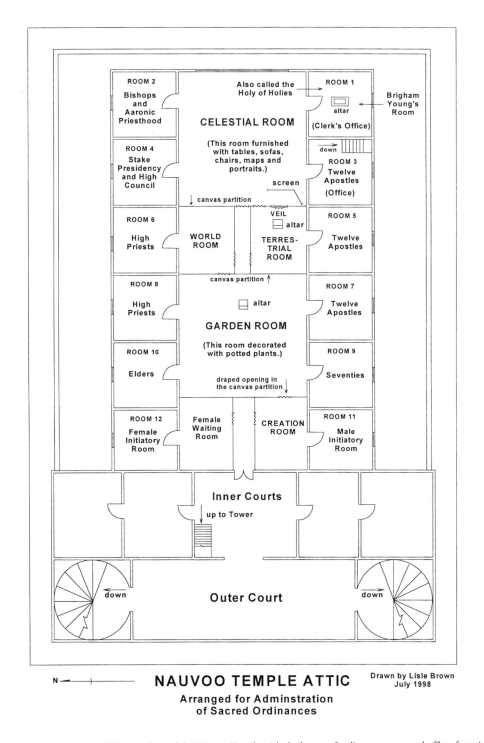

FIGURE 34. Reconstruction of the top floor of the Nauvoo Temple with the layout of ordinance rooms and offices for priesthood leaders.

dence that a revelation of endowment ordinances did indeed occur. There are also indications from a wide variety of historical sources that the Prophet, and a few other Saints, were aware of some of the ritual elements of the Nauvoo-era endowment long before it was first administered.[86]

During the Nauvoo period Joseph Smith had premonitions that he would not remain with the Saints on the earth very much longer. There are several historical sources which indicate that the Prophet was commanded by the Lord to proceed to bestow the endowment ordinances upon certain individuals before the Nauvoo Temple was completed.[87] And so on 3 May 1842 the Prophet gathered together a small group of brethren—Lucius N. Scovil, Shadrack Roundy, Noah Rogers, Dimick B. Huntington, Daniel Cairns, and Hosea Stout—and with them he prepared the upper room of his Red Brick Store so that it was arranged to represent "the interior of a temple as much as the circumstances would permit." The Prophet told these men that the room would be used for "giving endowments to a few Elders" and that he intended to "give unto them all the *keys of power* pertaining to the Aaronic and Melchizedek Priesthoods." Lucius Scovil recalled that during this preparatory work, which lasted throughout the day and was completed before noon on May 4th, the Prophet presented these brethren with "many items that were very interesting to us, which sank with deep weight upon my mind, especially after the temple was finished at Nauvoo, and I had received the ordinances."[88]

After the preparatory work had been completed, Joseph Smith gathered together a small group of priesthood leaders, which included Brigham Young, Heber C. Kimball, James Adams, Willard Richards, Newel K. Whitney, George Miller, William Marks, and William Law. The Prophet and his brother, Hyrum Smith, then spent the remainder of May 4th administering the ordinances of the temple endowment to these men. The *History of the Church* records that the Prophet and his brother spent the day,

> instructing them in the principles and order of the Priesthood, attending to washings, anointings, endowments and the communication of keys pertaining to the Aaronic Priesthood, and so on to the highest order of the Melchizedek Priesthood, setting forth the order pertaining to the Ancient of Days, and all those plans and principles by which anyone is enabled to secure the fulness of those blessings which have been prepared for the Church of the Firstborn, and come up and abide in the presence of the Eloheim in the eternal worlds. In this council was instituted the ancient order of things for the first time in these last days. And the communications I made to this council were of things spiritual, and to be received only by the spiritually minded.[89]

Without going into any inappropriate detail, we might offer a few brief remarks on some of the ritual elements that are mentioned in this quotation. The Prophet alluded on many public occasions to the "washings and anointings" that were given to the Saints as part of the temple ordinances.[90] In the *Encyclopedia of Mormonism* it is indicated that these washings and anointings are ceremonial in nature and are administered preparatory to donning "the sacred clothing of the temple."[91] All of those who participate in the temple endowment ceremonies are clothed with a white ceremonial garment.[92] They also put on "other priestly robes. The garment is worn at all times, but the robes are worn only in the temple." The garment bears "several simple marks" of a symbolic nature.[93]

The "order pertaining to the Ancient of Days," that is mentioned in the above quotation, may refer to the ritual drama of the endowment ceremony wherein temple patrons are taught about Adam, who is identified in latter-day scripture as "the ancient of days" (*see* D&C 27:11). The *Encyclopedia of Mormonism* notes that participants in the endowment rituals "assemble in ordinance rooms to receive . . . instruction and participate in the unfolding drama of the plan of salvation. They are taught of premortal life; the spiritual and temporal creation; the advent of Adam and Eve, and their transgression and expulsion into the harsh contrasts of the mortal probation."[94] Elder John A. Widtsoe has also stated that the temple endowment provides "information concerning the story of man, the creation of earth, [and] our first earthly parents."[95]

In the above quotation we also read that the temple endowment provides patrons with all of the "plans and principles" necessary to enable them to enter into the presence of exalted beings.[96] In speaking of the celestial glory, the Prophet Joseph Smith taught that "it is necessary for men to receive an understanding concerning the laws of the heavenly kingdom, before they are permitted to enter it."[97] Elder John A. Widtsoe taught that those who receive the endowment make a "covenant to obey the laws of eternal progress, and thereby give life to the knowledge received" during the ceremony.[98] Elder James E. Talmage informs us that the "ordinances of the endowment embody certain obligations on the part of the individual" and that with "the taking of each covenant and the assuming of each obligation a promised blessing is pronounced, contingent upon the faithful observance of the conditions."[99]

The "keys" that are mentioned in the above quotation are partly connected with the temple's function as "a house of prayer" (D&C 88:119; 109:8). As stated by the Lord in D&C 124, there are certain "keys" that have been ordained so that one may "ask and receive blessings" (vss. 95, 97). Elder Orson Pratt verified in the old foot-noting system of the Doctrine and Covenants that the "keys" mentioned in D&C 124 are "the order of God" for receiving certain blessings.[100] From Elder Charles C. Rich we learn that,

> It was a long time after the Prophet Joseph Smith had received the keys of the kingdom of God, and after Hyrum and others had received many blessings, that the Lord gave Joseph a revelation, to show him and others how they could ask for and receive certain blessings. We read in [Revelation 2:17] that the Saints are to receive a white stone, "and in the stone a new name written, which no man knoweth saving he that receiveth it." Joseph [Smith] tells us [in D&C 130:10–11] that this new name is a key word, which can only be obtained through the endowments. This is one of the keys and blessings that will be bestowed upon the Saints in these last days, for which we should be very thankful.[101]

The Prophet told a gathering of sister Saints, shortly before the temple ordinances were first given, that he was about to deliver "the keys of the Priesthood to the Church, and said that the faithful members of the Relief Society should receive them."[102] Sister Bathsheba W. Smith stated that when the Prophet was speaking during one of the Nauvoo fast-and-testimony meetings, he informed that gathering of Saints that in the temple rituals they would be taught certain principles pertaining to prayer.[103] In the *Encyclopedia of Mormonism* we read: "The prayer circle is a part of Latter-day Saint temple worship, usually associated with the endowment ceremony."[104]

Celestial Marriage

Celestial marriage was introduced as one of the temple ordinances after women began to receive the endowment ceremonies.[105] In sections 49, 131, and 132 of the Doctrine and Covenants we are presented with revelations and items of instruction concerning the Lord's law of marriage. In D&C 49:15–17 the Lord states that "marriage is ordained of God unto man. Wherefore, it is lawful that he should have one wife, and they twain shall be one flesh, and all this that the earth might answer the end of its creation; and that it might be filled with the measure of man, according to his creation before the world was made."[106] As mentioned previously in this chapter, when Elias appeared in the Kirtland Temple on 3 April 1836, he committed unto Joseph Smith and Oliver Cowdery the "dispensation of the gospel of Abraham" (D&C 110:12), which has been interpreted to mean the Abrahamic covenant. When the Lord established His covenant with Abraham, he promised the patriarch a posterity as numerous as the sand and the stars. The means of fulfilling such a promise would, of necessity, be attached to the practice of marriage. Hence, celestial or eternal marriage is associated with the Abrahamic covenant.

In D&C 131 we are informed that in the celestial kingdom "there are three heavens or degrees; and in order to obtain the highest, a man must enter into this *order of the priesthood* [meaning the new and everlasting covenant of marriage]; and if he does not, he cannot obtain it. He may enter into [a lower degree within the celestial world], but that is the end of his kingdom; he cannot have an increase" (vss. 1–4; emphasis added). In other words, the eternal marriage covenant of the temple is an order of the priesthood, and no one can achieve exaltation, or eternal life, without entering into it.

In section 132 of the Doctrine and Covenants the Lord provides a number of valuable insights into the doctrine of celestial marriage. Beginning in verse 3 it is explained that before the foundation of the world was laid, the members of the Godhead established certain laws and conditions that must be obeyed before one can receive specific blessings (vss. 5, 11). Among these laws is the *new and everlasting covenant* which, according to the Lord, is "instituted for the fulness of my glory." Without exception, all those who are to receive this fulness of glory *must* abide by this law (vs. 6). The Lord further states that "the conditions of this law are these: All covenants, contracts, bonds, obligations, oaths, vows, performances, connections, associations, or expectations, that are not made and entered into and sealed by the Holy Spirit of promise . . . both as well for time and for all eternity . . . through the medium of mine anointed . . . are of no efficacy, virtue, or force in and after the resurrection from the dead; for all contracts that are not made unto this end have an end when men are dead" (vs. 7). The Lord also issues the stern warning that all things in the world that are not done according to His word, which is His law, will be thrown down, shaken, and destroyed "and shall not remain after men are dead, neither in nor after the resurrection" (vss. 12–14). In short, all men and women who are not married and sealed by the power of the Holy Priesthood will be separate and single after the resurrection and will be appointed as "ministering servants" to those who have obeyed the law of marriage that God has ordained (vss. 15–18).[107]

For those who enter into the new and everlasting covenant of marriage, and endure in faithfulness unto the end, the Lord promises the marvelous blessings of exaltation.

> And again, verily I say unto you, if a man marry a wife by my word, which is my law, and by the new and everlasting covenant, and it is sealed unto them by the Holy Spirit of promise, by him who is anointed, unto whom I have appointed this power and the keys of this priesthood . . . [then they] shall come forth in the first

resurrection . . . and shall inherit thrones, kingdoms, principalities, and powers, dominions, all heights and depths . . . and they shall pass by the angels, and the gods, which are set there, to their exaltation and glory in all things, as hath been sealed upon their heads, which glory shall be a fulness and a continuation of the seeds forever and ever. Then shall they be gods, because they have no end; therefore shall they be from everlasting to everlasting, because they continue; then shall they be above all, because all things are subject unto them. Then shall they be gods, because they have all power, and the angels are subject unto them. Verily, verily, I say unto you, except ye abide my law ye cannot attain to this glory. (D&C 132:19–21)

By way of summarizing these doctrines, Joseph Smith taught that "a man and his wife must enter into [the everlasting] covenant in the world, or he will have no claim on her in the next world."[108] In addition, he said that "except a man and his wife enter into an everlasting covenant and be married for eternity, while in this probation, by the power and authority of the Holy Priesthood, they will cease to increase when they die; that is, they will not have any children after the resurrection. But those who are married by the power and authority of the priesthood in this life, and continue without committing the sin against the Holy Ghost will continue to increase and have children in the celestial glory."[109]

The Sealing of Generations

The sealing power restored by Elijah in the Kirtland Temple can be put to several different uses. In addition to sealing couples together for eternity, the Prophet Joseph Smith taught that Elijah's keys could be used to seal together all of the generations of the human family. Said the Prophet: "If you have power to seal on earth and in heaven, then [you] should . . . go and seal on earth your sons and daughters unto yourself, and [then seal] yourself unto your fathers" who are beyond the veil.[110] We will consider each of these concepts individually.

Children who are born to parents who have entered into the everlasting covenant of eternal marriage (also known as the Patriarchal Order of the Priesthood)[111] are said to be "born under the covenant." Such children are, by their lineage, legal heirs to all of the promises and blessings that are associated with the Abrahamic covenant. As stated by Brigham Young: "When a man and woman have received their endowments and sealings, and then [have] children born to them afterwards, those children are legal heirs to the kingdom and to all its blessings and promises."[112] President Ezra Taft Benson enumerated one of the benefits of being born under the covenant when he said: "Birth in the covenant entitles those children to a birthright blessing which guarantees them eternal parentage regardless of what happens to the [earthly] parents, so long as the children remain worthy of the blessings."[113]

Children who are not "born under the covenant" must, through the Law of Adoption, be grafted into the literal lineage of Abraham. From Orson Pratt we learn that "all who are born before their parents entered that new and everlasting covenant have to be made legitimate heirs. In what way? According to the ordinance and law of adoption."[114] Elder Pratt likewise stated that those who are outside of the covenant have to "enter into the law of adoption and be adopted into the Priesthood in order to become sons and legal heirs of salvation."[115] President Brigham Young expounded upon this doctrine in the following manner:

> [When] we come to other sealing ordinances, ordinances pertaining to the holy Priesthood, to connect the chain of the Priesthood from Father Adam until now, by sealing children to their parents, being sealed for our forefathers, etc., they cannot be done without a temple. When the ordinances are carried out in the temples that will be erected, men will be sealed to their fathers, and those who have slept, clear up to Father Adam. This will have to be done, because of the chain of the Priesthood being broken upon the earth. . . . This Priesthood has been restored again, and by its authority we shall be connected with our fathers, by the ordinance of sealing, until we shall form a perfect chain from Father Adam down to the closing up scene. This ordinance will not be performed anywhere but in a temple; neither will children be sealed to their living parents in any other place than a temple. For instance, a man and his wife come into the Church, and they have a family of children. These children have been begotten out of the covenant, because the marriage of their parents is not recognized by the Lord as [being] performed by his authority; they have, therefore, to be sealed to their parents, or else [the parents] cannot claim [the children] in eternity; [The children] will be distributed according to the wisdom of the Lord, who does all things right. When we had a temple prepared in Nauvoo, many of the brethren had their children, who were out of the covenant, sealed to them . . . . [When] parents, after receiving their endowments and being sealed for time and eternity, . . . have . . . children . . . they are begotten and born under the covenant, and they are the rightful heirs to the kingdom, they possess the keys of the kingdom. Children born unto parents, before the latter enter into the fulness of the covenants, have to be sealed to them in a temple to become legal heirs of the Priesthood. It is true they can receive the ordinances, they can receive their endowments, and be blessed in common with their parents; but still the parents cannot claim them legally and lawfully in eternity unless they are sealed to them. . . . [The] chain would not be complete without this sealing ordinance being performed.[116]

There are, of course, innumerable situations in the Church where converts do not have any family members to whom they can be sealed, and circumstances where inactivity makes sealing between some family members impossible. These problems should not be cause for discouragement, however. The Lord's plan of salvation will be fulfilled regardless of any obstacles that may currently prevail. No obedient servant of the Lord will be denied any of the gospel's glorious blessings. As Joseph Smith said: "All your losses will be made up to you in the resurrection, provided you continue faithful. By the vision of the Almighty I have seen it."[117]

After Joseph Smith died Brigham Young struggled with the complexities of joining generations together on both sides of the veil. In a visionary experience on 17 February 1847, Brigham Young saw Joseph Smith and he asked the Prophet to help him "understand the law of adoption or sealing principles." The Prophet explained to President Young, in a very earnest manner, that if the Saints would follow the guidance of the Spirit of the Lord they would find themselves

> "just as they were organized by our Father in Heaven before they came into the world. Our Father in Heaven organized the human family, but they are all disorganized and in great confusion." Joseph then showed me the pattern, how they were in the beginning. This I cannot describe, but I saw it, and saw where the Priesthood had been taken from the earth and how it must be joined together, so that there would be a perfect chain from Father Adam to his latest posterity.[118]

This quotation helps us to understand the ultimate purpose of sealing generations together. President George Q. Cannon expounded on this theme by saying that the temple sealing ordinance is the means by which "children will be sealed to their parents, one generation connected with another, and the whole human family be brought within the family of God, to be his recognized and acknowledged sons and daughters, bound together by the power of the everlasting Priesthood."[119] President Joseph F. Smith likewise taught that the sealing together of generations was meant to bring those who are sealed into the family of God. "The living cannot be made perfect without the dead, nor the dead be made perfect without the living. There has got to be a welding together and a joining together of parents and children and children and parents until the whole chain of God's family shall be welded together into one chain, and they shall all become the family of God and his Christ. The Lord revealed this doctrine to Joseph the Prophet."[120]

The early leaders of the LDS Church often described the connection between progenitors and posterity as a *chain*.[121] "There has been a chain of authority and power from Adam down to the present time," said the Prophet Joseph Smith.[122] This chain of the priesthood was complete in the premortal life when everyone belonged to the family of God. Here on the earth we must consciously choose to rejoin ourselves to God's family and place our link in the rebuilt chain by obeying all of the laws and ordinances of the priesthood. But as Elder Cannon points out above, in the resurrection, this chain will only include "recognized and acknowledged sons and

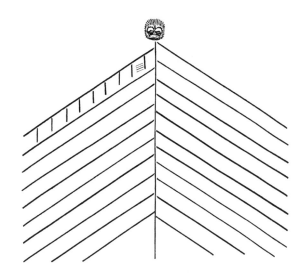

FIGURE 35. Elder Orson Hyde's symbolic diagram of the hierarchical structure of the Kingdom of God.

daughters." Elder Bruce R. McConkie taught that "son" and "daughter" are titles that are granted to those who become exalted in God's heavenly household.[123] Elder McConkie further taught that it is exalted Saints who will ultimately form the links of the great priesthood chain in the postmortal world. "Those who shall hereafter rule and reign in eternity as exalted beings will form a *patriarchal chain* which will begin with Father Adam and spread out until every exalted person is linked in."[124] Elder Orson Hyde published a diagram to visually illustrate how this chain of "kings and priests" would be linked together to form the command structure of the kingdom of God in eternity. "The eternal Father," said Elder Hyde, "sits at the head, crowned King of kings and Lord of lords. Wherever the other lines meet, there sits a king and a priest unto God, bearing rule, authority, and dominion under the Father. He is one with the Father, because His kingdom is joined to His Father's and becomes part of it."[125] And finally, we have Elder Bruce R. McConkie's comments on the great priesthood chain and its relationship to the lineage of father Abraham.

> Exaltation consists in the continuation of the family unit in eternity, and every family which so continues will find its proper place in the eternal organizational framework which the Almighty has ordained. None will be forgotten. Unworthy mortal links will be dropped in eternity, for there is no family in which all generations will attain exaltation; later generations of worthy families will be welded into the links formed by their ancestors who became worthy of a like exaltation with

them. All those after the day of Abraham (of whatever literal lineage they may be) who so live as to be worthy of a place in this great patriarchal chain will be welded into Abraham's lineage and shall rise up and bless him as their father. (Abraham 2:9–11)[126]

SUMMARY

The ordinances that are practiced in LDS temples were restored by the Lord through the Prophet Joseph Smith in Kirtland, Ohio and Nauvoo, Illinois. The Kirtland Temple ordinances centered on *time* and the building up of the Lord's earthly kingdom. The Nauvoo Temple ordinances were centered on *eternity* and pertained to the exaltation of the Saints in the celestial kingdom. In order for Latter-day Saints to receive the full benefit of these ordinances they must adhere to the laws and requirements that have been established by the Lord and then endure in faithfulness unto the end (*see* D&C 130:20-21; 82:10).

NOTES

1. *Joseph Smith—History*, 1:7–20, hereafter cited as *JS–H*.

2. Elder Orson Pratt reports that during this manifestation (which occurred on a Sunday evening) "a light burst into the room, becoming brighter by degrees, shining and then partially withdrawing, so that fear did not take possession of [Joseph's] bosom to any great degree. As he continued praying the light became brighter and brighter, and finally a personage clothed in a white robe stood before him" (*JD*, 15:182).

3. *JS–H*, 1:27–50. See Kent P. Jackson, "Moroni's Message to Joseph Smith," *Ensign*, August 1990, 13–16; W. Jeffrey Marsh, "Training from the Old Testament: Moroni's Lessons for a Prophet," *Ensign*, August 1998, 10–17.

4. *JS–H*, 1:41.

5. Oliver Cowdery wrote that "while those glorious things were being rehearsed, the vision was also opened, so that our brother [Joseph Smith] was permitted to see and understand much more full and perfect than I am able to communicate in writing" (*Messenger and Advocate*, vol. 1, no. 7, April 1835, 112).

6. The building of the Kirtland Temple should be viewed in conjunction with the attempt to build the temple in Jackson County, Missouri (or New Jerusalem), which was actually the first temple the Lord commanded to be built in this dispensation. For further reading, see Matthew B. Brown and Paul Thomas Smith, *Symbols in Stone: Symbolism on the Early Temples of the Restoration* (American Fork, Utah: Covenant Communications, 1997), 9–40; Richard O. Cowan, "The Great Temple of the New Jerusalem," in Arnold K. Garr and Clark V. Johnson, eds., *Regional Studies in Latter-day Saint Church History: Missouri* (Provo, Utah: BYU Department of Church History and Doctrine, 1994), 137–54.

7. *JD*, 2:31; emphasis in original.

8. See *HC*, 1:352.

9. Ibid., 1:353–54. It was at this time that the Kirtland Temple's foundation was dug, stone was hauled from the quarry, and the temple committee was directed to obtain building materials for the structure and commence to build it "immediately."

10. *JD*, 13:357. On another occasion Orson Pratt said: "When the Lord commanded this people to build a house in the land of Kirtland, in the early rise of this Church, he gave them the pattern by vision from heaven, and commanded them to build that house according to that pattern and order; to have the architecture, not in accordance with architecture devised by men, but to have everything constructed in that house according to the heavenly pattern" (ibid., 14:273). On 6 April 1837 Wilford Woodruff recorded in his journal: "The house of God is reared in beauty and splendor according to the pattern given by the visions of heaven and the revelations of Jesus Christ" (Dean C. Jessee, "The Kirtland Diary of Wilford Woodruff," *Brigham Young University Studies*, vol. 12, no. 4, Summer 1972, 392; hereafter cited as *BYUS*).

11. Truman O. Angell, *Autobiography*, 4–5, cited in the *Improvement Era*, October 1942, 630.

12. Orson F. Whitney, *The Life of Heber C. Kimball* (Salt Lake City: Bookcraft, 1992), 209–10. For a discourse by Joseph Smith on the three grades of the priesthood, see *TPJS*, 322–23.

13. For a detailed discussion on most of the symbols that are found within the Kirtland Temple, see Brown and Smith, *Symbols in Stone: Symbolism on the Early Temples of the Restoration*, 41–88. Some of the geometric emblems that are found inside of the Kirtland Temple remain unidentified. It should be noted that one of the geometric emblems from the Kirtland Temple can also be found on the facade of Brigham Young's Beehive House in Salt Lake City, Utah. Since Truman O. Angell took a leading role in the construction of both these buildings, it is possible that he was the source of the geometric designs.

14. On 6 February 1836 the Prophet stated that he was administering the Kirtland Temple rites according to "the order which God had shown to me" (*HC*, 2:391). On 15 December 1835 the Prophet petitioned the Lord that the Elders might "receive an endowment in thy house, even according to thine own order" (ibid., 2:334). On 12 November 1835 it is noted in the *History of the Church* that the Solemn Assembly in the temple was to be organized "according to the order of the house of God" (ibid., 2:309).

15. *HC*, 2:432.

16. See D&C 88:78. One participant in the Kirtland endowment proceedings informs us that on 6 April 1836 the Prophet "addressed the Elders for three hours. Clothed with the power and Spirit of God he . . . gave much instruction. He urged upon us the absolute necessity of giving strict heed to his teachings and counsel and the revelations of the Lord to the Church" (Jeremiah Willey Journal, 1836, 10–12, LDS Church Archives, Salt Lake City, Utah). The Prophet told those who were to receive the endowment rites: "Tarry at Kirtland until you are endowed with power from on high. You need a fountain of wisdom, knowledge, and intelligence such as you never had. . . . [God] can give you that wisdom, that intelligence, and that power, which characterized the ancient saints, and now characterizes the inhabitants of the upper world" (*HC*, 2:197). Wilford Woodruff records that those who were to receive the endowment rites received "counsel respecting [their] washing and anointing" and were then assigned to meet with a Church authority so that they could "have the perfumes and oil prepared against the day following" (Jessee, "The Kirtland Diary of Wilford Woodruff," 387). The *History of the Church* notes that a Solemn Assembly was called on 6 April 1836 "for the purpose of washing, anointing, washing of feet, receiving instructions, and the further organization of the ministry" (*HC*, 2:475). Solemn Assemblies are mentioned in D&C 88:70; 95:7; 108:4; 109:6, 10; 124:39; 133:6. Compare these references with Numbers 29:35; Deuteronomy 16:8; 2 Chronicles 7:9; Nehemiah 8:18; Joel 1:14; 2:15; Zephaniah 3:18.

17. Joseph Smith recorded that the washing ritual was done with "pure water" (*HC*, 2:379). Oliver Cowdery also reported that "pure water" was used in this rite (Leonard J. Arrington, "Oliver Cowdery's Kirtland, Ohio, 'Sketch Book,'" *BYUS*, vol. 12, no. 4, Summer 1972, 416, 419). Cowdery further noted that the purpose of this ordinance was to achieve "purification," and he said that those who were washed reflected upon "how the priests anciently used to wash always before ministering before the Lord," as recorded in biblical passages such as Exodus 29:4; 40:12, 30–32 (ibid., 416). After this washing the initiates' "bodies were perfumed with a sweet smelling odorous wash" that included cinnamon (ibid., 416, 419). The ancient Israelites mixed "sweet cinnamon" with their "holy anointing oil" (Exodus 30:23–25). Cowdery states that the washing rite was "preparatory to the anointing with the holy oil" (ibid., 419) and Wilford Woodruff spoke of "attending to the ordinance of washing the body

with clean water and perfumes that our bodies might be prepared for the anointing" (Jessee, "The Kirtland Diary of Wilford Woodruff," 387). The oil used in the anointing ceremony was considered to be holy because it was consecrated in the name of Jesus Christ, by those holding the holy priesthood of God, while their right hands were stretched toward heaven (*HC*, 2:379). The anointing oil was applied to the head of the recipient (ibid.). Cowdery stated that those who received their anointings were "anointed with the same kind of oil and in the manner that were Moses and Aaron, and those who stood before the Lord in ancient days" (Arrington, "Oliver Cowdery's Kirtland, Ohio, 'Sketch Book,'" 419; compare Exodus 29:7; 40:13–15).

18. Several different types of sealings took place in association with the Kirtland Temple. *The Sealing of Blessings*: The Prophet said of his father: "I then anointed his head with the consecrated oil, and sealed many blessings upon him." Joseph Smith Sr. then in turn anointed the head of the Prophet and sealed several blessings upon him (*HC*, 2:379–80). The Prophet said on another occasion: "I then poured the consecrated oil upon his head, in the name of Jesus Christ, and sealed such blessings upon him as the Lord put into my heart" (ibid., 2:382–83). Jeremiah Willey relates another method used in sealing blessings. The First Presidency, Twelve Apostles, and other priesthood quorums "met in solemn assembly and sealed upon us our washings, anointings and blessings with a loud shout of Hosannah to God and the Lamb" (Jeremiah Willey Journal, 1836, 10–12, LDS Church Archives, Salt Lake City, Utah). Oliver Cowdery likewise testified that "anointing blessings were sealed by uplifted hands and praises to God" (Arrington, "Oliver Cowdery's Kirtland, Ohio, 'Sketch Book,'" 422). Joseph Smith also speaks of the day's events being "sealed . . . by shouting hosanna, hosanna, hosanna to God and the Lamb, three times, sealing it each time with amen, amen, and amen" (*HC*, 2:427–28). And again, the Prophet said that "it became necessary to seal the anointing of those who had recently been anointed and not sealed" (ibid., 2:476). Stephen Post reports that the Hosanna Shout was connected with "acknowledging the Lord to be King" and was done "with uplifted hands unto the Most High, by the [Lord's] anointed" (Stephen Post Journal, 27 March 1836, LDS Church Archives, Salt Lake City, Utah; compare John 12:12–13). *Sealing Up to Eternal Life:* The Lord mentioned in a revelation on 1 November 1831 that he had granted unto his disciples the authority to "seal both on earth and in heaven" (D&C 1:8). During the same month he indicated that God the Father would reveal to his servants who should be sealed up "unto eternal life" by this power (D&C 68:12). The ordinance of the washing of feet was then introduced by the Lord as the means whereby someone could be rendered "clean from the blood of this generation" (D&C 88:138–141), and when Joseph Smith administered this ordinance, he stated that those who received it were not only "clean" in a ritual sense but were also "sealed up unto eternal life" (*HC*, 1:323–24; see also *MD*, 829–32). *The Sealing of Power and Authority*: "The Twelve then proceeded to anoint and bless the Presidency of the Seventy, and seal upon their heads power and authority to anoint their brethren" (*HC*, 2:383).

19. The Prophet recorded that during a 30 March 1836 endowment meeting in the Kirtland Temple, he proposed that those present should enter into a covenant. The covenant was then accepted and sealed "with a hosanna and an amen" (*HC*, 2:432). On an earlier occasion, 16 January 1836, the Prophet also proposed that a covenant be entered into by a group of priesthood leaders. Those present agreed to the covenant "by raising their hands to heaven in testimony of their willingness and desire to

enter into this covenant." They all then "took each other by the hand in confirmation of the covenant" they had mutually entered into (ibid., 2:375). Oliver Cowdery also recorded that on 16 January 1836 those who received endowment rites covenanted "to be faithful to God" (Arrington, "Oliver Cowdery's Kirtland, Ohio, 'Sketch Book,'" 416). Wilford Woodruff likewise refers to the making of covenants in the Kirtland Temple (see Jessee, "The Kirtland Diary of Wilford Woodruff," 388–89).

20. Stephen Post said: "we fasted until even[ing] when we partook of bread and wine in commemoration of the marriage supper of the Lamb" (Stephen Post Journal, 30 March 1836, LDS Church Archives, Salt Lake City, Utah). Edward Partridge also indicates that participants in the washing of feet ordinance "partook of bread and wine, a feast" (Edward Partridge Journal, 29–31 March 1836, LDS Church Archives, Salt Lake City, Utah). According to Zebedee Coltrin "the Sacrament was also administered at times when Joseph [Smith] appointed, after the ancient order; that is, warm bread to break easy was provided, and broken into pieces as large as my fist, and each person had a glass of wine and sat and ate the bread and drank the wine, and Joseph [Smith] said that was the way that Jesus and his disciples partook of the bread and wine and this was the order of the Church anciently" (*Salt Lake School of the Prophets: Minute Book 1883* [Salt Lake City: Pioneer Press, 1992], 53–54). D&C 27:1–4 is a revelation on the sacrament that was given to the Prophet by an angel of God (see the introduction to section 27 of the Doctrine and Covenants and also Lyndon W. Cook, *The Revelations of the Prophet Joseph Smith* [Salt Lake City: Deseret Book, 1985], 38; hereafter cited as *RPJS*).

21. Zebedee Coltrin reports that in the School of the Prophets, shortly after it was organized on 23 January 1833, Joseph Smith gave instructions to those assembled and then had them engage "in silent prayer, kneeling, with [their] hands uplifted" (*Salt Lake School of the Prophets: Minute Book 1883* [Salt Lake City: Pioneer Press, 1992], 54). Joseph Smith recorded that during one of the gatherings where endowment ordinances were bestowed, the meeting was closed by "invoking the benediction of heaven, with uplifted hands" (*HC*, 2:382). The Lord directed those in the School of the Prophets to use set wording, which he referred to as a "prayer and covenant," at specific times while raising both their hands toward heaven (D&C 88:128–137). Other ritual gestures employed by the Saints during the Kirtland period include raising the right hand toward heaven and the laying of both hands on the head of individuals (see *HC*, 2:379–82). Edward Partridge reports: "Joseph Smith, Jr., first anointed his father, pronouncing blessings upon him; then all the Presidents, beginning at the oldest, rubbed their hand over his head and face, which had been anointed. Then Brother Joseph prayed to the Lord to accept of the anointing and all the Presidency with right hand uplifted to heaven said 'Amen'" (Edward Partridge Journal, 21–22 January 1836, LDS Church Archives, Salt Lake City, Utah).

22. The washing of feet ordinance is mentioned by the Lord in D&C 88:139–141 (compare JST John 13:8–10). The Prophet Joseph Smith stated that after he had performed the washing of feet ordinance for several priesthood leaders, he "pronounced them all clean from the blood of this generation" by the power of the Holy Ghost. He then said that they were "sealed up unto eternal life" (*HC*, 1:323). Stephen Post spoke of "the last ordinance of the endowment viz: the ordinance of the washing of feet. This ordinance is administered to none but those who are clean from the blood of the generation in which they live" (Stephen Post Journal, 30 March 1836, LDS Church Archives, Salt Lake City, Utah). It is interesting to note that before a participant received the washing of feet ordinance, they first

cleansed their own hands, faces, and feet (*see* Kirtland Council Minute Book, 7–8, cited in *RPJS*, 186; Edward Partridge Journal, 29–31 March 1836, LDS Church Archives, Salt Lake City, Utah; compare *HC*, 1:323 where the Prophet mentions that each elder "washed his own feet first" and ibid., 2:430 where he says that those present "proceeded to cleanse [their] faces and [their] feet, and then proceeded to wash one another's feet"). Compare these actions with Exodus 29:4; 40:12, 30–32; D&C 88:74; JST John 13:8–10.

23. For a good overview of the spiritual manifestations that occurred among the Saints during the time of the dedication of the Kirtland Temple and the administration of the endowment ordinances, see Karl R. Anderson, *Joseph Smith's Kirtland: Eyewitness Accounts* (Salt Lake City: Deseret Book, 1989), 169–77. It is clear that the Saints were anticipating that they would experience "something similar to the Pentecost" in connection with their reception of the Kirtland Temple ordinances (Jessee, "The Kirtland Diary of Wilford Woodruff," 389; see Acts 2:1–4). "The Spirit [was] poured out. I saw the glory of God, like a great cloud, come down and rest upon the house, and fill the same like a mighty rushing wind. I also saw cloven tongues, like as of fire rest upon many" (Edward Partridge Journal, 27 March 1836, LDS Church Archives, Salt Lake City, Utah). "This eve[ning] the Spirit of the Lord rested on the congregation. Many spake in tongues, many prophesied, angels were in our midst and ministered unto some. Cloven tongues like unto fire rested upon those who spake in tongues and prophesied. When they ceased to speak the tongues ascended" (Stephen Post Journal, 27 March 1836, LDS Church Archives, Salt Lake City, Utah).

24. *JD*, 2:31.

25. Ibid., 19:15–16. George A. Smith provides much the same perspective: "The Lord poured his Spirit upon us, and gave us some little idea of the law of anointing, and conferred upon us some blessings. He taught us how to shout hosannah, gave Joseph the keys of the gathering together of Israel, and revealed to us, what? Why the fact of it was, he dare not yet trust us with the first key of the Priesthood" (ibid., 2:215).

26. *HC*, 2:432.

27. It is believed by some scholars that Sunday, April 3rd, is the actual date of the Lord's resurrection (see John P. Pratt, "Passover: Was It Symbolic of His Coming?" *Ensign*, January 1994, 44; John P. Pratt, "The Restoration of Priesthood Keys on Easter 1836, Part 1: Dating the First Easter," *Ensign*, June 1985, 67, nt. 40, 68; John P. Pratt, "The Restoration of Priesthood Keys on Easter 1836, Part 2: Symbolism of Passover and of Elijah's Return," *Ensign*, July 1985, 60, 64). If this is the case, it would make the Savior's declaration of his resurrected status on this occasion all the more significant—"I am he that liveth, I am he who was slain" (D&C 110:4).

28. Elder Erastus Snow identified the place where Christ and the other angels appeared in the Kirtland Temple as "the Holy of Holies" (A. Karl Larson and Katharine Miles Larson, eds., *Diary of Charles Lowell Walker* [Logan, Utah: Utah State University Press, 1980], 2:563).

29. According to President Wilford Woodruff, the "angels who appeared in the Kirtland Temple delivered the *keys of power* to the Prophet Joseph and they [are] now with the Priesthood" (Diary of L. John Nuttall, 20 April 1893, typescript, 4:537, Special Collections, Harold B. Lee Library, Brigham Young University, Provo, Utah; emphasis added). Joseph Smith specifically linked the "keys of power" with the "power of Elijah" (*WJS*, 331).

30. *HC*, 1:316.

31. *JD*, 14:273.

32. *CR*, April 1898, 17.

33. Even though the original manuscript of D&C 110 is found in Joseph Smith's journal, it is not in his handwriting but in the handwriting of Warren A. Cowdery, who served as one of the Prophet's scribes. It would therefore appear that section 110 is a dictated, and possibly abbreviated, account of the manifestation. See Robert J. Woodford, *The Historical Development of the Doctrine and Covenants*, doctoral dissertation, Brigham Young University, 1974, 3:1459–60.

34. See Brown and Smith, *Symbols in Stone: Symbolism on the Early Temples of the Restoration*, 61, 81–82 nts. 71–75; See also Paul K. Browning, "Gathering Scattered Israel: Then and Now," *Ensign*, July 1998, 58–59.

35. Brian H. Stuy, ed., *Collected Discourses* (Burbank, California: BHS Publishing, 1987), 1:69.

36. See the references in Rex E. Cooper, *Promises Made to the Fathers: Mormon Covenant Organization* (Salt Lake City: University of Utah Press, 1990), 73–75, 119–20.

37. *TPJS*, 307–308; emphasis added.

38. *WJS*, 213; emphasis added.

39. Ibid., 215; emphasis added.

40. See the note on dating various portions of D&C 107 in *RPJS*, 215. The Lord directly compared Joseph Smith to Moses in September of 1830 (see D&C 28:2). A revelation given on 24 February 1834 refers to the Latter-day Saints as "the children of Israel" who are to be led by a man who is like Moses (see D&C 103:15–18). The Prophet quoted Moses' biblical teachings on the gathering of Israel in November of 1835 (*HC*, 2:261). On 21 January 1836 (shortly before Moses appeared in the Kirtland Temple), Joseph Smith's father sealed upon him "the blessings of Moses, to lead Israel in the latter days, even as Moses led [Israel] in days of old" (ibid., 2:380). On 1 May 1842 the Prophet stated that Moses received the "keys" of the temple endowment "on the mountain top" (*WJS*, 119–20), and on 27 August 1843 he explained that "God cursed the children of Israel because they would not receive the last law from Moses" (ibid., 244).

41. *WJS*, 8, 13. Several LDS theologians have come to the conclusion that the "Elias" mentioned in D&C 110:12 was Noah (see, for example, Joseph Fielding Smith, *Answers to Gospel Questions* [Salt Lake City: Deseret Book, 1975], 3:138–41; hereafter cited as *AGQ*. See also Sidney B. Sperry, *Doctrine and Covenants Compendium* [Salt Lake City: Bookcraft, 1960], 600).

42. *JD*, 21:246.

43. *The Book of Jasher* (Salt Lake City: J. H. Parry and Co., 1887), 32. The reference is Book of Jasher, 12:61–63.

44. *MD*, 219–20; emphasis in original.

45. *NWAF*, 539.

46. *MD*, 13.

47. See Stephen D. Ricks, "The Appearance of Elijah and Moses in the Kirtland Temple and the Jewish Passover," *BYUS*, vol. 23, no. 4, Fall 1983, 483–86; John P. Pratt, "The Restoration of Priesthood Keys on Easter 1836, Part 1: Dating the First Easter," *Ensign*, June 1985, 59–68; John P.

Pratt, "The Restoration of Priesthood Keys on Easter 1836, Part 2: Symbolism of Passover and of Elijah's Return," *Ensign*, July 1985, 55–64; Ginzberg, *The Legends of the Jews*, 3:48.

48. The reader will no doubt notice the parallel between the appearance of Jesus Christ, Moses, and Elijah upon the raised pulpits in the Kirtland Temple and the gathering of the same group on the Mount of Transfiguration (see Matthew 17:1–9). Notice that footnote *b* for verse 3 of Matthew 17 clarifies that "Elias" should read "Elijah."

49. Notice in the text of D&C 110 that Moses, Elias, and Elijah each "committed" their keys to Joseph Smith and Oliver Cowdery. Unfortunately, the method whereby they "committed" these keys is not described. There is one late statement by Joseph Fielding Smith that claims "Elijah the prophet . . . laid his hands upon the head of Joseph Smith and upon the head of Oliver Cowdery, his fellow servant, and conferred upon them the keys which he held" (*CR*, October 1911, 121).

50. *TPJS*, 258.

51. Ibid., 337–38; emphasis added. The Prophet said that "the word *turn* [in Malachi 4:5–6] should be translated *bind*, or seal" (ibid., 330; emphasis in original).

52. Joseph Fielding Smith taught that Elijah restored "the keys of the sealing power." But he also noted that "some members of the Church have been confused in thinking that Elijah came with the keys of baptism for the dead or of salvation for the dead. Elijah's keys were greater than that. They were the keys of sealing, and those keys of sealing pertain to the living and embrace the dead who are willing to repent" (*DS*, 3:129–30). Joseph Smith seemed on one occasion to hint at what Elijah might have said during his visitation to the Kirtland Temple. "Let us suppose a case. Suppose the great God who dwells in heaven should reveal himself to Father Cutler here, by the opening heavens, and tell him, I offer up a decree that whatsoever you seal on earth with your decree, I will seal it in heaven; you have the power then; can it be taken off? No. Then what you seal on earth, by the keys of Elijah, is sealed in heaven" (*TPJS*, 338).

53. The Saints can be "sealed with the Holy Spirit of Promise, i.e., [with the sealing power of] Elijah. To obtain this sealing is to make our calling and election sure which we ought to give all diligence to accomplish" (*WJS*, 335). Even though "the Holy Spirit of Promise" is a *title* for the Holy Ghost in his capacity as the ratifier of all gospel blessings (see *MD*, 361–62), it is also the name of the *divine power* that has been delegated to authorized mortals so that they can seal individuals up to eternal life (see D&C 132:7, 19, 26). Elder Bruce R. McConkie has taught that "when the ratifying seal of approval is placed upon someone whose calling and election is thereby made sure—because there are no more conditions to be met by the obedient person—this act of being sealed up unto eternal life is of such transcendent import that of itself it is called being sealed by the Holy Spirit of Promise, which means that in this crowning sense, being so sealed is the same as having one's calling and election made sure. Thus, to be sealed by the Holy Spirit of Promise is to be sealed up unto eternal life; and to be sealed up unto eternal life is to be sealed by the Holy Spirit of Promise" (*DNTC*, 3:335–36; see also *MD*, 683).

54. *Millennial Star*, vol. 5, no. 10, March 1845, 151; hereafter cited as *MS*.

55. *HC*, 4:211; emphasis added. On another occasion the Prophet said that Elijah "restore[d] the *authority* and deliver[ed] the keys of the Priesthood, in order that *all the ordinances* may be attended to in righteousness" (*TPJS*, 172; emphasis added).

56. *HC*, 5:530. More specifically, Elijah turned "the hearts of the children to the covenant made with their fathers" (*WJS*, 242), or, as mentioned in D&C 2:2, to "the promises made to the fathers." According to Franklin D. Richards, the Prophet once rendered Malachi 4:5–6 as: "I will send Elijah the prophet and he shall reveal the covenants of the fathers to the children and [the covenants] of the children to the fathers that they may enter into covenant with each other" (ibid., 241).

57. Joseph Fielding Smith, comp., *Life of Joseph F. Smith* (Salt Lake City: Deseret News Press, 1938), 53. Joseph Fielding Smith repeated this idea by stating that "it is possible that there may have been others whose coming was not recorded [in D&C 110]. Whether this is so or not, we know, for the Lord has decreed it, that all the prophets came with their keys and authorities and restored them in this dispensation" (Joseph Fielding Smith, *Church History and Modern Revelation* [Salt Lake City: The Council of the Twelve Apostles, 1953], 2:42).

58. *DS*, 2:242.

59. *JD*, 2:214–15.

60. Ibid., 2:31–32.

61. *HC*, 3:286, 15 March 1839.

62. Ibid., 3:349. The Prophet relates that one time he prayed: "'Lord, what will thou have me to do?' And the answer was, 'Build up a city and call my Saints to this place!'" (*WJS*, 192).

63. See *WJS*, 4–6, 8–15, 37.

64. See Dean C. Jessee, "Joseph Smith's 19 July 1840 Discourse," *BYUS*, vol. 19, no. 3, Spring 1979, 390–94. Andrew Ehat and Lyndon Cook, in the first edition of *The Words of Joseph Smith*, questioned the accuracy of the date of this discourse and therefore placed it in an appendix of their book. But then Dean Jessee wrote a review of *The Words of Joseph Smith* and provided evidence that seems to support the reliability of the date (see *BYUS*, vol. 21, no. 4, Fall 1981, 529–34).

65. See *WJS*, 69.

66. *Times and Seasons*, vol. 2, no. 17, 1 July 1841, 456; hereafter cited as *TS*. A poem entitled "The Temple of God," published by Eliza R. Snow on 2 August 1841, may also pinpoint the revelation to this time period. In her poem Eliza notes that when Moses was appointed to build the ancient tabernacle, the Lord showed him a "true model—a pattern of heavenly things." Temples reared to the name of the Lord, she contended, "Must be built, by commandment, and form'd of his word, Or he will not accept it." She then stated that the Nauvoo Temple fit the proper criteria; "Hark! a scheme is divulg'd—'twas concerted on high; With divine revelation the saints have been bles't" (*TS*, vol. 2, no. 19, 2 August 1841, 493).

67. *HC*, 6:196–97. John Pulsipher, who received his endowment in the Nauvoo Temple, testified that the sacred edifice "was built according to the pattern that the Lord gave to Joseph [Smith]" (John Pulsipher Journal, cited in E. Cecil McGavin, *The Nauvoo Temple* [Salt Lake City: Deseret Book, 1962], 95). George A. Smith likewise stated that "the Saints were engaged in building a temple, the pattern of which was given by revelation, and which they were commanded to build" (*MS*, vol. 31, no. 38, 18 September 1869, 604). My thanks to Daniel B. McKinlay for bringing this source to my attention.

68. Martha P. J. Thomas, *Daniel Stillwell Thomas Family History* (Salt Lake City: Kate Woodhouse Kirkham, 1927), 30, Special Collections, Harold B. Lee Library, Brigham Young University, Provo, Utah.

69. *JD*, 2:44; John W. Gunnison reported in 1852 that the "pattern" of the Nauvoo Temple "was given to the prophet [Joseph Smith] by his angel, and all the details explained orally. A[n] . . . architect was employed to draft it by dictation. . . . Joseph insisted that the [architectural drawings] must be right . . . [because they were to illustrate] the 'Lord's design'" (John W. Gunnison, *The Mormons or Latter-day Saints in the Valley of the Great Salt Lake* [Brookline, Massachusetts: Paradigm Publications, 1993], 116). Another early source, originally written in 1855, is even more specific. "The design of the temple, Smith said, was given to him by the angel 'M[o]roni,' who explained all the details of the building to him" (Ellen E. Dickinson, *New Light on Mormonism* [New York: Funk and Wagnalls, 1885], 101).

70. Josiah Quincy, *Figures of the Past from the Leaves of Old Journals* (Boston: Roberts Brothers, 1896), 389.

71. Journal of Wandle Mace 1809–1890, typescript (1990), 105, Special Collections, Harold B. Lee Library, Brigham Young University, Provo, Utah. 1 Nephi 14:18–26 states that there are others who have been granted the privilege of seeing the vision that was given to the apostle John on the isle of Patmos.

72. *HC*, 5:2.

73. For a detailed discussion on the architectural symbolism of the Nauvoo Temple, see Brown and Smith, *Symbols in Stone: Symbolism on the Early Temples of the Restoration*, 89–116.

74. *TPJS*, 308.

75. Brian H. Stuy, ed., *Collected Discourses* (Burbank, California: BHS Publishing, 1987), 1:69. As indicated previously in the main text of this chapter, Joseph Smith was promised a vision of the Nauvoo Temple on 19 January 1841 (see D&C 124:42), and it appears from *TS*, vol. 2, no. 17, 456 that this vision may have occurred by 1 July 1841. It is very interesting to note that just a page earlier in this issue of the *Times and Seasons* (ibid., 455) the Nauvoo Temple's baptismal font is described in detail for the very first time, indicating that it was to be built after the pattern of the Brazen Sea in King Solomon's Temple. We may thus theorize that the Prophet had seen the baptismal font at the same time he saw his vision of the Nauvoo Temple.

76. See *WJS*, 37, 49; *HC*, 4:231.

77. "Who instructed [Joseph Smith] in . . . baptisms for the dead [?] . . . Angels and spirits from the eternal worlds" (*JD*, 2:44).

78. See *TPJS*, 179. The Prophet indicated on another occasion that some "very important things" had been "manifested" to him "respecting the doctrine of baptism for the dead" (ibid., 260).

79. Ibid., 180.

80. For a more detailed description of these rooms, see Lisle G. Brown, "The Sacred Departments for Temple Work in Nauvoo: The Assembly Room and the Council Chamber," *BYUS*, vol. 19, no. 3, Spring 1979, 361–74.

81. *HC*, 6:50; emphasis in original.

82. Ibid., 50–51. On another occasion the Prophet taught that "it is necessary for men to receive an understanding concerning the laws of the heavenly kingdom, before they are permitted to enter it: we mean the celestial glory" (*TPJS*, 51). And again, the Prophet taught that God gives the Saints "just

and holy laws, to regulate their conduct, and guide them in a direct way, that in due time he might take them to himself, and make them joint-heirs with his Son" (ibid., 54).

83. *TPJS*, 308. The ordinances of the temple are practiced in the seclusion of sacred space because they constitute "the mysteries of the kingdom" (McConkie, *Mortal Messiah*, 1:99). These ordinances, "though not secret, are of such a sacred nature as to be reserved for the eyes and ears and hearts of those whose attained spiritual maturity prepares them to receive the mysteries of the kingdom" (ibid., 1:104). "After people are converted and have the gift of the Holy Ghost to enlighten their minds it is time enough for them to learn the deeper things pertaining to exaltation in the eternal worlds. The sacred teachings revealed in temple ordinances, for instance, are mysteries reserved for selected and faithful members of the kingdom who have attained sufficient stability and background to understand them" (*DNTC*, 1:248–49). On the connection between the Melchizedek Priesthood and the "mysteries of the kingdom" see D&C 84:19–21; 107:18–19. Temple ordinances and teachings are also known as the "mysteries of godliness" (see Clyde J. Williams, ed., *The Teachings of Harold B. Lee* [Salt Lake City: Bookcraft, 1996], 575; Ezra Taft Benson, *The Teachings of Ezra Taft Benson* [Salt Lake City: Bookcraft, 1998], 245). The Prophet Joseph Smith urged the Saints to "go on to perfection, and search deeper and deeper into the mysteries of godliness" (*TPJS*, 364).

84. Larry E. Dahl and Donald Q. Cannon, eds., *The Teachings of Joseph Smith* (Salt Lake City: Bookcraft, 1997), 217.

85. On 22 January 1834 the Prophet Joseph Smith taught that "the ordinance or institution of offering blood in sacrifice, was only designed to be performed *till* Christ was offered up and shed his blood . . . that man might look forward in faith to that time" (*TPJS*, 60; emphasis added). On 5 October 1840, however, the Prophet delivered a discourse on Malachi 3:3, which speaks of the "sons of Levi" making an "offering in righteousness" in the latter days. This scripture does *not* say that blood sacrifices would be offered unto the Lord in the last days as many suppose. The Hebrew word used to designate the "offering" in this passage is *minchah,* which is commonly used in Old Testament temple texts to designate a "bloodless" sacrifice (James Strong, *The New Strong's Exhaustive Concordance of the Bible* [Nashville: Thomas Nelson Publishers, 1996], Hebrew and Aramaic Dictionary, 80, word #4503). Based upon the text of Malachi 3:3, and the reasoning that all of the priesthood ordinances performed in former dispensations had to be restored in the latter days, the Prophet taught that temple sacrifices—specifically those performed "prior to the law of Moses" and by the authority of the *Melchizedek Priesthood*—would be performed again "when the Priesthood is restored with *all* its authority, power and blessings" (*TPJS*, 172–73; emphasis added). The Lord helped to clarify the meaning of the Prophet's teachings when he revealed on 19 January 1841 that within the walls of the Nauvoo Temple he would restore "the *fulness* of the priesthood" (D&C 124:28; emphasis added), and there the latter-day "sons of Levi" would offer sacrifice in the manner of a *memorial,* meaning in symbolic fashion (vs. 39). On 6 September 1842, shortly after the Nauvoo temple ordinances were first bestowed, Joseph Smith quoted Malachi 3:2–3 and clearly stated that it was the "Latter-day Saints" who were to "offer unto the Lord an offering in righteousness" in the "holy temple." He also indicated that the offering he was referring to was of a bloodless nature (D&C 128:24).

Regardless of this evidence, there are those who still believe that blood sacrifices will be restored at some future time. Some LDS commentators believe that Latter-day Saints will perform them, some feel that they will be carried out by non-LDS Jews in Jerusalem, and still others feel that they will be performed by Jews who have converted to the LDS faith. A careful analysis of these statements reveals that they are inconsistent, ambiguous, and rely heavily on the Prophet's 5 October 1840 discourse to support their contentions. John A. Widtsoe, however, stated under the direction of the Quorum of the Twelve Apostles that the "coming of Jesus did away with sacrifices of blood" (John A. Widtsoe, *Priesthood and Church Government* [Salt Lake City: Deseret Book, 1939], 5). This doctrine is taught with great clarity in the scriptures. "Therefore, it is expedient that there should be a great and *last sacrifice*, and then shall there be, or it is expedient there should be, *a stop to the shedding of blood*; then shall the law of Moses be fulfilled; yea, it shall be all fulfilled, every jot and tittle, and none shall have passed away. And behold, this is the whole meaning of the law, every whit pointing to that great and *last sacrifice*; and that great and *last sacrifice* will be the Son of God, yea, infinite and eternal" (Alma 34:13–14; emphasis added). After the Savior had completed the Atonement, the Nephites heard his voice from heaven saying: "*And ye shall offer up unto me no more the shedding of blood; yea, your sacrifices and your burnt offerings shall be done away, for I will accept none of your sacrifices and your burnt offerings. And ye shall offer for a sacrifice unto me a broken heart and a contrite spirit*" (3 Nephi 9:19–20; emphasis added).

And what of the prophet Ezekiel's vision, which seems to indicate that blood sacrifice would be restored in a future Israelite temple? Professor Kent P. Jackson has made several astute observations about what Ezekiel said and saw. "As in other apocalyptic visions, the symbols often are not meant to portray literally the events, people, or things, but to characterize or idealize them. It seems that such is the case with this vision. It depicts the future glories of Israel's restoration in the most idealized images. Everything about the millennial day—including the land, the city, and the temple—would exceed by far the best of what had existed in earlier times. But the vision was limited by the level of the doctrinal understanding of its readers, who were still under the Law of Moses without a comprehension of the gospel of Christ and still rejected the words of the living prophets, as is so evident in the book of Ezekiel. Thus the vision showed a temple of the Law of Moses, patterned after the temples of ancient Israel. Officiating in it was the Aaronic Priesthood, as in biblical times (Ezekiel 43:13–27; 44:10–31), and burnt offerings, sin offerings, and fellowship ('peace') offerings are depicted (Ezekiel 43:18–27). But the scriptures make it clear that the Law of Moses and its sacrifices by the shedding of blood were ended with the atonement of Christ (Alma 34:13–14; Hebrews 10:18). Given this fact, it seems unlikely that a temple for the performance of Mosaic animal offerings will ever again be built, especially during the Millennium, when there will be no death. Future temples, both before and after the Second Coming, will presumably be similar to those with which we are familiar in the Church now, in which ordinances of the Melchizedek Priesthood will be performed for the living and the dead. . . . Ezekiel's vision portrayed the future temple by means of familiar Old Testament temple images. . . . The Lord communicates with people in their own language and according to their level of understanding (see D&C 1:24). In this vision he taught ancient Jews transcendent millennial things by using images drawn from their own time and experience" (Kent P. Jackson, "The Lord is There," in Kent P.

Jackson, ed., *Studies in Scripture: Volume Four, 1 Kings to Malachi* [Salt Lake City: Deseret Book, 1993], 316–17).

By way of summary I would emphasize the following five points. (1) The Lord stated after the completion of the Atonement that blood sacrifices had come to an end and he would no longer accept them. (2) There is no revelation from the Lord stating that blood sacrifices will ever be renewed. Any statements to the contrary are mere speculation. (3) The Lord has explicitly stated in his revelations that he considers Latter-day Saints to be "sons of Levi" and he has directed them to "offer an acceptable offering and sacrifice in the house of the Lord" in the manner of a *memorial* (D&C 84:31–34; 124:39). (4) Joseph Smith directly tied LDS temple worship to the fulfillment of Malachi's prophecy about the latter-day "sons of Levi" (see D&C 128:24). (5) The Prophet has indicated that the only sacrificial rites that would be restored in the latter days would be those practiced between the time of Adam and Moses and by the authority of the Melchizedek Priesthood. In the final analysis, it does not appear that there is any scriptural or doctrinal support for the reinstitution of blood sacrifice as part of the gospel of Jesus Christ.

86. This conclusion is supported by information that has been compiled in Matthew B. Brown, "Temple Restoration Timeline," unpublished paper, 1999, 24 pp. A portion of this timeline is presented in the appendix of this book.

87. "Many of the Apostles and Elders having returned from England, Joseph [Smith] washed and anointed as Kings and Priests to God . . . as he said he was commanded of God" (Letter, George Miller to James J. Strang, 26 June 1855, cited in H. W. Mills, "De Tal Palo Tal Astilla," *Annual Publications—Historical Society of Southern California*, vol. 10, no. 3 [Los Angeles: McBride Printing Co., 1917], 120–21). Orson Hyde reported that the Prophet said: "there is something going to happen; I don't know what it is, but the Lord bids me to hasten and give you your endowment before the temple is finished" (*TS*, vol. 5, no. 17, 15 September 1844, 651). Parley P. Pratt reported that the Prophet made a similar statement. "I know not why; but for some reason I am constrained to hasten my preparations, and to confer upon the Twelve all the ordinances, keys, covenants, endowments, and sealing ordinances of the priesthood, and so set before them a pattern in all things pertaining to the sanctuary and the endowment therein" (*MS*, vol. 5, no. 10, March 1845, 151).

88. Lucius N. Scovil, "The Higher Ordinances," *Deseret News Semi-Weekly*, vol. 19, no. 3, 15 February 1884, 2; emphasis added.

89. *HC*, 5:2. Even though it may appear awkward, the phrase "the Eloheim" is correct as it stands. *Elohim* is a plural form of *El* (the Hebrew word for "God") and when translated literally it means "Gods" (see *HC*, 6:475–76).

90. See, for instance, *TPJS*, 237, 308, 326, 330, 362–63.

91. Daniel H. Ludlow, ed., *Encyclopedia of Mormonism* (New York: Macmillan, 1992), 2:455, hereafter cited as *EM*. Elder Boyd K. Packer has stated that the "ordinances of washing and anointing are referred to often in the temple as initiatory ordinances. . . . [These] washings and anointings [are] mostly symbolic in nature, but promising definite, immediate blessings as well as future blessings. . . . In connection with these ordinances, in the temple you will be officially clothed in the garment and promised marvelous blessings in connection with it" (Boyd K. Packer, *The Holy Temple* [Salt Lake City:

Bookcraft, 1980], 154–55). "The words 'to endow' (from the Greek *enduein*), as used in the New Testament, mean to dress, clothe, put on garments" (*EM*, 2:454).

92. Carlos E. Asay, "The Temple Garment," *Ensign*, August 1997, 18-23. See also Packer, *The Holy Temple*, 75-79.

93. *EM*, 2:534. Another article in this encyclopedia mentions that all participants in the endowment ceremony "wear white temple robes" (ibid., 2:455).

94. Ibid., 4:1444.

95. John A. Widtsoe, *A Rational Theology* (Salt Lake City: Deseret Book, 1937), 126–27; See also James E. Talmage, *The House of the Lord*, rev. ed. (Salt Lake City: Deseret Book, 1974), 83.

96. In the *Encyclopedia of Mormonism* we read: "At the conclusion of the temple service, those participating in the endowment ceremony pass from the terrestrial room to the celestial room through a veil, which symbolizes the transition from time into eternity" (*EM*, 3:1430).

97. *TPJS*, 51.

98. Widtsoe, *A Rational Theology*, 125–26.

99. Talmage, *The House of the Lord*, 84. President Ezra Taft Benson said that in the temples Latter-day Saints "make solemn covenants pertaining to obedience, consecration, sacrifice, and dedicated service to our Heavenly Father" (Benson, *The Teachings of Ezra Taft Benson*, 251). From the pages of the *Encyclopedia of Mormonism* we read that altars in LDS temples "play a major role. Kneeling by them, Latter-day Saints participate in covenant-making ceremonies" (*EM*, 1:37).

100. *The Doctrine and Covenants* (Salt Lake City: George Q. Cannon and Sons, 1891), 441, ftnt. 2o. Footnote 2p calls these keys "the order, ordained of God."

101. *JD*, 19:250. According to Susan Easton Black, "a new name is often involved when a covenant relationship is formed. . . . We follow a similar pattern when entering into covenants with Christ in the waters of baptism. At that time, we take upon ourselves the name of Christ, and that becomes the name by which we are called (see Mosiah 5:7–12). The higher covenants of the temple also involve the giving and receiving of names. In each of these cases, the one giving the name assumes responsibility for protecting, loving, and nurturing the one receiving the new name. And the recipient of the name, in turn, is to honor the name-giver and follow his counsel" (*Ensign*, December 1988, 55).

102. *TPJS*, 226.

103. *Juvenile Instructor*, vol. 27, no. 11, 1 June 1892, 345.

104. *EM*, 3:1120. "As the ancients came to the altar to communicate and commune with God, so also do members of the Church, in a temple setting, surround the altar in a prayer circle" (ibid., 1:37).

105. See *WJS*, 293–94, nt. 11. See also Andrew F. Ehat, *Joseph Smith's Introduction of Temple Ordinances and the 1844 Mormon Succession Question*, master's thesis, Brigham Young University, 1981, 46–47.

106. In the *Encyclopedia of Mormonism* we read that while "kneeling opposite each other at the altar, the bride and groom are placed under mutual covenants to each other, and are married through the sealing power of Jesus Christ. . . . By apostolic authority, the blessings of Abraham, Isaac, and Jacob are explicitly invoked upon all marriages and sealings" (*EM*, 4:1445). Another article from this Encyclopedia states that "while kneeling at an altar in a temple, a man and woman make covenants with God and each other in a marriage ceremony that is to be binding both in mortality and in the eternal world" (ibid., 1:37).

107. In D&C 132:18 the Lord makes it clear that his house is "a house of order." Therefore, even if a couple decide to enter into a marriage covenant with each other "for time and for all eternity" it is not valid unless it is the covenant that the Lord has made available in his temple. Furthermore, no temple marriage covenants will be valid in eternity until they are "sealed by the Holy Spirit of promise, through him whom [the Lord has] anointed and appointed unto this power."

108. *HC*, 5:510.

109. *TPJS*, 300–301. "Not all women in the Church will have an opportunity for marriage and motherhood in mortality. But if those of you in this situation are worthy and endure faithfully, you can be assured of all blessings from a kind and loving Heavenly Father—and I emphasize *all blessings*" (Ezra Taft Benson, "To the Single Adult Sisters of the Church," *Ensign*, November 1988, 97; emphasis in original. See also *DS*, 2:65, 76–77; *AGQ*, 2:34–38).

110. *TPJS*, 340. On another occasion the Prophet indicated much the same thing when he said "the seals are in our hands to seal our children and our dead" (*WJS*, 346). President George Q. Cannon said of the Prophet: "He bestowed upon the faithful apostles and other chosen ones the endowments, and gave them the keys of the priesthood in their fulness as he had received them. He also taught and administered to them the sealing ordinances, explaining in great plainness and power the manner in which husbands and wives, parents and children are to be united by eternal ties, and the whole human family, back to Father Adam, be linked together in indissoluble bonds" (George Q. Cannon, *Life of Joseph Smith the Prophet* [Salt Lake City: Deseret Book, 1986], 516).

111. "Those married in the temple in the new and everlasting covenant of marriage become inheritors of all the blessings of Abraham, Isaac, and Jacob and all the patriarchs and thereby enter into the patriarchal order. If the participating parties abide in the eternal marriage covenant, they shall reap the full blessings of patriarchal heirship in eternity where the patriarchal order will be the order of government and rule" (*MD*, 559). "Celestial marriage is an 'order of the priesthood.' It is the patriarchal order that opens the door to a continuation of the family unit in eternity" (*NWAF*, 312).

112. *JD*, 11:118.

113. Benson, *The Teachings of Ezra Taft Benson*, 259.

114. *JD*, 16:258. Levi Savage, Jr. asked Daniel McAllister, president of the St. George Temple, the following questions regarding adoption. "Q[uestion]. Why is adoption necessary[?] Ans[wer]. To constitute the person a legal heir to the promises. Q[uestion]. What is the position of one not adopted, but yet has all the other blessings conferred upon him that can be conferred on man on earth[?] Ans[wer]. He is not legitimatized and cannot enjoy the blessings out of the order of the Priesthood" (Diary of Levi Savage, Jr., 7 September 1888, typescript, 134, Special Collections, Harold B. Lee Library, Brigham Young University, Provo, Utah).

115. Kenney, ed., *Wilford Woodruff's Journal*, 3:260.

116. *JD*, 16:186–87.

117. *TPJS*, 296.

118. Elden J. Watson, ed., *Manuscript History of Brigham Young, 1846–1847* (Salt Lake City: Elden J. Watson, 1971), 528–30.

119. *Deseret Evening News*, vol. 27, no. 150, 19 May 1894, 9.

120. *MS*, vol. 68, no. 40, 4 October 1906, 629.

121. See, for example, the statement by Brigham Young in *JD*, 12:165.

122. *HC*, 4:425.

123. "The sons of God are members of his family and, hence, are joint-heirs with Christ, inheriting with him the fulness of the Father (D&C 93:17–23). Before gaining entrance to that glorious household, they must receive the higher priesthood (Moses 6:67–68), magnify their callings therein (D&C 84:33–41), enter into the new and everlasting covenant of marriage (D&C 131:1–4; 132), and be obedient in all things (*DS*, 2:8–9, 37–41, 59, 64–65). Those who become the sons of God in this life (1 John 3:1–3) are the ones who by enduring in continued righteousness will be gods in eternity (D&C 76:58)" (*MD*, 745). "The temple ordinances, including celestial marriage, precede attainment of that membership in the household of God which makes one a daughter. Those who are adopted as daughters in this life will, if they continue faithful, gain exaltation in the world to come" (*MD*, 180).

124. *MD*, 558, emphasis in original.

125. Orson Hyde, "A Diagram of the Kingdom of God," *MS*, vol. 9, no. 2, 15 January 1847, 23–24.

126. *MD*, 558–59. Elder McConkie has taught plainly that the only family units that will exist in eternity will be among those who are exalted in the highest degree of the Celestial kingdom (see ibid., 117–18, 257–58, 273–74, 516–17, 670, 706, 751. *See especially NWAF*, 312–15, where Elder McConkie explains that these eternal families will consist of an exalted husband and wife and their spirit children).

CHAPTER SEVEN
The Gate of Heaven

At the groundbreaking ceremonies of the Logan Temple, Elder John Taylor paraphrased the biblical patriarch Jacob when he said: "Surely this is the House of God, and the gate of heaven" (*see* Genesis 28:17). He then stated that this "is not simply a metaphorical expression, but a reality, for it is in [the Lord's] House . . . that the most sacred ordinances of God are to be performed, which are associated with the interest and happiness of the human family, [both] living and dead."[1] Elder Lorenzo Snow invoked the same imagery when he offered a prayer at the dedicatory services of the Manti Temple. Elder Snow expressed his desire that the Father would hallow the Manti Temple and that it would serve the Saints "as one of the gates of heaven, opening into the straight and narrow path that leads to endless lives and eternal dominion."[2] In this chapter we will examine the role of the temple as "the gate of heaven" for both the living and the dead and how neither group can receive the blessings of exaltation without passing through its sacred portals. This chapter will also briefly touch upon the subject of temple work during the Millennial era.

THE EXALTATION OF THE SAINTS

President Joseph Fielding Smith has pointed out that according to the Lord's own revelations, His temples "are sanctuaries specially dedicated for sacred rites and ceremonies pertaining to exaltation in the celestial kingdom of God. . . . Temples are sanctified for the purpose of performing rites for and making covenants with the pure in heart, who have proved themselves by faithful service worthy of the blessings of exaltation."[3] It is within the Lord's holy houses, taught Elder A. Theodore Tuttle, that one can find "the covenants of exaltation." Elder Tuttle admonished all Latter-day Saints: "Teach your children that only by receiving these ordinances and making these covenants can they be exalted and become like our Heavenly Father."[4] President Joseph Fielding Smith likewise taught that it is necessary for each individual to receive the ordinances of the temple before they can be raised to a state of exaltation and obtain "the fulness of the glory of God."[5] The Prophet Joseph Smith once asked rhetorically: "Can we not be saved without going through with all those [temple] ordinances?" He answered: "No, not the fulness of salvation. . . . [A]ny person who is exalted to the highest mansion [within the Father's kingdom] has to abide a celestial law, and the whole law too."[6] In other words, said the Prophet, all of those "who become heirs of God and joint heirs with Jesus Christ will have to receive the fulness of the ordinances of his kingdom; and those who will not receive all the ordinances will come short of the fulness of that glory, if they do not lose the whole."[7]

President Spencer W. Kimball reminds us that "exaltation is available only to *righteous* members of the Church of Jesus Christ; only to those who accept the gospel; only to those who have their endowments; only to those who have been through the holy temple of God and have been sealed for eternity and who then continue to live righteously throughout their lives."[8] Elder Charles W. Penrose spoke of how such righteousness can be achieved.

> All these ordinances and ceremonies instituted by the Almighty and comprehended in that which is called the Gospel are necessary. There is no such thing as non-essential ordinances; every one of them is essential. Exaltation cannot be arrived at without them. But exaltation does not consist of the mere compliance to certain forms and ceremonies that the Almighty has instituted and placed in his Church. There is something more required, something superior to all this. What is it? It is the Spirit that comes from our Father to dictate us in every act, to make us righteous and holy unto the Lord, and to sanctify us and bring us into complete subjection to, and harmony with, the laws that govern the celestial kingdom.[9]

There are several doctrines that might be looked upon as the *doctrines of exaltation*. An understanding of these doctrines will greatly enhance one's understanding of the purpose and power of the temple. These doctrines include calling and election, the more sure word of prophecy, the Holy Spirit of Promise, being sealed up to eternal life, becoming kings and priests, the Second Comforter, and the Church of the Firstborn. Let us briefly examine each of these doctrines.

Making Your Calling and Election Sure

To make one's calling and election sure, says Bruce R. McConkie, "is, in effect, to have the day of judgement advanced, so that an inheritance of all the glory and honor of the Father's kingdom is assured prior to the day when the faithful actually enter into the divine presence."[10] The Prophet Joseph Smith admonished all Latter-day Saints to press forward and receive this highest of earthly blessings for themselves. "I would exhort you to go on and continue to call upon God until you make your calling and election sure for yourselves, by obtaining [the] more sure word of prophecy, and wait patiently for the promise until you obtain it."[11] "Oh! I beseech you," said the Prophet on another occasion, "to go forward, go forward and make your calling and your election sure."[12] Why was he so anxious that the Saints accomplish this? Because, according to Elder Bruce R. McConkie, "no one will ever gain exaltation, no one will ever have the family unit continue in eternity unless his calling and his election has been made sure, or in other words, unless he has gained the promise that he shall inherit eternal life."[13]

Elder McConkie further informs us: "In the temples the faithful enter into many covenants pertaining to exaltation. And so it goes, the more faithful and devoted a person is, the more of the covenants of the Lord he is enabled to receive, until he receives them in full and his calling and election is made sure."[14] But, he also reminds us, "these high blessings are not part of celestial marriage."[15] Put another way: "Making one's calling and election sure is in *addition* to celestial marriage and results from undeviating and perfect devotion to the cause of righteousness. Those married in the temple can never under any circumstances gain exaltation unless they keep the commandments of God and abide in the covenant of marriage which they have taken upon themselves."[16]

Elder Franklin D. Richards said that it "is by attending to certain ordinances that the blessings of eternity are sealed upon us, and by which, in the plain language of the scriptures, our calling and election [is] made sure."[17] The Prophet Joseph Smith informs us that "what you seal on earth, by the keys of Elijah, is sealed in heaven . . . the power of Elijah is sufficient to make our calling and election sure."[18] He also spoke of a time when "the servants of God are sealed in their foreheads, which signifies sealing the blessing upon their heads, meaning the everlasting covenant, thereby making their calling and election sure."[19]

Second Comforter

Perhaps the greatest blessing for mortals who make their calling and election sure is that they then qualify to receive the Second Comforter. Joseph Smith provides us with the following insights into this doctrine.

> After a person has faith in Christ, repents of his sins, and is baptized for the remission of his sins and receives the Holy Ghost, by the laying on of hands, which is the first Comforter, then let him continue to humble himself before God, hungering and thirsting after righteousness, and living by every word of God, and the Lord will soon say unto him, "Son, thou shalt be exalted." When the Lord has thoroughly proved him, and finds that the man is determined to serve Him at all hazards, then the man will find his calling and his election made sure, then it will be his privilege to receive the other Comforter. . . . Now what is this other Comforter? It is no more nor less than the Lord Jesus Christ Himself; and this is the sum and substance of the whole matter; that when any man obtains this last Comforter, he will have the personage of Jesus Christ to attend him, or appear unto him from time to time, and even He will manifest the Father unto him, and they will take up their abode with him, and the visions of the heavens will be opened unto him, and the Lord will teach him face to face, and he may have a perfect knowledge of the mysteries of the Kingdom of God.[20]

Elder Bruce R. McConkie has also provided us with information regarding the doctrine of the Second Comforter.

> After the true saints receive and enjoy the gift of the Holy Ghost; after they know how to attune themselves to the voice of the Spirit; after they mature spiritually so that they see visions, work miracles, and entertain angels; after they make their calling and election sure and prove themselves worthy of every trust—after all this and more—it becomes their right and privilege to see the Lord and commune with him face to face. Revelations, visions, angelic visitations, the rending of the heavens, and appearances among men of the Lord himself—all these things are for all of the faithful. They are not reserved for apostles and prophets only. God is no respecter of persons.[21]

The More Sure Word of Prophecy

According to latter-day scripture, the "more sure word of prophecy means a man's knowing that he is sealed up unto eternal life, by revelation and the spirit of prophecy, through the power of the Holy Priesthood" (D&C 131:5; *see also* 2 Peter 1:19). By way of explanation, the Prophet Joseph Smith said that even though a Latter-day Saint "might hear the voice of God and know that Jesus was the Son of God, this would be no evidence that their election and calling was made sure, that they had part with Christ, and were joint heirs with him. Then they would want that more sure word of prophecy, that they were sealed in the heavens and had the promise of eternal life in the kingdom of God."[22] On another occasion the Prophet spoke of "how to make our calling and election sure" and explained that this is equivalent to "obtain[ing] a promise from God for myself that I shall have eternal life. That is the more sure word of prophecy."[23] On yet another occasion the Prophet said,

> It is one thing to receive knowledge by the voice of God . . . and another to know that you yourself will be saved. To have a positive promise of your own salvation is making your calling and election sure. [It is to hear] the voice of Jesus saying, "My beloved, thou shalt have eternal life." Brethren, never cease struggling until you get this evidence. Take heed both before and after obtaining this more sure word of prophecy.[24]

The Holy Spirit of Promise

The Holy Spirit of Promise is the power of the Holy Ghost that binds certain acts that are performed on the earth so that they will be bound in heaven. This seal validates or ratifies all earthly "covenants, contracts, bonds, obligations, oaths, vows, performances, connections, associations, or expectations" so that they will have "efficacy, virtue, or force in and after the resurrection from the dead" (D&C 132:7, 18–19, 26). Thus, to have an earthly act sealed by the Holy Spirit of Promise is to receive a promise or assurance that the act so sealed will be valid for eternity.

This sealing power can be used to seal the Saints of God up "unto the day of redemption" (D&C 124:124; *see also* Ephesians 1:13–14), which is the day of the resurrection (*see* D&C 76:50–53). In this way the sealing power of the Holy Spirit of Promise is interwoven with the More Sure Word of Prophecy and making one's Calling and Election Sure. President Marion G. Romney said, "I know it is possible for men to so live that they may hear [God's] voice and know his words and that to receive 'the Holy Spirit of Promise' while here in mortality is possible. And so in the words of the Prophet Joseph [Smith] 'I exhort you to go on and continue to call upon God until (by the more sure word of prophecy) you make your calling and election sure for yourselves.'"[25]

Apostle Orson Pratt informs us that a person is "sealed with the [holy] spirit of promise through the ordinances of the house of God."[26] But, as Elder Bruce R.

McConkie has warned, even this seal can be broken through subsequent unrighteousness.

> Even if a person progresses to that state of near-perfection in which his calling and election is made sure, in which he is "sealed up unto eternal life" (D&C 131:5; 132:18–26), in which he receives "the promise . . . of eternal life" (D&C 88:3–4), in which he is "sealed up unto the day of redemption" (D&C 124:124; Ephesians 1:13)—yet with it all, these great promises are secured only if the "performances" are sealed by the Holy Spirit of Promise.[27]

The Fulness of the Priesthood

In section 124 of the Doctrine and Covenants, the Lord stated that the Nauvoo Temple would be a place where the "fulness of the priesthood" would be restored (D&C 124:28). Joseph Smith said: "If a man gets a fulness of the priesthood of God he has to get it in the same way that Jesus Christ obtained it, and that was by keeping all the commandments and obeying all the ordinances of the house of the Lord."[28] According to Joseph Fielding Smith, "the Lord has made it possible for every man in this Church, through his obedience, to receive the fulness of the priesthood through the ordinances of the temple of the Lord."[29] He likewise stated: "*No man can get the fulness of the priesthood outside the temple of the Lord.*"[30] And again: "If we want to receive the fulness of the priesthood of God, then we must receive the fulness of the ordinances of the house of the Lord and keep his commandments."[31] Why is the fulness of the priesthood necessary? Because, said Joseph Fielding Smith, there is "no exaltation in the kingdom of God without the fulness of the priesthood."[32]

President Ezra Taft Benson has declared that to "enter into the order of the Son of God is the equivalent today of entering into the fulness of the Melchizedek Priesthood, which is only received in the house of the Lord."[33] And from the Prophet Joseph Smith we learn that those "holding the fulness of the Melchizedek Priesthood are kings and priests of the Most High God, holding the keys of power and blessings."[34] In connection with this we read in the 76th section of the Doctrine and Covenants that those who are exalted in the celestial kingdom are "priests and kings, who have received of [God's] fulness, and of his glory" (D&C 76:56). They are additionally described as being "priests of the Most High, after the order of Melchizedek" (vs. 57). In speaking of the Nauvoo Temple, Joseph Smith said that he intended to—

> give the Elders of Israel their washings and anointings, and attend to those last and more impressive ordinances, without which we cannot obtain celestial thrones. But there must be a holy place prepared for that purpose. There was a proclamation

made during the time that the foundation of the [Nauvoo] Temple was laid to that effect, and there are provisions made until the work is completed, so that men may receive their endowments and be made kings and priests unto the Most High God, having nothing to do with temporal things, but their whole time will be taken up with things pertaining to the house of God.[35]

Elder Bruce R. McConkie has taught that it is "through the fulness of the ordinances of the temple [that we] receive the fulness of the priesthood and are ordained *kings and priests*."[36] He has also stated that as Christ obtained "the fulness of the Melchizedek Priesthood in order to gain exaltation, so must we." And then he adds that in "setting forth as much as can, with propriety, be spoken outside of the temple, the Lord says that 'the fulness of the priesthood' is received only in the temple itself. This fulness is received through washings, anointings, solemn assemblies, oracles in holy places, conversations, ordinances, endowments, and sealings (D&C 124:39)."[37]

The Church of the Firstborn

President Brigham Young stated emphatically that nobody can "dwell with the Father and Son, unless they go through those ordeals that are ordained for the Church of the Firstborn. The ordinances of the house of God are expressly for the Church of the Firstborn."[38] What is the Church of the Firstborn? Elder Bruce R. McConkie teaches that the Church of the Firstborn "is the Church which exists among exalted beings in the celestial realm."[39] He also states that "celestial marriage is the gate to membership in the Church of the Firstborn, the inner circle of faithful saints who are heirs to exaltation."[40] Elder McConkie has also penned the following insights on this important subject.

> Members of the Church of Jesus Christ of Latter-day Saints who so devote themselves to righteousness that they receive the higher ordinances of exaltation become members of the Church of the Firstborn. Baptism is the gate to the Church itself, but celestial marriage is the gate to membership in the Church of the Firstborn, the inner circle of faithful saints who are heirs of exaltation and the fulness of the Father's kingdom (D&C 76:54, 67, 71, 94, 102; 77:11; 78:21; 88:1–5; Hebrews 12:23).
>
> The Church of the Firstborn is made up of the sons of God, those who have been adopted into the family of the Lord, those who are destined to be joint-heirs with Christ in receiving all that the Father hath. "If you keep my commandments you shall receive of his fulness, and be glorified in me as I am in the Father; . . . And all those who are begotten through me are partakers of the glory of the same, and are the church of the Firstborn" (D&C 93:20–22).[41]

In D&C 76:54-58 we are told that those who become members of the Church of the Firstborn achieve the status of *gods*, even the *sons of God*. "Gods have an ascendency over the angels, who are ministering servants," said Joseph Smith. "In the resurrection, some are raised to be angels, others are raised to become Gods. These things are revealed in the most holy places in a temple prepared for that purpose."[42] Joseph Smith defined godhood by saying that "every man who reigns in celestial glory is a God to his dominions."[43]

THE REDEMPTION OF THE DEAD

The doctrine of the redemption of the dead began to be revealed to the Prophet Joseph Smith during the Kirtland period of Church history (*see* D&C 137). But the means and methods for accomplishing the full redemption of those who reside in the spirit world was not vouchsafed to the Church until the Nauvoo period, beginning with a series of revelations on baptism for the dead (*see* D&C 128). The Prophet taught: "It is not only necessary that you should be baptized for your dead, but you will have to go through all the ordinances [of the temple] for them, the same as you have gone through to save yourselves."[44] President Brigham Young learned by revelation that "it takes as full and complete a set of ordinances for the dead as for the living."[45]

President Joseph Fielding Smith explained that it "is in strict accordance with the divine will that the great work for the salvation of the dead was one assigned to those who lived in the dispensation of the fulness of times."[46] No doubt one of the major reasons for the assignment of this great work to the final dispensation is that technology created during this dispensation has made enormous amounts of genealogical data available on a worldwide scale, thus enabling a more rapid execution of the Lord's work.

Family Lineage

In an earlier period of Church history, President Brigham Young taught that once a family's genealogical lines had been accurately traced, a member of the family should be the one to perform the work of redemption in the temple for that line. The "proper person" to do such a work, he said, was "a blood relation" or "heir." If, for some reason, there were no persons within that family who were qualified to perform the work, then someone outside of that lineage could be duly authorized and appointed for the task.[47] The point that President Young was trying to make was that each family was ultimately responsible for the salvation of its lineage. When Lorenzo Snow was appointed as the president of the Salt Lake Temple, he too said that in the "performance of work for the dead the rights of heirship (blood relationship) should be sacredly regarded, when practicable."[48]

In more recent times Elder Mark E. Peterson has likewise taught that "each living person is responsible to assist in the salvation of his own deceased relatives. Our own salvation is largely dependent upon it. . . . [If] we go to the temple, and not for our own dead, we are performing only a part of our duty, because we are also required to go there specifically to save our own dead relatives and bind the various generations together by the power of the holy priesthood."[49] On one occasion, Elder Wilford Woodruff was attempting to do a great amount of proxy work for his deceased relatives in the St. George Temple. Being the only member of his family at the temple, he petitioned the Lord, in prayer, on 23 February 1877 to reveal to him how he could accomplish such a large task. In answer to his prayer the Lord granted permission for him to allow those outside of his own lineage to help him with the work. Said President Woodruff: "When I inquired of the Lord how I could redeem my dead, while I was in St. George, not having any of my family there, the Lord told me to call upon the Saints in St. George and let them officiate for me in that temple, and it should be acceptable unto him. . . . This is a revelation to us. We can help one another in these matters, if we have not relatives sufficient to carry this on, and it will be acceptable to the Lord."[50]

President George Q. Cannon had the following words to say on the need for all Latter-day Saints to do genealogy work and then offer their relatives the redemptive blessings of the gospel of Jesus Christ.

> It is your duty now to rise up, all of you, and trace your genealogies, and begin to exercise the powers which belong to the saviors of men, and when you do this in earnest, you will begin to comprehend how widespread, how numerous your ancestors are, for whom temple work has to be performed, in order that they may be brought into the fold; and when you get stopped, the Lord will reveal further information to you; and in this way the work of salvation and redemption will be accomplished, even from Father Adam down to the last one; or to speak more properly, down to the Prophet Joseph, who was the first of this dispensation. From Father Adam down to him, all being linked together by the sealing ordinances which God has restored, and the powers of which will be exercised in the temples of God, all being united together as brethren and sisters, for we are all begotten of God.[51]

Proxy Temple Work

The administration of proxy temple work and mortal temple work are very similar. In both cases the gospel of Jesus Christ must be preached to those who desire to hear its teachings. When Jesus Christ's body lay in the tomb after the crucifixion, his spirit went into the spirit world, and there He organized His faithful followers to teach the vast throngs in the spirit prison who had not yet been converted (*see* 1 Peter 3:19; 4:6; D&C 138:28–37). Because God is just, He offers the blessings of truth and salvation to all of His children and then, based upon their response to His offer, He can appropriately judge and reward their actions.

The priesthood organization on the other side of the veil is in charge of preaching the gospel of redemption to the spirits who are in the spirit prison. In speaking of the Holy Priesthood, President Wilford Woodruff taught that upon the earth there is

> a kingdom of priests raised up by the power of God to take hold and build up the kingdom of God. The same Priesthood exists on the other side of the veil. Every man who is faithful in his quorum here will join his quorum there. When a man dies and his body is laid in the tomb, he does not lose his position. The Prophet Joseph Smith held the keys of this dispensation on this side of the veil, and he will hold them throughout the countless ages of eternity. He went into the spirit world to unlock the prison doors and to preach the gospel to the millions of spirits who are in darkness, and every Apostle, every Seventy, every Elder, etc., who has died in the faith as soon as he passes to the other side of the veil, enters into the work of the ministry, and there is a thousand times more to preach there than there is here.[52]

Those spirits who are responsive to the message of the gospel are then eligible to receive its ordinances by means of a proxy on the earth. In the fall of 1857, a Swedish Latter-day Saint named John Peterson became extremely ill and one night was taken into the spirit world by a guide. While in the spiritual realms Brother Peterson saw Elder Parley P. Pratt and the New Testament apostle Matthias teaching the gospel of Jesus Christ to a large group of his forefathers. Elder Pratt preached on Malachi 4:5–6 and also "upon temple building and the ordinances to be performed therein in redeeming the dead." He told this group that if they "would receive the gospel they should be redeemed by their children on the earth, and if they did not receive it they could not" be redeemed. Brother Peterson was then asked if he would return to the earth and redeem his ancestors. He agreed to the task and was promised that his physical affliction would be healed.[53]

Once the ordinances of the Lord's house have been properly performed by a proxy on the earth "God has administrators in the eternal world to release those spirits from prison," said the Prophet Joseph Smith. "The ordinances being administered by proxy upon them, the law is fulfilled."[54]

The Second Chance Theory

Latter-day scripture informs us that when the ordinances pertaining to salvation for the dead were "ordained and prepared before the foundation of the world," the Lord stipulated that they would only be efficacious for those "who should die without a knowledge of the gospel" (D&C 128:5). It must be clearly understood that salvation for the dead is not a second chance to receive the blessings of the gospel in the spirit world. President Spencer W. Kimball has stated plainly that "vicarious work for the dead is for those who could not do the work for themselves. Men and women who live in mortality and who have heard the gospel here have had their day, their seventy years to put their lives in harmony, to perform the ordinances, to repent and to perfect their lives."[55] Elder Bruce R. McConkie has been even more specific about this issue. He points out that,

> There is no such thing as a second chance to gain salvation by accepting the gospel in the spirit world after spurning, declining, or refusing to accept it in this life. It is true that there may be a second chance to hear and accept the gospel, but those who have thus procrastinated their acceptance of the saving truths will not gain salvation in the celestial kingdom of God. Salvation for the dead is the system by means of which those who "die without a knowledge of the gospel" (D&C 128:5) may gain such knowledge in the spirit world and then, following the vicarious performance of the necessary ordinances, become heirs of salvation on the same basis as though the gospel truths had been obeyed in mortality. Salvation for the dead is limited expressly to those who do not have opportunity in this life to accept the gospel but who would have taken the opportunity had it come to them. . . . There is no promise in any revelation that those who have a fair and just opportunity in this life to accept the gospel, and who do not do it, will have another chance in the spirit world to gain salvation. On the contrary, there is the express stipulation that men cannot be saved without accepting the gospel in this life, if they are given opportunity to accept it. . . . Those who have a fair and just opportunity to accept the gospel in this life and who do not do it, but who then do accept it when they hear it in the spirit world will go not to the celestial, but to the terrestrial kingdom.[56]

FROM BEYOND THE VEIL

Certainly one of the strongest testimonies of the divine authenticity of temple work is the fact that those who are beyond the veil sometimes appear to mortals to request it, to help with it, and to witness it. The accounts that follow should serve to illustrate the point that the temple ordinances restored by the Prophet Joseph Smith are both vital and divine.

Righteous Spirits are Anxious for Temple Work

One elderly woman who worked in the Salt Lake Temple told President Harold B. Lee about a singular vision she once had while inside that sacred building. Because she had a debilitating medical condition, this sister wondered whether or not she should discontinue working as a proxy in the Lord's house. She took the matter up with the Lord in prayer and asked if there might perhaps be something else she could do with her life that would be of greater importance. President Lee tells her story.

> That day, as she went through as a worker in the temple from one room to another, she came into one of the rooms, and, she said, "I suddenly had a strange feeling come over me, and I thought I was going to faint." She said, "All my life I'd never fainted." She said, "I thought to myself, 'Well, I mustn't make a spectacle, so I'd better seek a chair here to sit down,'" and as she sat down, the walls of the temple seemed to move out. Behind her was a great concourse of people dressed in white robes. When she sat down and stopped, they had to stop and wait. And then the whole impression of it came upon her: only could they move forward when she moved forward. And after musing upon the singularity of that vision which was shown her, the walls came back.[57]

Joseph Smith is reported to have said a few words about the gratitude of those for whom temple ordinances are performed. "In the resurrection," said the Prophet, "those who had been worked for [will] fall at the feet of those who had done their work, kiss their feet, embrace their knees and manifest the most exquisite gratitude. We do not comprehend what a blessing to them these ordinances are."[58]

Some Spirits Help with Genealogy

There are times when those in the spirit world are allowed to part the veil and directly assist mortals with genealogical matters that are vital to temple work. One

LDS bishop, named A. J. Graham, was visited from beyond the veil by his deceased parents who brought books of genealogy with them.

> One night while in the hospital after an operation and in the act of praying I felt someone present in my room. I opened my eyes and the room was light, the door closed and near my bed stood my mother. She smiled and said:
>
> "I am glad to see you are better." She held in her hand a book. I asked what it was. She replied that it was a book of genealogies. Father then appeared with three books in his hand, saying, "I am glad you are better."
>
> "You must get well, for I have three volumes of names that are ready to have work done for them in the temple. We have connected up our family so you can do their work. Ways and means will open for you if you will."
>
> I asked how I was to find these records. He said, "If you will work in the temple, you shall know but it will take money." I said, "Father, I haven't any money and have been out of work since May 1."
>
> He said, "Never mind my boy, money will come to you if you are determined to work in the temple for these poor people who are held back and can't go on. They pray as earnestly for you, that you might have money and the necessities of life, and that your heart will be moved so that you will do this work for them, just as sincerely as you pray for things you need. Don't forget, they cannot go on until their work is done."
>
> With a smile of confidence and content they both faded from my mortal vision.[59]

Some Spirits Request Temple Work

In November of 1914, Lerona A. Wilson was stricken with a life-threatening medical condition and decided that it would be prudent to exercise her faith in prayer to God. Even though she offered up her prayer when it was midday she noticed that her room began to fill with a soft, bright light.

> Immediately her father who had been dead seven years came into her room accompanied by her mother who had been dead thirty years, and by her sister and her daughter-in-law who had both been dead two years, and two men whom her father introduced as Dr. Robiou and Dr. Trabue, his ancestors of the French Hugenot people of Virginia.
>
> Her father addressed her saying, "We have come to talk to you about the temple work for our people who are now in the spirit world."
>
> Her father told [her] about her ancestors. They were a worthy people, he said, and had accepted the Gospel in large numbers, and were waiting with anxious hope for the ordinance of baptism to be performed for them.

He then said the time had come for these ordinances to be performed and he desired her to take up the work. She promised she would.

After she made the promise, her father required her to repeat it and then warned her in these words: "If you do not, I will move you out of the way and raise up someone who will."

He used great emphasis in urging that baptisms be performed at once for all the people she had records of. "The time is short," he said, "our people cannot be put off. Their work must be done so they can be ready for the coming of the Savior."

On another occasion, while Lerona was asleep, this same group of visitors returned in a vivid dream and seemed to take her into the spirit world where she was shown a vast congregation of her relatives who had been confined within walls. Once Lerona and her spirit visitors had positioned themselves upon an elevated stand, Lerona's father informed the confined masses that she had promised to have their temple work done for them.[60]

Soon after the Manti Temple had been dedicated, Bishop George Farnworth of Mount Pleasant, Utah, who was the only member of the Church in his family, had a singular experience while driving a team of horses toward the city of Manti.

The morning of the 16th of July, 1888, about 10 o'clock while I was traveling between Pigeon Hollow and the Ephraim graveyard I felt a very strange sensation such as I never before experienced. Under this influence I went along and chancing to raise my eyes, it seemed that right in front of me there was a vast multitude of men; to the right and a little in front stood a large man about the size of my father, who weighed two hundred and forty-two pounds. This man waved his right hand towards the multitude and said:

"These are your kindred! And we have been waiting, waiting, waiting! Waiting for your temple to be finished. It is now dedicated and accepted by our Father. You are our representative, and we want you to do for us what we cannot do for ourselves. You have had the privilege of hearing the gospel of the Son of God; we had not that great blessing."

As he ceased, I looked at the great concourse and realized that they were all men, and thought it strange there were no women. I tried to recognize some of them but could not as I knew none. The thought came strongly into my mind, "How can I find out their names, who and what they are?" Then a voice seemed to answer in my ears, "When that will be required it will be made known."

I felt while looking at them, "Oh, shall I be worthy to help them?" whereupon I found tears were rolling down my cheeks and in the humility of my soul I shouted, "God help me!" adding aloud, "God being my helper I will do all I can;" and it seemed as if the whole host shouted with one voice, "Amen!"

Once Bishop Farnworth reached Manti, and rested from the weakness brought on by this powerful vision, he made his way to the Manti Temple. There he related this spiritual manifestation to President Wells and several others. Eventually the story reached the ears of the temple recorder whose name was Frank Farnsworth. The recorder found the bishop and said that while he was doing genealogical research for his own family lineage, he had run across many Farnworths. And even though these people were not related to his family line he felt the impulse to gather their names anyhow. "Now," said the temple recorder, "you are welcome to these names for they are evidently your own kindred."[61]

Another large group of spirits who appeared to request temple ordinances were the signers of the Declaration of Independence. President Wilford Woodruff, who told of this well-known incident, prefaced his remarks by encouraging the Saints to "build these temples now underway, to hurry them up to completion. The dead will be after you, they will seek after you as they have after us" because "we held the keys and power to redeem them." President Woodruff stated that in March of 1877, George Washington and the signers of the Declaration of Independence called upon him "as an Apostle of the Lord Jesus Christ, in the temple at St. George, two consecutive nights, and demanded at my hands that I should go forth and attend to the ordinances of the House of God for them." President Woodruff stood in as the baptismal proxy for these noble men and when he had finished the work for them he had himself baptized for fifty other "eminent men," including religious leaders and presidents of the United States. He later saw to it that they all received their temple endowments as well.[62]

In addition to these group visitations there are stories from the early history of the Church of individual family members making appearances to request that their temple ordinance work be done. A temple worker once related such a story to Elder Rudger Clawson of the Quorum of the Twelve Apostles who, in turn, related the story to the Saints attending General Conference.

> I saw in vision, upon one occasion, my father and mother, who were not members of the Church, who had not received the gospel in life, and I discovered that they were living separate and apart in the spirit world, and when I asked them how it was that they were so, my father said: "This is an enforced separation, and you are the only individual that can bring us together; you can do this work; will you do it?"—meaning that he should go into the house of the Lord and there officiate for his parents who were dead, and by the ordinance of sealing bring them together and unite them in the family relation beyond the veil.

The temple worker informed Elder Clawson that after this manifestation occurred he attended to the necessary temple ordinance that would seal his parents together for eternity. Then he and Elder Clawson rejoiced in the knowledge that one of the keys of life and salvation had been turned on behalf of those who had passed beyond the veil.[63]

Frederick William Hurst was one of the painters of the Salt Lake Temple when it was being built. At the beginning of March in 1893, he was visited in succession by two of his dead brothers who requested that temple work be performed in their behalf. The first brother, Alfred, who was not a member of the Church when he died, entered the room where Frederick was and sat on the opposite side of a table from him. It is interesting to note that Alfred did not look like a spirit to Frederick, but was very natural in appearance.

> He said: "I have just come from the Spirit World, this is not my body that you see, it is lying in the tomb. I want to tell you that when you were on your mission you told me many things about the Gospel, and the hereafter, and about the Spirit World being as real and tangible as the earth. I could not believe you, but when I died and went there and saw for myself I realized that you had told the truth. I attended the Mormon meetings [in the Spirit World]." He raised his hand and said with much warmth: "I believe in the Lord Jesus Christ with all my heart. I believe in faith, and repentance and baptism for the remission of sins, but that is as far as I can go. I look to you to do the work for me in the temple."

During their lengthy conversation Frederick was informed that his kindred beyond the veil were fully aware of everything that he did on the earth. He was also told that "there are a great many spirits who weep and mourn because they have relatives in the Church here who are careless and are doing nothing for them." When their conversation was complete, the spirit of Frederick's deceased brother arose and left through the same door that he had entered. Frederick continues his account.

> As I sat pondering upon what I had seen and heard, with my heart filled with thanks and gratitude to God, the door opened again and my brother Alexander walked in and sat down in the chair that Alfred had occupied. He had died in 1852 in New Zealand. I did the work for both he and Father in April 1885. He had come from a different sphere, he looked more like an angel as his countenance was beautiful to look upon. With a very pleasant smile he said: "Fred, I have come to thank you for doing my work for me, but you did not go quite far enough," and he paused. Suddenly it was shown to me in large characters, "No man without the woman, and no woman without the man in the Lord."

I looked at him and said: "I think I understand, you want some person sealed to you."

He said: "You are right, I don't need to interpret the scriptures to you, but until that work is done I cannot advance another step."

I replied that the [Salt Lake] Temple would be completed and dedicated in about four weeks, and then I would attend to it as quickly as possible.

"I know you will," he said, and then got up and left the room, leaving me full of joy, peace, and happiness beyond description.[64]

Another interesting account is that of a dying mother who was requested by her son, who was not a member of the Church and skeptical about life after death, to return to the earth if possible and tell him about what lay beyond. She agreed, and shortly after her funeral she visited her son in broad daylight while he was out riding his horse. She "appeared by his side, about eight or ten feet from him. She told him she had come to redeem her pledge; and she desired that he should go, on the following Thursday, and be baptized by his Bishop, taking with him two witnesses, whom she named. She further desired him to be faithful and eventually receive his endowments and help to do the work for her dead friends, which she had failed to accomplish."[65]

Some Spirits Witness Proxy Ordinances

On the afternoon of 19 March 1914, Horatio Pickett, who was a worker in the St. George Temple, saw a vision of those for whom proxy baptisms were being performed that day. This experience was sparked by a question that those who do proxy temple work often ask themselves.

One day while at the font confirming, when a large list of women were being baptized for, the thought again came into my mind: Do those people for whom this work is being done, know that it is being done for them, and, if they do, do they appreciate it? While this thought was running through my mind I happened to turn my eyes toward the southeast corner of the font room and there I saw a large group of women. The whole southeast part of the room was filled; they seemed to be standing a foot or more above the floor and were all intently watching the baptizing that was being done; and as the recorder called a name, one of them—a rather tall, very slim woman, apparently about 35 years of age, gave a sudden start and looked at the recorder. Then her eyes turned to the couple in the water, closely watching the baptism; then her eyes followed the sister that was being baptized as she came up out of the water and was confirmed, and when the ordinance was completed the happy, joyous expression that spread over her countenance was lovely to behold.[66]

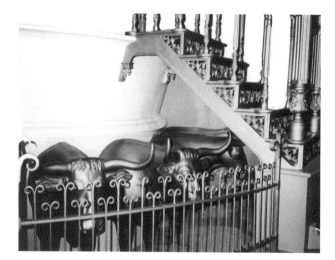

FIGURE 36. Baptismal font from the Logan Temple used for the performance of proxy baptisms. LDS temple baptismal fonts are built after the pattern of the Brazen Sea that was placed in the courtyard of King Solomon's Temple.

In the historical record of the Salt Lake Temple, it is recorded that "Elder Wilford Woodruff, Jr., in a morning meeting in the temple annex, told the congregation that, after he had gone through the veil one day, the dead man for whom he had taken endowments appeared to him and thanked him therefor."[67] M. F. Farnsworth, a long-time worker and recorder for the St. George Temple, testified that persons had also told him "of seeing their dead friends for whom they have officiated, manifesting themselves to them."[68]

In the Terrestrial Room of the Salt Lake Temple on 20 July 1893, a sister reported seeing "the personages of a spiritual prayer circle assembled above the brethren and sisters who were then being conducted in the prayer circle service of the temple, and heard their voices repeating the words of the prayer that was then being uttered. A sister, who was with her, heard the spirit voices also, but she did not see the personages in the spirit circle."[69]

A Salt Lake Temple recorder by the name of Joseph H. Smith reported an instance of spirit couples being seen in attendance at their vicarious marriage sealings.

> Brother Joseph Warburton and his daughter were doing sealings in the Salt Lake Temple on December 1, 1898. After having completed their labors in the sealing room, they walked up to President John R. Winder and expressed their appreciation for his having performed these sealings for them.
>
> After they had gone into the next room the daughter turned to her father and asked, "Did you see those three couples in the sealing room with us?" His answer was, "No, I did not."
>
> She then said: "There were three couples in the room. They were dressed in temple clothing, and the room was illumined by a supernatural light. As we knelt at the altar, and the names were called of the people for whom we were being sealed, each couple in turn knelt by our side. As the ordinance was performed they showed by the expression on their faces how pleased they were. When we walked up to

thank President Winder, they came up also, and after we had completed our expression of thanks to him they disappeared.[70]

J. Hatton Carpenter, the Recorder of the Manti Temple, also reported a vision of those who were being sealed together as husband and wife for time and all eterntity.

A certain brother and his wife, whom we will call Mr. F., were acting as proxies at the altar for some six or seven couples who were being sealed as husband and wife and who were living in England some 250 or more years ago.

Mr. F. told me that when he had reached the second couple he did not seem to notice his wife or much of the ceremony and words that the [officiator] said [while he] was performing the sealing, for his spiritual eyes were opened, and he gazed into a room about the size of the one he was in, and saw some twelve or thirteen couples standing there dressed in their temple clothes. This number corresponded to the number to be sealed that day, as

FIGURE 37. Sealing altar from the Manti Temple. Altars play an important role in several of the ordinances that are performed within LDS temples.

there was another list of six couples to be sealed after Mr. F. was finished. Mr. F. told me he had never seen anything so wonderful, or felt so enraptured in his life, as when the sealing ordinance of the second couple was ended, and he saw them embrace one another, and witnessed the heavenly joy and happiness that their countenances exhibited. Yes, when we think of husbands and wives being separated for 200 and 300 years from each other, we are unable to describe the joy they would have in the thought that from now on [neither] time nor eternity [can] separate them.[71]

One other ordinance for which we have record of spirit-world witnesses is the family sealing stories that demonstrate the desire of those beyond the veil to have this ordinance performed. The following incident occurred in the Cardston Temple in Canada. The witness of this manifestation was President Duce, who for several years had been an active worker in the Logan Temple. He was sitting inside a sealing room when this manifestation occurred.

He stated that he saw the main corridor to the sealing room filled with people looking into the sealing room and taking note as sealing ordinances were administered for one person after another, in the relationship of wives to husbands or children to parents.

He said that he saw plainly as each person's work was done he or she would shake hands with the people still waiting in the corridor and would apparently go away. When the work in the sealing room was finished, he still saw very many waiting in the corridor. They were apparently very much disappointed in knowing that the work was finished for the day and no work was done for them.

This leads us to believe that there are a good many people in the Spirit World who know just what is being done in the temple, and that when the work is not done for them, they are greatly disappointed.[72]

In more recent times a wonderful story was publicly related by Lynn A. McKinlay who had once accepted the invitation to act as a proxy for an elderly woman and her daughter who had come to the Lord's house from Boston to seal their family together for eternity.

It was late at night. They had not understood the instructions properly and when they came to the temple, though their [genealogical] sheets were made out well, they had made no provision for a proxy. So the officiator of the temple came to me and said, "Would you like to act as proxy for this family?" I was in a perfect spirit to do that very thing. I went into the sealing room. On the one side was this little lady well, I'm sure, in her eighties, snow white hair, bright blue eyes, skin almost transparent, beauty in age—she had it. When it came time for the sealings we gripped our hands across the altar and as the ordinance was performed her chin quivered and her eyes filled up with tears, and so did mine. Then her daughter came over, their only child, and placed her hand upon our hands. This time when the ordinance of sealing the child to the parents was being performed she was not looking at me. She looked up and beyond me, and through her tears there was a smile. This was a sacred moment for me but I knew it was sacred to these two people so I just withdrew and I was on my way going down to change my clothing to leave the temple when I felt an arm slip through mine. I turned around and saw this little lady. She said, "I probably will never see you again in this life but I wanted to explain something as well as to thank you. Did you know what happened there tonight?" I said, "No. I knew that this was a sacred experience, but I don't know what occurred." She said, "When my husband and I were being sealed, suddenly your face seemed almost transformed into his. It's as if we were when [my husband and I] were married the first time. And then when our daughter was sealed to us you noticed I didn't look at you, I looked beyond you. My husband was standing there smiling approval and love." And she said, "I probably will never get back to the West again. I'm too old. But I'm not afraid to die now. [My husband] will be waiting for me, and together we'll wait for our daughter there."[73]

THE LAWS OF HEAVEN

While many things have been revealed about the temple work that is to be performed upon the earth, we know considerably less about what happens in connection with this work on the other side of the veil. What we do know is sketchy but it still helps us to begin to understand how God governs the glorious process of salvation.

The Law of Redemption

The Lord revealed to President Wilford Woodruff that there is a Law of Redemption connected with temple work. President Woodruff relates that his son was drowned in northern Idaho while President Woodruff was serving in the St. George Temple. "He was 21 years of age, and was a faithful young man. He had a warning of this. In a dream he was notified how he would die. We had testimony of that after his death. I asked the Lord why he was taken from me. The answer to me was, 'You are doing a great deal for the redemption of your dead; but the law of redemption requires some of your own seed in the spirit world to attend to work connected with this.' That was a new principle to me; but it satisfied me why he was taken away."[74] President Heber J. Grant further informs us that President Woodruff was told by the Lord that "this boy of his was needed on the other side to carry the gospel to his relatives for whom brother Woodruff was to do the vicarious labor in the temples when they were completed."[75]

An account related by a missionary serving in 1901 adds considerable insight into President Woodruff's experience. While serving his mission in the British Isles, James A. LeSueur received word that his younger brother Frank had been killed. Frank had recently been called as a missionary by the First Presidency of the Church but he had not yet been assigned to his field of labor. In pleading with the Lord for comfort and consolation during this tragedy, James asked the Lord why his brother's life had been taken and whether it had been the will of the Lord that this had occurred. His prayer was answered by a clear and penetrating voice from above him, which said,

> "Your brother is called for a similar purpose as President Woodruff's son."
> I recalled immediately how President Woodruff's son, one on whom he had laid

a great hope of an eventual earthly career, had been drowned in Idaho. President Woodruff had gone to the temple and asked the Lord why this son was taken, when an angel of the Lord stood before him and asked this question,

"Which of all your sons would you prefer to have charge of the missionary work of preaching the gospel to your kindred in the spirit world?"

President Woodruff spoke the name of the son who was drowned and the angel passed out of his sight.

So then I knew that my brother, Frank, had been called to take charge of the missionary work among my kindred who had passed on.[76]

The Law of Agency

Even when proxy ordinances are performed in the temple for the dead, their agency is not infringed upon. The law of free agency cannot be violated under any circumstances because that would contradict the whole purpose of the plan of salvation, which is to provide everyone with the opportunity to choose their own destiny (*see* 2 Nephi 2:27; 10:23). President Gordon B. Hinckley has made this point very clear. Those who reside in the spirit world "are free to accept or reject those earthly ordinances performed for them, including baptism, marriage, and the sealing of family relationships. There must be no compulsion in the work of the Lord, but there must be opportunity."[77]

According to Elder Orson Pratt, the spirits in prison are taught about all of the blessings of the gospel that are available to them and they are then left to decide their own course of action. "When these holy and sacred institutions are made known to the spirits in prison by holy messengers holding the priesthood, they will be left to their own agency either to receive or reject these glad tidings, and will be judged according to men in the flesh who have the privilege of hearing the same things."[78]

Spirit World Ratification

It is clear from the scriptural record and eyewitness accounts that there are temples in the spiritual world. Even though we are not aware of precisely what goes on inside those heavenly buildings, we have been informed by latter-day prophets that some form of work is performed that ratifies the temple work that is performed upon the earth. President Ezra Taft Benson taught that the "work we are performing here has [a] direct relationship to the work over there. Someday you will know that there are ordinances performed over there, too, in order to make the vicarious work which you do effective. It will all be done under the authority and power of the priesthood of God."[79] And from President John Taylor we learn that,

God is looking upon us, and has called us to be saviors upon Mount Zion. And what does a savior mean? It means a person who saves somebody. Jesus went and preached to the spirits in prison; and he was a Savior to that people. When he came to atone for the sins of the world, he was a Savior, was he not? Yes. And we are told in the revelations that saviors should stand upon Mount Zion [see Obadiah 1:21]; and the kingdom shall be the Lord's. Would we be saviors if we did not save somebody? I think not. Could we save anyone if we did not build temples? No, we could not. . . . If we are saviors, what have we to do? Build temples. What then? Administer in them; and others in the heavens are engaged in the same work as we, but in another position and in other circumstances. They preach to spirits in prison; they officiate in ordinances with which we have nothing to do. We administer in ordinances which God has revealed to us to attend to; and when we attend to them correctly, God sanctions them.[80]

TEMPLE WORK DURING THE MILLENNIUM

From the writings of Brigham Young, we sense something of the grand scope and scale of the temple work to be performed during the Millennium. During this time, said President Young, "the brethren and sisters will go into the temples of the Lord, to officiate for those who have died without the gospel from the days of Father Adam to the winding-up scene, until everyone is officiated for; who can or will receive the gospel so that all may have the opportunity and privileges of life and salvation. Don't you think we have a work to perform? Yes, and it will take a thousand years to accomplish it."[81]

The Millennium will be a great and glorious season to engage in temple work because heaven and earth will combine more closely in carrying out the Lord's plan. President Charles W. Penrose informs us that "we shall have plenty of work to do, in the millennial season, the one thousand years, the one 'day of the Lord,' when we get communications from the priesthood behind the veil to the priesthood [on] the earth, in the temples that will be erected."[82] President Anthon H. Lund voiced his opinion that during the Millennium, the veil "will be much thinner between the spirit world and this [world]; and we will work for the dead, not only in faith that those for whom we labor will accept the gospel, but with an actual knowledge that they are longing for the work to be done."[83] President John Taylor taught that revelations "from the heavens will be received in regard to our labors, how we may perform them, and for whom."[84] Elder Orson Pratt verified this teaching when he said that we "shall learn by the spirit of revelation whom to be baptized for, and whom to officiate for in the holy ordinances of the gospel."[85]

Elder Pratt also identified another of the methods whereby the heavenly and earthly worlds will be brought together in the greatest work of the last days.

> The Most High says, "I deign to reveal unto you hidden things, things that have been kept hid from the foundation of the world." Among these hidden things that are to be revealed are the books of genealogy, tracing individuals and nations among all people back to ancient times. It may be inquired, "How can all this be done?" We answer, by the Urim and Thummim, which the Lord God has ordained to be used in the midst of his holy house, in his temple. . . . When that instrument is restored to the house of God, to the temple of the Most High, our ancestry, that is, the ancestry of all the faithful in the Church of Jesus Christ of Latter-day Saints, will be made manifest. Not all at once, but by degrees. Just as fast as we are able to administer for them, so will the Lord God make manifest, by the manifestation of holy angels in his house, and by the Urim and Thummim, those names that are necessary, of our ancient kindred and friends, that they may be traced back to the time when the Priesthood was on the earth in ancient days.[86]

Perhaps this is the reason why President Wilford Woodruff, after having dedicated the Manti Temple, "consecrated" one of Joseph Smith's personal seerstones upon one of the temple's sacred altars.[87]

It has also been made known that during the Millennium heavenly messengers will part the veil between the worlds and bring vital information directly to those who are engaged in the salvation of the human family. Joseph Fielding Smith, for example, has stated that some of those who will be alive during the Millennium "will be in daily communication with those who have passed through the resurrection, and they will come with this information, this knowledge that we do not have, and will give it to those who are in mortality saying, 'Now go into the temples and do this work. When you get this done we will bring you other names,' and in that way every soul who is entitled to a place in the celestial kingdom of God will be ferreted out, and not one soul shall be overlooked."[88] President Brigham Young also had a few words to say on this issue.

> You will enter into the temple of the Lord and begin to offer up ordinances before the Lord for your dead. Says this or that man, I want to save such a person— I want to save my father; and he straightway goes forth in the ordinance of baptism, and is confirmed, and washed, and anointed, and ordained to the blessings of the

holy Priesthood for his ancestors. Before this work is finished, a great many of the Elders of Israel in Mount Zion will become pillars in the temple of God, to go no more out; they will eat and drink and sleep there; and they will often have occasion to say—"Somebody came into the temple last night; we did not know who he was, but he was no doubt a brother, and told us a great many things we did not before understand. He gave us the names of a great many of our forefathers that are not on record, and he gave me my true lineage and the names of my forefathers for hundreds of years back. He said to me, 'You and I are connected in one family: there are the names of your ancestors; take them and write them down, and be baptized and confirmed, and save such and such ones, and receive of the blessings of the eternal Priesthood for such and such an individual, as you do for yourselves.'"[89]

There are, of course, certain laws and stipulations that govern such revelations as these. As Elder Melvin J. Ballard reminds us, such manifestations are not warranted until we have first done everything that is in our power to move the work forward. When we do the work for our dead ancestors, said Elder Ballard, "we will reach a limit after a while. That limit will be after we have gone as far as records are kept. I have said that when any man or woman goes into this work earnestly the Lord will provide ways and means for them to obtain the information they seek. Our understanding will be opened and sources of knowledge will be made manifest. Why? Because the dead know a great deal more than we do about existing records."[90]

Finally, it should be apparent from the preceding quotations that temple work will not have to be performed for everyone who lives upon the earth. The ordinances of the temple are only designed to bestow glory and honor upon those who inherit the Celestial kingdom of God. President Joseph Fielding Smith reminds us of this important truth.

> I want to correct an idea that prevails very largely in the minds of many members of the Church . . . [regarding] whether or not the temple work will have to be performed for everybody upon the earth. I want to say to you no, absolutely no. Now let us get this plainly in our minds. . . . All of the ordinances of the gospel pertain to the celestial kingdom of God. We are not preaching the gospel with the idea of trying to save people in the terrestrial world. Ours is the salvation of exaltation. . . . We are not going to do the temple work for everybody because it does not pertain to them. We are going to do the temple work for those who are entitled, through their faith and their repentance, to enter into the celestial kingdom.[91]

SUMMARY

In this chapter it has been established that temple ordinances are directly connected with making one's calling and election sure and thus becoming exalted in the Celestial kingdom of God. These ordinances are so vital to one's eternal destiny that those who have passed beyond the veil are sometimes permitted to return to the mortal sphere to encourage this work, to request that it be done, or to witness its completion. The Millennial era will be devoted in large measure to carrying out the rituals of redemption for those who accept the gospel of Jesus Christ and who desire to pass through the gate of heaven.

NOTES

1. *JD*, 19:35. Elder Franklin D. Richards has taught that "the houses of our God, when acceptably dedicated, become to us the gates of heaven. They are esteemed most holy unto the Lord of all places upon the earth; therein the faithful approach nearest unto God" (*JD*, 25:231).

2. *Millennial Star*, vol. 50, no. 25, 18 June 1888, 389; hereafter cited as *MS*.

3. *DS*, 2:231.

4. *CR*, April 1984, 33.

5. Joseph Fielding Smith, "The Duties of the Priesthood in Temple Work," *The Utah Genealogical and Historical Magazine*, vol. 30, no. 1, January 1939, 4.

6. *TPJS*, 331. On another occasion the Prophet said, "There are mansions for those who obey a celestial law, and there are other mansions for those who come short of the law, every man in his own order" (ibid., 366).

7. Ibid., 309.

8. Edward L. Kimball, ed., *The Teachings of Spencer W. Kimball* (Salt Lake City: Bookcraft, 1998), 51; emphasis in original.

9. *JD*, 21:353.

10. *DNTC*, 3:330–31.

11. *TPJS*, 299.

12. *HC*, 6:365.

13. Bruce R. McConkie, "Making Our Calling and Election Sure," in *Speeches of the Year 1968–69* (Provo, Utah: Brigham Young University Press, 1969), 8. For further reading on the doctrine of making one's calling and election sure, see especially Bruce R. McConkie, "Make Your Calling and Election Sure," *DNTC*, 3:323–53; Roy W. Doxey, "Accepted of the Lord: The Doctrine of Making Your Calling and Election Sure," *Ensign*, July 1976, 50–53.

14. *MD*, 167.

15. Ibid., 110.

16. Ibid., 118; emphasis in original.

17. *JD*, 26:1.

18. *HC*, 6:252. President Ezra Taft Benson expressed his desire for God to "bless us to receive all the blessings revealed by Elijah the prophet so that our callings and election will be made sure" (*Ensign*, August 1985, 10).

19. *HC*, 5:530.

20. *TPJS*, 150–51. Joseph Fielding Smith has taught: "If a man gets knowledge enough to have the companionship of the Son of God, the chances are his call[ing] and election would be sure" (*DS*, 1:55).

21. Bruce R. McConkie, *The Promised Messiah* (Salt Lake City: Deseret Book, 1981), 575.

22. *TPJS*, 298.

23. *WJS*, 209.

24. Ibid., 208.

25. Marion G. Romney, "Making Our Calling and Election Sure," *Improvement Era*, December 1965, 1116; hereafter cited as *IE*. Joseph Fielding Smith explained that "the Holy Spirit of Promise is not the Second Comforter. The Holy Spirit of Promise is the Holy Ghost who places the stamp of approval upon every ordinance that is done righteously; and when covenants are broken he removes the seal" (*DS*, 1:55).

26. *JD*, 2:260.

27. *MD*, 362.

28. *TPJS*, 308. "Every bearer of the Higher Priesthood should receive the blessing of the temple endowment. . . . The temple endowment is a priestly ordinance" (John A. Widtsoe, *Priesthood and Church Government* [Salt Lake City: Deseret Book, 1939], 353).

29. *DS*, 3:132–33.

30. Ibid., 3:131; emphasis in original.

31. Ibid.

32. *IE*, June 1970, 66. Orson Pratt is reported to have preached: "The Saints will not receive their crowns of glory until after the resurrection. . . . No person will be crowned with power in the eternal world (we are to be kings and priests to God to all eternity), unless they have been ordained thereto in this life, previous to their death, or by some friend acting as proxy for them afterwards, and receiving it for them. What is it to be kings and priests? It is to have honor, authority and dominion, having kingdoms to preside over, and subjects to govern, and possessing the ability ever to increase their authority and glory, and extend their dominion" (*Times and Seasons*, vol. 6, no. 10, 1 June 1845, 920).

33. Ezra Taft Benson, "What I Hope You Will Teach Your Children About the Temple," *Ensign*, August 1985, 8.

34. *HC*, 5:555. In speaking of the Melchizedek Priesthood, Brigham Young said: "For any person to have the fulness of that priesthood, he must be a king and priest" (ibid., 5:527).

35. *TPJS*, 362–63.

36. *MD*, 425; emphasis in original.

37. *NWAF*, 315.

38. *JD*, 8:154. Parley P. Pratt said that "in the holy sanctuary, must be revealed, ordained, and anointed the kings and queens of eternity" (Parley P. Pratt, *Key to the Science of Theology* [Salt Lake City: Deseret Book, 1978], 104). Just as men can become *kings and priests*, so too, can women become *queens and priestesses*. Joseph F. Smith once told a gathering of Saints: "Some of you will understand when I tell you that some of these good women who have passed beyond have actually been anointed queens and priestesses unto God and unto their husbands, to continue their work and to be the mothers of spirits in the world to come. The world does not understand this—they cannot receive it—they do not know what it means, and it is sometimes hard for those who ought to be thoroughly imbued with the spirit of the gospel—even for some of us, to comprehend, but it is true" (Joseph F. Smith, *Gospel Doctrine* [Salt Lake City: Bookcraft, 1998],461). For other statements on queens and priestesses, see Daniel H. Ludlow, ed., *The Encyclopedia of Mormonism* (New York: Macmillan, 1992), 1:276; *MD*, 424, 594, 613.

39. *DNTC*, 3:230.

40. Ibid.

41. *MD*, 139–40; emphasis in original. According to Elder James E. Talmage, the Holy of Holies in the Salt Lake Temple "is reserved for the higher ordinances in the Priesthood relating to the exaltation of both [the] living and [the] dead" (James E. Talmage, *The House of the Lord*, rev. ed. [Salt Lake City: Deseret Book, 1976], 163). Joseph Fielding Smith has stated: "When [a Latter-day Saint] has proved himself by a worthy life, having been faithful in all things required of him, then it is his privilege to receive other covenants and take upon himself other obligations which will make him an heir, and he will become a member of the '*Church of the Firstborn.*' Into his hands 'the Father has given all things.' He will be a king and a priest, receiving of the Father's fulness and of his glory" (Joseph Fielding Smith, *The Way to Perfection* [Salt Lake City: Deseret Book, 1963], 208; emphasis in original).

42. *TPJS*, 312. In the Joseph Smith Diary, kept by Willard Richards, this sentence says, "Some are resurrected to become god[s] by such revelations as God gives in *the most holy place* in his temple" (*WJS*, 212; emphasis added). "The holy of holies in the Lord's earthly houses are symbols and types of the Eternal Holy of Holies which is the highest heaven of the celestial world" (*DNTC*, 3:589).

43. Ibid., 374.

44. Ibid., 366.

45. Letter, Brigham Jarvis to Susa Young Gates, 8 November 1926, Susa Young Gates papers, Utah State Historical Society, Salt Lake City, Utah.

46. *IE*, April 1966, 273.

47. *JD*, 16:188.

48. Letter of instructions on temple work written by President Lorenzo Snow, "Salt Lake Temple, Salt Lake City, June 23rd 1893," reproduced in *Church News*, 5 December 1964, 15.

49. Mark E. Peterson, "The Message of Elijah," *Ensign*, May 1976, 15–16.

50. *MS*, vol. 56, no. 22, 28 May 1894, 341. President Woodruff mentions this revelation in his journal. See Kenney, ed., *Wilford Woodruff's Journal*, 7:329, 331.

51. *JD*, 22:130.

52. Ibid., 22:333–34.

53. *Juvenile Instructor*, vol. 41, no. 20, 15 October 1906, 609–10; hereafter cited as *JI*.

54. *WJS*, 372.

55. Kimball, ed., *The Teachings of Spencer W. Kimball*, 542.

56. *MD*, 685–87; emphasis in original. See also D&C 76:72–74; Bruce R. McConkie, "The Seven Deadly Heresies," in *Classic Speeches* (Provo, Utah: Brigham Young University Press, 1994), 174–75. In connection with the Second Chance Theory is the Progression Between Kingdoms Theory. President George Albert Smith has taught plainly that there is no progression from kingdom to kingdom after the resurrection. "There are some people who have supposed that if we are quickened telestial bodies that eventually, throughout the ages of eternity, we will continue to progress until we find our place in the celestial kingdom, but the scriptures and revelations of God have said that those who are quickened telestial bodies cannot come where God and Christ dwell, worlds without end" (*CR*, October 1945, 172; *see* D&C 76:112). Melvin J. Ballard has likewise taught: "Those whose lives have entitled them to terrestrial glory can never gain celestial glory. One who gains possession of the lowest

degree of the telestial glory may ultimately arise to the highest degree of that glory, but no provision has been made for promotion from one glory to another. Let us be reasonable about it" (Melvin J. Ballard, *Three Degrees of Glory* [Salt Lake City: Joseph Lyon and Associates, 1975], 30–31). See also McConkie, "The Seven Deadly Heresies," 175–76; *DS*, 2:28–29; Kimball, ed., *The Teachings of Spencer W. Kimball*, 50.

57. Clyde J. Williams, ed., *The Teachings of Harold B. Lee* (Salt Lake City: Bookcraft, 1996), 569–70.

58. Nels B. Lundwall, comp., *The Vision or The Degrees of Glory* (Independence, Missouri: Zion's Printing and Publishing Co., 1945), 141.

59. *Deseret News*, Church Section, 25 June 1932, 2.

60. Ibid., 16 July 1932, 6.

61. *Young Woman's Journal*, vol. 1, no. 7, April 1890, 214–15.

62. *JD*, 19:229; *CR*, 10 April 1898, 89–90.

63. *CR*, October 1908, 74.

64. Samuel H. Hurst and Ida Hurst, comps., *Diary of Frederick William Hurst*, privately published, 1961, 204–205, Harold B. Lee Library, Brigham Young University, Provo, Utah.

65. *JI*, vol. 16, no. 3, 1 February 1881, 29.

66. Lundwall, comp., *The Vision or The Degrees of Glory*, 142–43.

67. Salt Lake Temple Historical Record, no date given, cited in *A Book of Remembrance: A Lesson Book for First Year Junior Genealogical Classes* (Salt Lake City: The Genealogical Society of Utah, 1936), 78.

68. *The Contributor*, vol. 16, no. 1, November 1894, 64.

69. Salt Lake Temple Historical Record, 20 July 1893, cited in *A Book of Remembrance: A Lesson Book for First Year Junior Genealogical Classes*, 78.

70. *A Book of Remembrance: A Lesson Book for First Year Junior Genealogical Classes*, 77–78. This account is also recorded in the Salt Lake Temple Historical Record.

71. J. Hatten Carpenter, "Temple Manifestations," *The Utah Genealogical and Historical Magazine*, vol. 11, no. 3, July 1920, 121.

72. *A Book of Remembrance: A Lesson Book for First Year Junior Genealogical Classes*, 80–81.

73. Lynn A. McKinlay, "The Celestial Family," transcript of lecture given at Brigham Young University, 15 January 1971, 16–17. My thanks to Lynn A. McKinlay for providing this account for publication.

74. *MS*, vol. 58, no. 47, 19 November 1896, 742.

75. *IE*, February 1931, 189.

76. Michele R. Sorenson and David R. Willmore, *The Journey Beyond Life* (Midvale, Utah: Sounds of Zion, 1988), 1:149.

77. Gordon B. Hinckley, *Teachings of Gordon B. Hinckley* (Salt Lake City: Deseret Book, 1997), 632.

78. *The Seer*, vol. 1, no. 9, September 1853, 141–42.

79. Ezra Taft Benson, *The Teachings of Ezra Taft Benson* (Salt Lake City: Bookcraft, 1998), 252–53.

80. *JD*, 22:308–309.

81. Ibid., 19:45.

82. *CR*, October 1923, 14.

83. Ibid., October 1903, 82.

84. *JD*, 25:185.

85. Ibid., 7:86.

86. Ibid., 16:260–61. Joseph F. Smith said that "it is revealed that the great work of the Millennium shall be the work in the temples for the redemption of the dead; and then, we hope to enjoy the benefits of revelation through the Urim and Thummim, or by such means as the Lord may reveal concerning those for whom the work shall be done, so that we may not work by chance, or by faith alone, without knowledge, but with the actual knowledge revealed unto us" (*IE*, December 1901, 146–47).

87. Kenney, ed., *Wilford Woodruff's Journal*, 8:500.

88. Joseph Fielding Smith, "Heirs to Exaltation," *The Utah Genealogical and Historical Magazine*, vol. 26, no. 2, April 1935, 62. See also *DS*, 2:251–52.

89. *JD*, 6:295.

90. Ballard, *Three Degrees of Glory*, 23.

91. *DS*, 2:190–91; emphasis in original. On another occasion President Smith said: "We are not preaching a salvation for the inhabitants of the terrestrial or the telestial kingdoms. *All of the ordinances of the gospel pertain to the celestial kingdom, and what the Lord will require by way of ordinances, if any, in the other kingdoms he has not revealed*" (ibid., 2:329; emphasis in original). And yet again: "Some people think we have got to do the work in the temple for everybody. *Temple work belongs to the celestial kingdom, not to the other kingdoms.* There will be millions of people, countless as the sands upon the seashore, who will not enter into the celestial kingdom. That we are told in these revelations [*see* D&C 76:108–112]. *There will be no need to do temple work for them*" (ibid., 2:176; emphasis in original).

CHAPTER EIGHT

Stand Ye in Holy Places

In a latter-day revelation the Lord has commanded his disciples: "Wherefore, stand ye in holy places, and be not moved, until the day of the Lord come; for behold, it cometh quickly, saith the Lord" (D&C 87:8; *see also* D&C 45:32). What are these "holy places" and why is it necessary for the Latter-day Saints to stand within them? A partial answer can be found in a revelation wherein the Lord explained,

> Behold, it is my will, that all they who call on my name, and worship me according to mine everlasting gospel, should gather together, and stand in holy places;
>
> And prepare for the revelation which is to come, when the veil of the covering of my temple, in my tabernacle, which hideth the earth, shall be taken off, and all flesh shall see me together. . . .
>
> Again, verily I say unto you, I will show unto you wisdom in me concerning all the churches, inasmuch as they are willing to be guided in a right and proper way for their salvation—
>
> That the work of the gathering together of my saints may continue, that I may build them up unto my name upon holy places; for the time of harvest is come, and my word must needs be fulfilled.
>
> Therefore, I must gather together my people, according to the parable of the wheat and the tares, that the wheat may be secured in the garners to possess eternal life, and be crowned with celestial glory, when I shall come in the kingdom of my Father to reward every man according as his work shall be. (D&C 101:22–23, 63–65; emphasis added)

The exact nature of these "holy places" is hinted at in these passages but they are more readily identified by the revelation that is known as section 115 of the Doctrine and Covenants. The Lord states in this revelation that the land of Far West, Missouri, was holy unto Him and as such needed to be consecrated. "Therefore," said the Lord, "I command you to *build a house unto me*, for the *gathering* together of my saints, that they may *worship me*" (D&C 115:7–8; emphasis added). Taken together, these scriptures indicate that the Saints are to gather to the House of the Lord in order to worship Him and be properly guided in the way of salvation so that they might be enabled to eventually receive a celestial crown and everlasting life. Joseph Smith told the Saints: "You need an endowment . . . in order that you may be prepared and able to overcome all things. . . . the Saints will be gathered out from among [the workers of iniquity], and stand in holy places ready to meet the Bridegroom when he comes."[1]

A HOUSE OF ORDER

The temples of the Most High God are houses of order and not of confusion (*see* D&C 88:119; 109:8; 132:8). The Lord requires that His disciples put their lives in proper order before they enter within the courts of His sanctuaries. But it is just as important to have one's mind properly prepared before one encounters the divine atmosphere and holy ordinances of the Lord's house.

Proper Preparation

It is never too early to begin to prepare to enter the House of the Lord. President Harold B. Lee taught that we must "teach the membership of the Church to become temple minded from the time they are little children as they grow to maturity."[2] President Howard W. Hunter concurs by recommending that we should "share with our children the spiritual feelings we have in the temple. And let us teach them more earnestly and more comfortably the things that we can appropriately say about the purposes of the house of the Lord."[3] President Ezra Taft Benson shared some of his insightful thoughts on this important subject.

> The temple is a sacred place, and the ordinances in the temple are of a sacred character. Because of its sacredness we are sometimes reluctant to say anything about the temple to our children and grandchildren.
>
> As a consequence, many do not develop a real desire to go to the temple, or when they go there, they do so without much background to prepare them for the obligations and covenants they enter into.

I believe a proper understanding or background will immeasurably help prepare our youth for the temple. This understanding, I believe, will foster within them a desire to seek their priesthood blessings just as Abraham sought his.[4]

Elder John A. Widtsoe pointedly reminds us that it is not just the youth who need to be properly and adequately prepared for their temple experience. More mature members of the Church are in equal need of meaningful preparation.

[W]e should give more attention to preparing our young people and some of the older people, for the work they are to do in the temple. . . . It is not quite fair to let the young girl or young man enter the temple unprepared, unwarned, if you choose, with no explanation of the glorious possibilities of the first fine day in the temple. Neither is it quite fair to pass opinion on temple worship after one day's participation followed by an absence of many years. The work should be repeated several times in quick succession, so that the lessons of the temple may be fastened upon the mind.[5]

The Language of Symbolism

Since the ordinances of the temple are filled with the language of symbolism it is necessary for each Latter-day Saint who enters the Lord's house to understand that language. Only then can they fully understand and appreciate what has been revealed from the heavens for their benefit. "The holy endowment is deeply symbolic," said Elder John A. Widtsoe. Temple worship requires "a great effort of mind and concentration if we are to understand the mighty symbols that pass in review before us." Elder Widtsoe also taught that the "form of the endowment is of earthly nature, but it symbolizes great spiritual truths. . . . The endowment itself is symbolic; it is a series of symbols of vast realities." Continuing, he states that nobody "can come out of the temple endowed as he should be, unless he has seen, beyond the symbol, the mighty realities for which the symbols stand." Finally, he informs us that the "endowment which was given by revelation can best be understood by revelation; and to those who seek most vigorously, with pure hearts, will the revelation be greatest." To the "man or woman who goes through the temple, with open eyes, heeding the symbols and the covenants, and making a steady, continuous effort to understand the full meaning, God speaks his word, and revelations come."[6]

Blessings of the Temple

Those who faithfully follow and abide in the prescribed order of the Lord's house are assured that they will receive heavenly blessings (*see* D&C 130:20–21). President

Ezra Taft Benson spoke of some of the blessings that flow from temple worship.

> When you attend the temple and perform the ordinances that pertain to the house of the Lord, certain blessings will come to you: You will receive the spirit of Elijah, which will turn your hearts to your spouse, to your children, and to your forebears. You will love your family with a deeper love than you have loved before. You will be endowed with power from on high as the Lord has promised. You will receive the key of the knowledge of God (see D&C 84:19). You will learn how you can be like Him. Even the power of godliness will be manifest to you (see D&C 84:20). You will be doing a great service to those who have passed to the other side of the veil in order that they might be "judged according to men in the flesh, but live according to God in the spirit" (D&C 138:34; 1 Peter 4:6). Such are the blessings of the temple and the blessings of frequently attending the temple.[7]

Peace is another of the blessings received by those who advance the Lord's cause in His sacred sanctuaries. Because a temple is literally a house of the Lord, it is a holy space, and within it the Prince of Peace sheds forth His Spirit in great abundance. Haggai 2:9 tells us that the temple is a place where the Lord bestows peace upon His people. "We believe in the gift of healing," said President James E. Faust. "To me, this gift extends to the healing of both the body and the spirit. . . . The Lord has provided many avenues by which we may receive this healing influence. I am grateful that the Lord has restored temple work to the earth. . . . Our temples provide a sanctuary where we may go to lay aside many of the anxieties of the world. Our temples are places of peace and tranquility. In these hallowed sanctuaries God 'healeth the broken in heart, and bindeth up their wounds' (Psalm 147:3)."[8]

With our hearts and minds in a peaceful state we are more susceptible to the workings of the Spirit upon us and more capable of advancing along the road toward sanctification. From President Ezra Taft Benson we learn that we "will not be able to dwell in the company of celestial beings unless we are pure and holy. The laws and ordinances which cause men and women to come out of the world and become sanctified are administered only in these holy places" known as temples.[9] Elder Bruce R. McConkie likewise testifies that the "purpose of the endowment in the house of the Lord is to prepare and sanctify [the Lord's] Saints so they will be able to see his face, here and now, as well as to bear the glory of his presence in the eternal worlds."[10] Bishop Glenn L. Pace wrote that in order "to bring us to ultimate sanctification, we need the higher ordinances, which are received in the temple. Becoming a Melchizedek Priesthood holder won't bring sanctification about. It is the ordinances of the Melchizedek

Priesthood that bring this to pass. Hence, male and female alike receive the sanctifying power as they receive their endowments in the temple." Bishop Pace further states that if a person wants to become sanctified, "he or she must participate in the higher ordinances of the temple, receiving the endowment given there, and remain true to the covenants made there." He also explained that "an infusion of the sanctifying Spirit comes to those who have gone to the temple that is not available to those who have only received the gift of the Holy Ghost." Bishop Pace further informs us that after we receive the blessings of the temple "the Spirit begins to perfect us in ways not available to someone who has been baptized but not endowed. A new level of revelation becomes available to those who make—and keep—the covenants and who perform the ordinances of the temple. They begin to live by celestial laws and thereby receive celestial blessings."[11]

A HOUSE OF LEARNING

Temples are houses of learning and revelation (*see* D&C 88:119; 109:8). The Prophet Joseph Smith listed three basic reasons for building temples. These beautiful and holy buildings are constructed, said the Prophet, so that God can reveal unto His people the ordinances of His house, the glories of His kingdom, and the way of salvation.[12] President Gordon B. Hinckley has taught,

Surely these temples are unique among all buildings. They are houses of instruction. They are places of covenants and promises. At their altars we kneel before God our Creator and are given promise of his everlasting blessings. In the sanctity of their appointments we commune with him and reflect on his Son, our Savior and Redeemer, the Lord Jesus Christ, who served as proxy for each of us in a vicarious sacrifice in our behalf. Here we set aside our own selfishness and serve for those who cannot serve themselves. Here we are bound together in the most sacred of all human relation-

FIGURE 38. Stained glass representation of the Lord Jesus Christ. The Savior is at the center of all LDS temple activities and ideology.

ships—as husbands and wives, as children and parents, as families under a sealing that time cannot destroy and death cannot disrupt.[13]

The services of the temple center on the Lord Jesus Christ. President Howard W. Hunter has said that as we "attend the temple, we learn more richly and deeply the purpose of life and the significance of the atoning sacrifice of the Lord Jesus Christ. Let us make the temple, with temple worship and temple covenants and temple marriage, our ultimate earthly goal and the supreme mortal experience."[14] President Spencer W. Kimball likewise taught that "every element in the design, decoration, atmosphere, and program of the temple contributes to its function, which is to teach. The temple teaches of Christ. It teaches of his ordinances. It is filled with his Spirit."[15] Heber C. Kimball once said that "in the endowments, there is not a solitary thing but what is an imitation of the Son or the Father in some way or other."[16] Elder David B. Haight has made a similar statement.

> Each of the ordinances of the Lord's house bears witness "of him who triumphed o'er the grave"—of the reality of his atonement and his resurrection. We are taught of immortality and eternal life, which are realities for us through his atonement. We are blessed by covenants and ordinances to prepare us to eventually reenter his divine presence.[17]

Finally, we have the testimony of Elder David E. Sorensen. "Our temple worship today includes many symbolic references to Christ. . . . All temple ordinances are centered in Jesus Christ and his divine mission, and they are performed by the authority of the Melchizedek Priesthood. . . . Each ordinance is calculated to reveal to us something about Christ and our relationship to God."[18]

Why does the temple center on Jesus Christ? President Ezra Taft Benson taught that the "temple ceremony was given by a wise Heavenly Father to help us become more Christlike."[19] President Brigham Young spoke of participating with the Savior in the work of salvation by engaging in temple work. "The feeling experienced by those who have participated in the blessings administered in the temple is something which cannot be described to your understanding. Those only who have shared with us in the temple ordinances know for themselves the satisfaction there is in realizing that we are indeed coworkers with our Lord and Savior; that we bear a humble part in the great work of salvation."[20]

A HOUSE OF GLORY

The Lord promised the Saints in the city of Kirtland that once the temple had been built there to His holy name, and was kept in a state of spiritual sanctity, He would manifest both His "glory" and His "presence" to those who worshipped within its walls (*see* D&C 94:8; 97:15–17; 109:5, 12–13; 110:6–8; 124:27). There are at least three different ways whereby the Lord's "presence" can be experienced in His temples. He can be present in Spirit, in the ordinances, and in person.

Spiritual Presence

The Lord is continually present in His temples by the power of His Spirit. The Spirit of the Lord, or Light of Christ as it is sometimes called, "proceedeth forth from the presence of God to fill the immensity of space" and "is in all things" (D&C 88:12–13). Because this Spirit permeates all things, the Lord "comprehendeth all things, and all things are before him" (D&C 88:41; compare D&C 130:6–7). This principle is illustrated in 1 Kings 9:3, where

FIGURE 39. This sculpture of the all-seeing eye of God adorns the east center tower of the Salt Lake Temple. To King Solomon, the Lord promised that His eyes would continually see all that transpired within the walls of His holy house.

we read that the Lord appeared to King Solomon after the Jerusalem Temple had been dedicated and promised: "mine eyes and mine heart shall be there perpetually" (*see also* 1 Kings 8:29). Elder John A. Widtsoe provides us with the following thoughts regarding the spiritual presence of God in the temples.

> A temple is a place where God will come; a place where the pure in heart shall see God. . . . It is a great promise that to the temples God will come, and that in them man shall see God. What does this promised communion mean? Does it mean that once in a while God may come into the temples, and that once in a while the pure in heart may see God there; or does it mean the larger thing, that the pure in heart who go into the temples, may, there, by the Spirit of God, always have a wonderfully rich communion with God? I think that is what it means to me and to you

and to most of us. We have gone into these holy houses, with our minds freed from the ordinary earthly cares, and have literally felt the presence of God. In this way, the temples are always places where God manifests himself to man and increases his intelligence. A temple is a place of revelation.[21]

Sometimes the Spirit of the Lord is magnified so strongly within the walls of His sacred sanctuaries that it becomes visible to mortals as a heavenly light or a cloud. When the temple was being dedicated in ancient Jerusalem, a cloud appeared within its precincts and radiated the Lord's glory (*see* 1 Kings 8:10–11; Ezekiel 43:1–5). The Prophet Joseph Smith petitioned the Father to allow the Kirtland Temple to also be filled with His glory (*see* D&C 109:37). Oliver Cowdery testified that on 27 March 1836, when he was present in the Kirtland Temple, the Spirit of God was poured out and he "saw the glory of God, like a great cloud, come down and rest upon the house, and fill the same like a mighty rushing wind. I also saw cloven tongues, like as of fire rest upon many . . . while they spake with other tongues and prophesied"[22] (compare D&C 84:5; 109:36–37).

Ritual Presence

In the Old Testament there are many scriptures indicating that the Lord puts His *name* upon His holy houses.[23] Such references to the temple as a house for "the name" of the Lord, says Elder Dallin H. Oaks, "obviously involve something far more significant than a mere inscription of his sacred name on the structure. The scriptures speak of the Lord's putting his name in a temple because He gives authority for his name to be used in the sacred ordinances of that house. That is the meaning of the Prophet's reference to the Lord's putting his name upon his people in that holy house (*see* D&C 109:26)."[24]

Physical Presence

In Exodus 20:24 the Lord promised that "in all places where I record my name I will come unto thee, and I will bless thee." In the latter days He has said much the same thing. In regard to the building of the Kirtland Temple the Lord said: "And inasmuch as my people build a house unto me in the name of the Lord, and do not suffer any unclean thing to come into it, that it be not defiled, my glory shall rest upon it; yea, and my presence shall be there, for I will come into it, and all the pure in heart that shall come into it shall see God" (D&C 97:15–16). Once the Kirtland Temple was dedicated, the Lord did indeed appear in His house and made this statement: "For behold, I have accepted this house, and my name shall be here; and I will manifest myself to my people in mercy in this house. Yea, I will appear unto my servants, and speak unto them with mine own voice, if my people will keep my commandments, and do not pollute this holy house" (D&C 110:7–8; *see also* D&C 109:5). Elder Bruce R. McConkie verified this profound concept.

> What is a temple? It is a house of the Lord; a house for Deity that is built on earth; a house prepared by the saints as a dwelling place for the Most High, in the most literal sense of the word; a house where a personal God personally comes. It is a holy sanctuary, set apart from the world, wherein the saints of God prepare to meet their Lord; where the pure in heart shall see God, according to the promises. . . . When the Lord comes from heaven to the earth, as he does more frequently than is supposed, where does he make his visitations? Those whom he visits know the answer; he comes to one of his houses. Whenever the Great Jehovah visits his people, he comes, suddenly as it were, to his temple.[25]

There are several recorded accounts of the Lord making a personal appearance within the hallowed halls of His temples. The account that follows was related by the granddaughter of President Lorenzo Snow.

> One evening while I was visiting grandpa Snow in his room in the Salt Lake Temple, I remained until the doorkeepers had gone and the night-watchmen had not yet come in, so grandpa said he would take me to the main front entrance and let me out that way. He got his bunch of keys from his dresser. After we left his room and while we were still in the large corridor leading into the celestial room, I was walking several steps ahead of grandpa when he stopped me and said: "Wait a moment, Allie, I want to tell you something. It was right here that the Lord Jesus Christ appeared to me at the time of the death of President Woodruff. He instructed me to go right ahead and reorganize the First Presidency of the Church at once and not wait as had been done after the death of the previous presidents, and that I was to succeed President Woodruff."
>
> Then grandpa came a step nearer and held out his left hand and said: "He stood right here, about three feet above the floor. It looked as though He stood on a plate of solid gold."
>
> Grandpa told me what a glorious personage the Savior is and described His hands, feet, countenance and beautiful white robes, all of which were of such a glory of whiteness and brightness that he could hardly gaze upon Him.
>
> Then he came another step nearer and put his right hand on my head and said: "Now granddaughter, I want you to remember that this is the testimony of your

grandfather, that he told you with his own lips that he actually saw the Savior, here in the Temple, and talked with Him face to face."[26]

In addition to this wonderful account of the Savior's visit to one of the earth's most sacred structures, we also have the testimony of President Harold B. Lee who said, "I know that this is the Lord's work, I know that Jesus Christ lives, and that he's closer to this Church and appears more often in holy places than any of us realize excepting sometimes to those to whom He makes personal appearance."[27]

TO BE CROWNED WITH JESUS CHRIST

The ordinances of the temple will play a decisive role in determining where an individual will spend eternity and under what conditions that eternity will be spent. Through latter-day revelation it has been made known that after the resurrection there will be three levels of glory or reward known as the telestial, terrestrial, and celestial kingdoms (*see* D&C 76:11–117). It has also been revealed that there are three levels or degrees of glory within the celestial realm (*see* D&C 131:1–4).

President Joseph Fielding Smith has stated that "baptism is the door into the celestial kingdom [*see* John 3:3–5]. All the ordinances of the gospel pertain to the celestial kingdom, and any person who is faithful to the covenant of baptism will be entitled to enter there, but no person can receive an exaltation in the celestial kingdom without the ordinances of the temple. The endowments are for advancement in that kingdom, and the sealings for our perfection, provided we keep our covenants and obligations."[28] Section 132 of the Doctrine and Covenants speaks of this graduated order. Verses 15 through 17 indicate that Latter-day Saints who are not sealed to a spouse by the law and covenant that has been ordained by God will be "appointed *angels* in heaven, which *angels* are ministering servants, to minister for those who are worthy of a far more, and an exceeding, and an eternal weight of glory." They will "remain separately and singly, without exaltation . . . [for] all eternity; and from henceforth are not *gods*, but are *angels* of God forever and ever" (emphasis added). President Spencer W. Kimball clarifies:

Now, the angels will be the people who did not go to the temple, who did not have their work done in the temple. And if there are some of us who make no effort to cement these ties [through the sealing ordinances], we may be angels for the rest of eternity. But if we do all in our power and seal our wives or husbands to us . . . then we may become gods and pass by the angels in heaven.[29]

President George Q. Cannon asked, "Can a man attain celestial glory without receiving his endowments?" In answer he stated categorically that "men and women cannot receive celestial glory without having the ordinances that pertain to the endowments."[30] President Brigham Young likewise told a gathering of Saints, "I wish you to understand, with regard to the ordinances of God's house . . . that no man from the days of Adam, no woman from the days of Eve to this day, who have lived, and who are now living upon the earth will go into the kingdom of their Father and God, *to be crowned with Jesus Christ*, without passing through the same ordinances of the House of God [that] you and I have obeyed. I wish you distinctly to understand that."[31]

FIGURE 40. Painting of Brigham Young with a crown above his head from the old Summit Stake Tabernacle in Coalville, Utah. The crown symbolizes the potential reward for those who partake of the blessings that are found only in the House of the Lord.

SUMMARY

The Lord has commanded His disciples to stand in holy places. This commandment is designed to center their attention on, and draw them toward, the holiest of all places—the House of the Lord. The sacred space of the temple has been divinely designated as a school where the faithful can be taught lessons that have eternal consequences. It is within the hallowed walls of the Lord's house that the Saints learn the laws of exaltation and are entrusted with knowledge that will enable them to reach their full potential by partaking of the divine nature. The temple is a holy place; we enter it so that we, too, may become holy.

NOTES

1. *TPJS*, 91–92. According to President Ezra Taft Benson, the temple "is one of the holy places in which the Savior commanded the faithful to stand. It is a holy place because it is a house of covenants" (Ezra Taft Benson, *The Teachings of Ezra Taft Benson* [Salt Lake City: Bookcraft, 1998], 250).

2. Clyde J. Williams, ed., *The Teachings of Harold B. Lee* (Salt Lake City: Bookcraft, 1996), 243. On page 576 of this same source we read: "As I have gone throughout the Church, I have been concerned to know why there are so many of our young people who do not avail themselves of the opportunity of going to the temple. I have asked our leaders as I have gone about to stake conferences, and they have given me several answers. The most frequent reason given is that young people do not have proper encouragement from their homes. Unfortunately, many . . . have not been impressed in their childhood with the sacred privileges of the temple. Parents who themselves have lightly regarded their temple covenants can expect little better from their children because of their bad example. Little children should not be taught to reverence the temple itself but to look forward reverently to the holy experiences which one day might be theirs."

3. Clyde J. Williams, ed., *The Teachings of Howard W. Hunter* (Salt Lake City: Bookcraft, 1997), 237.

4. Ezra Taft Benson, "What I Hope You Will Teach Your Children About the Temple," *Ensign*, August 1985, 8.

5. John A. Widtsoe, "Temple Worship," *The Utah Genealogical and Historical Magazine*, vol. 12, no. 2, April 1921, 64.

6. Ibid., 60, 61, 62, 63.

7. Benson, *The Teachings of Ezra Taft Benson*, 254.

8. James E. Faust, "Spiritual Healing," *Ensign*, May 1992, 7.

9. Benson, *The Teachings of Ezra Taft Benson*, 252.

10. Bruce R. McConkie, *The Promised Messiah* (Salt Lake City: Deseret Book, 1988), 583. President Harold B. Lee stated that we are meant to "be uplifted and sanctified by the temple ceremony" (Williams, ed., *The Teachings of Harold B. Lee*, 582).

11. Glenn L. Pace, *Spiritual Plateaus* (Salt Lake City: Deseret Book, 1991), 68, 69, 72.

12. *TPJS*, 308.

13. Gordon B. Hinckley, "Why These Temples?" *Ensign*, August 1974, 41.

14. Williams, ed., *The Teachings of Howard W. Hunter*, 236.

15. Edward L. Kimball, ed., *The Teachings of Spencer W. Kimball* (Salt Lake City: Bookcraft, 1998), 534–35.

16. *JD*, 10:44. On another occasion Heber C. Kimball is reported to have said: "All the ordinances are signs of things in the heavens" (*Improvement Era*, September 1910, 991).

17. David B. Haight, "Come to the House of the Lord," *Ensign*, May 1992, 17.

18. David E. Sorensen, "Small Temples—Large Blessings," *Ensign*, November 1998, 65.

19. Benson, *The Teachings of Ezra Taft Benson*, 250–51.

20. *JD*, 19:1–2.

21. John A. Widtsoe, "Temple Worship," *The Utah Genealogical and Historical Magazine*, vol. 12, no. 2, April 1921, 55–56.

22. Leonard J. Arrington, "Oliver Cowdery's Kirtland, Ohio, 'Sketch Book,'" *Brigham Young University Studies*, vol. 12, no. 4, Summer 1972, 426. Stephen Post, who was also present on this occasion, likewise testified that after receiving instructions from Joseph Smith, "the Spirit of the Lord rested on the congregation. Many spake in tongues, many prophesied, angels were in our midst and ministered unto some. Cloven tongues like unto fire rested upon those who spake in tongues and prophesied. When they ceased to speak the tongues ascended" (Stephen Post Journal, 27 March 1836, LDS Church Archives, Salt Lake City, Utah). On another occasion Milo Andrus reported that he "saw the Spirit in the form of cloven tongues as a fire descend in thousands, and rest upon the heads of the Elders, and they spoke with tongues and prophesied" (Autobiography of Milo Andrus, 1814–1875, LDS Church Archives, Salt Lake City, Utah).

23. *See* Deuteronomy 12:11; 14:23–24; 1 Kings 3:2; 5:5; 8:16–20, 29, 44, 48; 9:3; 1 Chronicles 22:8–10, 19; 29:16; 2 Chronicles 2:4; 6:5–10, 20, 34, 38; 7:16. Notice that the Lord's name in the temple is equated with his presence in 2 Chronicles 20:7–9.

24. Dallin H. Oaks, "Taking Upon Us the Name of Jesus Christ," *Ensign*, May 1985, 81.

25. Bruce R. McConkie, *The Mortal Messiah* (Salt Lake City: Deseret Book, 1979), 1:98–99.

26. LeRoi C. Snow, "An Experience of My Father's," *Improvement Era*, September 1933, 677.

27. *Living Prophets for a Living Church* (Salt Lake City: Church Educational System, 1974), 119.

28. *DS*, 2:45.

29. Edward L. Kimball, ed., *The Teachings of Spencer W. Kimball* (Salt Lake City: Bookcraft, 1998), 51; emphasis added.

30. Jerreld L. Newquist, ed., *Gospel Truth: Discourses and Writings of President George Q. Cannon* (Salt Lake City: Deseret Book, 1974), 1:119.

31. General Conference address, 8 October 1854, Brigham Young Papers, MS d 1234, box 48, fd. 12, LDS Church Archives, Salt Lake City, Utah. President Young also said: "Your *endowment* is, to receive all those ordinances in the House of the Lord, which are necessary for you, after you have departed this life, to enable you to walk back to the presence of the Father, passing the angels who stand as sentinels, being enabled to give them the key words, the signs and tokens, pertaining to the Holy Priesthood, and gain your eternal exaltation" (*JD*, 2:31; emphasis in original).

CONCLUSION

As this book comes to a close it is my sincere hope that the reader has found the material presented within it to be both informative and thought-provoking. It is also my hope that this volume has provided its audience with a better understanding of the scriptures, a clearer vision of the past, and a stronger conviction of the reality of the Restoration.

There are at least five overall conclusions that can be drawn from the information that has been presented in this book.

1. *The temple is of heavenly origin.* God is a physical being who rules His countless creations from a throne that is located in a heavenly temple. The temples of ancient Israel were constructed after the pattern of the Lord's celestial sanctuary and hence were looked upon as a sort of "heaven on earth." It was decreed in the premortal councils of heaven that temples would be built upon the earth so that the children of God would have access to knowledge that pertained to the plan of salvation and ordinances that were designed to bring them back into God's presence.

2. *Temples and their attendant blessings have been on the earth from the beginning.* The Garden of Eden was the earth's first temple. It was a place where those who dwelled on the earth could stand in the presence of God. After Adam and Eve were driven from the Garden of Eden, they were taught the plan of salvation and were made familiar with its redeeming and exalting ordinances. Ancient Jewish traditions and biblical scholarship support latter-day revelations which proclaim that the patriarchs and the children of Israel were aware of the plan of salvation and the ordinances of the Lord's house. The Prophet Joseph Smith taught that the "order of the house of God has been, and ever will be, the same, even after Christ comes; and after the termination of the thousand years it will be the same; and we shall finally enter into the celestial kingdom of God, and enjoy it forever."[1]

3. *The early Christians did not abandon the temple after the Atonement of Jesus Christ.* The scriptural and historical records clearly indicate that there was a continuity between the rituals practiced in the temples of ancient Israel and those practiced by the early disciples of Jesus Christ. Contrary to what many modern Christian denominations believe, the earliest Christians did not abandon the Israelite temple after the Atonement was completed. Instead, they went to the temple daily and only left its hallowed courts when their enemies forced them to go.

4. *The biblical temple pattern has been restored.* Critics of the LDS Church contend that the rituals that are practiced within LDS temples are not biblical and therefore cannot represent a restoration of God-ordained rites. For those with "eyes to see" it should be evident that this argument simply cannot be sustained. Elder W. Grant Bangerter has testified that "nothing is said or done in the temple which does not have its foundation in the scriptures."[2] The temple rituals and doctrines that have been provided to the Church by Joseph Smith are one of the strongest evidences that he was indeed a true prophet of God and that there has been a legitimate restoration of the ancient temple pattern.

5. *The temple is the gate of heaven.* President Thomas S. Monson eloquently asked, "How far is heaven? It is not very far. In the temples of God, it is right where you are."[3] "Temples are really the gateways to heaven," taught President Ezra Taft Benson, because "it is in the temples that we obtain God's greatest blessings pertaining to eternal life."[4] The blessings of the temple are so vital in the determination of one's future state and status that those beyond the veil are sometimes permitted to visit the mortal sphere in order to request them, to witness them, or even to assist in their accomplishment.

The scriptures inform us that "the gate of heaven is open unto all, even to those who will believe on the name of Jesus Christ, who is the Son of God" (Helaman 3:28). It is, therefore, appropriate to end this book with the invitation that is recorded in the second chapter of the book of Isaiah. "Come ye, and let us go up to the mountain of the Lord, to the house of the God of Jacob; and he will teach us of his ways, and we will walk in his paths. . . . O house of Jacob, come ye, and let us walk in the light of the Lord" (Isaiah 2:3, 5).

NOTES

1. *TPJS*, 91.

2. *Ensign*, May 1982, 72. President Ezra Taft Benson made a similar statement. "Everything we learn in the holy places, the temples, is based on the scriptures" (Ezra Taft Benson, *The Teachings of Ezra Taft Benson* [Salt Lake City: Bookcraft, 1998], 245).

3. *Ensign*, November 1986, 99.

4. Benson, *The Teachings of Ezra Taft Benson*, 255.

APPENDIX

The LDS Temple and Freemasonry

Critics of the Prophet Joseph Smith have long claimed that he plagiarized ritual and symbolic elements from a fraternal organization known as Freemasonry in order to fabricate the Nauvoo temple endowment ceremony.[1] In making this claim, these critics have accused Joseph Smith of both intellectual theft and religious fraud. This appendix will briefly address the various aspects of this criticism by providing answers to a series of short questions. While space will not allow for an in-depth treatment of every relevant point, the information presented on these pages should be sufficient to introduce the subject to the non-specialist.

• *What is Freemasonry?*

Probably the best-known definition of Freemasonry refers to it as "a peculiar system of morality, veiled in allegory and illustrated by symbols."[2] But perhaps a more precise way to describe the Masonic institution would be to say that it is an organization that offers its adherents an elaborate system of rituals that are designed to bring about the "transformation of the human personality from a state of primitive darkness to a higher level of human consciousness." This transformation is brought about through the teaching of Hermetic-Rosicrucian principles that have been mixed together with the rationalistic-deistic beliefs of the Enlightenment. This "peculiar system" has been superimposed upon

FIGURE 41. A Masonic emblem displaying the working tools of the stonemason's craft: compass, square, level, trowel, and hammer. In later years, the emblem was simplified and several of the tools were removed.

some of the biblical and medieval traditions that pertain to stonemasons, with particular emphasis on the story of the building of King Solomon's Temple.[3] It would therefore be accurate to say that Freemasonry consists of various philosophical beliefs that
have been mingled together with the scriptures.

• *Where and when did the Masonic institution originate?*

Freemasons have debated their own origin for several hundred years and have still
not reached a consensus. There are currently several divergent views on this issue,
some based on mythology and some based on history. The origins of the Masonic
institution can only be properly understood after one separates popular mythology
from historical fact.[4] One must also come to the realization that the origin of the
Masonic *institution* is separate and distinct from the origin of many of the *rituals and
symbols* that have come to be identified as "Masonic." The Masonic institution was
formally created in London in the year 1717 A.D., but the symbols and rites that have
been borrowed by Freemasons to create their ritual system are much older.

Since the early 1700s Masonic initiates have been taught that their initiation rituals originated during the building of King Solomon's Temple. Today many Masonic
historians understand that this is just an imaginative legend and that "the claim that
Freemasonry took its origin at the building of the [Solomonic] Temple is without any
historical authority." But incredibly, "despite all indications to the contrary . . . we
find this tradition to be believed in at the present time."[5]

Another popular myth about Masonic origins claims that the organization
descended from the old European stonemason guilds of the Middle Ages. While it
appears that Freemasonry has in fact borrowed some of its rituals and symbols from
the operative stonemasons, the idea that there was a direct descent between the two
groups has been discredited.[6] Yet another popular Masonic myth goes so far as to
claim that Freemasonry originated in the Garden of Eden and that Adam was the first
Mason. Again, this claim cannot be sustained by any historical record and is generally
held to be nothing more than a popular myth that is perpetuated by those who wish
to claim an ancient and distinguished origin for the Masonic institution.[7] Two eminent Masonic historians have lamented that "an immense amount of ingenuity has
been expended on the exploration of possible origins of Freemasonry, a good deal of
which is now fairly generally admitted to have been wasted." They also note that "not
only has no convincing evidence yet been brought forward to prove the lineal descent
of [Freemasonry] from any ancient organization," but "it is excessively unlikely that

there was any such parentage."⁸ Anyone who desires to understand the historical origin of Freemasonry must also consider this bleak, but honest, evaluation from a
member of the world's most respected Masonic research society.

> When, Why, and Where did Freemasonry originate? There is one answer to
> these questions: we do not know, despite all the paper and ink that has been
> expended in examining them. Indeed, the issues have been greatly clouded by well-
> meaning but ill-informed Masonic historians themselves. . . . Whether we shall ever
> discover the true origins of Freemasonry is open to question.⁹

Once it is acknowledged that the traditional origins of Freemasonry are mythical,
it is possible for one to begin to catch a glimpse of its true origins from the historical
record. For instance, it is known that around 1640 A.D. "operative" stonemason
lodges in Scotland and England began to accept non-operative "gentlemen" or aristo-
crats into their ranks.¹⁰ In 1717 A.D. four lodges of stonemasons, each of which consisted of a mixture of "operative" freestone masons (hence the title "Freemasons") and
"accepted/gentlemen/speculative" Masons, joined together in London to form a
"Grand Lodge." By 1721 A.D. sixteen lodges had joined together in this group and
the "speculative" Masons, who were mostly intellectuals of the Enlightenment, had
taken over the leadership positions of the Grand Lodge.¹¹ Over time the Grand Lodge
changed from a mixture of "operative/speculative" Masons to an organization that
consisted almost exclusively of "speculative" Masons. Thus, the modern institution of
Speculative Freemasonry was born.

• *Where did the rituals and symbols of Freemasonry come from?*
   Many of Freemasonry's original initiation rituals and symbols (they have been
greatly expanded and modified over time) can be traced to ancient Hebrew and
Christian sources. This should not be surprising since the two men who are credited
with forming the ritual and mythology of Speculative Freemasonry were both
Christian ministers.¹² Masonic historians have established that these two men, along
with a few others who formed a committee, "adapted certain simple rites and customs
which they gathered from documents of the operative craft of former times [called the
Old Charges or Gothic Constitutions] and to give an aura of respectable antiquity
they maintained and believed they were merely continuing an unbroken line of
masonic practice and philosophy. . . . [S]peculative Masons have drawn upon material from former times, from the freestone masons, the Bible and from ancient sources

unconnected with either. . . . By a long process of refinement, by adding and discarding, a system has been developed."[13]

The operative stonemason documents, or Old Charges, that the first speculative Freemasons drew material from are of great interest because of their clear Christian character and the fact that some of the ritual elements found within them are closely

associated with persons from the Bible. The speculative Masons simply took these ritual elements out of these documents and recast them in a way that would facilitate their purposes.[14] Part of the reason why Masonic historians have such trouble reconstructing their history and determining the true origin of their rites is because some of the Old Charges were deliberately burned by operative stonemasons who did not want the speculative Freemasons to have access to the legends, lore, rituals, and symbols that were preserved upon their pages.[15]

Despite the tragic loss of these valuable documents, Masonic commentators regularly reexamine the Old Charges that have survived and debate what they might reveal about Speculative Freemasonry's origins. The results of these investigations are of interest to those who understand the Apostasy and Restoration. For instance, one Masonic commentator has presented detailed and convincing evidence that some of the dramatic elements employed in Masonic rites were borrowed straight from the Christian mystery plays of the Middle Ages.[16] Other Masonic authors have produced evidence that some of Freemasonry's ritual words and gestures can be traced to the Bible, to medieval Christian monks, and to Jewish records of ancient practices that were carried out in the Jerusalem Temple.[17] Some Masonic historians even believe that a great deal of Freemasonry's ritual elements came from orthodox Christian sources. Their theory is that—

FIGURE 42. The Apostle Thomas with a builder's square. The square was commonly associated with Thomas in the Middle Ages after a legend arose about his architectural exploits.

> within the English monasteries there was an inner sancta, with membership restricted to senior and learned brethren, in which time-honored rites were practiced; that on dissolution of the monasteries by Henry VIII in 1538, followed by the disendowment of the religious fraternities in 1547, while most disappeared, some survived as secret cells until late in the sixteenth or early seventeenth century. Then, on more favorable conditions, they emerged, expanded and gradually evolved into the form of Speculative Freemasonry known to us today.[18]

• *When and how was Freemasonry established in Nauvoo, Illinois?* [19]

The available evidence seems to indicate that Freemasonry was established in Nauvoo, Illinois, at the instigation of John C. Bennett. Ebenezer Robinson, who lived in Nauvoo during its early years, records that up until Bennett's arrival in the city the leaders of the LDS Church had "strenuously opposed secret societies," including Freemasonry, but "after Dr. Bennett came into the Church a great change of sentiment seemed to take place."[20] Bennett, who was a former Masonic officer and also a prominent member of Nauvoo society, was asked to temporarily fulfill the responsibilities of Sidney Rigdon as a counselor in the First Presidency of the LDS Church while Rigdon recovered from an ailment.[21] Two months after taking on this position, Bennett contacted the Bodley Masonic Lodge in Quincy, Illinois, and asked its leaders to recommend to the Grand Lodge of Illinois that the Masonic organization be officially established in Nauvoo.[22] Even though his motives for taking this action are presently unclear, it is noteworthy that at this time Bennett was a disgraced Mason who had been ejected from his former lodge for conduct unbecoming a member of the Masonic fraternity. Bennett had not informed the residents of Nauvoo of his degraded standing within Masonic circles, and it may be that he wanted to establish a lodge in Nauvoo so that he could clandestinely regain his former status and standing.[23]

The following timeline will help readers to understand how Freemasonry came to be established in the city of Nauvoo and will also indicate when Joseph Smith is known to have become involved with the Masonic fraternity.

• 15 October 1841. Abraham Jonas, Grand Master of the Grand Lodge of Illinois, agreed to the creation of a Masonic lodge in Nauvoo, Illinois. He granted a dispensation to George Miller, John D. Parker, and Lucius N. Scovil, who were Freemasons prior to joining the LDS Church and who had petitioned to be the main officers of the new lodge.

• 29 December 1841. Eighteen Mormons who were Freemasons prior to joining the LDS Church met in the business office of Hyrum Smith to elect officers and to draft bylaws for the future Nauvoo Lodge.

• 30 December 1841. The bylaws for the future Nauvoo Lodge were adopted. A group called the Committee of Investigation was formed by Heber C. Kimball, Newel K. Whitney, and John C. Bennett. It was their job to investigate the character of all those who petitioned for admission into the Nauvoo Lodge. Among others on this day, Joseph Smith and Sidney Rigdon petitioned in writing for admission into the future Nauvoo Lodge and paid an initiation fee of five dollars.

• 3 February 1842. The petitions of Joseph Smith, Sidney Rigdon, and others received approval from the Committee of Investigation and were voted upon by all Masons in attendance. The vote was found favorable but no further action was taken at this time.

• 17 February 1842. It was resolved that the Nauvoo Lodge of Freemasons would be officially installed at the next regular meeting, that John C. Bennett would act as Grand Marshall for the proceedings, and that the First Presidency of the LDS Church and the Quorum of Twelve Apostles would be invited to participate in the public exercises of the day. Joseph Smith was also invited to serve as the Grand Chaplain during these public activities.

• 15 March 1842. Grand Master Abraham Jonas presided at the official installation of the Nauvoo Lodge of Freemasons. A thirty-day waiting period was usually required before a Mason was allowed to advance from one degree of initiation to another. This was so that he could demonstrate proficiency in the knowledge that he had previously acquired. But Grand Master Jonas granted a "special dispensation" in the cases of Joseph Smith and Sidney Rigdon, giving them permission to advance through the three degrees of initiation in the Ancient York Rite "as speedily as the nature of the case will admit," while strictly adhering to the organization's established order of prior approval through balloting. After being voted upon, both Joseph Smith and Sidney Rigdon were initiated, in the evening, into the first degree of Freemasonry.

• 16 March 1842. Joseph Smith and Sidney Rigdon both signified their desire for further advancement in the Masonic initiation rites. After their proficiency in the first degree was vouched for (and they were properly voted upon), they were both initiated into Freemasonry's second degree. In the afternoon the Prophet applied for initiation into the third Masonic degree and after being balloted for, he was initiated and signed the Nauvoo Lodge's bylaws. In the evening Sidney Rigdon went through the same process.

• *Why did Joseph Smith and so many other early Church members join the Masonic fraternity?*

There seem to be three basic reasons why Joseph Smith became a Freemason and then encouraged a large number of LDS men to follow his example. These reasons were to get security for the Church as a whole, to obtain influence in the United States and abroad, and to prepare the general LDS population for the introduction of the temple endowment ceremony.

1. *To Get Security.* The Saints were frequently persecuted by their enemies and were even driven from their own homes by murderous mobs on several occasions. Saints like John Taylor understood that "Freemasonry is one of the strongest binding contracts that exists between man and man."[24] This fraternal bond is sometimes referred to in Masonic circles as "the mystic tie."[25] Whenever necessary, a Mason is expected to render assistance to any other needy Mason who is in good standing because, as Heber C. Kimball put it, they are all "bound under the strongest obligations to be true and faithful to each other in every case and under every circumstance, the commission of crime excepted."[26]

2. *To Obtain Influence.* Looking back on the Nauvoo period, Lorenzo Snow "spoke of Joseph, the prophet, and others of the brethren joining the Freemasons in order to obtain influence in furtherance of the purposes of the Lord."[27] It is possible that the Prophet hoped that being bound to a worldwide fraternal organization would bring the Church broader recognition and help in opening doors for the spreading of the gospel and the building of the kingdom of God.

3. *To Prepare the Saints to Receive the Temple Endowment.* Shortly before he started introducing the Nauvoo-era temple ceremonies, Joseph Smith told the Saints that they did not have more of the secrets of the Lord revealed unto them because they were not very skillful at keeping secrets.[28] But, he noted: "The secret of Masonry is to keep a secret."[29] On one of the occasions when the Prophet spoke to the Relief Society sisters about giving them the temple endowment, he said he would tell them of a private matter that was to be kept among them and then see if they could be "good Masons" and be "sufficiently skilled in Masonry [so] as to keep a secret."[30]

Along with the desire to teach the Saints to keep silent about certain matters, the Prophet apparently encouraged men in the Church to become Freemasons in order to help them learn the ancient language of ritual and symbolism, which was fairly unfamiliar to most people living on the American frontier at this time. Joseph Fielding, an English convert who received the temple endowment from Joseph Smith and also became a Freemason during the Nauvoo period, said: "Many have joined the Masonic institution. This seems to have been a stepping stone or preparation" for the reception of the temple ceremonies.[31]

• *What did Joseph Smith teach the early Saints about the origin of Freemasonry?*

When Joseph Smith administered the Nauvoo temple endowment ceremony for the first time, he chose to bestow it upon a small group of priesthood leaders who had

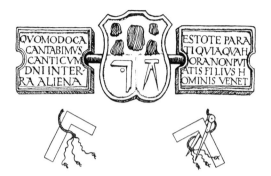

FIGURE 43. Compass and square designs from the pulpit and staircase of an ancient Christian church in San Lesmes, Burgos, Spain (ca. 866-910 A.D.).

either been long-time Masons or who had just recently been initiated into Freemasonry's rites. Questions would have naturally arisen when these men saw some similarities between the two rituals, and it is evident that the Prophet explained these similarities by teaching them that the Masonic rites contained fragments of priesthood ordinances that had come down through the ages; some fragments had been corrupted by apostasy, others not. Only a few weeks after the Prophet gave this set of men their endowments, Elder Heber C. Kimball wrote to his fellow apostle Parley P. Pratt and said,

> We have received some precious things through the Prophet on the Priesthood that would cause your soul to rejoice. I cannot give them to you on paper for they are not to be written, so you must come and get them for yourself. . . . There is a similarity of Priesthood in Masonry. Brother Joseph says Masonry was taken from Priesthood but has become degenerated. But many things are perfect.[32]

Benjamin F. Johnson, who was a close friend of Joseph Smith, reports that the Prophet taught him the very same thing.

> In lighting him to bed one night he showed me his garments and explained that they were such as the Lord made for Adam from skins, and gave me such ideas pertaining to endowments as he thought proper. He told me Freemasonry, as at present, was the apostate endowments, as sectarian religion was the apostate religion.[33]

President Brigham Young assigned the Masonic institution the same pedigree when he stated that the Freemasons "were Christians originally."[34] Joseph Fielding was taught during the Nauvoo period that the ancient priesthood ordinances of the temple that were restored through Joseph Smith were "the true origin of Masonry."[35]

• *Is it true, as critics of the LDS Church claim, that there is no record of Joseph Smith receiving a divine revelation restoring the temple ordinances, thus increasing the likelihood that he simply pilfered Masonic material shortly after his initiation into that fraternity?*

Certainly not. Even though the Prophet was only able to record the *History of the Church* up through 1838 before his death, there are clear indications from other sources that the temple ordinances were indeed restored through him by divine revelation sometime before 4 May 1842 (when he first administered them to others). Such a restoration was promised to the Prophet in a revelation given to him on 19 January 1841 which is now known as section 124 of the Doctrine and Covenants. In this revelation the Lord not only promised to "show" the Prophet "all things" pertaining to the Nauvoo Temple at some future time, but he also provided a fairly detailed list of what the Nauvoo-era temple ceremonies would include (*see* D&C 124:28, 34, 39-42, 95, 97). How were the various elements of the temple ceremonies restored to Joseph Smith? Several sources indicate that the restoration of these things occurred through heavenly messengers and the gift of seership. Elder Parley P. Pratt stated in early 1845 that Joseph Smith had given the Quorum of the Twelve Apostles "a pattern in all things pertaining to the sanctuary and the endowment therein" and explained to them that this pattern had been shown to him in a "heavenly vision."[36] On another occasion Elder Pratt asked: "Who instructed [Joseph Smith] in the mysteries of the Kingdom, and in all things pertaining to Priesthood, law, philosophy, sacred architecture, ordinances, sealings, anointings, baptisms for the dead, and in the mysteries of the first, second, and third heavens, many of which are unlawful to utter? Angels and spirits from the eternal worlds."[37] Elizabeth A. Whitney likewise stated her understanding, in a Church periodical, that an angel of God committed the temple rituals to Joseph Smith.[38] Eliza Mariah Munson records that Joseph Smith told her grandmother Elizabeth Warren Allred, who was a seamstress by trade, that he had seen an angel wearing temple clothing and needed her assistance in reconstructing the pattern of what he saw.[39] This story is corroborated by Esther Johnson, sister of Benjamin F. Johnson, who recounts that the Prophet informed a group of Saints in Nauvoo that he had been visited by an angel who instructed him to have them "wear the garments of the Holy Priesthood, a sample of which the angel showed him."[40] And then there is the testimony of the Prophet himself that he learned some ritual elements of the temple rites through the "Urim and Thummim."[41]

It appears from the following statement by Elder Franklin D. Richards that the Prophet's involvement in Freemasonry may have acted as a trigger for the reception of some of the revelations that restored the temple ceremonies.

> Joseph, the Prophet, was aware that there were some things about Masonry which had come down from the beginning and he desired to know what they were,

hence the lodge. The Masons admitted some keys of knowledge appertaining to Masonry were lost. Joseph enquired of the Lord concerning the matter and he revealed to the Prophet true Masonry, as we have it in our temples. Owing to the superior knowledge Joseph had received, the Masons became jealous and cut off the Mormon lodge.[42]

• *Isn't the fact that Joseph Smith introduced the Nauvoo temple endowment ceremony shortly after his initiation into Freemasonry a clear indication that the similarities between the two rites are the result of plagiarism on the part of the Prophet?*

There is a substantial amount of evidence that the Prophet, and other Latter-day Saints, knew of various elements of the Nauvoo-era temple rituals long before either Joseph Smith's Masonic initiation (15–16 March 1842) or the day when the Prophet first revealed the temple rites to others (4 May 1842).[43] While it is not possible, nor prudent, to enumerate all of this evidence in this short appendix, I offer the following timeline for consideration.[44]

• 16 February 1832 (D&C 76:50–70): Joseph Smith learned by vision about being sealed by the Holy Spirit of Promise, Kings and Priests, the Church of the Firstborn, and godhood.

• 22 September 1832 (D&C 84:18–26, 31–34): Joseph Smith learned by revelation that Moses knew of Melchizedek Priesthood ordinances that would enable one to enter into the Lord's presence.

• 2 February–2 July 1833 (JST Exodus 34:1–2): Joseph Smith learned of "the holy order, and the ordinances thereof." He also learned that these ordinances would enable a person to enter into the presence of the Lord. The Nauvoo period temple ceremonies are referred to in some contemporary historical documents as the "Holy Order."[45]

• 2 February–2 July 1833 (JST Isaiah 34:16): Joseph Smith learned that none of those whose names are written in the book of the Lord "shall want [i.e., lack] their mate," suggesting the permanent sealing together of husband and wife.[46]

• 5 July 1835 (*HC*, 2:235–36): The Church acquired several ancient Egyptian papyrus scrolls that contained, among other things, the writings of Abraham and Joseph. It has been demonstrated that some of the material on these scrolls is related to Egyptian temple ceremonies (compare Abraham 1:26; *see* explanations to facsimile 2).

• 20 January 1836 (*HC*, 2:377–78): The Prophet conducted a marriage ceremony "after the order of heaven." The couple took each other by the hand, and the Prophet invoked upon them "the blessings of Abraham, Isaac, and Jacob."

• 3 April 1836 (D&C 110): Keys pertaining to the temple ordinances that were eventually practiced in the Nauvoo period were restored to Joseph Smith and Oliver Cowdery in the Kirtland Temple.

• 15 March 1839 (*HC*, 3:286): Joseph Smith informed a member of the Church: "I never have had [an] opportunity to give [the Saints] the plan that God has revealed unto me."

• 27 June 1839 (*WJS*, 6): The Prophet made the first of several known references to methods of discerning between spiritual beings sent from God and deceptive spirits who attempt to pass themselves off as heavenly messengers. These methods were considered to be some of "the keys of the kingdom of God." The Prophet's teachings are now published in section 129 of the Doctrine and Covenants.

• 18 June 1840 (*HC*, 4:137): Joseph Smith stated his desire to continue translating the Egyptian papyrus scrolls obtained by the Church in 1835.

• 15 August 1840 (*WJS*, 37, 49; *HC*, 4:231): During a funeral sermon the Prophet read 1 Corinthians 15:29 and announced that baptism for the dead would be practiced in the Nauvoo Temple.

• 31 August 1840 (*HC*, 4:184–87): The First Presidency stated in a general letter to all Latter-day Saints that the priesthood was yet to be established in its fulness and the Kingdom of God built up in all of its glory. They announced that they had been given "the pattern and design" to accomplish this and emphasized that everything the Saints had accomplished so far would pale in comparison to what was about to occur. In connection with this they spoke of the necessity of building the Nauvoo Temple.

• 19 January 1841 (D&C 124:28, 34, 38-41, 95, 97): The Lord revealed that the fulness of the priesthood would be restored and practiced in the Nauvoo Temple, spoke of certain "keys" whereby one could ask for and receive blessings, and provided a detailed outline of what the Nauvoo Temple ordinances would consist of. The Lord also stated that the ordinances that were about to be restored were once practiced in the tabernacle built by Moses and in the temple constructed by king Solomon.

• 5 May 1841: William Appleby visited the Prophet who showed him the three Egyptian facsimiles that are now published in the Book of Abraham and evidently showed him written explanations of their various parts. These explanations, as recorded in Appleby's journal, closely match the printed explanations that now accompany the Book of Abraham facsimiles. Appleby recorded that one part of Facsimile #2 represented "the Lord revealing the Grand Key Words of the Holy

Priesthood to Adam in the Garden of Eden, as also to Seth, Noah, Melchizedek, Abraham, and to all whom the Priesthood was revealed."[47]

• 31 October 1841 (*HC*, 4:443–44): Hyrum Smith informed a group of Latter-day Saints that within the Nauvoo Temple "the key of knowledge that unfolds the dispensation of the fulness of times may be turned, and the mysteries of God be unfolded."

• 4 March 1842 (*HC*, 4:543): The Prophet gave Reuben Hedlock instructions regarding the "explanations" that were to accompany Facsimile #2 when it was published in the *Times and Seasons*. These "explanations" made mention of "the grand Key-words of the Holy Priesthood" and also indicated that this Egyptian hypocephalus contained "writings that cannot be revealed unto the world but [are] to be had in the holy temple of God."

I will end the timeline here because it is at this point that Joseph Smith becomes initiated into Masonic secrets (on the 15th and 16th of March 1842). It should be abundantly clear to the discerning reader of the timelines in this appendix and chapter 6 of this book that Joseph Smith knew quite a bit about the Nauvoo Temple endowment before he learned the secrets of Freemasonry. It should also be remembered when studying this material that of the 250 *known* public addresses given by Joseph Smith during his lifetime we have *nonverbatim notes* from only about 50 of them.[48] This is to say nothing of his private sermons and teachings. In other words, Joseph Smith's claim to be a restorer, and not a plagiarist, could undoubtedly be strengthened if more historical sources concerning his teachings were available.

• *Why did early Church leaders end up cutting their ties to the Masonic fraternity?*

Friction began to build between the Nauvoo Masons and other Illinois Masons shortly after the Nauvoo Lodge opened. The Nauvoo Lodge experienced an explosive amount of growth in a relatively short period of time. The other Masonic Lodges in Illinois saw this as a threat to the balance of power, and it also appears that some jealousy arose over the Nauvoo Lodge's phenomenal success. Charges of noncomformity to Masonic rules were leveled against the Nauvoo Lodge, but after an investigation by the Grand Lodge of Illinois these charges were found to be almost groundless.

In any event, an atmosphere of antagonism had been created between Nauvoo Masons and the other Masons in the state of Illinois. That antagonism reached its apex when a few Freemasons joined in with the mob that murdered Joseph and Hyrum Smith. Heber C. Kimball informs us that "Joseph and Hyrum Smith were

Master Masons, yet they were massacred through the instrumentality of some of the leading men of that fraternity."[49] Brigham Young lent credence to this claim when he said that "Joseph and Hyrum Smith . . . were put to death by Masons or through their instigation. [Joseph Smith] gave the [Masonic] sign of distress and he was shot by Masons while in the act."[50]

Within a year of Joseph and Hyrum Smith's murders, the Quorum of the Twelve Apostles decided that, since the Masonic leaders of Illinois were becoming increasingly hostile toward the Latter-day Saints, the Nauvoo Masonic Lodge should be closed down. Instead of finding the support, fraternity, and brotherhood they had hoped for, the Lord's people had only found more enemies. Once the Saints had left Nauvoo and settled in the Great Salt Lake valley, President Brigham Young decided that the Church as a whole no longer needed an association with the Masonic fraternity. "The truth is," he said, "that we have got to look to the Lord God of Israel to sustain us and not to any institution or kingdom or people upon the earth except the kingdom of God."[51] Or, as stated by Elder Matthias F. Cowley, the "fraternity sought for in [Freemasonry] was superseded by a more perfect fraternity found in the vows and covenants which the endowment in the House of God afforded members of the Church."[52]

NOTES

1. The "critics" that I refer to include those within and without the LDS Church. The charge that Joseph Smith plagiarized ritual and symbolic elements from Freemasonry has traditionally come from anti-Mormons who either never were members of the LDS Church or who had left the LDS community by one means or another. But this situation has changed. Some people on the fringes of Mormonism have now adopted and published the anti-Mormon point of view on Mormonism and Freemasonry. For a paper that briefly examines this truly strange phenomenon, see Matthew B. Brown, "Of Your Own Selves Shall Men Arise," *FARMS Review of Books*, vol. 10, no. 1, 1998, 97–131.

2. James Hastings, ed., *Encyclopaedia of Religion and Ethics* (New York: Charles Scribner's Sons, 1951), 6:120.

3. Mircea Eliade, ed., *The Encyclopedia of Religion* (New York: Macmillan, 1987), 5:418. For further reading on Hermeticism and its relationship to Freemasonry, see Hugh W. Nibley, "One Eternal Round: The Hermetic Version," in Hugh W. Nibley, *Temple and Cosmos* (Salt Lake City: Deseret Book and FARMS, 1992), 379–433.

4. As Dr. Hugh W. Nibley has noted: "The most consistent thing about histories of Freemasonry by its most eminent historians is the noncommittal position in the important matter of origins" (Nibley, *Temple and Cosmos*, 419).

5. Alex Horne, *King Solomon's Temple in the Masonic Tradition* (Wellingborough, England: Aquarian Press, 1977), 37–38.

6. One Masonic writer admits that Freemasons "cannot in truth claim to be a continuation of medieval operative masonry" (Eric Ward, "In the Beginning Was the Word," *Ars Quatuor Coronatorum*, 83 [1970]: 301).

7. "The first history of [Freemasonry] appeared, with official sanction, as part of the first *Constitutions*, compiled and published on behalf of the premier Grand Lodge by the Revd. Dr. James Anderson in 1723. Anderson's work is largely a legendary history of the builder's craft from Adam in the Garden of Eden down to the formation of the premier Grand Lodge of England in 1717. Anderson makes no distinction between operative and speculative Masonry, implying that the one was a continuation of the other. Anderson has often been harshly criticised for his history . . . He was not writing a history as we would term it today but producing an *apologia* to give a relatively new institution an honourable descent. He did not even claim to have written an original work but, as he explained in the second edition (1738) of the *Constitutions*, had simply digested the old Gothic Constitutions." Anderson's "history" of Freemasonry is thus nothing more than "an *apologia* constructed from legend, folklore and tradition" (John Hamill, *The History of English Freemasonry* [Addlestone, England: Lewis Masonic Books, 1994], 20; emphasis in original).

8. Fred L. Pick and G. Norman Knight, *The Pocket History of Freemasonry*, rev. ed. (London: Frederick Muller Ltd., 1977), 13.

9. Hamill, *The History of English Freemasonry*, 19, 29.

10. These aristocratic gentlemen are labeled "speculative masons" because they had strong inter-

ests in such things as architecture, mathematics, alchemy, numerical mysticism, Hermeticism, and Rosicrucianism. The first known "speculative" masons, Sir Robert Moray in Edinburgh (1641) and Elias Ashmole in Warrington, Lancashire (1646), were both founding members of the Royal Society (see Margaret C. Jacob, *The Radical Enlightenment: Pantheists, Freemasons and Republicans* [London: George Allen and Unwin, 1981], 116–17). Some of the early Masonic documents, including the Book of Constitutions, "suggest a strong link with the new science of the Royal Society" (ibid., 119).

11. "Prior to 1715, accepted or speculative Masons constituted a small minority within the ranks of operative lodges and were not very active in lodge affairs. Speculative Masons, for the most part, were 'gentlemen-scholars,' being admitted to Operative Masonry in light of their interest in architecture and mathematics. . . . The precise connection between Operative and Speculative Freemasonry from 1715 to 1717 is still in dispute. Yet, one thing is clear. With the admittance of more accepted members into Operative lodges between 1715 and 1717, some Speculative Masons evidently wished to create their own Masonic organization and in 1717 realized this aim, establishing the Modern Grand Lodge of London. . . . The Modern Grand Lodge emerged and functioned as an enlightenment institution in early Hanoverian London" (R. William Weisberger, *Speculative Freemasonry and the Enlightenment* [Boulder, Colorado: Eastern European Monographs, 1993], 23–24).

12. These two men were James Anderson and Jean Desaguliers. Anderson was a Presbyterian minister from Scotland while Desaguliers was a Huguenot minister from France and a member of the Royal Society.

13. Eric Ward, "In the Beginning Was the Word," *Ars Quatuor Coronatorum*, 83 (1970): 302. Even though the founders of Speculative Masonry have "drawn freely" from biblical texts, it must be understood that they have also infused that material with "significantly new meanings" (ibid., 306). Biblical elements are so pervasive in early Masonic ritual that in one of Freemasonry's earliest printed initiation texts one can detect well over one hundred of these elements in the first three initiation rites alone (*see* Jabez Richardson, *Richardson's Monitor of Freemasonry* [Harwood Heights, Illinois: Charles T. Powner Co., 1994], 5–41).

14. The Masonic handclasps, embrace, and transmittal of an esoteric word can all be found in an early Masonic document called the *Graham Manuscript*. The ritual elements in this document are associated with the biblical patriarch Noah. This document has a strong Christian character but the original source of the material found within it remains unknown to Masonic scholars (see Horne, *King Solomon's Temple in the Masonic Tradition*, 336–45).

15. James Anderson "tells us, in the second edition of the *Book of Constitutions*, that in the year 1719, 'at some private Lodges several very valuable manuscripts concerning the Fraternity, their Lodges, Regulations, Charges, Secrets, and Usages, were too hastily burnt by scrupulous Brothers, that these papers might not fall into strange hands'" (Albert G. Mackey, *The History of Freemasonry* [New York: The Masonic History Co., 1906], 1:13). See also Hamill, *The History of English Freemasonry*, 29; Pick and Knight, *The Pocket History of Freemasonry*, 72.

16. See the article by N. Barker Cryer, "Drama and Craft: The Relationship of the Mediaeval Mystery and Other Drama to the Practice of Masonry," *Ars Quatuor Coronatorum*, 87 (1974): 74–95.

17. It is admitted by one Masonic author that Freemasonry's passwords have been taken from bib-

lical texts (see A. C. F. Jackson, "Masonic Passwords: Their Development and Use in the Early 18th Century," *Ars Quatuor Coronatorum*, 87 [1974]: 106–7, 123, 125, 128, 130). Other writers note that some Masonic ritual gestures were adopted from the Bible (*see* Eric Ward, "In the Beginning Was the Word," *Ars Quatuor Coronatorum*, 83 [1970]: 309; see also Colin F. W. Dyer, *Symbolism in Craft Masonry* [London: Lewis Masonic, 1983], 49). A well-known Masonic historian mentions that some within his fraternity believe that Masonry's ritual gestures may have been derived from a system of signs that were employed by medieval Christian monks (see Albert G. Mackey, *An Encyclopaedia of Freemasonry*, rev. ed. [Philadelphia: L. H. Everts and Co., 1887], 715). Regarding Masonic penalty gestures: "Some eminent brethren of the Fraternity insist that the penalty had its origin in the manner in which the lamb was sacrificed under the charge of the captain of the temple" in ancient Jerusalem (Albert G. Mackey, *An Encyclopaedia of Freemasonry*, rev. ed. [Chicago: The Masonic History Co., 1925], 2:551; see also Albert G. Mackey, ed., *The American Quarterly Review of Freemasonry* [New York: Robert Macoy, 1859], 2:269). For an article that briefly addresses the origin of Masonic ritual aprons, see Matthew B. Brown, "Girded about with a Lambskin," *Journal of Book of Mormon Studies*, vol. 6, no. 2, 1997, 124–51. This list of elements that were "borrowed" by the Freemasons from Hebrew and Christian sources is by no means complete and could be considerably expanded. It has been frankly admitted by some Masonic historians that Freemasonry has "borrow[ed] its symbols from every source" (Albert G. Mackey, *An Encyclopaedia of Freemasonry*, rev. ed. [Philadelphia: L. H. Everts and Co., 1887], 99).

18. Cyril N. Batham, "The Origin of Freemasonry: (A New Theory)," *Ars Quatuor Coronatorum*, vol. 106, 1993, 17. Batham is not alone in believing this particular theory. Page 47 of this same source lists other Masonic scholars who share this view. On page 23 of this same source we read: "Some masonic catechisms before 1730 show a very strong Christian influence."

19. The material in this section has been digested from the following three sources: Mervin B. Hogan, ed., *The Founding Minutes of Nauvoo Lodge* (Des Moines, Iowa: Research Lodge No. 2, 1971); Mervin B. Hogan, ed., *The Official Minutes of Nauvoo Lodge* (Des Moines, Iowa: Research Lodge No. 2, 1974); Mervin B. Hogan, *Mormonism and Freemasonry: The Illinois Episode* (Salt Lake City: Campus Graphics, 1980).

20. Ebenezer Robinson, ed., *The Return*, vol. 2, no. 6, June 1890, 287.

21. "John C. Bennett was presented, with the First Presidency, as Assistant President *until* President Rigdon's health should be restored" (*HC*, 4:341; emphasis added). Both John C. Bennett and Sidney Rigdon were disciples of Alexander Campbell in 1830 and were acquainted with each other before Rigdon's conversion to the LDS Church (see Andrew C. Skinner, "John C. Bennett: For Prophet or Profit?" in H. Dean Garrett, ed., *Regional Studies in Latter-day Saint Church History: Illinois* [Provo, Utah: BYU Department of Church History and Doctrine, 1995], 250). Bennett's first letters to Joseph Smith in the early 1840s were co-addressed to Sidney Rigdon (see *HC*, 4:168–170, 172). Perhaps it was Rigdon who recommended that Bennett serve in his place in the First Presidency. This conclusion is bolstered by the fact that on the day before Bennett was presented to the Church as Rigdon's temporary replacement, "President Rigdon arose and stated that, in consequence of weakness from his labors of yesterday, *he* would call upon General John C. Bennett to officiate in his place" (ibid., 4:339; emphasis added).

22. The leaders of the Bodley Lodge refused to offer this recommendation because they did not know anyone in Nauvoo who was a Freemason, including Bennett. Had they known Bennett they probably would not have supplied the recommendation anyway since Bennett had been expelled from his Masonic Lodge for conduct unbecoming a Mason.

23. In this regard it should be noticed that when the Nauvoo Lodge was established, Bennett immediately became one of its officers. John A. Widtsoe claims that the Nauvoo Masonic Lodge was established "with the acquiescence of the Prophet" who was looking for "means to quell the rising tide of opposition" and persecution against the Church (John A. Widtsoe, *Evidences and Reconciliations* [Salt Lake City: Bookcraft, 1987], 357–59).

24. *JD*, 10:125.

25. *Times and Seasons*, vol. 5, no. 13, 15 July 1844, 585.

26. Orson F. Whitney, *The Life of Heber C. Kimball* (Salt Lake City: Bookcraft, 1992), 11.

27. Stan Larson, ed., *A Ministry of Meetings: The Apostolic Diaries of Rudger Clawson* (Salt Lake City: Signature Books in association with Smith Research Associates, 1993), 316. Directly preceding this quote, President Snow provided an important perspective. He said he had allowed his daughter to act as the queen of an Elks Lodge carnival under this reasoning: "The general idea was that we might, as a people, get influence with a large organization of influential men in the nation—and yet, he said, he did not feel to give them aid, or encouragement, or endorsement further than this."

28. *TPJS*, 195, 19 December 1841.

29. Ibid., 329.

30. *Minutes of the Nauvoo Relief Society*, LDS Church Archives, Salt Lake City, Utah. This citation comes from an entry found under the date of 8 September 1842, but the actual minutes are from a meeting that was held on 30 March 1842.

31. Andrew F. Ehat, "'They Might Have Known That He Was Not a Fallen Prophet'—The Nauvoo Journal of Joseph Fielding," *Brigham Young University Studies*, vol. 19, no. 2, Winter 1979, 145; hereafter cited as *BYUS*.

32. Letter, Heber C. Kimball to Parley P. Pratt, 17 June 1842, Parley P. Pratt Papers, LDS Church Archives, Salt Lake City, Utah. Helen Mar Whitney reports: "The Prophet Joseph, after becoming a Mason, said that Masonry had been taken from the Priesthood" (*Woman's Exponent*, vol. 12, no. 4, 15 July 1883, 26).

33. Benjamin F. Johnson, *My Life's Review* (Provo, Utah: Grandin Book, 1997), 85.

34. *JD*, 11:327.

35. Ehat, "'They Might Have Known That He Was Not a Fallen Prophet'—The Nauvoo Journal of Joseph Fielding," 145; see also 147. The fact that the early Saints were taught that the temple ceremonies were "the true origin of Masonry" probably accounts for Heber C. Kimball's description of the temple rites as "the true Masonry" (Stanley B. Kimball, "Heber C. Kimball and Family, the Nauvoo Years," *BYUS*, vol. 15, no. 4, Summer 1975, 458). Matthias F. Cowley also spoke of "Freemasonry as being a counterfeit of the true masonry of the Latter-day Saints" (Larson, ed., *A Ministry of Meetings: The Apostolic Diaries of Rudger Clawson*, 380).

36. *Millennial Star*, vol. 5, no. 10, March 1845, 151.

37. *JD*, 2:44.

38. "It was during the time we lived at the Brick Store that Joseph received the revelation pertaining to celestial marriage; also concerning the ordinances of the House of the Lord. He had been
strictly charged by the angel who committed these precious things into his keeping that he should only
reveal them to such persons as were pure, full of integrity to the truth, and worthy to be trusted with
divine messages" (Elizabeth A. Whitney, "A Leaf from an Autobiography," *Woman's Exponent*, vol. 7,
no. 14, 15 December 1878, 105).

39. "It was while they were living in Nauvoo that the Prophet came to my grandmother, who was
a seamstress by trade, and told her that he had seen the angel Moroni with the garments on, and asked
her to assist him in cutting out the garments" (Eliza Mariah Allred Munson, MS d 4558, no. 5, 1-2,
LDS Church Archives, Salt Lake City, Utah).

40. MS d 4057, fd. 2, LDS Church Archives, Salt Lake City, Utah. Like the Eliza Munson
account, this one relates that the Prophet "had a garment made after the exact pattern the angel showed
him."

41. William Clayton recorded that the Prophet "spoke concerning key words. The g[rand] key
word was the first word Adam spoke and is a word of supplication. He found the word by the Urim
and Thummim" (George D. Smith, ed., *An Intimate Chronicle: The Journals of William Clayton* (Salt
Lake City: Signature Books in association with Smith Research Associates, 1995), 134.

42. Larson, ed., *A Ministry of Meetings: The Apostolic Diaries of Rudger Clawson*, 42. The reference
in this quote to lost Masonic knowledge is an important point for consideration. When Freemasons
are initiated they are taught that certain elements of their rituals have been lost "and that certain substituted secrets were adopted 'until time or circumstance should restore the former'" (Hamill, *The
History of English Freemasonry*, 19–20). In 1842, shortly after he had apostatized from the LDS Church,
John C. Bennett accused Joseph Smith of "pretend[ing] that God has revealed to him the real Master's
word . . . [as part of the] 'restoration of the ancient order of things'" (John C. Bennett, *History of the
Saints* [Boston: Leland and Whitney, 1842], 275–76. The entry in *HC*, 5:1–2 records the bestowal of
the temple endowment for the first time in Nauvoo and refers to it as "the ancient order of things").
One anti-Mormon in the nineteenth century said that "Joseph Smith out-Masoned Solomon himself
and declared that God had revealed to him a great key-word, which had been lost, and that he would
lead Masonry to far higher degrees, and not long after [the] charter [of the Nauvoo Lodge] was revoked
by the Grand Lodge [of Illinois]" (John H. Beadle, *The Mysteries of Mormonism* [Philadelphia: National
Publishing, 1878], 409). John W. Gunnison and Richard F. Burton—two non-LDS writers who visited Salt Lake City in 1852 and 1862 respectively—were evidently informed by members of the LDS
faith that Masonry was an apostate institution that had originated with the Christian church and that
an angel had restored to Joseph Smith the lost key-words of several Masonic degrees (*see* John W.
Gunnison, *The Mormons, or Latter-day Saints, in the Valley of the Great Salt Lake* [Brookline,
Massachusetts: Paradigm Publications, 1993], 59–60; Richard F. Burton, *The City of the Saints* [Niwot,
Colorado: University Press of Colorado, 1990], 350–51).

43. In their desperation to discredit the Prophet, some of his critics have suggested that he learned
the secrets of Freemasonry long before the Nauvoo period from (1) members of his own family or other

Saints who were Masons, (2) from reading printed exposés of Masonry or, (3) by seeing public reenactments of Masonic rites by those who were antagonistic toward the fraternity. There is no doubt that Joseph Smith knew *something* about the teachings of Freemasonry prior to his own initiation. Otherwise he would have had no interest in joining its ranks. But there is no hard evidence whatsoever that he knew the secrets of the Masonic organization before he himself became a member. All Freemasons are required to swear an oath of nondisclosure, agreeing never to divulge the secrets of Masonry to anyone other than to another Mason who is qualified to know such things (this is clearly spelled out in the Nauvoo Lodge's founding minutes). The breech of this promise would bring about the punishment and possible expulsion of the violator. There is no evidence that any Latter-day Saint who was a Mason ever told the Prophet about Freemasonry's secrets. Heber C. Kimball, for one, affirmed: "I have been true . . . to my Masonic brethren" *(JD, 9:182)*. There is also no evidence that Joseph Smith ever read an exposé on Masonic ceremonies or ever witnessed a public reenactment of Freemasonry's rituals.

44. The information presented here is based upon Matthew B. Brown, "Temple Restoration Timeline," unpublished paper, 1999, 24 pp.

45. See, for example, Stanley B. Kimball, ed., *On the Potter's Wheel: The Diaries of Heber C. Kimball* (Salt Lake City: Signature Books in association with Smith Research Associates, 1987), 56, 79, 88, 93, 98–99, 101, 105, 109, 112–13, 118–20, 123, 127, 131, 133, 161–62, 164.

46. For evidence that Joseph Smith was aware of the doctrine of eternal marriage during the Kirtland period of Church history, see Danel W. Bachman, "New Light on an Old Hypothesis: The Ohio Origins of the Revelation on Eternal Marriage," *Journal of Mormon History*, vol. 5, 1978, 19–32 and Danel W. Bachman, "The Authorship of the Manuscript of Doctrine and Covenants Section 132," *Sidney B. Sperry Symposium: A Sesquicentennial Look at Church History* (Salt Lake City: Church Educational System, 1980), 27–44.

47. William I. Appleby Journal, 5 May 1841, MS d 1401, fd. 1, p. 72, LDS Church Archives, Salt Lake City, Utah.

48. *See BYUS*, vol. 21, no. 4, Fall 1981, 529.

49. Whitney, *The Life of Heber C. Kimball*, 11. In this same source Orson F. Whitney interjects: "Yes, Masons, it is said, were even among the mob that murdered Joseph and Hyrum in Carthage jail. Joseph, leaping the fatal window, gave the masonic signal of distress. The answer was the roar of his murderer's muskets and the deadly balls that pierced his heart" (ibid., 11–12). Brigham Young claimed that "there were delegates from the various [Masonic] lodges in the Union to see that [Joseph Smith] was put to death. . . . They have got the blood of the prophets upon their heads and they have got to meet it" (Kenney, ed., *Wilford Woodruff's Journal*, 5:482–83). This statement finds some support in another source. "Josephine Rigdon Secord, the last surviving grandchild of Sidney Rigdon, made the following statement to Noel B. Croft on the afternoon of 23 August 1972: 'Near the turn of the century my Aunt Athalia Robinson, wife of George W. Robinson, told me that the killing of Joseph Smith was the result of a complex political plot which included, among others, the Masons, John C. Bennett and George W. Robinson'" (Richard S. Van Wagoner, *Sidney Rigdon: A Portrait of Religious Excess* [Salt Lake City: Signature Books, 1994], 347, nt. 45). Of the nine men who were indicted for the murders

of Joseph and Hyrum Smith, four of them sought refuge from justice at the Masonic Lodge in Warsaw, Illinois. These men were Thomas C. Sharp, Jacob C. Davis, Levi Williams, and Mark Aldrich. Williams was a colonel in the state militia while Davis, Aldrich, and Sharp were all captains under him. Aldrich had been a Freemason for many years, and after the martyrdom he sat on the Committee of Investigation that was assigned to determine the character of the other three men before they were admitted as members of the Warsaw Lodge. Once the Grand Lodge of Illinois discovered that these men had taken refuge in the Warsaw Lodge, and that the members of that Lodge had been fully aware that these men were under indictment for murder, it demanded the surrender of the Warsaw Lodge's charter and the Lodge ceased to function. A report from the investigation conducted by the Grand Lodge is cited in E. Cecil McGavin, *Mormonism and Masonry* (Salt Lake City: Stevens and Wallis, 1947), 23–25. Dallin H. Oaks and Marvin S. Hill note that "the defendants were apparently trying to strengthen their position by new allegiances within the influential Masonic order. . . . How much advantage the defendants expected to derive from this association is unclear, though it is a fact that many of the most influential men in the county and state at this time were Masons. The list includes Justice Richard M. Young of the Illinois Supreme Court, who was to be the judge at the trial . . . [and] former circuit judge O. C. Skinner, who was to be among the defense counsel at the trial" (Dallin H. Oaks and Marvin S. Hill, *Carthage Conspiracy: The Trial of the Accused Assassins of Joseph Smith* [Urbana, Illinois: University of Illinois Press, 1975], 66). All of the men who were indicted for the murders of Joseph and Hyrum Smith were acquitted.

50. Scott G. Kenney, ed., *Wilford Woodruff's Journal* (Midvale, Utah: Signature Books, 1984), 5:482. An editorial printed in the *Times and Seasons* shortly after the murders said much the same thing: "with uplifted hands [Joseph and Hyrum Smith] gave such signs of distress as would have commanded the interposition and benevolence of Savages and Pagans. They were both Masons in good standing. Ye brethren of 'the mystic tie,' what think ye! Where is our good Master Joseph and Hyrum? . . . Joseph's last exclamation was, '*O Lord my God!*'" (*Times and Seasons*, vol. 5, no. 13, 15 July 1844, 585; emphasis in original). All of the men who were being held in the Carthage jail—Joseph Smith, Hyrum Smith, John Taylor, and Willard Richards—were Master Masons in good standing and thus entitled to receive assistance from other Masons when in distress. Dan Jones reminded Governor Thomas Ford of Illinois shortly before the martyrdom: "The Messrs. Smith are American citizens, and have surrendered themselves to your Excellency upon your pledging your honor for their safety; they are also master masons and as such I demand of you the protection of their lives" (Andrew Jenson, *Latter-day Saint Biographical Encyclopedia* [Salt Lake City: Publishers Press, 1971], 3:659).

51. Kenney, ed., *Wilford Woodruff's Journal*, 5:483.

52. Matthias F. Cowley, *Wilford Woodruff: History of His Life and Labors* (Salt Lake City: Bookcraft, 1964), 160.

ILLUSTRATION SOURCES

CHAPTER 2: *The Patriarchal Pattern*

Figure 1, page 25.   Creator with compass. Miniature from the Trèsor of Brunetto Latini. *Ars Quatuor Coronatorum* (Margate: Kebel's Gazette Office, 1895), 8:89.

Figure 2, page 28.   Diagram illustrating the geometric space associated with the Garden of Eden. Drawing by Jessica A. Warner and Matthew B. Brown.

Figure 3, page 36.   Facsimile #2 from the Book of Abraham. *Times and Seasons,* vol. 3, no. 10, 15 March 1842, 720.

Figure 4, page 40.   Abraham and Isaac standing before a sacred portal with an altar in the foreground. Christian glass dish decorated in gold (ca. 400 A.D.). Carl M. Kaufmann, *Handbuch der Christlichen Archäologie* (Paderborn: Ferdinand Schöning, 1905), 336.

CHAPTER 3: *The Tabernacle of Jehovah*

Figure 5, page 62.   Diagram of the position of the twelve tribes of Israel encamped around the tabernacle complex. Drawing by Jessica A. Warner and Matthew B. Brown.

Figure 15, page 87. The breastplate of the high priest of the temple. William W. Rand, *A Dictionary of the Holy Bible* (New York: American Tract Society, 1859), 72.

Figure 16, page 89. Incense ladle with hand carved on the back of the cup. Drawing by Matthew B. Brown.

CHAPTER 4: *The Temple on Mount Zion*

Figure 17, page 119. Reconstruction of the capitals that adorned the pillars *Jachin* and *Boaz*. George Rawlinson, *History of Phoenicia* (New York: Longmans, Green, and Co., 1889), 210.

Figure 18, page 120. Reconstruction of the brazen sea from King Solomon's Temple. Eduard Riehm, *Handwörterbuch des Biblischen Altertums für Gebildete Bibelleser* (Bielefeld: Velhagen and Klasing, 1884), 2:969.

Figure 19, page 127. Coin showing King Charles the Great (Charlemagne). William Smith and Samuel Cheetham, eds., *A Dictionary of Christian Antiquities* (Hartford, Connecticut: J. B. Burr Publishing Co., 1880), 2:1307, figure 51.

Figure 20, page 128. Keys carried upon the shoulder of an Egyptian merchant. James M. Freeman, *Handbook of Bible Manners and Customs* (New York: Nelson and Phillips, 1877), 263.

Figure 21, page 129. Royal headdress from a sculpture at Persepolis with a long ribbon hanging from the back. Patrick Fairbairn, ed., *The Teachers' and Students' Bible Encyclopedia* (Toledo, Ohio: Browning-Dixon, 1902), 2:86.

Figure 31, page 189. Entering paradise through a curtain. P. Sixte Scaglia, *Manuel D'archéologie Chrétienne* (Turin: Pierre Marietti, 1916), 387.

CHAPTER 6: *The Restoration of the Temple*

Figure 32, page 208. First floor of the Kirtland Temple. Drawing by Jessica A. Warner and Matthew B. Brown.

Figure 33, page 219. Daguerreotype of the Nauvoo Temple believed to have been taken in 1847 by Louis R. Chaffin. Artifact is in the possession of the Daughters of Utah Pioneers, Cedar City, Utah.

Figure 34, page 223. Reconstruction of the top floor of the Nauvoo Temple. Drawing by Lisle G. Brown, used by permission.

Figure 35, page 231. Diagram by Orson Hyde of the hierarchical structure of the kingdom of God. *Millennial Star,* vol. 9, no. 2, 15 January 1847, 23.

CHAPTER 7: *The Gate of Heaven*

Figure 36, page 266. Proxy baptismal font with oxen from the Logan Temple. Artifact on display in the LDS Church Museum of History and Art, Salt Lake City, Utah. Photograph by Matthew B. Brown.

Figure 37, page 267. Sealing altar from the Manti Temple. Artifact on display in the LDS Church Museum of History and Art, Salt Lake City, Utah. Photograph by Matthew B. Brown.

CHAPTER 8: *Stand Ye in Holy Places*

Figure 38, page 285. Stained glass representation of the Lord Jesus Christ.

Artifact on display in the LDS Church Museum of History and Art. Photograph by Matthew B. Brown.

Figure 39, page 287. All-Seeing Eye of God looking out from behind a veil. Salt Lake Temple, east center tower. Photograph by Jerry Silver, used by permission.

Figure 40, page 291. Brigham Young with crown. Photograph #6633 courtesy of the Utah State Historical Society. Used by permission. All rights reserved.

APPENDIX: *The LDS Temple and Freemasonry*

Figure 41, page, 299. Masonic emblem. G. W. Speth, ed., *Ars Quatuor Coronatorum* (Margate: Keble's Gazette Office, 1890), 3:171.

Figure 42, page, 302. The Apostle Thomas with a builder's square. Fulcran Vigouroux, *Dictionnaire de la Bible* (Paris: Letouzey et Ané, 1912), 5:2198.

Figure 43, page 306. Compass and square designs. *Ars Quatuor Coronatorum* (Margate: W. J. Parrett, 1919), 32: 57, 59.

SELECTED BIBLIOGRAPHY

REFERENCE WORKS

Atiya, Aziz S. *The Coptic Encyclopedia*, 8 vols. (New York: Macmillan), 1991.

Botterweck, Johannes G. and Helmer Ringgren, eds., *Theological Dictionary of the Old Testament*, 6 vols. (Grand Rapids, Michigan: Eerdmans), 1974–1990.

Bromiley, Geoffrey W. ed., *The International Standard Bible Encyclopedia*, rev. ed., 4 vols. (Grand Rapids, Michigan: Eerdmans), 1979–88.

Buttrick, George A., ed., *The Interpreter's Bible*, 12 vols. (New York: Abingdon Press) 1952–57.

Charlesworth, James H. *The Old Testament Pseudepigrapha*, 2 vols. (New York: Doubleday), 1983.

Ehat, Andrew F. *Joseph Smith's Introduction of Temple Ordinances and the 1844 Mormon Succession Question*, master's thesis (Provo, Utah: Brigham Young University), 1981.

Frankel, Ellen and Betsy Platkin Teutsch. *The Encyclopedia of Jewish Symbols* (Northvale, New Jersey: Jason Aronson), 1992.

Freedman, David Noel, ed. *The Anchor Bible Dictionary*, 6 vols. (New York: Doubleday), 1992.

Ginzberg, Louis. *The Legends of the Jews*, 7 vols. (Philadelphia: The Jewish Publication Society of America), 1937.

Goodenough, Erwin R. *Jewish Symbols in the Greco-Roman Period*, 13 vols. (New York: Pantheon Books), 1953–1968.

Harris, R. Laird, ed., *Theological Wordbook of the Old Testament*, 2 vols. (Chicago: Moody Press), 1980.

Hennecke, Edgar and Wilhelm Schneemelcher, eds., *New Testament Apocrypha*, 2 vols. (Philadelphia: Westminster Press), 1965.

Kenney, Scott G., ed., *Wilford Woofdruff's Journal*, 9 vols. (Midvale, Utah: Signature Books), 1984.

Kittel, Gerhard, ed., *Theological Dictionary of the New Testament*, 10 vols. (Grand Rapids, Michigan: Eerdmans), 1964–76.

Ludlow, Daniel H., ed., *The Encyclopedia of Mormonism*, 4 vols. (New York: Macmillan), 1992.

Mowinckel, Sigmund. *The Psalms in Israel's Worship*, 2 vols. (Nashville: Abingdon Press), 1979.

Roth, Cecil, ed., *Encyclopaedia Judaica*, 17 vols. (Jerusalem: Keter Publishing House), 1971.

Smith, Joseph, Jr. *History of the Church of Jesus Christ of Latter-day Saints*, 7 vols., B. H. Roberts, ed. (Salt Lake City: The Church of Jesus Christ of Latter-day Saints), 1932–51.

Smith, William and Samuel Cheetham. *A Dictionary of Christian Antiquities*, 2 vols. (Hartford, Connecticut: J. B. Burr Publishing Co.), 1880.

Strong, James. *The New Strong's Exhaustive Concordance of the Bible* (Nashville: Thomas Nelson Publishers), 1996.

VanGemeren, Willem A., ed., *The New International Dictionary of Old Testament Theology and Exegesis*, 5 vols. (Grand Rapids, Michigan: Zondervan), 1997.

Watt, George D., et. al., eds., *Journal of Discourses* (Liverpool, England: Franklin D. Richards and Sons), 1854-86.

Whiston, William, trans. *The Works of Josephus: Complete and Unabridged*, updated ed. (Peabody, Massachusetts: Hendrickson Publishers), 1987.

Wilson, William. *Old Testament Word Studies* (Grand Rapids, Michigan: Kregel Publications), 1978.

Woodford, Robert J. *The Historical Development of the Doctrine and Covenants*, 3 vols., doctoral dissertation (Provo, Utah: Brigham Young University), 1974.

BOOKS

Albright, William F. *Archeology and the Religion of Israel* (Baltimore: Johns Hopkins Press), 1953.

Barker, Margaret. *The Older Testament: The Survival of Themes from the Ancient Royal Cult in Sectarian Judaism and Early Christianity* (London: SPCK), 1987.

Bentzen, Aage. *King and Messiah* (London: Lutterworth Press), 1955.

Borsch, Frederick Houk. *The Son of Man in Myth and History* (Philadelphia: Westminster Press), 1967.

Brown, Matthew B. and Paul T. Smith, *Symbols in Stone: Symbolism on the Early Temples of the Restoration* (American Fork, Utah: Covenant Communications) 1997.

Brown, William. *The Tabernacle: Its Priests and Services*, updated ed. (Peabody, Massachusetts: Hendrickson), 1996.

Cassuto, Umberto. *A Commentary on the Book of Exodus* (Jerusalem: Magnes Press, Hebrew University), 1983.

Chilton, Bruce and Craig A. Evans, *Jesus in Context: Temple, Purity, and Restoration* (Leiden: E. J. Brill), 1997.

Clifford, Richard J. *The Cosmic Mountain in Canaan and the Old Testament* (Cambridge, Massachusetts: Harvard University Press), 1972.

Cook, Lyndon W. *The Revelations of the Prophet Joseph Smith* (Salt Lake City: Deseret Book), 1985.

de Vries, Ad. *Dictionary of Symbols and Imagery*, 2d ed. (London: North-Holland), 1976.

Edersheim, Alfred. *The Temple: Its Ministry and Services*, updated ed. (Peabody, Massachusetts: Hendrickson Publishers), 1994.

Ehat, Andrew F. and Lyndon W. Cook, eds., *The Words of Joseph Smith* (Orem, Utah: Grandin Book), 1991.

Elliot, J. K. *The Apocryphal New Testament* (Oxford: Clarendon Press), 1993.

Farbridge, Maurice H. *Studies in Biblical and Semitic Symbolism* (New York: E. P. Dutton & Co.), 1923.

Goldman, Bernard. *The Sacred Portal* (Detroit: Wayne State University Press), 1966.

Gorman, Frank H. *The Ideology of Ritual* (Sheffield, England: JSOT Press), 1990.

Graves, Robert and Ralph Patai, *Hebrew Myths: The Book of Genesis* (New York: Crown Publishers), 1983.

Haran, Menahem. *Temples and Temple Service in Ancient Israel* (Oxford: Clarendon Press), 1978.

Hayward, C. T. R. *The Jewish Temple: A Non-Biblical Sourcebook* (New York: Routledge), 1996.

Himmelfarb, Martha. *Ascent to Heaven in Jewish and Christian Apocalypses* (New York: Oxford University Press), 1993.

Hollis, F. J. *The Archeology of Herod's Temple* (London: J. M. Dent and Sons), 1934.

Hugenberger, Gordon Paul. *Marriage as a Covenant* (Leiden: E. J. Brill), 1994.

Isaacs, Marie E. *Sacred Space: An Approach to the Theology of the Epistle to the Hebrews* (Sheffield, England: JSOT Press), 1992.

Jenson, Philip P. *Graded Holiness* (Sheffield, England: JSOT Press), 1992.

Johnson, Aubrey R. *Sacral Kingship in Ancient Israel* (Cardiff: University of Wales Press), 1967.

Koester, Craig R. *The Dwelling of God* (Washington, D. C.: The Catholic Biblical Association of America), 1989.

Kramer, Samuel N. *The Sacred Marriage Rite* (Bloomington: Indiana University Press), 1969.

L'Orange, Hans P. *Studies on the Iconography of Cosmic Kingship in the Ancient World* (New Rochelle, New York: Caratzas Brothers), 1982.

Levenson, Jon L. *Sinai and Zion* (Minneapolis: Winston Press), 1985.

Madsen, Truman G., ed., *The Temple in Antiquity* (Provo, Utah: Brigham Young University Religious Studies Center), 1984.

McConkie, Bruce R. *Mormon Doctrine* , 2d ed. (Salt Lake City: Bookcraft), 1979.

_____. *A New Witness for the Articles of Faith* (Salt Lake City: Deseret Book), 1985.

McGavin, E. Cecil. *The Nauvoo Temple* (Salt Lake City: Deseret Book), 1962.

Milgrom, Jacob. *Leviticus 1–16* (New York: Doubleday), 1991.

Mitchell, Leonel L. *Baptismal Anointing* (Notre Dame: University of Notre Dame Press), 1978.

Mullen, E. Theodore, Jr. *The Assembly of the Gods: The Divine Council in Canaanite and Early Hebrew Literature* (Chico, California: Scholars Press), 1980.

Nibley, Hugh W. *The Message of the Joseph Smith Papyri: An Egyptian Endowment* (Salt Lake City: Deseret Book), 1975.

_____. *Mormonism and Early Christianity* (Salt Lake City: Deseret Book and FARMS), 1987.

_____. *Temple and Cosmos* (Salt Lake City: Deseret Book and FARMS), 1992.

Pace, Glenn L. *Spiritual Plateaus* (Salt Lake City: Deseret Book), 1991.

Parry, Donald W., ed., *Temples of the Ancient World: Ritual and Symbolism* (Salt Lake City: Deseret Book and FARMS), 1994.

Riley, Hugh M. *Christian Initiation* (Washington, D. C.: The Catholic University of America Press), 1974.

Robinson, James M., ed., *The Nag Hammadi Library*, rev. ed. (New York: Harper Collins), 1990.

Sarna, Nahum M. *Exploring Exodus* (New York: Schocken Books), 1986.

Smith, Joseph Fielding, comp., *Teachings of the Prophet Joseph Smith* (Salt Lake City: Deseret Book), 1989.

Smith, Morton. *The Secret Gospel* (New York: Harper and Row), 1973.

Strong, James. *The Tabernacle of Israel: Its Structure and Symbolism*, rev. ed. (Grand Rapids, Michigan: Kregel), 1987.

Tabor, James D. *Things Unutterable: Paul's Ascent to Paradise in its Greco-Roman, Judaic, and Early Christian Contexts* (New York: University Press of America), 1986.

Talmage, James E. *The House of the Lord*, rev. ed. (Salt Lake City: Deseret Book), 1976.

Van Dam, Cornelis. *The Urim and Thummim: A Means of Revelation in Ancient Israel* (Winona Lake, Indiana: Eisenbrauns), 1997.

Vellian, Jacob. ed., *Studies on Syrian Baptismal Rites* (Kottayam: C.M.S. Press), 1973.

Viberg, Ake. *Symbols of Law* (Stockholm: Almqvist and Wiksell International), 1992.

Welch, John W. *Illuminating the Sermon at the Temple and Sermon on the Mount: An Approach to 3 Nephi 11–18 and Matthew 5–7* (Provo, Utah: Foundation for Ancient Research and Mormon Studies), 1999.

Widengren, G. *The King and the Tree of Life in Ancient Near Eastern Religion* (Uppsala: A. B. Lundequistka Bokhandeln), 1951.

Widtsoe, John A. *A Rational Theology* (Salt Lake City: Deseret Book), 1937.

Wijngaards, J. N. M. *The Dramatization of Salvific History in the Deuteronomic Schools* (Leiden: E. J. Brill), 1969.

Yarnold, Edward. *The Awe-Inspiring Rites of Initiation: Baptismal Homilies of the Fourth Century* (Great Britain: St. Paul Publications), 1971.

ARTICLES

Anderson, David T. "Renaming and Wedding Imagery in Isaiah 62," *Biblica*, vol. 67, no. 1, 1986, 75–80.

Asay, Carlos E. "The Temple Garment," *Ensign*, August 1997, 18–23.

Avigad, Nahman. "The Inscribed Pomegranate from the 'House of the Lord'," *Biblical Archeologist*, September 1990, 157–66.

Avi-Yonah, M. "The Facade of Herod's Temple, an Attempted Reconstruction," in Jacob Neusner, ed., *Religions in Antiquity*, (Leiden: E. J. Brill, 1968), 327–35.

Bachman Danel W. "New Light on an Old Hypothesis: The Ohio Origins of the Revelation on Eternal Marriage," *Journal of Mormon History*, vol. 5, 1978, 19–32.

Barker, Margaret. "Transformations in the Post-Exilic Period: (2) The Eden Stories," in Margaret Barker, *The Older Testament: The Survival of Themes from the Ancient Royal Cult in Sectarian Judaism and Early Christianity* (London: SPCK, 1987), 233–45.

Brown, Kent S. and Wilfred C. Griggs. "The Messiah and the Manuscripts," *Ensign*, September 1974, 68–73.

_____. "The 40-Day Ministry," *Ensign*, August 1975, 6–11.

Brown, Lisle G. "The Sacred Departments for Temple Work in Nauvoo: The Assembly Room and the Council Chamber," *Brigham Young University Studies*, vol. 19, no. 3, Winter 1979, 360–74.

Brown, Matthew B. "Girded about with a Lambskin," *Journal of Book of Mormon Studies*, vol. 6, no. 2, 1997, 124–51.

_____. "Of Your Own Selves Shall Men Arise," *FARMS Review of Books*, vol. 10, no. 1, 1998, 97–131.

Compton, Todd M. "The Handclasp and Embrace as Tokens of Recognition," in John M. Lundquist and Stephen D. Ricks, eds., *By Study and Also By Faith*, 2 vols. (Salt Lake City: Deseret and FARMS, 1990), 1:611–42.

Cooke, Gerald. "The Israelite King as Son of God," *Zeitschrift Fur Die Alttestamentliche Wissenschaft*, vol. 73, 1961, 202–25.

Cross, Frank, M. "The Priestly Tabernacle in the Light of Recent Research," in Truman G. Madsen, ed., *The Temple in Antiquity* (Provo, Utah: BYU Religious Studies Center, 1984), 91-105.

Eissfeldt, Otto. "Renaming in the Old Testament," in Peter R. Ackroyd and Barnabas Lindars, eds., *Words and Meanings* (Cambridge: University Press, 1968), 69–79.

Fekkes III, Jan. "'His Bride has Prepared Herself': Revelation 19–21 and Isaian Nuptial Imagery," *Journal of Biblical Literature*, vol. 109, no. 2, Summer 1990, 269–87.

Fishbane, Michael A. "The Sacred Center: The Symbolic Structure of the Bible," in Michael A. Fishbane and Paul R. Flohr, eds., *Texts and Responses* (Leiden: E. J. Brill, 1975), 6–27.

Fletcher-Louis, Crispin. "The High Priest as Divine Mediator in the Hebrew Bible: Daniel 7:13 as a Test Case," *Society of Biblical Literature 1997 Seminar Papers* (Atlanta, Georgia: Scholars Press, 1997), 161–93.

Friedman, John Block. "The Architect's Compass in Creation Miniatures of the Later Middle Ages," *Traditio: Studies in Ancient and Medieval History, Thought, and Religion*, vol. 30, 419–29.

Gane, Roy. "'Bread of the Presence' and Creator-in-Residence," *Vetus Testamentum*, vol. 42, no. 2, 1992, 179–203.

Garber, Paul L. "Reconstructing Solomon's Temple," *Biblical Archaeologist*, vol. 14, no. 1, February, 1951, 2–24.

Griggs, Wilfred C. "The Tree of Life in Ancient Cultures," *Ensign*, June 1988, 26–31.

Hamblin, William J. "Aspects of an Early Christian Initiation Ritual," in John M. Lundquist and Stephen D. Ricks, eds., *By Study and Also By Faith*, 2 vols. (Salt Lake City: Deseret Book and FARMS, 1990), 1:202–21.

———. "Temple Motifs in Jewish Mysticism," in Donald W. Parry, ed., *Temples of the Ancient World: Ritual and Symbolism* (Salt Lake City: Deseret Book and FARMS, 1994), 440–76.

Hayman, Peter. "Some Observations on Sefer Yesira: (2) The Temple at the Center of the Universe," *Journal of Jewish Studies*, vol. 37, no. 2, Autumn 1986, 176–82.

Hilton, Lynn M. "The Hand as a Cup in Ancient Temple Worship," *Newsletter and Proceedings of the Society for Early Historic Archeology*, no. 152, March 1983, 1–5.

Himmelfarb, Martha. "The Temple and the Garden of Eden in Ezekiel, the Book of Watchers, and the Wisdom of ben Sira," in Jamie Scott and Paul Simpson-Housley, eds., *Sacred Places and Profane Spaces* (New York: Greenwood Press, 1991), 63–78.

———. "Apocalyptic Ascent and the Heavenly Temple," in Kent H. Richards, ed., *Society of Biblical Literature 1987 Seminar Papers* (Atlanta: Scholar's Press, 1987), 210–17.

———. "Heavenly Ascent and the Relationship of the Apocalypses and the Hekalot Literature," *Hebrew Union College Annual*, vol. 59, 1988, 73–100.

Honeyman, A. M. "The Evidence for Regnal Names Among the Hebrews," *Journal of Biblical Literature*, vol. 67, 1948, 13–25.

Houtman, C. "On the Pomegranates and the Golden Bells of the High Priest's Mantle," *Vetus Testamentum*, vol. 40, no. 2, April 1990, 223–29.

———. "On the Function of the Holy Incense (Exodus 30:34–38) and the Sacred Anointing Oil (Exodus 30:22–33)," *Vetus Testamentum*, vol. 42, no. 4, 1992, 458–65.

Hurowitz, Victor Avigdor. "Inside Solomon's Temple," *Bible Review*, April 1994, 24–37, 50.

Hyde, Orson. "A Diagram of the Kingdom of God," *Millennial Star*, vol. 9, no. 2, 15 January 1847, 23–24.

Johnson, Aubrey R. "Hebrew Conceptions of Kingship," in S. H. Hooke, ed., *Myth, Ritual, and Kingship* (Oxford: Clarendon Press, 1958), 204–35.

Kearney, Peter J. "Creation and Liturgy: The P Redaction of Exodus 25–40." *Zeitschrift Fur Die Alttestamentliche Wissenschaft*, vol. 89, 1977, 375–87.

Lundquist, John M. "What Is a Temple? A Preliminary Typology," in Donald W. Parry, ed., *Temples of the Ancient World: Ritual and Symbolism* (Salt Lake City: Deseret Book and FARMS, 1994), 83–117.

May, Herbert G. "The King in the Garden of Eden: A Study of Ezekiel 28:12–19," in Bernhard W. Anderson and Walter Harrelson, eds., *Israel's Prophetic Heritage* (New York: Harper and Brothers, 1962), 166–76.

Meservy, Keith. "Four Accounts of the Creation," *Ensign*, January 1986, 50–53.

Mettinger, Tryggve N. D. "YHWH SABAOTH—The Heavenly King on the Cherubim Throne," in Tomoo Ishida, ed., *Studies in the Period of David and Solomon* (Winona Lake, Indiana: Eisenbrauns, 1982), 109–38.

Milgrom, Jacob. "Of Hems and Tassels," *Biblical Archeology Review*, May/June 1983, 61–65.

_____. "The Temple in Biblical Israel: Kinships of Meaning," in Truman G. Madsen, ed., *Reflections on Mormonism: Judaeo-Christian Parallels* (Salt Lake City: Bookcraft and BYU Religious Studies Center, 1978), 57–65.

Nibley, Hugh W. "Evangelium Quadraginta Dierum: The Forty-day Mission of Christ—The Forgotten Heritage," in Hugh W. Nibley, *Mormonism and Early Christianity* (Salt Lake City: Deseret Book and FARMS, 1987), 10–44.

_____. "The Early Christian Prayer Circle," in Nibley, *Mormonism and Early Christianity*, 45–99.

_____. "Baptism for the Dead in Ancient Times," in Nibley, *Mormonism and Early Christianity*, 100–67.

_____. "Christian Envy of the Temple," in Nibley, *Mormonism and Early Christianity*, 391–434.

_____. "Sacred Vestments," in Nibley, *Temple and Cosmos*, 91–138.

_____. "One Eternal Round: The Hermetic Version," in Nibley, *Temple and Cosmos*, 379–433.

_____. "On the Sacred and the Symbolic," in Donald W. Parry, ed., *Temples of the Ancient World: Ritual and Symbolism* (Salt Lake City: Deseret Book and FARMS, 1994), 535–62.

_____. "A House of Glory," in Parry, ed., *Temples of the Ancient World: Ritual and Symbolism* 29–47.

North, C. R. "The Religious Aspects of Hebrew Kingship." *Zeitschrift Fur Die Alttestamentliche Wissenschaft*, vol. 50, 1932, 8–38.

Ostler, Blake. "Clothed Upon: A Unique Aspect of Christian Antiquity," *Brigham Young University Studies*, vol. 22, no. 1, Winter 1982, 31–45.

Parry, Donald W. "Garden of Eden: Prototype Sanctuary," in Donald W. Parry, ed., *Temples of the Ancient World: Ritual and Symbolism* (Salt Lake City: Deseret Book and FARMS, 1994), 126–51.

_____. "Sinai as Sanctuary and Mountain of God," in John M. Lundquist and Stephen D. Ricks, eds., *By Study and Also By Faith*, 2 vols. (Salt Lake City: Deseret Book and FARMS, 1990), 1:482–500.

_____. "Ritual Anointing with Olive Oil in Ancient Israelite Religion," in Stephen D. Ricks and John W. Welch, eds., *The Allegory of the Olive Tree* (Salt Lake City: Deseret Book and FARMS, 1994), 262–89.

_____. "Temple Worship and a Possible Reference to a Prayer Circle in Psalm 24," *Brigham Young University Studies*, vol. 32, no. 4, 1992, 57–62.

Parry, Jay A. and Donald W. Parry, "The Temple in Heaven: Its Description and Significance," in Donald W. Parry, ed., *Temples of the Ancient World: Ritual and Symbolism* (Salt Lake City: Deseret Book and FARMS, 1994), 515–32.

Patai, Ralph. "Hebrew Installation Rites," in Ralph Patai, *On Jewish Folklore* (Detroit: Wayne State University Press, 1983), 110–73.

Patrich, Joseph. "Reconstructing the Magnificent Temple Herod Built." *Bible Review*, October 1988, 16–29.

Polzin, Robert. "HWQY^c and Covenantal Institutions in Early Israel." *Harvard Theological Review*, vol. 62, no. 2, April 1969, 227–40.

Pratt, John P. "The Restoration of Priesthood Keys on Easter 1836—Part 1: Dating The First Easter," *Ensign*, June 1985, 59–68; "The Restoration of Priesthood Keys on Easter 1836 —Part 2: Symbolism of Passover and of Elijah's Return," *Ensign*, July 1985, 55–64.

_____. "Passover: Was it Symbolic of his Coming?" *Ensign*, January 1994, 38–45.

Rice, George E. "Hebrews 6:19: Analysis of Some Assumptions Concerning *Katapetasma*," *Andrew University Seminary Studies*, vol. 25, no. 1, Spring 1987, 65–71.

Ricks, Stephen D. "The Appearance of Elijah and Moses in the Kirtland Temple and the Jewish Passover," *Brigham Young University Studies*, vol. 23, no. 4, 1983, 483–86.

_____. "Oaths and Oath Taking in the Old Testament," in *A Symposium on the Old Testament*, (Salt Lake City: The Church of Jesus Christ of Latter-day Saints, 1983), 139–42.

_____. "Liturgy and Cosmogony: The Ritual Use of Creation Accounts in the Ancient Near East," in Donald W. Parry, ed., *Temples of the Ancient World: Ritual and Symbolism* (Salt Lake City: Deseret Book and FARMS, 1994), 118–25.

_____. "The Garment of Adam in Jewish, Muslim, and Christian Tradition," in Parry, ed., *Temples of the Ancient World: Ritual and Symbolism*, 705–39.

_____. "The Law of Sacrifice," *Ensign*, June 1998, 24–29.

Robinson, Stephen E. "The Esoteric Teaching (the Temple)," in Stephen E. Robinson, *Are Mormons Christians?* (Salt Lake City: Bookcraft, 1991), 96–103.

Schultz, Joseph P. "Angelic Opposition to the Ascension of Moses and the Revelation of the Law," *The Jewish Quarterly Review*, vol. 61, no. 4, April 1971, 282–307.

Schwartz, Joshua. "Jubilees, Bethel and the Temple of Jacob," *Hebrew Union College Annual*, vol. 56, 1985, 63–85.

Scott, R. B. Y. "The Pillars Jachin and Boaz," *Journal of Biblical Literature*, vol 58, 1939, 143–49.

Seely, David Rolph, "The Raised Hand of God as an Oath Gesture," in Astrid B. Beck, ed., *Fortunate the Eyes That See* (Grand Rapids, Michigan: Eerdmans, 1995), 411–21.

Smith, Robert F. "Some 'Neologisms' from the Mormon Canon," in *Conference on the Language of the Mormons* (Provo, Utah: Language Research Center, 1973), 64–67.

Terrien, Samuel. "The Omphalos Myth and Hebrew Religion," *Vetus Testamentum*, vol. 20, no. 3, July 1970, 315–38.

Toorn, Karel van der. "The Significance of the Veil in the Ancient Near East," in David P. Wright, David N. Freedman and Avi Hurvitz, eds., *Pomegranates and Golden Bells* (Winona Lake, Indiana: Eisenbrauns, 1995), 327–39.

Tvedtnes, John A. "Science and Genesis," in Wilford M. Hess, Raymond T. Matheny, and Donlu D. Thayer, eds., *Science and Religion: Toward a More Useful Dialogue* (Geneva, Illinois: Paladin House, 1979), 39–60.

_____. "Egyptian Etymologies for Biblical Cultic Paraphernalia," in Sarah Israelit-Groll, ed., *Scripta Hierosolymitana*, vol. 28, 1982, 215–21.

_____. "Olive Oil: Symbol of the Holy Ghost," in Stephen D. Ricks and John W. Welch, eds., *The Allegory of the Olive Tree: The Olive, the Bible, and Jacob 5* (Salt Lake City: Deseret Book and FARMS, 1994), 427–59.

_____. "Priestly Clothing in Bible Times," in Donald W. Parry, ed., *Temples of the Ancient World: Ritual and Symbolism* (Salt Lake City: Deseret Book and FARMS, 1994), 649–704.

Ulansey, David. "The Heavenly Veil Torn: Mark's Cosmic Inclusio," *Journal of Biblical Literature*, vol. 110, no. 1, Spring 1991, 123–25.

_____. "Heavens Torn Open," *Bible Review*, August 1991, 32–37.

Von Rad, Gerhard. "The Royal Ritual in Judah," in Gerhard Von Rad, *The Problem of the Hexateuch and Other Essays* (New York: McGraw-Hill, 1966), 222–31.

Von Wellnitz, Marcus. "The Catholic Liturgy and the Mormon Temple," *Brigham Young University Studies*, vol. 21, no. 1, Winter 1981, 3–35.

Welch, John W. and Claire Foley, "Gammadia on Early Jewish and Christian Garments," *Brigham Young University Studies*, vol. 36, no. 3, 1996–97, 252–58.

Wenham, Gordon J. "Sanctuary Symbolism in the Garden of Eden Story," in *Proceedings of the Ninth World Congress of Jewish Studies* (Jerusalem: World Union of Jewish Studies, 1986), 19–25.

Widengren, Geo. "King and Covenant," *Journal of Semitic Studies*, vol 2, no. 1, January 1957, 1–32.

_____. "Royal Ideology and the Testaments of the Twelve Patriarchs," in F. F. Bruce, ed., *Promise and Fulfilment* (Edinburgh: T. and T. Clark, 1963), 202–12.

Wilkinson, Richard H. "The *stylos* of Revelation 3:12 and Ancient Coronation Rites," *Journal of Biblical Literature*, vol. 107, no. 3, September 1988, 498–501.

Wyatt, N. "The Significance of the Burning Bush," *Vetus Testamentum*, vol. 36, no. 3, July 1986, 361–65.

Young, Frances M. "Temple Cult and Law in Early Christianity," *New Testament Studies*, vol. 19, no. 3, April 1973, 325–38.

INDEX